FOUNDATIONS OF THE AMERICAN CENTURY

FOUNDATIONS OF THE AMERICAN CENTURY

The Ford, Carnegie, and Rockefeller Foundations in
the Rise of American Power

INDERJEET PARMAR

COLUMBIA UNIVERSITY PRESS   *New York*

Columbia University Press
Publishers Since 1893
New York   Chichester, West Sussex
cup.columbia.edu

Library of Congress Cataloging-in-Publication Data
Parmar, Inderjeet.
   Foundations of the American century : the Ford, Carnegie, and Rockefeller Foundations in the rise of American Power / Inderjeet Parmar.
      p. cm.
   Includes bibliographical references and index.
   ISBN 978-0-231-14628-9 (cloth : alk. paper) — ISBN 978-0-231-51793-5 (e-book)
   1. Ford Foundation—History   2. Carnegie Foundation for the Advancement of Teaching—History.   3. Rockefeller Foundation—History.   4. United States—Foreign relations—20th century.   I. Title.

   HV97.F62P37   2011
   327.73009′04—dc23

                                                                                        2011029190

Columbia University Press books are printed on permanent and durable acid-free paper.
This book is printed on paper with recycled content.
Printed in the United States of America

c 10 9 8 7 6 5 4 3 2 1

CONTENTS

ACKNOWLEDGMENTS

It is a pleasure to acknowledge debts incurred on the way to researching and writing this book. It has been many years in the making; indeed, we have become somewhat attached to each other. I do wonder how I will get along without it, this simultaneously enjoyable, stimulating, educational, but occasionally frustrating long-term relationship.

I have received enormous assistance at various stages of this book project. Colleagues and friends have generously given up their time to discuss ideas, read draft chapters or conference papers, and listen to my not uniformly upbeat accounts of the book's progress. Thanks to all of the following for their time and patience: Bob Arnove, Paul Cammack, Phil Cerny, Mick Cox, Nick Cullather, Michael Doyle, Rosaleen Duffy, John Dumbrell, Donald Fisher, Nicolas Guilhot, Jon Harwood, Doug Jaenicke, Matthew Jones, Dino Knudsen, John Krige, Mark Ledwidge, Leo McCann, Linda Miller, Mick Moran, Craig Murphy, Alex Nunn, Pierre-Yves Saunier, Giles Scott-Smith, Diane Stone, Srdjan Vucetic, and Japhy Wilson. I owe a significant debt to Ralph Young, a wonderfully warm and insightful former colleague, who asked me the question during a seminar presentation that led to my thinking of U.S. foundations as an aspect of American political development. If I have forgotten anyone I've exploited over the years, please do forgive me. Any errors or omissions are my responsibility—although, as a sociologist, I appreciate the social basis of those impostors, "success" and "failure"!

I am very grateful to the archivists who take care of and make available to scholars the historical records of the Big Three foundations. In particular, Alan Divack and Anthony Maloney were absolutely wonderful during the several weeks I spent in the basement reading room at the Ford Foundation. I especially enjoyed our chats over doughnuts and coffee on Friday mornings. I remember our hopeful discussions about John Kerry's chances of defeating George W. Bush for the White House in 2004. Alan's knowledge and understanding of the foundation's records was incredibly helpful, as were his comments regarding the nature of the foundation itself. Anthony was just amazing; he was always there for me, making my time at Ford productive and congenial. Thanks to you both. At a later stage, Idelle Nissila seamlessly took over from Anthony, assisting me with locating documents long after I had begun writing this manuscript.

Tom Rosenbaum at the Rockefeller Archive Center was always helpful, encouraging, interested in my work, and very knowledgeable. I missed him during my last visit and hope he is enjoying his retirement. Darwin Stapleton's friendly helpfulness was also much appreciated. The station wagon that the RAC uses to ferry researchers to and from Tarrytown station was also very welcoming and helpful. Thank you!

The records of the Carnegie Corporation and other Carnegie philanthropies are located at the Rare Books and Manuscripts Collection at the Butler Library, Columbia University. It is a marvelous facility with an excellent staff. Thanks to you all, especially Brenda Hearing and Jane Gorjevsky, curators of the Carnegie collections, for your untiring efforts. Despite the wintry conditions that often prevailed in the reading room (thanks to a superefficient air conditioning system), I always felt very warmly welcome there.

The British Academy, the Arts and Humanities Research Board, and the University of Manchester provided funds and research leave, which enabled me to spend several months in the United States over many years. Some aspects of the book benefited from the work of the SSRC's initiative on think tanks, led by Nicolas Guilhot and Tom Asher, in the wake of the Iraq War. I am in their debt. Finally, generous research leave from the university upon completing a term as head of politics was essential to the completion of this book.

At Columbia University Press, Peter Dimock proved an excellent commissioning editor, sharp publishing adviser, and all-round caring and warm human being. We met after a conference panel at the International Studies Association convention in Chicago in 2007 (I think) and, during our chat, he suggested I put together a book proposal for Columbia to consider. To say that that was a very welcome invitation would be an understatement— it was music to my ears! Thanks also to Peter's assistant, Kabir Dandona.

Since Peter's departure, Philip Leventhal has been extremely helpful with editorial advice and, not to mention, generous with granting greatly appreciated deadline extensions!

Much of the time taken to research and write this book was stolen from my family. My children—Rohan, Nikhil, and India—were very young (four and two years and not even a twinkle in the eye, respectively) when work on this book began in the late 1990s. In their own ways, they have contributed to the book's completion. India is a welcome distraction, giggling chaos and random observations on legs; Rohan, a keen historian. Nikhil was especially helpful without knowing it: his ability to focus and dedicate every spare moment—when still a primary-school pupil—including fleeting moments in the car park before school to additional homework was inspiring. Because of him, I began using the car as a study space as well.

But I dedicate this book to my wife and best friend, Meera: she enables everything, including me.

FOUNDATIONS OF THE AMERICAN CENTURY

1

THE SIGNIFICANCE OF FOUNDATIONS IN U.S. FOREIGN POLICY

And it may be that he who bestows the largest amount of time and money on the needy is doing the most by his mode of life to produce that misery which he strives in vain to relieve.
—Henry David Thoreau, *Walden* (1854)

American expansion has been characterized not by the acquisition of new territories but by their penetration. . . . a variety of organizations, governmental and nongovernmental, have attempted to pursue the objectives important to them within the territory of other societies.
—Samuel P. Huntington, "Transnational Organizations in World Politics" (1973)

When [Bill] Gates first started the charity organization, he sought advice from Vartan Gregorian, president of the $2.2-billion-US Carnegie Corporation of New York . . . "Bill Gates always has believed that with wealth comes responsibility, the same as Andrew Carnegie," said Gregorian. "There are people who deal with symptoms—somebody is poor, you give money. That's charity. Philanthropy . . . is to solve problems through investment and planning, not (just) through generosity."
—CTV.CA News, "Bill Gates to Devote More Time to Charity Work"

It is difficult to believe that philanthropy—literally, "love of all mankind"—could possibly be malignant. When one reads of the millions of dollars donated to health schemes by the Rockefeller and Bill and Melinda Gates foundations, for example,[1] it is close to sacrilegious to suggest that such initiatives might be other than they seem. Yet I claim something close in this book, in which I analyze the influence of American foundations on U.S. foreign affairs from the 1930s to the "war on terror." Philanthropic foundations, I argue, have been a key means of building the "American century," or an American imperium, a hegemony constructed in significant part via cultural and intellectual penetration. This is as much the case within the United States—where a powerful East Coast foreign policy Establishment "penetrated" other regions and social strata—as it is in the world.

Despite their image of scientific impartiality, ideological-political neutrality, and being above the market and independent of the state, the "Big 3" foundations (Ford, Rockefeller, and Carnegie) have been extremely influential in America's rise to global hegemony over the past century.[2] This book shows that they are intensely political and ideological and are steeped in market, corporate, and state institutions—that they are a part of the power elite of the United States. Working today in a much more crowded field, they continue to innovate, inspire emulation, and collaborate with newer philanthropies.

Historically, the Big 3 foundations represented a strategic element of the East Coast foreign policy Establishment and the core of the latter's mindset, institutions, and activities, manifested by active leadership in organizations like the Council on Foreign Relations and the Foreign Policy Association. Principally, the Big 3 were at the heart of the Establishment's efforts to strengthen and mobilize, as necessary, the American academy behind its programs for American-led global hegemony, including the specialized study of foreign areas likely to be of concern to makers of foreign policy, as well as through developing the discipline of international relations. Foundation leaders were drawn from various sections of American elite society and were closely connected with the country's biggest industrial corporations and elite cultural, religious, political, and state institutions. At the turn of the twentieth century, that elite focused its attention on America's global role—as well as toward domestic political reform, to build a stronger federal executive. They sought to unite American society to build and catalyze anti-isolationist and globalist opinion (elite, attentive, and mass public), to build state capacities and political capital in the area of foreign affairs, and to improve the study of foreign areas and international relations in the universities. The foundations built the domestic intellectual and political bases that would assist America's rise to global leadership. In addition, the foundations were directly engaged in extending and consolidating U.S. hegemony around the globe, especially during the Cold War, influencing intellectual, political, and ideological developments that transformed Chile, for example, from a welfare democracy into a neoliberal pioneer state under General Augusto Pinochet, following the bloody military coup of 1973.

America's journey to global leadership may be tracked through the rise of the major foundations through three overlapping but distinct stages, with each stage socializing elites at home and abroad and embedding liberalism into national and international institutions: Stage 1, at the domestic level, lasted from the 1920s to the 1950s, during which time the foundations helped construct the hegemony of liberal internationalism, marginalized isolationism, and built up the institutional capacities of the federal government, especially in foreign affairs. Stage 2 partially overlapped the first stage and lasted from the 1930s to the 1970s, during which time foundations helped socialize and integrate American and foreign elites and developed formal and informal international organizations. Stage 3 began in the late 1980s, when foundations helped reconceptualize American hegemony, promoted democracy and "global civil society," and fostered "democratic challenges" to neoliberal globalization.[3] The international orders constructed or aimed at were, and are, congenial to American interests.[4]

The crucial point is that despite claims to the contrary, the Big 3's large-scale aid programs for economic and political development failed to alleviate poverty, raise mass living standards, or better educate people. What that aid generated were sustainable elite networks that, on the whole, supported American policies—foreign and economic—ranging from liberalism in the 1950s to neoliberalism into the twenty-first century.

FOUNDATIONS AND FOREIGN AFFAIRS: A NEGLECTED AREA

There is only one other book-length treatment of American foundations' roles in U.S. foreign policy, and it was published in 1983.[5] Edward H. Berman's excellent monograph provides a great deal of original evidence, which makes easier a more comprehensive and complementary coverage of the issues relating to philanthropic foundations. It is appropriate, however, that the issue is revisited in light of subsequent scholarly and political concerns, including the increased attention to nonstate actors in international relations and to the power of knowledge networks.

Despite the importance of foundations, their role in foreign affairs is underresearched. This is puzzling. However, the very definition of what counts as "politics" marginalizes philanthropy. "Governmental" institutions and the "state" constitute key concerns in political science and IR, but foundations are often understood as independent of the state. "Political parties" are central to political science, but foundations are specifically, or so they claim, nonpartisan. The same might be said for other concerns like ideology and organized and special interests: American foundations are self-professedly "nonideological" and beholden to no "sectional" interests—they focus on all mankind. Of course, the study of foreign affairs is state-centric, reinforcing the idea that foreign policy is especially the remit of a few state experts with inside information. Foundations and even foreign affairs think tanks, therefore, do not appear important, by definition, when one thinks in statist ways.

In addition, the study of elites—and foundations are quite elitist—has fallen by the wayside.[6] It has been just over fifty years since the publication of C. Wright Mills's *The Power Elite*, and no major event appears to have been arranged to mark that anniversary. A conference at the University of Manchester recently aimed to revive elite studies. Foundations as elite institutions therefore have not been studied by sociologists, for example, despite a lively debate on their role between Donald Fisher and Martin Bulmer back in the 1980s.[7]

Of course, the nonstate actors' approach was urged by Robert Keohane, Joseph Nye, and Samuel Huntington in the 1970s, noting the importance of philanthropic foundations as transnational actors.[8] The private actor in world affairs was not displacing the state, but it had transformed the institutional environment of interstate politics to such a degree that the mutual interactions of private and public spheres required investigation. The upsurge of interest since 1989 in nonstate actors in global politics and the construction of global civil society, however, maintains the sharp distinction between states and private organizations in international affairs. In tandem with and related to this distinction, an attachment to pluralistic approaches to the study and understanding of power at the global (and domestic) levels remains—note the *pluralistic* character of America's expansion as claimed by Huntington[9]—led by governmental and nongovernmental actors in service of their selfish interests.[10] Extant research on foundations' roles in the construction of twenty-first-century global civil society continues to be based on assumptions that governed scholarship on foundations during earlier periods. Prewitt argues, for example, that foundations represent a "third sector" in society that is beyond the state and the marketplace. As such, they operate not for the purposes of profit or politics but to make a broad contribution to enhancing the essential features of a pluralistic society.[11] Anheier and Leat profess similar sentiments, arguing that foundations' nonstate, nonmarket character "makes them independent forces of social change and innovation."[12] Given their global character, Anheier claims that foundations "are one of the main sources of support for global civil society organizations" that are, in turn, building a more open global order and trying to "humanize globalization."[13] These arguments about philanthropy as a benign, progressive, nonpolitical, and nonbusiness force are being challenged by an increasing body of research.

In what follows, I offer a detailed, archive-based critique that takes a long view of U.S. foundations' position in U.S. foreign policy. The book advances part of an agenda encouraged by Keohane and Nye in the 1970s, although there remain normative and theoretical differences between their approaches and those favored here. Four characteristics—or "fictions"—of the Big 3 foundations account for their significance, all related to their apparent *independence*: first, the "nonstate" fiction, at odds with their trustees' statist mindset and their governmental connections; second, the "nonpolitical" fiction, despite the foundations' connections with both main political parties; third, the "nonbusiness" fiction, even as foundations' trustees serve as corporate directors and earn income from them; and finally, the "scientific/nonideological" fiction, despite the Big 3's attachment to and promotion of the ideology of Americanism as liberal internationalism.[14] Additionally, the foundations' adaptability and sense of historic mission—changing tactics, same program[15]—meant that they successfully negotiated their way through the frequently hostile environment of American domestic politics and the equally turbulent wider world. Such agility during the isolationist 1920s and 1930s provides insights into how foundation programs and tactics would successfully adapt in states designated as "anti-American" during the Cold War era. In each such case, foundations showed tenacity and adaptability in allying with any nonhostile agency that furthered their goals and prepared for a more permissive climate.

Holding such fictions as articles of faith permits foundations to act as unifiers of a political system divided by sovereignties and characterized by mass democracy and group competition. The Ford, Rockefeller, and Carnegie philanthropies *mediate* among the concerns of the state, big business, party politics, and foreign policy–related academia; *articulate* a divided system; and constitute and create forums for constructing elite *expertise, consensus*, and *forward planning*. Nevertheless, foundation networks did not always succeed and, importantly, were most successful during conditions of crisis,[16] such as the Japanese attack on Pearl Harbor in 1941, the outbreak of the Korean War, and after 1989. However, the foundations are adept at network building and well prepared to interpret and promote crises as opportunities to policy makers and public alike.[17]

FOUNDATIONS AND THE AMERICAN STATE

The foundations enjoyed a close relationship with the American state even if there were times when they found themselves marginalized—particularly during the 1920s and early 1930s. Despite its "private" character, U.S. philanthropy sees itself as directed at the "public" good. Philanthropic foundations have served as a catalyst for powerful reform movements—including temperance, social assistance for the poor, health and safety legislation, against corruption in politics, educational reform, and "Americanization" programs for immigrants. This publicly oriented self-concept emerged as opposition to the "local" and support for the "national." Powerfully opposed to parochialism, the party machine, the congressional pork barrel, and mass politics, the foundations favored the construction and strengthening of the *federal executive branch* and the mobilization of elite opinion[18]—academics, policy makers, journalists, students, corporate directors, the attentive publics— initially behind programs of American globalism and, after the Cold War, behind globalization, democracy promotion, and global civil society building. In short, *the foundations were created and led by self-conscious Progressive-era state builders, private citizens who backed state power for globalist ends; today, they are self-conscious global civil society builders.*

The foundations were established when America's federal executive institutions and "national" consciousness were weak and the individual states strong; the foundations spent hundreds of millions of dollars in encouraging private parastate institutions to carry out functions such as urban renewal, improving schools, and promoting health and safety in workplaces, which were later subsumed and developed by the federal state, as well as to develop a supportive base in public opinion; the foundations helped to "nationalize" American society. Today, they are trying to achieve similar aims at the global level. Where the global system is institutionally relatively weak and nation-states jealously guard their sovereignty, the foundations are assisting in global institution building and in constructing a global "civil society" that sustains and develops such institutions,[19] and this is also part of developing the infrastructure for continued American hegemony.

FOUNDATIONS AND NETWORKS

Domestically, the big foundations sponsored a vast range of programs that, inter alia, transformed the American academy, sustained an array of globalist foreign policy think tanks, and vigorous foreign affairs media coverage. Foundation sponsorship helped the State Department to improve the training of its foreign-service officers as well as funding academics to boost the department's research capacities. In the universities, the foundations pioneered area studies and IR programs in elite academies such as Harvard, Yale, and Princeton. Additionally, and perhaps more profoundly, such new disciplines were armed with positivistic social-scientific methods that, despite their scientific claims, were particularly effective in generating results of policy-related use. Foundation leaders, in effect, helped to create and perpetuate elite networks of academics, think tanks, publicity organizations, emerging mass media, and public officials. These networks proved powerful in constructing and mobilizing a globalist elite and broader support in the United States, a nation renowned for its strongly "isolationist" tendencies, on the political left and right.[20]

Overseas, the foundations were active in network building and perhaps even more influential, especially in the areas of political and economic development, in promoting capitalist "modernization."[21] Through the mobilization of academics in area studies, political science, economics, and sociology, the big foundations built elite academic institutions overseas, networks of scholars focused around "centers of excellence," academic hubs radiating intellectual influence well beyond the levels of financial investment by the foundations. Such networks were established in strategically important countries and regions—such as Indonesia, Chile, and Nigeria—specifically to ensure a regional and continental multiplier effect: cadres of academics imbued with knowledge and training aimed at orienting them toward a pro-American/Western approach to "modernization" and "development" as opposed to nationalist or procommunist strategies. In addition, and relatedly, some regions/countries were targeted by foundations as strategically important but especially prone to anti-Americanism (or superpower "neutralism") and, therefore, appropriate recipients of funding for American Studies programs. Of course, foundations' investments did not always achieve their goals and sometimes even generated unintended opposition to American influence. This, however, had relatively little effect in the long run and was often viewed as a "bearable" cost of American power.

A significant analytical thread that runs throughout this book is the idea of foundations' knowledge networks as *both* the ends and means of hegemonic social and political forces. Useful here in conceptualizing the role of networks are some of the critical ideas of Pierre Bourdieu, Robert Brym, and Manuel Castells. Castells argues that knowledge flows are unequal: some actors are excluded from knowledge flows, while others are included; some kinds of knowledge are valued, while others are marginalized; some intellectuals are central, while others peripheral. Knowledge flows, however, are not just unequal: they also reorient "mentalities" or "mind sets," particularly by shifting scholars' reference points from their locale to a broader or global logic. In *The Informational City*, Castells advances an appealing argument on the denationalizing impact of metropolitan core-based foundation sponsorship and network building on Third World scholars. Castells argues that as global networks strengthen, "local" actors' logic becomes increasingly divorced from their local culture and preoccupations and more locked in to relative "placelessness," with the latter incorporated into the "hierarchical logic of the organization," in our case the logic of the global knowledge network.[22]

Pierre Bourdieu's notions of *fields* (or networks or social arenas within which struggles occur for scarce resources) and *symbolic capital* deepen our understanding of the network not only as a system of knowledge flows—an instrument or means—but also as an important phenomenon in its own right. Foundation networks may therefore be seen as fields, as specific social spaces constructed by foundation elites that reproduce themselves (those spaces) to socialize the current generation and to pass on a set of ideas, practices, orientations, habits of interaction with those who are likeminded, and habits of intellectual-political combat with others, to strengthen self-awareness and develop common cultural codes. The prestige associated with those social spaces (networks)—of scholars, policy makers, corporate lawyers—transforms those ideas, practices, and habits into symbolic capital that is seen as legitimate in the wider global social system, thereby reinforcing power relations and elite cohesiveness.

Bourdieu's concept of *habitus*, a system of dispositions that originate in social structures but are so deeply internalized by actors that they generate behavior even after the original structural conditions may have changed, is also useful.[23] In the context of U.S. foundation networks, habitus suggests that merely establishing and maintaining the structural properties, internal hierarchies, intellectual-academic predispositions, and spaces of a network is likely to socialize scholars with specific dispositions about "realistic" or "scientific" research, favoring policy-oriented research strategies. This would then encourage a hierarchy of intellectual-academic endeavors that privileges positivistic and pragmatic approaches over overtly normative or value-oriented ones.

Finally, Bourdieu's ideas about the role of intellectuals in modern societies, especially as it is a specific type of intellectual—the (broadly) policy-related academic researcher or scholar—that U.S. philanthropy seeks to mobilize, are useful for us here. Intellectuals occupy a contradictory position as owners of cultural capital in a system in which cultural capital is subordinated to economic capital. Yet their functions in unequal social systems are vital, especially in defining the social world in ways that lend credibility to the status quo. Should the subordination of intellect to financial-economic power be found in the case studies below regarding the relative power positions of corporate philanthropy and university researchers, the assertions to the contrary of Karl and Katz,[24] two leading "conservative" scholars of philanthropy, would be undermined. It is precisely the increasing role in intellectual production that large-scale bureaucratic organizations—favoring technocratic expertise—have come to play that Bourdieu emphasizes and that have more and more subordinated independent intellectual efforts. In effect, philanthropic foundations are among the strategic-leading players in the intellectual field: they have great influence in determining—through grants—who defines what is legitimate and illegitimate knowledge. Their power to establish new disciplines—such as international relations, for example—as well as their theoretical, methodological, and empirical preoccupations are not "simple contributions to the progress of science . . . [they] are *also* always 'political' maneuvers that attempt to establish, restore, reinforce, protect, or reverse a determined structure of relations of symbolic domination."[25]

It is also the case, according to Robert Brym, that intellectual institutions and knowledge networks are, at least in part, aimed at the incorporation and employment of intellectuals, thereby consolidating their attachment to existing political arrangements and processes of change.[26] Intellectual unemployment or underincorporation within elite cultural and political institutions has long been associated with political radicalism, while integration tends to lead to greater levels of political moderation and stability. U.S. foundations' role in the modernization of Third World nations has been motivated by the conviction that "anything less than their [intellectuals'] smooth and complete integration in the economic, political and cultural spheres will produce radicalism—that is, collective attempts to speed up the retarded pace of modernization by political means, sometimes of a violent nature." In more highly modernized and integrated systems such as the United States, where there has occurred "increasing absorption of intellectuals into various parts of the 'establishment,'" intellectuals engage in "conflict . . . within rather narrowly defined limits."[27]

Robert Brym's ideas converge with those elaborated by the Italian Marxist Antonio Gramsci.[28] Gramsci argues that intellectuals play a vital role in developing their specific social group's or class's economic, political, and social self-awareness and ideas about organizing society, so as better to consolidate class positions. The intellectuals' own political-ideological development is determined by their primary, secondary, and tertiary socialization as well as by the posteducational structure of opportunities available to intellectuals to become occupationally and politically tied to a variety of social groups. U.S. philanthropic foundations have attempted to create strong networks precisely to recruit and mobilize the most promising academic intellectuals for a whole range of large-scale projects, including assisting the development of the American state in domestic and foreign affairs. The intellectuals so mobilized are provided with strong career-building opportunities, well-funded programs, opportunities for policy influence, and are systemically well integrated, and they tend therefore to produce research of a utilitarian, technocratic character that is methodologically compatible with the positivistic orientations of foundation leaders.[29] *This is not to suggest that foundations directly interfere with researchers or research results, let alone pressure researchers. It is only to suggest that given the conditions of perpetual financial crisis within academic institutions, the large-scale funding programs of foundations prove very attractive to researchers and influence the selection of research topics, research questions, and methodologies.*[30] It is plainly possible that, as Berman points out, researchers could always draw conclusions radically at odds with foundations' implicit or explicit intentions, thereby challenging hegemonic thinking.[31]

Overall, such organic intellectuals' work functions largely to elaborate a consensus for the "harmonization" of divergent social and economic forces and the perpetuation of unequal systems of national and global power. By constructing knowledge networks, the most powerful states, in which the richest foundations are based, develop a system of flows of people, ideas, and money suited to the maintenance of the existing global hierarchy of power.

Third World intellectuals are incorporated into network spaces constructed, funded, and heavily influenced by—if not led and populated with—scholars and foundation, corporate, and state elites from the metropolitan core. The former are, to an extent, transformed into cosmopolitans or transnational forces that respond, to an increasing degree, to extranational, global logics. Crudely, such "extraction" of intellectuals approximates the extraction of resources, the global flows of wealth from the underdeveloped to developed nations. Foundations have helped to develop spaces which "house" global elites and within which elites circulate and communicate with one another, developing ideas, programs, and, most of all, symbolic capital. The World Social Forum provides an interesting example of this process.[32]

For American foundations, the construction of global knowledge networks is almost an end in itself; indeed, *the network appears to be their principal long-term achievement.* Although foundation-sponsored networks *also* attempt to operate as means of achieving particular ends, *generally speaking, those ends are not necessarily the ones publicly stated.* However, despite their oft-stated aims of eradicating poverty, uplifting the poor, improving living standards, aiding economic development, and so on, even the U.S. foundations' own assessments of their impact show that they largely have failed in these efforts. On the other hand, those very reports lay claim to great success in building strong global knowledge networks that sustain foundation investments, such as their funded research fellows, research programs, and lines of communication across universities, think tanks, makers of foreign policy, and foreign academics.

Network Building, Not Solving Social Problems

According to Landrum Bolling, a researcher closely linked with the Council on Foundations, Third World university network building was a key objective of U.S. philanthropy—creating "strong universities in a few of the strategically located and potentially important developing countries . . . [with the hope] that these investments could help bring about . . . a critical mass of scholars [as] instruments for broad national development."[33] However, despite his support for the foundations' aims, Bolling concludes that their well-intentioned programs failed to improve the lives of ordinary people. Even as American philanthropy successfully created "professionally elite universities," critics felt that the "'trickle down' benefits to the whole society were not sure enough or fast enough."[34]

Bolling cites Francis X. Sutton, who long served the Ford Foundation (1954–1983), to demonstrate that one of the main achievements of Ford in Latin America was the development of *networked cadres of social scientists*. Ford backed the formation of professional and scholarly associations to train, cohere, and incorporate Latin American social scientists, including the Latin American Social Science Council and the Brazilian Society of Agricultural Economics.[35]

Additionally, Bolling demonstrates the extensive system of sponsorship and network building that U.S. philanthropy established across kindred overseas organizations. The Ford Foundation provided funding to organizations that back development programs similar or complementary to its own: the Overseas Development Institute, to develop expertise (at Oxford and Cambridge universities) and public discussion on development issues in Britain; the Royal Institute of International Affairs, an elitist counterpart to the U.S. Council on Foreign Relations, to research Latin American development issues; the German Institute for Developing Countries, to train technical experts to serve overseas; and the Organization for Economic Cooperation and Development.[36]

From a Gramscian viewpoint, Robert Arnove argues that foundations' sponsorship of expert-training programs across the world was largely aimed at developing leadership and "competence" in the professions, the managerial classes, and in government and was undergirded by the technocratic belief that societies only change and develop if they have competent leaders. The Rockefeller Foundation saw as its most coherent historical mission "the development of institutions to train professional people, scientists and scholars in the applied disciplines, who in turn will train succeeding generations of students, advance the state of knowledge in their fields." This approach sidelines "mass-based" programs and networks, preferring to invest instead in elite institutions and networks, an inherently elitist political and ideological strategy.[37] Hence, Ford funded the construction of "centers of excellence" that were to "induct [scholars] into regional and international networks . . . conducting the type of research the Ford Foundation thinks is appropriate and useful." Ford grants for research, travel, conferences, and journals integrated and assimilated regional and international scholars with specific standard literatures, dominant disciplinary assumptions, and appropriate research methodologies. And to ensure that its funded students are not neglected after graduation, Third World scholars return from the United States, according to Ford's annual report in 1975, "often to be employed in an emerging network of Foundation-supported research centers."[38]

What was the impact of network construction on actual economic development and raising mass living standards? "The ultimate goal of institution-building is of course national development—*to widen the range of choice open to the general population, improve the quality of life, and serve the most important needs of the people*," according to the Ford and Rockefeller foundations.[39] That this, on the whole, did not occur is well recognized by foundation officials and their scholarly sympathizers. A Rockefeller-backed assessment of the role of Third World universities in national development criticized them as "dysfunctional and disoriented," which was attributable to their adoption of American and other Western university structures "with little thought or effort given to questions of how this mode of academic organization would fit or serve existing conditions."[40] This suggests that the foundations' success even in a core objective—building strong, effective institutions for development—must be qualified.

A major report in 1976 by Kenneth W. Thompson (a former vice president of the Rockefeller Foundation) also added its voice to "disillusionment . . . within the agencies [of foreign aid] because it was believed that assistance had not yielded the hoped-for results." Indeed, he noted the persistence of structural and social inequality. Further, he commented that "most institutions of higher education abroad were ivory towers, elitist in character, and . . . unresponsive to the urgent needs of their people."[41] Instructively, the way forward identified by Thompson was based on the cooperation of Western and Third World scholars, i.e., human capital that American philanthropy and other aid agencies had developed since the 1950s. That is, established networks were to be used to redefine the mission of the university in development, despite their failure to meet the needs of Third World peoples. It was hoped that a more cooperative style of First World–Third World negotiation would help develop better economic planning and lead quite quickly to the alleviation of poverty.

Yet, the main thrust of Thompson's report remained focused on network development through further aid to universities for innovative ideas, "career security for staff . . . and strategies to meet the problem of the brain drain." It was recommended that "agencies should continue to help build a reservoir of scholars, faculty members, and development-oriented educators in developing countries." One way to do so might be "to maintain and strengthen the *present* network of educators in developing countries."[42] And when we look closely at the network assembled by Thompson, it is clear that it is thoroughly enmeshed in the foundation-sponsored community: representatives from the foundations themselves (such as David Court of the Carnegie Corporation, Rockefeller's Michael Todaro and George Harrar, and Ford's F. Champion Ward), from universities and institutes long funded by the foundations (such as Universidad del Valle, Cali, Colombia; and University of Ife, Nigeria), and from scholars and university leaders who had received funding from U.S. philanthropy (Indonesia's Soedjatmoko and a host of African university leaders).[43] The network endured even as failures were revealed and development strategies were refined: its members were considered "highly respected and responsible Third World educators"[44] who would produce legitimate and fundable knowledge. As Arnove argues, the principal benefits lay in the incorporation of Third World scholars "into regional and international networks of individuals and institutions conducting the type of research the Ford Foundation [among others] thinks is appropriate and useful."[45] Arnove further contends that foundation knowledge networks "facilitate the movement of ideas among nationals of a region and between the metropolitan centers and the periphery." The production and consumption of policy-related "network" ideas is thereby separated from the locale and the "masses" and incorporated within elite discourses.[46] In this way, even the relatively radical ideas they generate may become diluted, domesticated, and metamorphosed into incremental reforms that fail to address the structural conditions of global inequality.

Foundations build networks for their own sake because they produce results by virtue of merely being constructed (i.e., due to a range of "internal" functions they perform) and, second, because networks achieve ends other than those publicly stated (their "external" functions). Foundation networks foster and create frames of thought that cohere the network; they generously finance spaces for the production and legitimization of particular types of knowledge; networks build careers and reputations; they fund key scholars, policy makers, universities, journals, professional societies, and associations, connecting scholars from the "core" metropolitan centers with those in the "periphery"; networks provide sources of employment for intellectuals within a system of "safe" ideas, strengthening some ideas, combating others, and, merely through generating and disseminating ideas and empirical research preventing, or at least making a lot less likely, "other thoughts"; networks identify and develop pro-U.S. elite cadres that, in the

Cold War, backed (and benefited from) capitalist modernization strategies and that, today, back and benefit from neoliberal globalization strategies.

Foundation networks are system-maintenance systems that, *usually* after a sufficient period of foundation patronage, self-perpetuate (as most organizations try to do). Their self-perpetuation becomes a vested interest of the networks' key constituencies. Networks produce "legitimate" scholars linked with "legitimate" ideas and policies endorsed by or at least engaged with "legitimate" organizations such as the International Monetary Fund, World Bank, and U.S. Department of State, among others. They help to maintain the status quo and, more frequently, act as intrasystemic reformers.

Conceptualizing the State-Private Network

Though links between states and private transnational actors are recognized in numerous empirical studies, there is little conceptualization of such relationships. This constitutes a genuine problem in the study of foundations that, on one hand, appear to straddle the "state-private" divide while, on the other, appear to be fiercely independent of the state. However, a number of international historians have developed the concept of "state-private networks" to conceptualize the interconnections and consensus-building activities between a range of civil-society organizations and the (American) state.[47] Such an approach is among several that offer much more persuasive and novel ways of understanding "how power works," with special reference to philanthropic foundations, at both domestic and global levels, and a number of those approaches—such as epistemic communities, parastates, corporatism, the Establishment, Gramscian hegemony theory—are further explored in this chapter. I will argue, however, that Gramscian analysis provides the most comprehensive framework for this study and that the other perspectives may be subsumed within it.

The cooperative relationship of the modern American state with elite foreign affairs and other organizations blurs the distinction between the public and private sectors and calls into question theories (such as pluralism, statism, and instrumental Marxism)[48] that advance a *zero-sum* view of power and pit the state *against* private interest groups or vice versa. Yet, cooperative state-private elite networks have played a powerful historical role in mobilizing for U.S. global expansionism, and such networks can best be appreciated by examining concepts that emphasize shared and mutual state-private elite interests and go beyond the conventional theories of state interests and private interests in competition. The advantages to the state of such arrangements were/are that official policy objectives could be met, or at least advanced, especially in "sensitive" areas, by purportedly unofficial and nongovernmental means. American foundations are and historically have been particularly close to the state and therefore provide ideal illustrative cases of public-private "bridging" organizations.

According to Michael Mann, one of the most significant powers of the modern state is its infrastructural capacity, in addition to its considerable and growing coercive power. That is, the state's power has increased to reach deeply into its "own" society and draw upon reservoirs of legitimacy and popular goodwill, in addition to extracting tax revenues and using the benefits of a productive economy, such as bank loans.[49] Gramsci, on the other hand, maintains that one of the most significant powers of dominant *classes* is the ability to establish private institutions that become fundamental to the exercise of state power. Elite self-organization and the organization of private life by state agencies creates the basis of interpenetrated organizations and networks of political, ideological, and cultural power, and this has far-reaching consequences for practically every sphere of modern life. Such interpenetrations have forced historians and political scientists to reevaluate and reconceptualize state-private relations and to develop a better understanding of how power works in modern democracies such as the United States.

Each of the following four conceptual frameworks stands against theories that posit an all-powerful state (such as statism or realism) or that posit a weak state against all-powerful private interests (pluralism). Each of the four formulations of the private-state network go beyond the zero-sum view of power that strong state/weak group theories and strong group/weak state theories favor (although corporatism does retain certain elements of its pluralist origins).[50] This chapter explores these four major conceptualizations and then argues that, although each of them advances useful ways of understanding the behavior of the American state and elite private groups, *their insights may be subsumed within the more comprehensive view of power advanced by a neo-Gramscian analysis of power. The role of the following four conceptualizations, therefore, is principally to place more empirical/historical flesh on what are broader and more abstract Gramscian categories and notions, such as historic bloc, hegemonic project, and state spirit.*

THE ESTABLISHMENT

According to the historian Godfrey Hodgson, the Establishment, which he dates back to World War II (but in this book is shown to have a longer lineage), is "the group of powerful men who know each other . . . who share assumptions so deep that they do not need to be articulated; and who continue to wield power outside the constitutional or political forms: the power to put a stop to things they disapprove of, to promote the men they regard as reliable; the power, in a word, to preserve the status quo."[51] More precisely, at its heart, the Establishment is made up of three core groups: internationally minded lawyers, bankers, and corporate executives from New York; government officials from Washington, D.C.; and elite university academics (including the heads of the major philanthropic foundations). These three groups were united, Hodgson argues, by a common history, policy, aspiration, instinct, and technique.

The *historical* origins and unity of the postwar Establishment lay in winning World War II, developing and implementing the Marshall Plan, founding NATO, and confronting the Soviet Union. Their agreed *policy* was to oppose isolationism and to promote "liberal" internationalism, to deprecate national chauvinism but press the case for American power, advocate restraint but admire the use of high-tech military force, and to act with conscience but not permit it to prevent robust action. Their shared *aspiration* was to nothing less than "the moral and political leadership of the world"— to fill the vacuum left by the British Empire. To Hodgson, the fundamental *instinct* of the Establishment was for the political center, "between the yahoos of the Right and the impracticalities of the Left." Finally, Hodgson believes that the Establishment's *technique* was to use the executive branch of government—the White House, National Security Council, the Central Intelligence Agency—rather than the U.S. Congress and public opinion. The Establishment claims to take private action for the public good.

Although Hodgson mentions the place of foundations only in passing, his conceptualization fits several aspects of the foreign policy roles of the Big 3, who saw themselves as bipartisan and ideology free, opposed isolationism, supported liberal internationalism, and worked tirelessly for American global leadership. Foundation leaders were drawn from similar social and educational backgrounds to those of Hodgson's Establishment. In effect, Hodgson identifies the cohesive elite forces that dominate American foreign policy and that bridged the gap between state and society. Although neo-Gramscians would expect a historic bloc to be broader than Hodgson's Establishment, they would certainly find Hodgson's concept useful within a broader formulation, because it permits the specific historicization of Gramscian abstractions. It is also important, of course, in showing that non-Gramscians too recognize that, despite the rhetoric of democracy and egalitarianism, there is indeed disproportionate power wielded in America by unelected, unaccountable, unrepresentative, and highly secretive elites who work outside "the constitutional or political forms."[52]

THE CORPORATIST SCHOOL

Corporatism is a variant of pluralist theory, sharing its idea that the American state is essentially weak, incapable of independent action, and dominated by private interests. Nevertheless, where pluralism focuses on political conflict and competition, corporatism emphasizes mechanisms for conflict management and collaboration between functional blocs (corporations, government, organized labor, agribusiness). Functional blocs cooperate better to manage economic and political transformations, harmonize conflicting interests, and promote political stability.

Corporatists such as Michael Hogan and Ellis Hawley trace the history of functional blocs to the Progressive era, a period of rising corporate power, mass immigration, rapid urbanization, and perceived social chaos.[53] Consequently, big business and government became increasingly intertwined, creating an "organizational sector" above party competition and narrow sectional interests. The "organizational sector" is viewed as "an enlightened social elite," a benign source of policies favoring the whole nation, seeking a *middle way* between "laissez-faire . . . and . . . paternalistic statism." Specifically, the interpenetration of functional blocs and government agencies enhanced the possibilities of pragmatic New Deal reform and an internationalist foreign policy, because the blocs were focused on capital-intensive industrial and financial institutions and with organized labor, all of which had a stake in economic growth and international stability. Such structural changes, in effect, led to the emergence of new elites—an aspect neglected within corporatist literature—that transformed America internally and projected their New Dealism abroad. Michael Wala's analysis of the role of the Council on Foreign Relations is an excellent example of a corporatist account that can be applied to philanthropic foundations.[54]

The corporatist analysis, also, in some ways, fits within a neo-Gramscian framework. Indeed, the corporatists Thomas Ferguson and Thomas Mc-Cormick allude to concepts used in both perspectives. Ferguson actually uses the term "historic bloc" for the New Deal coalition built by Franklin Delano Roosevelt.[55] Certainly, the enlightened self-image of the "organizational sector" accords with Gramscian "state spirit," and the corporatist emphasis on the coalescence of interests between internationally oriented, capital-intensive industries and financial institutions as well as organized labor are fundamental elements of Gramsci's historic bloc. What is missing, however, in corporatist analysis is any compelling account of the role of intellectuals and knowledge institutions. A Gramscian approach adds much by analyzing knowledge-network construction and mobilization of intellectuals by philanthropy.

PARASTATES

As noted previously, the Progressive era witnessed the rise of a variety of reform-oriented and modernizing organizations. Broadly, reformists concentrated on attempts to relieve poverty, promote moral renewal, reform government and politics, and transform America's place in the world.[56] Eldon Eisenach calls these organizations "parastates" because they stood for the "national public good," claiming to represent "the authentic nation." Working outside the established channels of the party machine and electoral politics, parastates favored extending federal executive authority into labor rights, health and safety at work, slum clearance, public health, and so on.[57]

In fact, parastates made no distinction between themselves and "the state," which they saw in Hegelian terms as the embodiment of the faith of a people. In this view, it was taken for granted that "the state must be no external authority which restrains and regulates me, but it must be myself acting as the state in every smallest details of life." The "good citizen," therefore, is "state oriented" in the sense of seeking to achieve a larger public good in his or her everyday actions. But this, in the Progressive era, was the aspiration, not the fact. The interests of a weak federal state and of active parastates coalesced around the mobilization of public opinion: the parastates would educate public opinion behind a reformist agenda at home, through a strong federal state, and via the export of American values abroad. "Good citizens" would also staff the most statist public offices as well as exercise citizenship in publicly oriented private organizations (foundations, charities, etc.). Parastates backed New Deal reform, globalism, and the institutions that underpinned them—the universities, foundations, churches, and public opinion.

The parastates' state orientation is remarkably similar to Gramsci's state spirit. What this suggests is that Gramsci's concepts have a great deal to offer in analyzing power in the United States. Also, it is apparent that the greater comprehensiveness of Gramsci's theoretical framework effectively subsumes but also articulates the concepts outlined above, permitting a more comprehensive, compelling, coherent, and critical study of power.

EPISTEMIC COMMUNITIES

Epistemic (or knowledge) communities play an important role in policy processes. The concept is considered here because it relates to state-private networks, especially in one of its particular forms. Epistemic communities are "networks of specialists with a common world view about cause and effect relationships which relate to their domain of expertise, and common political values about the type of policies to which they should be applied."[58] Understood this way, epistemic communities appear to be value/knowledge-based special interests, very much in the pluralistic mold, who seek to influence the state. Influence, if any, flows from the private group to the state.

A nuanced version of the concept of epistemic communities argues for a "two-tier" dynamic within knowledge groups: the first tier consists of government officials, international agencies, and corporate executives; the second, of academics, lawyers, and journalists. Both tiers share a common conceptual framework but operate within an agreed division of labor: government officials have access to policy making and use the second tier to publicize/disseminate their ideas, legitimate them as "objective and scientific," and to elaborate on them. Additionally, the second tier's ideas are brought to government officials and decision makers as evidence of a growing consensus. When such interactions conclude successfully, they lead to the institutionalization of the epistemic community's "policy paradigm" and the incorporation of experts into direct state service.[59]

In relation to Gramscian thought, the concept of epistemic communities is limited—it contains no general theory of power or the state nor of the multiple sources of power in the corporate economy, the academy, and so on. The present argument differs from Haas's pluralism and the lack of articulation of epistemic communities with other aspects of power, especially the power of the purse, and the rather casual way in which Haas suggests that knowledge networks "emerge" in response to "demand" without examining the precise mechanisms by which effective demand for information is distributed and whether there are any agencies that both generate demand and foster the growth and development of suppliers of knowledge. Haas implicitly works within a notion of a free market of ideas. This book argues that certain strategic institutions with financial power try to foresee problems and foster the scholars that may assist in problem conceptualization and solution. Placed in a Gramscian context, however, the epistemic-community approach becomes a more usable empirical concept that might have something to say about the precise character of state-private networks and relations.

The concepts of Establishment, the corporatist organizational sector, parastates, and epistemic/knowledge communities have much in common, and they may usefully be applied to American foreign relations to help us understand the relationship between key elements of private elite and other organizations and interests with various agencies of the American state. Each concept clearly shares the view that there are numerous and significant overlaps in outlook and interests between the state and elite sectors of society. Despite the use of different language and vocabularies, each concept highlights the utility of blurring the distinction between state and society, moving beyond ideas of state power that set up the state against society and vice versa. They suggest that political outcomes, policies, and state behavior are better understood as an alliance between state and society; even more, they suggest that state penetration of society and vice versa are so deep and comprehensive—physically, politically, ideologically, psychologically, and organizationally—that it is almost impossible to say where one ends and the other begins.

Political reform is another leitmotif of the four concepts examined here. Enlightened, elite-led change is central to each concept. But the changes/reforms sought and campaigned for are not purely for the sake of change: their aim is to establish a new order, combat "chaos" and "disorder," and create a new regime in which there will be "stability" and "progress." Even though Hodgson's Establishment and the corporatists' organizational sector aspire to stability, they are at heart reformers who challenged the status quo (of isolationism and untrammeled competition, respectively); undermined it through political, economic, and social critiques; and eventually overcame their foes. They then became the upholders of stability—to defend *their* new order.

Relatedly, each concept also favors elite-led, top-down, technocratic change. The masses do not make a positive appearance in any of the concepts examined. There is an underlying assumption of the superiority of expertise, certified knowledge, status, position, social origins, and intellect. The Progressives, the Establishment, etc. shared the view that the masses were poor judges of public issues—indeed, they sink to the level of "primitives" when examining matters of politics, according to Schumpeter,[60] an elite democrat—and were too emotional, unstable, and too easily swayed by rabble rousers and demagogues. In each of the concepts, except the corporatist, the people are the objects of surveillance, elite guidance, and mobilization.[61]

If they frown on the dangers of electoral politics, elites are more optimistic about those men who occupy the higher echelons of the state, for it is the higher executives who are considered as enlightened as they, who indeed are often drawn from the same corporations, elite universities, private schools, foundation boards, churches, and so on. Relatively insulated from the vagaries of electoral politics and public opinion's mood swings, to some extent at least and especially in foreign affairs, the executive branch offers the opportunity of great influence, of realizing goals of political, economic, and administrative reform. The revolving door from Wall Street and Cambridge, Massachusetts, to the corridors of Washington, D.C., expresses and symbolizes the easy circulation of Establishment men in the exercise of power: the symbiosis of private elites and public power.[62]

A NEO-GRAMSCIAN PERSPECTIVE

Hodgson's Establishment and the corporatists' organizational sector are the most economistic of the four concepts, favoring the idea that elites are, at least in part, drawn from the ranks of capital-intensive international manufacturers and bankers. By recognizing the importance of economic interests to politics and the political system, the two relevant concepts move closer to a more radical interpretation of power: Gramscian thought. The latter framework is far more comprehensive and certainly more critical than any of the ones examined above, and it is a better way of explaining state-society relations. In addition, Gramsci's rarely examined notion of "state spirit" offers new insight into understanding state-society relations that is hinted at in several of the four concepts examined above but never satis-factorily articulated.

Gramsci made more explicit what Karl Marx argued: "The ideas of the ruling class are in every epoch the ruling ideas."[63] Gramsci, however, lo-cated ideological, political, and cultural struggle more centrally into Marxist thought, thereby creating space for intellectuals. It is the role of "organic in-tellectuals"—thinkers who are connected with the dominant class, for exam-ple, within the universities, or the church, mass media, political parties—to develop, elaborate, and disseminate dominant ideas, values, and norms and to make "natural," "commonsensical," and psychologically satisfying to the whole society what are, in reality, ideas that principally support the ruling class.

Through struggle, compromise, and the building of enduring coalitions that cut across class, ethnic, and racial cleavages is formed the prevailing idea of "reality," the dominant concept that underlies a particular regime. As political regimes—or hegemonic projects and alliances—are made up of cross-class coalitions, they require for their formation and sustenance mobilizations of public opinion to convince the masses—or at least a criti-cal proportion of them—that they have a stake in current arrangements. In short, the historic bloc is generated and sustained by leadership based on the "consent of the governed," under the hegemonic leadership of politi-cians and intellectuals of the capitalist class.

As the "consent of the governed" is so vital to political arrangements, it is engineered[64] by intellectual, political, and cultural elites through numer-ous channels that involve not only the state but also the sort of organiza-tions that Hodgson's Establishment, the corporatists' organizational sector, Eisenach's parastates, and the epistemic communities would recognize: the major private and public universities, the Council on Foreign Relations, and the great philanthropic foundations—Ford, Carnegie, and Rockefeller.

In Gramscian terms, elite and popular authority are constructed by an alliance of state and private agencies in order to undermine the old or-der and to usher in the new. Central to the motivation of private elites is Gramsci's concept of "state spirit." In essence, state spirit inspires leaders to take personally the concerns of the nation and state and to subordinate narrow economic and political interests to the broader, long-term interests of the state/nation as a whole. State-spirited leaders contextualize them-selves in the broad sweep of national and global historical development:

their outlook "presupposes 'continuity,' either with the past, or with tradition, or with the future; that is, it presupposes that every act is a moment in a complex process, which has already begun and which will continue."[65] According to Gramsci, such leaders may even come to believe "that they *are* the State."[66]

Studies of the American state's and private elites' foreign policy behavior that do not adequately appreciate the importance of state-private networks must be questioned. Private elites played key roles in the making of foreign policy, opinion mobilization, and overseas policy implementation, with the direct and indirect support of the American state. Indeed, foundations and think tanks often were able to operate under the fiction that they were independent nonstate institutions in sensitive countries and regions. The best way to conceptualize and appreciate this phenomenon is through frameworks that provide adequate cognizance of the importance of consensus building and network construction—and the state spiritedness that motivates the state-private network—both within the American Establishment and in its relations with subordinate social classes.

However, the dominant conceptualizations of the position, roles, and history of the Big 3 foundations provide a stark contrast to the critical analysis advanced by neo-Gramscians. "Mainstream" scholars of foundations, as well as foundation insiders, tend to view American philanthropy as comprising benign, enlightened, and selfless forces for the betterment of the nation and world; as above politics and ideology, beyond big business and the state, and part of a third sector above and independent of both;[67] as led by and dependent upon university academics and other intellectual institutions rather than mobilizing the former to advance any ideopolitical agenda; and as builders of a more open and pluralistic America and a democracy-enhancing global civil society (the latter since the late 1980s). They argue, for example, that foundation trustees do not "interfere" with university research and teaching, either within or beyond the United States because American academic professional associations predated the foundations and had, by the time the foundations were established, developed an intellectual autonomy that could not be and was not diminished by philanthropy.[68] They also raise a fundamental objection to Gramscian theory (along with other European elite theories) as inapplicable (or at least less applicable) to the American case, owing to critical differences between the two cultures. In Europe, they argue, intellectuals were mobilized by political parties, but in the United States, parties were different and less legitimate organizations and were shunned by intellectuals. Philanthropy and academia, therefore, steered clear of politics and even government, remaining above partisanship, patronage, and parochialism.[69] Karl and Katz, therefore, react to a Gramscian analysis of foundations by reverting to the more optimistic interpretations of foundation insiders, who claim that foundations merely sponsor good ideas or knowledge for its own sake, rather than for political, strategic, or ideological ends.[70] Karl and Katz et al., therefore, would expect to find, in the case of the foundations' roles in the cases considered in this study, disinterested, apolitical, and nonideological grant-making and investment initiatives that were independent of the American state; that is, they would expect to find evidence to confirm the foundation's own *publicly stated* claims about their role. *Foundations of the American Century* fundamentally challenges such interpretations.

QUESTIONS AND METHODS

Given this radically divided set of ideas and arguments about the position, roles, and history of the Big 3 foundations, in what follows I directly address several questions:

> Are foundations above governmental and corporate interests, or are they part of an unrepresentative East Coast Establishment and part of a hegemonic ruling elite?
>
> What are and historically have been the roles of philanthropic foundations—at home and abroad—in U.S. foreign policy?
>
> Are American foundations and their increasingly powerful networks of global philanthropy actively creating a politically and ideologically skewed "global civil society" that sustains American (and Western) hegemony? Are the foundations now building the organizations and civil-society infrastructure that support U.S.-led globalization?
>
> What does the evidence suggest about "how power works" in the United States, particularly regarding the role of knowledge and knowledge networks?

These questions are addressed through a series of detailed case studies of the foundations' roles from the 1930s to the "war on terror" after 9/11 by analyzing relevant comprehensive historical and contemporary primary evidence from foundation records. Those foundations' roles break down into the following kinds: first, policy making and building state research capacity, especially focusing on the foundations' support for think tanks and other policy-related intellectual institutions, such as the Council on Foreign Relations (CFR), Carnegie Endowment for International Peace, Yale Institute of International Studies, and the American Committee on International Studies; second, elite opinion formation and mobilization efforts through the examination of, for example, the activities of the CFR's regional committees, Foreign Policy Association, and Institute of Pacific Relations, as well as university IR programs' outputs; third, the building of formal and informal international organizations in and through which American influence and hegemony was exercised; fourth, direct overseas interventions in coordination with the U.S. state in promoting American ideas, values, and methods in regard to economic-development strategies in specific cases, including interventions in Indonesian, Chilean, and Nigerian universities during the Cold War, as well as promoting Americanism and combating anti-Americanism more generally; and, finally, in post–Cold War promotion of neoliberal globalization and strategies of democracy promotion.

Foundations' records are an extremely rich source of knowledge and insights as to the mindset of their leaders and the rationale, scope, and effectiveness of their funding programs. They yield information on their policy-making committees' main preoccupations and assumptions, including the boards of trustees; documents on internal conferences for clarifying aims/objectives; grant files charting the funding of particular programs, projects, and institutions; grant impact evaluation reports; internal correspondence and memoranda chronicling policy debates; correspondence between officials and grantees; external referees' reports; annual reports; officers' and trustees' oral histories; and correspondence with relevant sections of the State (and other) Departments. These records have yielded much evidence—links with U.S. universities' area studies and IR programs, elite opinion mobilization activities, and the foundations' own overseas operations in support of U.S. hegemony—to shed light on the key questions. The case studies (from the 1930s/World War II years, the Cold War, and the post–Cold War periods) reveal the difference to U.S. foreign affairs made by philanthropy over a long historical period; provide evidence of their political-ideological characteristics and their relationships with the American state and corporations; their perception of the roles and effect of the knowledge networks they historically constructed; their role in globalization, democracy promotion, and global civil society construction and, thereby, in "mobilizing bias" in certain policy-related and ideological directions and away from others; and in addressing the final question as to what the evidence tells us about "how power works" in a major liberal democracy and through its increasingly "globalized" reach.

The whole study permits consideration of the first question regarding the foundations' third-sector claims. Most specifically, however, the question will be addressed by an original analysis of the political, religious, educational, occupational, and corporate backgrounds of the foundation trustees and officers. By examining the connections of scores of foundation leaders with the rest of American society, politics, state, and economy, I analyze trustees' wider linkages and changes over time. It is explicitly recognized, though not in any overly deterministic way, that social origins have far-reaching consequences. It is also recognized that socialization processes are lifelong in duration and effect: each time individuals enter a new phase of their lives or enter new institutional cultures, they undergo subtle reeducation in their self-concept.

The second question—the historical and contemporary roles of U.S. foundations in American foreign affairs—will be explored in a number of related ways. For example, I analyze the foundations' contributions to enhancing the American state's policy-making functions, through financing initiatives to increase the research/knowledge-construction capacities of the state; improving official policy makers' linkages with experts and think tanks; increasing the supply of academic policy-related expertise useful to policy makers; and increasing the supply of better-trained graduates from U.S. foreign policy–related area studies and IR programs.

Additionally, I will explore this issue at the level of the foundations' roles in forming and mobilizing elite, attentive, and public opinion. As the U.S. political system is especially responsive to public opinion, American elites developed sophisticated means of engineering consent. The role of the foundations in opinion formation will be considered through their financing of important prointernationalist and anti-isolationist publicity organizations; women's conferences, labor unions, and business associations; workshops and educational materials for school teachers and students; research on internationalist public opinion formation strategies and the effectiveness of specific kinds of radio broadcasts; and building connections with interest groups promoting policies such as the abolition of American neutrality legislation in the late 1930s and American belligerence before the Japanese attacks on Pearl Harbor in December 1941.

The book also considers how the Big 3 foundations directly promoted American hegemony through their networks of U.S. universities' area studies programs and linkages with overseas universities in countries strategically vital to American interests. In particular, the project explores three case studies (of regionally and strategically pivotal countries: Indonesia, Nigeria, and Chile) to show how the foundations constructed knowledge networks that promoted specific forms of economic development strategies (capitalist modernization), positivistic social-scientific research methodologies, and financed American-foreign university collaborations.

The flows of *people* (academics, doctoral students, policy practitioners), *ideas* (capitalist economic and political development via international loans, aid, and investment), and *money* (foundation grants) that the networks facilitated were the means by which foundations concretely built American hegemony. Research suggests that the construction of networks is both a *means* of hegemony construction as well as an *end in itself* because, once established, the network connects and maintains flows of people, ideas, and finances, ensuring that Third World elites remain within the orbit of powerful American/Western institutions.

The third question—the roles of foundations in globalization, democracy promotion, and global civil society—will be addressed by examining an emerging secondary literature on philanthropy in the twenty-first century[71] as well as the activities of the International Network of Strategic Philanthropy, the Asia-Pacific Philanthropy Consortium, and the major American foundations and their European counterparts (Soros's Open Society Network, Europe in the World, and the European Foundation Centre). Such networks of philanthropy—and philanthropic *networks* of networks—have played a major role in the development of globalization forums such as the World Economic Forum and World Social Forum, in addition to significant funding for the United Nations' globalization-related institutions and the World Bank's development and poverty-reduction programs.[72] Finally, global philanthropy—following the American domestic model—is claiming to develop international nongovernmental and transnational advocacy organizations and coalitions that constitute part of a more representative and accountable "pluralistic" global civil society that plugs the "democratic deficit," a claim challenged by new research.

The chapter structure of the book aims systematically to address the issues above: chapter 2 examines the historical origins and aims, sociology, and worldview of the foundations' leadership groups, considering the case for the foundations being central components of an East Coast foreign policy Establishment.

Chapter 3 covers the period from the 1930s to the end of World War II, considering the ways in which, in a period of "isolationism" in U.S. foreign policy, the foundations fostered liberal internationalism and combated the forces of isolationism. It will also discuss how philanthropy assisted the United States' rise to globalism during World War II by opposing neutrality legislation and sponsoring elite interventionist organizations like the Council on Foreign Relations, the development of university-based IR programs, and of realism as a dominant discourse within the IR discipline. It also examines in some detail the construction of elite knowledge networks and their planning for a new world order.

Subsequent chapters of the book cover the Cold War period from 1950 to the late 1980s and consist of detailed analyses of the foundations' promotion of Americanism and undermining of anti-Americanism through the development of an American Studies network, including the Salzburg Seminar in American Studies, Henry Kissinger's Harvard International Seminar, and the rise of the British and European associations for American Studies (chapter 4). Chapter 5 explores the role of the Ford Foundation in Indonesia and the establishment of an Asian studies network; in particular, the chapter investigates the functions of the Cornell University Modern Indonesia Project and the role of the so-called Berkeley Mafia or Beautiful Berkeley Boys in the transfer of power from the leftist Sukharno to the military regime of Suharto and in the beginnings of the globalization of the Indonesian economy. Chapter 6 details the development by the Ford, Carnegie, and Rockefeller foundations of a capitalist modernizing elite in Africa, with special but not exclusive reference to Nigeria, and the development of an African studies network. Chapter 7 considers the roles of the Big 3 in Chile and the Latin American studies network, with special reference to Ford and the "Chicago Boys," USAID, and the economics departments at the University of Chile and the Catholic University. In addition, chapter 7 examines the transition from Allende to Pinochet (1970–1975), the rise of neoliberalism, and the role of Ford's economists.

Chapter 8 examines the roles of American foundations in the post–Cold War and post-9/11 era: development and promotion of neoliberal globalization, democracy, and global civil society; combating the upsurge in post-9/11 anti-Americanism; and developing a post–Bush era approach to global power. Chapter 9 concludes the book by considering the significance of American foundations to the development and consolidation of the American Century of imperial hegemony; the foundations' appreciation of the power of politically motivated elite knowledge networks; and the theoretical implications of the historical and contemporary evidence.

2 | AMERICAN FOUNDATION LEADERS

This chapter considers the historical context of modern American philanthropy, the men who created and led the foundations, and the views of the world that shaped their activities. The evidence shows that foundation leaders were a core part of the power elite of the United States—unrepresentative, unaccountable, yet highly influential in the nation's foreign relations, undermining pluralistic notions of competing elites. The evidence supports the Gramscian case that the foundations were part of a historic bloc of private and state elites cohered by a long-term globalist hegemonic project. The evidence challenges accounts of American philanthropy that argue that the foundations were disinterested investors in ideas for their own sake or for the betterment of society or mankind in general. The leaders of U.S. philanthropy were both products and producers of history, playing a vital role in America's rise to globalism, despite their neglect by mainstream political science and international relations.[1]

American foundations occupy a distinct place in national life, though one at odds with some of its core values. In a society dedicated to democratic accountability and responsibility, they are answerable to no shareholders, market forces, or electors. Just as the great concentration of corporate wealth and power worried Americans raised on the ideal of the "small manufacturer, artisan and unrestricted competition," so are there periodic anxieties about the robber barons' philanthropic largesse.[2] They are blocs of concentrated "venture" capital generating "political" and intellectual influence, weighty players skewing the "free market of ideas," violating a value and expressing a contradiction that sits at the heart of the American liberal tradition. Foundation leaders' attitudes reflect their vaunted positions: they tend to be "democratic elitists" who take a rather dim view of the "masses." The latter are seen as objects fit for philanthropy-funded experts' investment and intervention but not as subjects in their own right.[3]

Of course, the Big 3 foundations are not without their democratic or liberal features: they value free speech, intellectual inquiry, and pluralistic features of the political system, including the role of public opinion. The foundations also claim to be meritocratic, with trustees recruited from all walks of life. Each of those characteristics, however, is hemmed in by qualifications. Their commitment to intellectual freedom is bounded by their political centrism, their opposition to the left, right, and isolationists, for example. Their commitment to public opinion is fundamentally a belief in the pervasiveness of popular ignorance and the consequent need for elites to "educate" the people in "right thinking." Their meritocratic outlook is tempered by the consistent practice of recruiting white, male trustees overwhelmingly from elite social and economic backgrounds. And those trustees recruited from nonelite backgrounds are normally already acculturated and assimilated to elite culture.[4]

That such organizations have developed in a relatively open political democracy may at first appear to be a contradiction. In fact, for elites, such organizational forms are an absolute necessity in democracies, in which public opinion is valued and potentially very influential at decisive historical moments.[5] Elite interests in democratic polities are protected precisely by well-organized small groups that build networks to promote particular kinds of thinking among publics, adherence or acquiescence among the masses, coherence and consensus among elites, and specific political programs at the level of the state. Such patterns of organization may specifically be sourced in the institutional innovations developed by the "founding fathers" of American philanthropy. This chapter shows that Carnegie, Rockefeller, and Ford were at their most innovative in *engineering systems of organization, the technologies of power: combination, centralization, networking vast corporate undertakings across America and the world, modernizing America into a single "system" suited to their own corporate purposes, building a new "administrative" state at home, and, looking outward, increasingly internationalizing their power.* Their philanthropies were molded in the slipstream of organizational innovations fundamental to managing and maximizing the power of gigantic corporations with global reach. "Giving"—in the "scientific" and systematic ways that characterized early twentieth-century philanthropy—was in very large part also a means of increasing the power and influence of the givers. While their appetite for wealth could be sated, in most cases, philanthropists' "desire for power . . . was not subject to the same law of diminishing returns," as Wall argues. Philanthropists' appetites were imperial in character and content—they wanted to reign supreme.[6] This was particularly important at a time when the institutional capacity of the American federal government, though developing, was limited.

Plainly, the changing position of the United States in the world, allied with profound domestic transformations, played a fundamental role in giving birth to modern American philanthropy. The personal and impersonal forces of history created the contexts for emerging elites in the United States to see their country differently from the late nineteenth and early twentieth centuries onward. For East Coast elites, America was economically, politically, and morally superior, ready not merely to sit at the "high table" of world politics but to supersede moribund colonialism by exporting the "American dream" to the world.[7] Born in anticolonial revolt, the United States laid claim to being a relatively mature democracy, an attractive and open society based on individual opportunity.[8] In today's language, East Coast elites believed that the United States had an abundance of "soft power."[9] Foundation elites wanted better to project *their* "soft power" alongside their aspiration that the American state develop and promote its *own* soft and hard power.

Two of the Big 3 American foundations or, rather, "families" of foundations—Rockefeller and Carnegie—were formed at the very end of the nineteenth and beginning of the twentieth centuries. The Ford Foundation was formed in 1936 but only became a national organization in the early 1950s, and it was constructed on the Rockefeller/Carnegie model. Therefore, the foundations were active through two world wars, the "roaring" (and isolationist) 1920s, the Great Depression, and the Cold War. They remain highly activist in today's post–Cold War, post-9/11 world, a world characterized by the American-led "global war on terror." They are seasoned organizations that have learned skillfully to adapt to their environments as well as to play key roles in shaping those very environments, domestically and internationally.

It is all the more remarkable, then, to note that despite the tumultuous events of the twentieth century, the foundations' overall strategic goals with

regard to promoting America's position in the world have remained virtually unchanged. There have clearly been organizational and programmatic
developments and adaptations, but their commitment to a strategic mission has remained constant. This tactical dynamism has been essential to
their survival, development, and influence. As liberal internationalists in
the 1920s and 1930s, for example, Rockefeller and Carnegie philanthropies
found themselves marginalized in an era of relative isolationism in U.S. foreign policy. Yet their modus operandi proved highly adaptive. Rather than
giving up, foundation leaders strenuously incubated an internationalist
"counterhegemony" to the prevailing (and, admittedly, uneven) isolationist
mainstream.[10]

The Big 3 are adept at fending off political attacks from left and right
on their very existence, including their claims to "Americanism." In 1915,
for example, the fledgling Rockefeller Foundation was attacked in the U.S.
Congress from the left, as being an undemocratic influence in the American
body politic. In the McCarthyite 1950s and the neoconservative-dominated
post-9/11 years, the Big 3 foundations were and are still challenged from the
right for acting in anti- or "un-American" ways, such as "losing" China in
1949 and supporting Palestinian "terrorists" since 9/11.

Of course, wars have had a major influence on foundations' activities,
accentuating their central strategic mission. The drive to war in the mid-
to-late 1930s and the opportunities offered and threats posed to the United
States influenced the precise mechanics of Rockefeller and Carnegie's mission but did not alter the mission itself. World War II, the onset and demise
of the Cold War, and the terrorist attacks on September 11, 2001, worked in
much the same way on the foundations' strategic thinking and operations.
The onset of the era of globalization affected foundations' programs but not
their underlying rationale: the promotion of American power.

Finally, the point about tactical dynamism and strategic consistency may
also be made with reference to the character of the foundations' leadership cadres—boards of trustees and organizational managers: elite, white,
and male. Of course, in an era of globalization and transnationalization,
i.e., since the 1980s, the foundations have recruited some women, African Americans, and foreign nationals to their boards.[11] Yet their elitism
remains intact; the foundations leaders remain wedded to the institutions
and aspirations to global preponderance of the American foreign policy
Establishment.

THE INTERNATIONAL CONTEXT

It hardly needs to be stressed here that the structure of world economic, political, and military power was undergoing profound change in the late nineteenth and early twentieth centuries, when the foundations emerged. By 1950, the contours of world power were almost unrecognizable by the benchmarks of the 1890s or even the Great War. Britain famously declined from heading a global empire to being a power struggling to find a role, as Dean Acheson, an arch-Anglophile, remarked.[12] The flip side to one power's decline, of course, is frequently another's ascendancy. The United States benefited enormously from Britain's pyrrhic military victories, principally economically and financially. While Britain used up its blood and treasure, the United States operated as the "arsenal of democracy" (not to mention its bank)—the producer of the materiel of war but itself guaranteed protection by oceans to east and west and weak powers to its north and south.

America's economic and financial transformation following the Civil War (1861–1865) is remarkable. The facts are well known: agricultural output expanded in all areas—wheat (by 256 percent) and refined sugar (460 percent), for example. Coal production increased by 800 percent between 1865 and 1898, while steel-rail production burgeoned by over 500 percent. In 1901, when they were sold to J. P. Morgan, Andrew Carnegie's mills alone produced more steel than the entire British steel industry.[13]

By 1937, the United States accounted for one-fifth of the world's total manufactured exports; by 1939, the nation's overseas capital stood at over $12 billion, outstripping Britain's holdings by $3 billion. As early as 1918, the United States had become the world's largest creditor nation: the world owed the United States $1.2 billion, not including government loans. By the late 1930s, the City of London's preeminent position as the world's financial center was overtaken by New York's Wall Street.[14]

Such preeminence created the basis for a more assertive and nationalistic foreign policy. Many economic, commercial, and other interest groups demanded that the United States "punch its weight" in global affairs. According to Hofstadter, the Europeans' "scramble for Africa" in the 1890s was viewed with alarm by many American elites, fearing that the carve-up of the world would exclude the United States from a share of the spoils.[15] Presidents McKinley (1897–1901) and Roosevelt (1901–1909) were particularly assertive, militarily defeating Spain in 1898, facing down German encroachments in Venezuela in 1902, generally enforcing the Monroe Doctrine of 1823 ("America for the Americans"), and intervening in Latin America as it suited U.S. interests. As Paul Kennedy argues, however, American policy makers were also more active in global affairs beyond the Western hemisphere: 2,500 American troops were dispatched to "restore order" in China in 1900; Roosevelt acted as mediator in the Russo-Japanese War of 1904–1905 (for which he won the Nobel Peace Prize) and insisted on American participation in the Algeciras Conference in 1906 over the future of Morocco.[16] Roosevelt was an Anglo-Saxonist imperialist who believed that "backward" peoples needed the tutelage of superior races. "More and more," he argued in 1902, "the increasing interdependence and complexity of international political and economic relations render it incumbent on all civilized and orderly powers to insist on the proper policing of the world."[17] Roosevelt was no outlier but was strongly representative of a dominant tendency within an emerging East Coast foreign policy elite.

THE DOMESTIC CONTEXT

According to Hofstadter, the United States was in the middle of a "psychic crisis" by the beginning of the twentieth century, on the very eve of the birth of the Rockefeller and Carnegie foundations.[18] Indeed, the gigantic industrial concerns headed by Andrew Carnegie and John Davison Rockefeller, Sr. and Jr., were both cause and symptom of that crisis. There were several aspects to the psychic crisis brought about by massive industrialization, mass immigration, and rapid urbanization: first, large-scale protest movements across the country—Populism, violent strikes and industrial unionism, in particular—fueling fears among elites that revolutionary tendencies were at large, "the specter . . . of drastic social convulsions";[19] second, the concentration of production to such an extent as to fuel fears that the days of open market competition and opportunity were over; third, the closing of the American frontier, the prevalent belief that the principal outlet for frustrated energies had disappeared; and fourth, the pervasive belief that corruption in business, politics, and government was rampant. All this signaled a radical change to the Victorian-era sense of order that prevailed in middle-class circles. One result of the psychic crisis was, as noted above, America's desire to expand beyond its frontiers: the "tonic of a foreign adventure," as Theodore Roosevelt put it, to unite the nation and overcome its internal upheavals and convulsions. The other result was "an intensification of protest and humanitarian reform. Populism, utopianism, the rise of the Christian Social gospel, the growing intellectual interest in socialism, the social settlement movement."[20] *Philanthropy was implicated both in the sources of the psychic crisis—as we shall see, Carnegie's and Rockefeller's industrial power and practices of labor relations were powerful drivers—and in proposing how to address some of the symptoms of the crisis through social reform and by amelioration of the harsher elements of capitalist industrialization.*[21]

The industrial fortunes upon which Rockefeller and Carnegie philanthropies are based were constructed through organizational innovation and honest endeavor as much as by the exploitation of labor. Carnegie's steel mills dominated the industry. In 1892, Carnegie Steel was capitalized at $25 million; Andrew Carnegie earned $4 million per year.[22] In 1898, Carnegie's profits amounted to $10 million, $3 million higher than in the previous year, an almost 50 percent return on total capitalization.[23]

However, the exploitation of labor—low wages, long hours, unsafe working conditions, and the on-again-off-again battle against organized labor—led to outbreaks of bloody industrial conflict, a rich source of clues as to some of the underlying values of Rockefeller and Carnegie and some understanding of the underlying ameliorative aims of their philanthropies. All was well with the world of the "robber barons" like Carnegie, but, as Josephson argues, labor opposition was developing "in most menacing form" by the 1880s. "Against the threat of labor's growing might, and its demands which they held intolerable, the barons exerted themselves with . . . an unflinching ruthlessness. In the United States, as in almost no other industrial nation, the encroachments of organized labor were halted or neutralized or completely nullified."[24] Carnegie proved no exception to this rule.

The Homestead strike/lockout of June–July 1892 is instructive of the methods of Andrew Carnegie. Prior to this, Carnegie was often thought of as a benevolent employer; the handling of the strike tarnished his reputation. Briefly, Carnegie's steel plant at Homestead, Pennsylvania, was unionized. Carnegie wanted to break the union and to reduce worker levels and wages.[25] Faced with resistance, Carnegie's manager, Henry Frick, locked out the workers, recruited nonunion strikebreakers, and hired hundreds of armed men from the Pinkerton National Detective Agency, a nineteenth-century private military contractor.[26] The ensuing gun battle left twelve men dead or wounded; the state militia was called in to protect strikebreakers; after four months the strikers returned to work, and all strike leaders were blacklisted and many charged with murder; the union was broken. Despite

Carnegie's later expressions of regret, the episode furnishes an important contradiction: as Joseph Frazier Wall argues, Carnegie was "torn between wanting to pose as a great democrat and liberal and at the same time wanting to make sure Carnegie Steel came out on top."[27]

The Rockefeller family wealth was based on Standard Oil of Ohio, established in 1870, which effectively grew to control the production, refining, and distribution of oil in the United States by the 1890s. Capitalized at a modest $70 million, it produced earnings of $10 million per annum in 1882; by 1890, earnings had almost doubled. In 1882, the trust wholly owned fourteen other companies and partly owned twenty-six others, including the National Transit Company, with a capitalization of $30 million. By that time, the trust earned 53 percent of its income from transportation and just 36 percent from refining.[28] It was a multiheaded organism spanning the United States, and, as it grew, it confronted organized labor even more ruthlessly than did Carnegie.

The dispute at Rockefeller's Colorado Fuel and Iron Company (CFI, in which they owned 40 percent of the shares) in 1913–1914 was even bloodier than the lockout at Homestead. Up to sixty-six strikers and their family members were killed when National Guardsmen attacked the "tent city" that strikers had built upon eviction from their homes in CFI's company town at Ludlow. John D. Rockefeller Jr.'s role was identical to that played by Carnegie before and during the Homestead dispute: he backed the company's managers in breaking the strike and in forcing down wages. In October 1913, Rockefeller commended the correctness of CFI's action in refusing to unionize the mines and in bringing in private armed guards.[29] Rockefeller congratulated management for "fighting the good fight, *which is not only in the interest of your own company but of other companies of Colorado and the business interests of the entire country and the laboring classes* quite as much." Rockefeller promptly employed a public relations firm—headed by one of the profession's pioneers, Ivy Lee—to handle the issue in the American press, indicating a shrewd understanding of the political significance of public-opinion "management" in the United States. Lee's stream of bulletins and press releases, purporting to be from local Colorado coal operators rather than from Junior's office, were sent to opinion leaders across the country, leading to broadly favorable coverage in the American press.[30]

There were protests across the country, including outside Rockefeller's offices in New York City. The Ludlow killings renewed public attention to the Rockefeller Foundation and John D. Rockefeller, principally as a result of an ongoing congressionally authorized investigative Commission on Industrial Relations, under the chairmanship of the attorney Frank P. Walsh.[31] The Walsh Commission, among others, concluded that the newly established Rockefeller Foundation was being used by Rockefeller industrial interests to develop propaganda for deployment during industrial disputes. In addition, the Rockefellers had been receiving direct advice on the CFI dispute by the Canadian labor expert and future prime minister William L. MacKenzie King, who was subsequently employed by the foundation to undertake an "impartial" "Investigation of Industrial Relations to Promote Industrial Peace."[32] King's testimony to the Walsh Commission was instructive on the relationship between technical expertise and corporate funding: he argued that the technical character of his work meant that he was impartial, although he was placing the results of his studies at the disposal of powerful interests.[33]

These two episodes provide useful antidotes to any (understandably) relaxed acceptance of the altruistic public rhetoric of Carnegie and Rockefeller philanthropy. At the very least, the bloody disputes at Homestead and Ludlow suggest that the motives of philanthropists are complex and worthy of deeper analysis. The argument of this chapter does not depend, however, on the personal "psychology" and motivations of the foundations' benefactors. Feelings of "guilt" and the desire to "give something back" to society are less interesting to the argument here than the underlying aims, operations, and influences of philanthropy in the long run. In providing brief accounts of the histories of the industrialists who endowed the foundations, this chapter seeks, at least partly, to show the means by which they clawed their way to the top—through ruthlessness; the deployment of bribery, corruption, and violence; and outright exploitation. As important, however, to the character of their philanthropic ventures was the industrialists' organizational vision as *architects of massive, centralized corporate-bureaucratic national and global networks.* That is, their "normal" (and mainly legal) business activities and experiences are the other key to an understanding of Rockefeller, Carnegie, and Ford philanthropy.

Origins, Aims, and Founders

As noted above, part of the psychic crisis of the 1890s reflected the country's breakneck pace of capitalist industrialization and accompanying social polarization, generating great fears among elites. Some of those fears resulted in the flowering of calls for reform: slum clearance, labor laws, and so on. Others turned to charity. Still others, including Rockefeller and Carnegie, turned their minds to establishing philanthropic foundations to help tackle the ills of American society, economy, and politics. The flurry of new foundations reflected the rapid increase in the number of millionaires—rising from an estimated one hundred in 1880 to forty thousand by the middle of the Great War. Individual fortunes were remarkable. Carnegie's personal wealth stood at $300 million in 1901, while John D. Rockefeller's stood at $900 million in 1913, making him the richest man in history.[34]

Although the Rockefeller Foundation was formed in 1913, the family's philanthropic efforts had begun with the University of Chicago (1892), the Rockefeller Institute of Medical Research (1901), and the General Education Board (1903). This was augmented by the Laura Spelman Rockefeller Memorial (LSRM) in 1918 and the Rockefeller Brothers' Fund in 1940. Andrew Carnegie's philanthropic efforts include the Carnegie Institution of Washington (1902), Carnegie Institute of Technology (1905), Carnegie Foundation for the Advancement of Teaching (1905), Carnegie Endowment for International Peace (1910), and the Carnegie Corporation of New York (1911). Other philanthropic foundations formed in that period include Russell Sage (1907) and the Cleveland Foundation (1914).

The Carnegie Corporation (CC) was founded in 1911, with an endowment of $135 million, for the provision of "information and understanding," especially adult education. As it was tax exempt, it was forbidden from supporting political causes or engaging in propaganda.[35] CC's trustees claimed to supply no ideas; they hoped merely to supply "fertilizer" to scholars.[36] On the other hand, trustees were clear that public opinion "bears heavily upon the thinking of [the American people's] representatives" and aimed, therefore, to "educate" the people to support the United States in playing "effectively its role of leadership in world affairs."[37] The Carnegie Endowment for International Peace (CEIP, founded in 1910) was even more directly concerned with "educating" public opinion. One of its founding spirits, U.S. Senator Elihu Root, noted in 1915 that there was a compelling need for the CEIP and others to "inform the minds and educate the attitude of this great new sovereign [public opinion] that is taking charge of foreign affairs."[38]

The Rockefeller Foundation (RF, founded in 1913) was far less modest: it claimed to promote nothing less than the welfare of all mankind. It was set on a scientifically driven mission to develop solutions to America's and the world's most intractable problems: sickness, poverty, underdevelopment, and ignorance.[39] The Ford Foundation (FF), like its older counterparts, aimed to develop human potential, promote peace and freedom, and aid global political and economic development.[40]

KEY FOUNDATION LEADERS

This section considers the biographies of the principal pioneers and leaders of Carnegie, Rockefeller, and Ford philanthropy: the men who made, funded, and led the foundations. The evidence from these brief biographies combines to show that the foundations were, from the very earliest days of their creation, part of and builders of the American East Coast Establishment.

JOHN D. ROCKEFELLER SR. (1839–1937)

JDR Sr. was born in Richford, near Binghamton, New York, the second of six children in a German-American family. He was educated at local schools, the Owego Academy, and a local commercial college in Cleveland, Ohio. After graduating from high school, he worked as a clerk at the age of sixteen. As a Northern Baptist, he paid 10 percent of his earnings to charity, despite relatively low income and extensive family responsibilities. Rockefeller's father, William, a confidence trickster, among other things, was an embarrassment to his family.[41] Rockefeller's mother, a somewhat stern Scottish Protestant, was a powerful influence in shaping JDR Sr.'s habits of thrift, personal responsibility, hard work, and religious faith.[42] According to one view, JDR learned from his father, William, somewhat surprisingly, the importance of honesty in business affairs, honoring contracts, and prompt settlement of bills. William claimed to teach his children the realities of life by "skinning them in financial matters as frequently as possible."[43]

According to Nevins, this heritage helped "mould" the purpose and to establish JDR as one of the giants of American industrial history. Nevins, a highly sympathetic biographer, concludes that JDR's career was marked by "his single-mindedness; his sharpness of insight; his cool disdain of emotional factors; his instinct for the future . . . ; his breadth of ambition; and his skill (which to opponents sometimes seemed merciless) in finding novel weapons to attain his ends—his strategic ingenuity."[44] He was a churchgoing materialist, a charitable citizen but ruthless entrepreneur, and a Republican who did not enlist in the Civil War (too many depended on his business). He was a single-minded, ambitious, strategic thinker on the scale of the arch–Empire builder Cecil Rhodes.[45] He understood more clearly and was moved by the forces of "combination and concentration"; he knew how to marshal "the right clout at the right point in the system, making the appropriate alliance, engaging the vulnerable opponent." Collier and Horowitz surely are right when they argue that JDR's principal contributions "had far less to do with the technology of oil than with the *technology of power*." His passion was to "work on different kinds of structures, like the creation of the corporate trust,"[46] a powerful system of networked power.

JDR's greatest achievement was the Standard Oil Company of Ohio, which not only destroyed all other competition in Cleveland within a few months but went on to become one of the world's largest multinational corporations. In an age of restrictions on interstate ownership of corporations, Rockefeller pioneered the "trust," a new form of organization that permitted him centralized control of America-wide business interests, breaking the shackles (or safeguards) of the internal political organization—into dozens of states—of the United States. He not only nationalized his corporation; he *internationalized* it—steps followed by others. JDR was a ruthless competitor able to use the very system of competition itself to crush opposition and "progress" beyond it to one that was dominated by huge conglomerations, a new stage of capitalism. Standard Oil's foreign policy, as it were, reflected its domestic policy: "The Standard fought for overseas markets with the same ferocious intensity as it had for domestic concessions . . . defying foreign governments as routinely as it had state legislatures at home."[47] Through intense price cutting and other activities, Standard Oil managed to control 60 percent of the European oil market by the early twentieth century. Interestingly for this study of Rockefeller and other American philanthropy, Standard's overseas behavior found more congeniality with the objectives of the federal administration, because, in faraway lands, Standard's "prosperity was America's prosperity; its manifest destiny was at one with the nation's." Enjoying remarkable access to State Department field reports on the Middle East and Southeast Asia, Standard Oil "functioned as a shadow government with a foreign policy of its own," according to Collier and Horowitz.[48]

After much-criticized monopolistic, competition-busting practices, in addition to well-documented cases of "buying" congressmen and senators to abort threatening legislation, Standard Oil was broken up by order of the Supreme Court in 1911.[49] JDR became America's first dollar billionaire as Standard's share price skyrocketed. As Abels fawningly summarizes the organizational achievements of JDR, Standard Oil was a truly integrated and networked system: "As the operations in oil extended vertically by integration, the trust owned its wells at the source and sold the end product at wholesale and retail, transporting oil through its own pipelines, by its tankers at sea, and by its own tank wagons on the streets of cities, even in foreign countries."[50] His and John D. Rockefeller Jr.'s philanthropy would also be pioneering in its own right: they would transform the purposes, organization, and scale of "giving" much as JDR had the corporate landscape of America. His was a *scientific* philanthropy; a networked globe-spanning system; efficient, concentrated power for maximum impact; and a "social dividend."[51] He would nationalize and globalize America and, indeed, begin the processes that would lead U.S. philanthropy to try to Americanize the globe.

JOHN D. ROCKEFELLER JR. (1874–1960)

It was John D. Rockefeller Jr., however, who was mainly responsible for running the family's philanthropic enterprises. He lived and worked in his father's shadow, sharing many of the same attitudes and ideals. Junior's life was driven by a desire to detach in the public mind the Rockefeller name from social irresponsibility and privilege and adorn it with responsibility and service; hence his employment of Ivy Lee as a permanent senior adviser after the Colorado dispute.[52] Yet he was also committed to big business and to leaving behind as large a fortune to his children as he had received from Senior.[53]

Privately tutored until the age of ten, Junior attended successively the New York School of Languages, the Cutler, and then the Browning private schools. He graduated from Brown University in 1897[54] and joined his father's financial staff under the tutelage of the Reverend Frederick T. Gates, who also drove and managed Senior's numerous philanthropic projects.[55] Much later, Junior made a number of appointments to assist his philanthropic and other enterprises that, in effect, replicated the modern corporate committee system with which Senior had run the tightly networked Standard Oil. The influence of Gates was supplemented by Junior's appointment of a number of "informal" associates, including Raymond Fosdick and Beardsley Ruml, men who were progressive modernizers, builders of organizations, networks, and a new "administrative state."[56] Junior weaved Rockefeller interests into the very institutional fabric of American life.[57]

He had a view of global affairs and alignments that derived from the work with which Fosdick and Gates had acquainted him, which was being done by the elitist and internationalist Institute of Pacific Relations (IPR), the Foreign Policy Association (FPA), and the Council on Foreign Relations (CFR), among other leading organizations that had resulted directly from the Great War.[58] Swimming with the tide of modernization, Junior put Rockefeller money behind programs of centralization, scientific management, and "the internationalization of American influence and power."[59] His work with the Protestant churches, missions, and charitable trusts, as with his philanthropy, was of a piece. And it continued to be funded by Junior's stock holdings of Standard Oil and by the profits from his forays into banking and finance, through the acquisition of Chase Manhattan Bank (1930) and the Equitable Trust Company (1911).[60] Junior ended up building a network of philanthropies and other emblematically American entities that are every bit as impressive as the Standard Oil monopoly. Yet, at heart, there was never any contradiction for him in "giving" while pursuing greater wealth; indeed, giving was seen a way of "taking" more power or, at least, exercising greater influence over the great social and other movements—combination, concentration, centralization, and internationalization—that he believed would dominate the future.

Andrew Carnegie (1835–1919)

Andrew Carnegie was born in Dunfermline, Scotland, to a caring family. He never knew grinding poverty firsthand and never empathized with those who did. According to Wall, Carnegie's references to the nobility of poverty in his *Gospel of Wealth* betrayed his inability ever really to appreciate others' experiences: his life of care and protection had made him largely egocentric, unusually so.[61] Educated at local schools, Carnegie was a voracious reader. Both parents were lapsed Calvinists, his father a supporter of Chartism—a radical reformist organization that campaigned for democracy in nineteenth-century Britain. Ironically, it was at the very moment that the Chartists seemed to be raising the temperature of protest that the family emigrated to the United States. For Andrew, who also was "educated" in the political democratic demands of Chartism, the United States was just about the world's best system, and he wanted to utilize to the full the opportunities open to him. Like John D. Rockefeller Sr., Carnegie became the supporter of his family at a young age, as his weaver father, William, rued the industrial revolution that rendered his handloom obsolete. There was little inkling in those days that Andrew Carnegie was destined to be one of the pioneers and powerhouses of the American industrial revolution.

Starting as a telegraph messenger at the Pittsburgh branch of the Ohio Telegraph Company in 1851, Carnegie's hard-working nature and eye for opportunities saw him promoted to superintendent. He began making money through investing in stocks and shares. Progressing into the railroad industry, Carnegie served in the Civil War as superintendent of military railways and telegraphs. His biggest windfall came with earnings of $1 million on a $40,000 investment in 1864, which Carnegie used astutely to move into the iron and steel industry, given the lucrative government contracts available for railroads, bridges, and armaments to defeat the Confederate armies.

Like Rockefeller, Carnegie was an organizational innovator: he vertically integrated steel production with its raw materials' supply chain, bought up rival corporations, and built the biggest steel company in the world. When he sold out to J. P. Morgan in 1901, Carnegie received $480 million.[62] The sale led to the emergence of the United States Steel Corporation, the world's first billion-dollar company.[63] Upon retirement, Carnegie vowed to "give away" the bulk of his money before his death.

The Rockefellers and Carnegie modernized charitable giving into "scientific" philanthropy. The foundations they established were in the proper sense investments and investors—in ideas, scholarship, and research institutions. Just as they revolutionized American industrial organization and reaped the dividends, so they transmogrified "giving," hoping to reap dividends in the form of social peace and stability, particular forms of progress, ideological legitimation for the American system, and ameliorative reform—making America modern through the rule of expertise to cohere the elite, build a stronger federal executive, and "manage" the masses.

HENRY FORD (1863–1947)

The Ford Foundation, in its "modern" form, on the other hand, was only the indirect work of the man who gave it its name, Henry Ford. Although funded by an endowment of over $2.3 billion in 1936—a sum that dwarfed the Carnegie and Rockefeller philanthropies—from Ford Motor Company profits and shares, the foundation is not a direct extension of the Ford family. While Andrew Carnegie and the Rockefellers conceptualized and built their foundations, the Ford Foundation's mission resulted from an "expert" commission headed by Rowan Gaither, a Los Angeles attorney, in 1950. While Henry and Edsel (Henry's only son) were original founders, the foundation as a major institution developed under the relatively hands-off Henry Ford II, the grandson. To some extent, therefore, the Ford Foundation suggests more than Carnegie and Rockefeller a "separation" of ownership and control emblematic of the modern corporation. That the Ford Foundation has operated since 1950 very much on the lines of the other major philanthropies indicates that though its early history may differ, its strategic mission, its operating style, and its goals differed very little. It is of a piece with the-then Big 2.[64]

Despite the humane character of Ford's own general reputation, especially the five-dollar-a-day wage in 1914 and his admiration of honest hard work, he was implacably opposed to organized labor. The Ford Service Department (FSD) intimidated workers attracted by unions, as well as using "bribery, liquor, and easy women" to deal with anyone threatening Ford interests. Headed by Harry Bennett, an ex-boxer, FSD was thoroughly involved with the criminal gangs of the Detroit underworld and in political corruption. During the 1930s, Bennett unleashed "terror" against union organizers and sympathizers, employing thugs, spies, and agents provocateurs.[65]

Rugged individualism, unsurprisingly, was Ford's underlying value: if you don't like something, change it or change yourself. He loathed charity as degrading and as a drug that fostered perpetual dependency and did not address the root causes of problems such as poverty.[66] The answer to poverty was not charity but industrial growth, development, and service to society. Philanthropy—particularly of the wrong sort—was wasteful and unproductive: Ford argued that "no matter how noble its motive, [philanthropy] does not make for self-reliance." However, it is possible to develop philanthropy that is more acceptable if it "spends its time and money in helping the world to do more for itself."[67] Yet Ford's views were not dissimilar to those of Carnegie and Rockefeller; many of Ford's innovations were underpinned by specific kinds of middle-class family values, even when their principal motivations were increased efficiency and profitability.[68] The Ford sociology department's aim was to uplift workers' culture to conform to Ford's standards: clean, male-dominated nuclear families, English speaking and fully Americanized.[69]

The latter point is quite basic to understanding the principal characteristic of the "founding fathers": they were "systems engineers" adept at diagnosing the problems of organization so as better to achieve their industrial objectives. More than this, they were able to implement their diagnoses with spectacular success and apply them to entirely new fields of organization—through their philanthropy to American society and to other parts of the world itself. *Indeed, if they helped produce the American system, they saw in the world a need for global-systemic elements within which the American system itself would flourish.* They were not alone in such thinking: the philosophy of Taylorism, or scientific management, had by the turn of the century come to predominate in the United States.[70] The activities of philanthropy will be examined later in this study; for now, it is to the leadership of the Big 3 that attention must be paid.

THE ROCKEFELLER FOUNDATION AND THE AMERICAN ELITE, 1930–1951

Social background influences behavior.[71] What people do and what and how they think about their society and the world is heavily influenced by their place and time of birth, "historical generation," social class, schooling, race, gender and ethnicity, religion, and their degree of assimilation in American society. The social composition of a group creates a particular subculture and mindset that affects not just decision making on grants and programs but also on the kinds of people, values, and ideas that are considered "acceptable." The backgrounds and networks of the leaders of the Big 3, therefore, are explored in the sections below, beginning with the Rockefeller Foundation.

A survey was conducted of Rockefeller Foundation trustees for three sample years—1930, 1945, and 1951, a pivotal period of U.S. foreign policy transformation. Data were collected from *Who's Who* and *Who Was Who* on background factors on twenty-nine trustees, including region and decade of birth, university education, profession, corporate directorships, service in government, connections with other elite political-intellectual organizations, and membership in elite clubs.

Several of the trustees were major figures in the world of business, the press, or government service. John D. Rockefeller Jr. was trustee from 1913 to 1940. Junior's father-in-law, Winthrop W. Aldrich, served as trustee from 1935 to 1951, alongside his leading role at the Rockefeller bank, Chase National. The publisher of the *New York Times*, Arthur Hays Sulzberger, served from 1939 to 1957, while John Foster Dulles was trustee from 1935 until 1952, when President Eisenhower appointed him to serve his administration as secretary of state, a post he held from 1953–1960.

The majority (fifteen) were East Coast born—particularly New York and Pennsylvania—while the rest were reasonably evenly distributed across the rest of the country: two in the southeast and southwest and two abroad. All of the trustees, bar one, were born after the Civil War and before 1900, indicating a shared generational experience in those decades of "psychic crisis" mentioned earlier. The period also featured, of course, an evangelical awakening and the Darwinian revolution in science, effects that may already be clearly visible in the character of American philanthropy.

Educationally, the Rockefeller trustees exhibited powerful elitist characteristics, with nineteen having attended Ivy League (fourteen at Harvard and Princeton) and other elite universities (five), including Chicago and Johns Hopkins.

The foundations' trustees were dominated by the legal and educational professions, with ten lawyers from major "blue-blood" New York firms such as Sullivan and Cromwell (where Dulles was partner) and Davis, Polk, Wardwell, Gardner, and Reed (where John W. Davis was senior partner). The presidents of Yale University (James R. Angell), Princeton (Harold W. Dodds), Chicago (Max Mason), and the University of California–Los Angeles (Robert G. Sproul) were trustees during the 1930–1951 period. In addition to Aldrich and Rockefeller Jr., there were several major figures from the world of business and finance, for example Chester I. Barnard, the president of the Bell Telephone Company; Lewis W. Douglas, the president of the Mutual Life Insurance Company; and Owen D. Young, of General Electric.

Corporate directorships among the trustees—excluding John D. Rockefeller Jr.—totaled thirty-four; just fourteen trustees accounted for that number. Some of the most important corporations were "represented" by trustees, including General Electric, AT&T, Westinghouse, and Equitable Life Insurance.

Government service was another key factor that many trustees had in common. Several had served as U.S. ambassadors, for example, including Winthrop Aldrich, John W. Davis, and Lewis Douglas (all of whom served as ambassadors to Britain). John Foster Dulles served under Eisenhower; he was also distinguished by having an uncle (Robert Lansing) and grandfather (John W. Foster) who had served as secretary of state, and his brother Allen Welsh was CIA director in the 1950s. Additionally, of course, Dulles served numerous U.S. presidents from the Great War onward, bringing an important perspective to the Rockefeller board of trustees.

Most trustees (eighteen) of the Rockefeller Foundation served numerous other Rockefeller philanthropies—such as the General Education Board and the Rockefeller Institute for Medical Research. Four trustees were also on the boards of several Carnegie philanthropies, including the Carnegie Corporation and CEIP. In addition, several were more broadly connected with other philanthropies, including Karl T. Compton, who was a trustee of five other foundations, including the Ford Foundation. There were numerous links with organizations that regularly received large grants from the Rockefeller Foundation, including the Council on Foreign Relations (nine trustees), the Institute of Pacific Relations (two), and the Brookings Institution (two).

Finally, twenty-five trustees accounted for over one hundred elite club memberships, including New York City's Century (eighteen), Harvard (five), and Metropolitan (four), and four trustee members at the Cosmos Club in Washington, D.C. John W. Davies was the most clubbable, with nine memberships.[72] In 1940, the Century Club was a hotbed of prowar organizers mainly drawn from the leading members of the Council on Foreign Relations.[73]

THE CEIP AND THE AMERICAN ELITE, 1939–1945

The original leadership of the Carnegie Endowment for International Peace was drawn from a narrow East Coast elite, with twenty-seven of its twenty-eight trustees having been born before the Civil War.[74] According to its third president, Alger Hiss, the endowment had changed little fundamentally almost forty years later, when he took office. The CEIP's trustees were "interlocked," he claimed, with the charitable bodies, the New York public library, the Metropolitan Museum, the Metropolitan Opera, and the Rockefeller Foundation. It was through such interlocking that the attitudes of a small section of the United States predominated culturally and otherwise.[75]

A detailed survey of the trustees of the CEIP for the years 1939 to 1945 (inclusive) provides an indication of its elite socioeconomic and other characteristics, such as corporate directorships, educational background, region of residence and birth, membership in other foreign policy organizations, elite clubs, and political and religious affiliations. On average, the CEIP trustees numbered twenty-eight for each year between 1939 and 1945, although the sample studied totals thirty-five owing to turnover. At least some information of the kind sought was available for thirty-three of the thirty-five men in the sample, from sources such as *Who Was Who* and Shoup and Minter's study of the Council on Foreign Relations.[76]

Of the twenty-seven trustees upon whom generational and regional information was available, seven had been born during the 1860s, ten in the 1870s, and nine in the 1880s. Only one had been born during the 1890s. The age group of the trustees was therefore between fifty to seventy, whose formative years were those of post–Civil War America, the rise of U.S. national and global corporations, U.S. imperialism, and progressivism. The CEIP's President Butler was the most senior in age, having been born in 1862.

The majority of the trustees had been born *outside* the eastern seaboard (which accounted for twelve trustees). The East Coast, however, provided the largest single group (by birth) compared with the other regions (Midwest, seven; West, three; South, four; born abroad, three). By residence, however, most trustees were located on the East Coast: sixteen compared with six from the Midwest and three from each of the West and South. This still left twelve trustees in the regions outside the East Coast, a much larger representation than Robert Divine suggests in his general comments on the CEIP.[77] Given the CEIP's focus on public opinion, it was essential that the organization had representation across America.

Data for schooling is sparse, with information on only seven trustees, one of whom (Harper Sibley, the agribusinessman) had listed the elite school, Groton, founded by the puritanical Endicott Peabody, who aimed to recreate the English public school on American soil.[78] The university data are more complete, however, and pride of place goes to the Ivy League universities. Fifty universities and colleges were listed by the trustees (many attended more than one). Twenty-one of the fifty university registrations were with Ivy League institutions, with Columbia (seven) and Harvard (six) the most popular. Other elite colleges accounted for a further eighteen registrations, including the University of Chicago, MIT, the University of California, and Georgetown. In addition, ten registrations were for foreign, mostly European, universities.

Almost 50 percent of the sample of trustees were "career" businessmen (sixteen of thirty-three) and were involved in a wide range of economic sectors, with one of the best examples being Pittsburgh's Howard Heinz, the president of H. J. Heinz Company from 1919 to 1941; another was Alanson B. Houghton, the chairman of the Corning Glass Works Co. from 1918.

Thomas J. Watson was president of International Business Machines (IBM). These sixteen men were businessmen by occupation, but, in all, thirty-three trustees were either presidents or directors of at least eighty-four industrial, commercial, or financial concerns across America. The corporations included General Electric, U.S. Steel, Mutual Life Insurance Co. of New York, and several banks.

Closely connected with the business world were the nine lawyers within the sample, five of whom were partners within their own practices. Two names stand out among this group: the first was John W. Davis, of Davis, Polk, Wardwell Gardiner, and Reed of Wall Street, New York. Davis was the president of the Council on Foreign Relations, a former U.S. congressman for West Virginia (1911–1913) and former U.S. solicitor general (1913–1918), and a Democratic presidential candidate in 1924. Second, there was John Foster Dulles, partner in Sullivan and Cromwell of Wall Street, a leading lawyer of his generation and future secretary of state.

Several CEIP trustees were highly active in business organizations. The most active was Watson, of IBM, who played a leading role in the International Chamber of Commerce (as its president) and was a former director of the U.S. Chamber of Commerce and of the National Association of Manufacturers (NAM). In addition, Watson was a member of organizations such as the Business Advisory Council of the U.S. Department of Commerce, the National Foreign Trade Council, the National Industrial Conference Board, and the Economic Club of New York. Eliot Wadsworth was the president of the Boston Chamber of Commerce (1937–1939), chairman of the U.S. section of the International Chamber of Commerce (1937–1945), and a director of the U.S. Chamber of Commerce (1934–1940). Watson and Wadsworth were joined on the CEIP board by the former U.S. Chamber of Commerce presidents Harper Sibley and Silas H. Strawn, the Chicago banker and lawyer.

Thirty-three trustees had at least forty-two "associations" with government/politics; three had been U.S. congressmen and one, a state governor. Two trustees had held the position of assistant secretary to the Treasury, and another two the post of U.S. solicitor general. The largest single agency of the federal government with which CEIP trustees were connected was the State Department (seven links), although there were three with the War Department, and one each with the Office of War Information (OWI) and the Office of Strategic Services (OSS). Four trustees had held the position of ambassador extraordinary and plenipotentiary, five had been in the U.S.

delegation to the Paris Peace Conference of 1919, and three had attended the San Francisco Conference in 1945. Six trustees had been members or leaders of U.S. delegations at the numerous international, financial, economic, and disarmament conferences of the 1920s and 1930s. In short, of the forty-two "governmental connections" identified, thirty-two (or 76 percent) were directly concerned with America's foreign relations. Carnegie Endowment trustees were predominantly Republicans (eight), with four declaring themselves registered Democrats.

The academic world was underrepresented when seen in the light of the business, legal, and governmental connections of Carnegie trustees. Ten lectureships were declared by trustees, constituting over 30 percent of the sample, although only six trustees were career academics (18 percent). There were, however, several outstanding academics of that generation represented, including Professor James T. Shotwell, the historian and expert on international affairs (Columbia); Philip C. Jessup, the international-law professor (Columbia); and Ben Cherrington, the director of the Social Science Foundation at the University of Denver. Each of these men were exceptional academics as well as activists for the globalist cause. In addition, there were three university presidents among the trustees: Butler (Columbia, 1901–1945), Henry M. Wriston (Brown, 1937–1955), and Francis P. Gaines (Washington and Lee, 1930–1959).

There were ten trustee connections with the press and radio. One of the most important publishers among the trustees was William W. Chapin, a Quaker from Philadelphia. He owned a number of regional newspapers in Chicago, Seattle, and San Francisco, as did Peter Molyneaux of Texas. By the 1940s, Molyneaux was a radio commentator and editor of several influential news and financial periodicals. The importance of these connections is clear for an organization interested in the enlightenment of public opinion.

Carnegie Endowment trustees were connected with a number of other prominent foreign affairs organizations, usually in a leading capacity, such as the Institute of Pacific Relations, the League of Nations Association, the Commission to Study the Organization of Peace and the Woodrow Wilson Foundation. There were sixteen such connections, but over half (nine) were with one organization alone—the Council on Foreign Relations (CFR). Of these nine trustees, six were CFR directors: Philip C. Jessup of Columbia University; Philip D. Reed of General Electric; Henry Wriston (president of Brown University); the banker Norman H. Davis; the lawyer John W. Davis;

and the international lawyer, financial expert, and General Electric and U.S. Steel Corporation director (among others) Leon Fraser.

CEIP and RF trustees were steeped in a series of relationships with a broader business, political, academic, and foreign policy elite. They were leaders and activists, editors and directors, lawyers and businessmen, politicians and their advisors. All of them were leaders in at least two fields— their occupations and as trustees—and many of them were active across a whole range of issues and organizations.

Several overlapping memberships of the two philanthropies are also important: John W. Davis and John Foster Dulles were trustees, along with Douglas S. Freeman, of both RF and CEIP. The elite think tank with which trustees of both RF and CEIP are most commonly associated is the elitist and internationalist Council on Foreign Relations, with which each foundation had nine trustee connections. Government service is another common factor: CEIP and RF trustees had impressive histories of serving numerous administrations in times of peace, crisis, and war. Between them, there were over 130 governmental positions, up to and including a secretary of state. Forty-one of the RF's trustees' total of ninety governmental connections were within the realm of foreign affairs; for CEIP, thirty-two of its trustees' forty-two governmental posts were in foreign affairs. Finally, the two sets of trustees most frequently belonged to one elite club: New York's Century Club, which proved to be a key venue in 1940 for CFR elites in developing a manifesto in support of American intervention into World War II. Thus we can see reasonably strong specific shared experiences and interconnections between private foundations, an elite think tank, and the federal government's foreign policy apparatus.

FORD FOUNDATION TRUSTEES, 1951–1970

The Ford Foundation (FF) had sixty-nine appointed trustees in the period from 1951 to 1970, half of whom (thirty-five) served several terms, leaving an actual total of forty-four trustees over the first twenty years of its modern existence. Information from *Who's Who, Who Was Who,* and other biographical sources was available on thirty-three trustees; their collective portrait is summarized below.

The cohort of Ford Foundation trustees analyzed here were a microcosm of the Cold War American power elite. Their number included four national security advisers and National Security Council members (including McGeorge Bundy); three presidents of the World Bank (including John J. McCloy, sometimes referred to as "the chairman of the American Establishment"); two major newspaper publishers (John Cowles and Mark Ethridge); the chairmen of Shell, General Electric, Standard Oil, and the Ford Motor Company (John Loudon, Charles E. Wilson, Frank W. Abrams, and Robert S. McNamara, respectively); five university presidents; and a secretary of defense (McNamara).

By region of birth, Ford trustees were widely distributed: from the East Coast (seven), Midwest (eight), West (six) and South (five). They were born mainly between 1890 and 1920, the period of "psychic crisis" mentioned above as a significant factor in generational socialization, coming to maturity from 1914 through to the 1939–1945 war; almost half of the trustees (sixteen) served in the armed forces in the two world wars. Educated mainly at elite private schools—at least four trustees had attended either Groton, Hotchkiss, or Phillips Exeter Academy—they went on to Ivy League universities in large numbers, with a total of twenty-one registrations recorded at such institutions, including Princeton, Yale, and Columbia. Harvard alone records fourteen trustees as alumni. The remainder studied at the University of California, University of Chicago, MIT, and a host of other elite academies. In total, thirty-three trustees recorded fifty university registrations, indicating high levels of postgraduate study.

Academia features very strongly as a source of employment among trustees, with twenty-four academic appointments. On the whole, however, the cohort of trustees under consideration consisted of men active across a range of professions—including banking, law, and business. They were leaders of several business organizations, including the U.S. Chamber of Commerce, the Business Council, and the Conference Board. In total, there were thirteen trustee leadership connections with significant business organizations. Between them, the trustees held at least seventy-six corporate directorships in concerns that included household names like General Electric, Shell, Studebaker, Standard Oil, Chemical Bank, Chase Manhattan, and Bechtel.

The quality and quantity of linkages of the Ford trustees with the American state were impressive. Mention has already been made of Secretary of Defense McNamara (1960–1968) and connections with the National Security Council. There was, in addition, one undersecretary of state (William H. Donaldson, in the Nixon administration), twelve links with the State

Department, and seventeen with the Department of Defense. McGeorge Bundy was Ford Foundation president (1966–1979) after serving as national security advisor to presidents Kennedy and Johnson. He attended the elite Groton School, like so many of his fellow Boston Brahmins, and graduated from Yale, where he was a member of the exclusive Skull and Bones society. As a political scientist at Harvard, Bundy was recruited by President Kennedy in 1961 and played a key role in the most important foreign policy decisions of the time—the failed attempt to overthrow the Castro administration in Cuba and the decision to escalate the Vietnam war. In total, Ford trustees had 104 connections with the American state, at least thirty-three of which were with foreign affairs and national security agencies.

Ford trustees were overwhelmingly Protestant, Republican, and white; there was just one black trustee—Vivian Wilson Henderson, an economist. The trustees were well connected with other foundations' boards, including Carnegie philanthropies and the Sloan and May foundations (six links in all). In addition, Ford trustees were connected with the RAND Corporation—the U.S. Air Force's think tank—as well as with the Brookings Institution and the Council on Foreign Relations (six leading members were found among trustees). As expected, trustees belonged to a range of elite country and gentleman's clubs, including Cosmos, Metropolitan, and Century.

According to Waldemar Nielsen, a former Ford Foundation staff director, "foundations are at or near the centre of gravity of the American Establishment,"[79] and this applies to a far broader range of foundations than just the Big 3. Ben Whitaker found, for example, that over 50 percent of trustees from the thirteen largest U.S. foundations were educated at Harvard, Princeton, or Yale; were aged between fifty-five and sixty-five years; and were either Episcopalians or Presbyterians.[80] Additionally, foundations' trustees were heavily interlinked, flowing steadily between powerful institutions. As Mary Colwell demonstrates, foundation trustees were equally closely linked with organizations that received philanthropic largesse. The elitist Council on Foreign Relations, she shows, received one quarter of its income in 1961 from the Big 3. At the very same time, on the CFR's membership roster were ten of the fourteen Carnegie, ten of the fifteen Ford, and twelve of the twenty Rockefeller trustees. In 1964, John J. McCloy was simultaneously chairman of the CFR, chairman of the Ford Foundation, a trustee of the Rockefeller Foundation, and chairman of Chase Manhattan.[81] According to Shoup and Minter, almost half of all top foreign policy officials in Washington, D.C., between 1945 and 1972 were CFR members.[82]

There is little doubt that America's Big 3 were close to the apex of elite power in the period from the Great Depression to end of the 1960s. Their trustees were drawn from among the largest corporations, the most prestigious universities, and Wall Street's most strategic law firms and financial institutions, and from public officials, especially from the State and Defense departments, and they had extensive wartime service. Among trustees were some of the most important architects of the Cold War, such as John Foster Dulles, Dean Rusk, and John J. McCloy. Rusk served longer as secretary of state (1961–1969) than anyone other than Dean Acheson and served as Rockefeller trustee and president of the Rockefeller Foundation (1950–1961). He was a Rhodes Scholar at Oxford and studied law at the University of California–Berkeley. McCloy was a graduate of Harvard Law School, president of the World Bank (1947–1949), U.S. high commissioner in Germany (1949–1952), chairman of the Rockefellers' Chase Manhattan Bank (1953–1960), trustee of the Rockefeller Foundation (1946–1949 and 1958), and chairman of the Ford Foundation (1958–1965). He chaired the Council on Foreign Relations from 1954 to 1970. McCloy served in advisory capacities to presidents Kennedy, Johnson, Nixon, Carter, and Reagan.[83] John Foster Dulles graduated from Princeton University and George Washington University, was a leading Wall Street lawyer (Sullivan and Cromwell), a founding member of the Council on Foreign Relations, chairman of the CEIP, and served President Eisenhower as secretary of state (1953–1959). In the latter capacity, Dulles was strongly involved in the CIA-backed decision to overthrow Iran's premier, Mohammed Mossadegh, in 1953, part of Dulles's commitment to move U.S. policy beyond "containment" and to embrace "rollback."

Such experience and connections are more than of passing interest to organizations such as the Big 3: they are a rich source of collective expertise, organizational experience, and global knowledge as well as of "inside knowledge" of matters at the heart of the American state. These are the men who "know the world" and frame foundations' programs, whose very raison d'être is to promote the networked institutions of "knowledge for use": universities, research institutes, think tanks, policy-advocacy groups, professional scholarly societies, journals, and conferences. It should occasion little surprise that such knowledge makers are thoroughly interconnected with the foreign affairs apparatus of the American state in numerous "state-private" networks.[84]

Since that time, of course, there have been numerous momentous changes in the world: the defeat in Vietnam, a land laid waste by saturation bombing—the result of strategies masterminded by Robert McNamara, among others; a second Cold War under President Ronald Reagan; the fall of the Berlin Wall; the onset of economic globalization; the terror attacks of 9/11, and an illegal war in Iraq that began in 2003. How have the foundations' boards reflected such historic transformations? To be sure, they are keenly interested in the world and America's place within it. The financiers of movements in support of America's "rise to globalism" after 1945—helping build the postwar international infrastructure (IMF, World Bank, United Nations)—have embraced globalization and transnationalism. This is reflected in their leadership: the Ford Foundation increased its trustees drawn from (ethnic and racial) minorities from 6 percent in the 1980s to 24 percent in the 1990s and its complement of women from 13 percent to 18 percent, and it recruited foreign nationals, such as Nigeria's General Obasanjo (who went from supporting a military coup in the 1970s to becoming the country's elected president at the turn of the twenty-first century). Ford's Susan Berresford, a graduate of Vassar and Radcliffe colleges, was appointed the first woman head of any Big 3 foundation in 1996. In 2008, almost 50 percent of the Ford board of trustees was composed of women, while eight of eighteen trustees in the Rockefeller and Carnegie corporations were female. This constitutes a major change for the Big 3, of course, though a brief perusal suggests that by practically all other indicators, the women recruited are elites who were educated in the very same exclusive institutions as the men who ran the foundations for most of their history.

The Big 3's recruitment among foreign nationals has been of a piece with its increasing appointment of senior women. Ms. Mamphela Ramphele, the World Bank's managing director, was recruited by Rockefeller, in addition to Fernando Henrique Cardoso, the former academic champion of leftist "dependency" theory and by 2001 the former president of Brazil and a neoliberal economic reformer. At the same time, the recruitment by the Big 3 among U.S. elite males continued apace: RF was joined by the trustee Thomas J. Healey, formerly of Goldman Sachs, a senior fellow at Harvard's Kennedy School, President Reagan's assistant secretary to the treasury, and a Hoover Institution board member. Thomas H. Kean was first appointed a Carnegie Corporation board member in 1991, rising to chair in 1997. In December 2002, Kean was appointed by President George W. Bush to direct the National Commission on Terrorist Attacks on the United States (the "9/11 Commission"), a bipartisan group charged with investigating the terrorist attacks on New York and Washington, D.C., in 2001. Kean subsequently served as the chairman of the 9/11 Public Discourse Project, a nonprofit entity created with private funds to continue the commission's work of guarding against future attacks. He rejoined the board of CC trustees in 2005.

Foundation programs have not visibly shifted their focus because of such recruitment. Instead, such recruitment serves to underline their ability to adapt to new environments and largely continue their historic mission of promoting U.S. elite interests. The evidence presented above paints a portrait of deep and powerful oligarchic tendencies in American society and government, challenging the notion of discrete, fundamentally competitive forces battling it out. That is not to say that there are no battles; it is merely to argue that consensus building is also central to an understanding of how power works in the United States and that the major philanthropic foundations were, and are, central to the elite consensus-building project.[85]

THE WORLDVIEW OF FOUNDATION LEADERS

The broad outlines of a worldview among foundation leaders is now visible: most notable, of course, is the firm, indeed unshakeable, attachment to American global leadership, a "hardwired" attitude that will be systematically portrayed in the empirical chapters to follow. Suffice it here to say that David Rockefeller, son of Junior and his true heir, sums up the position very well:

> The world has now become so inextricably intertwined that the United States can no longer go it alone. . . . We are the world's sole superpower and its dominant nation economically. One of our principal duties is to provide judicious and consistent leadership that is firmly embedded in our national values and ideals. To do otherwise is to guarantee a return to the conflict that characterized the blood-drenched twentieth century.[86]

The American system of values—free enterprise, individualism, limited government—is deeply ingrained in the foundations' own benefactors and originators: indeed, the Rockefellers, Carnegie, and Ford built their industrial empires in the very spirit of the American "dream." Below is an attempt to sketch out a collective portrait of the kinds of views that prevailed among foundation elites and that contextualize the kinds of mission the foundations pursued, how they saw themselves and others at home and abroad, and how they wanted to go about "doing" philanthropy. Four interrelated themes are clear from such an exploration of foundation leaders' subculture: their religiosity, scientism, racism, and elitism.

"God gave me my wealth," John D. Rockefeller Sr. once responded to critics who demanded he admit the "tainted" character of his vast fortune.[87] Foundation leaders are overwhelmingly drawn from "among the believers": Protestants, an elect group, the chosen few, in their own eyes, the real "owners" of America. Being among the most successful people of their generation, such a self-image is hardly surprising. It is a short step from this to a belief in their own superiority—as a social group, a national elite, as opposed to the "lower" classes in America or, equally, over "lesser" peoples overseas. The linkage of religion and the "elect," self-made earthly success and their movement in restricted social and racial milieus associated with elite schools, Ivy-covered universities, "blue-blood" law firms and pinstriped State Department officialdom mixes a potent cocktail that tends both to cohere the "in" group and to cast among the damned everyone else: nonelite white Americans, non-Protestants—let alone African Americans and swarthy, non-Anglo-Saxon foreigners. The "in" group "knows" and "decides"; the "out" groups are the objects of knowledge.

Andrew Carnegie stands out as broadly secular and even opposed to religion and theology. His conversion to this state, however, rendered him righteous enough merely to have replaced the Christian missionary with a biological evolutionist missionary who, at least superficially, championed "social Darwinism" and the ideas of Herbert Spencer. According to Stephen Wall, Carnegie had long searched for a credible faith to replace Scottish Presbyterianism.[88] His utopia, it seems, was the triumph of capitalist industrialism—as exemplified by his steel plants at Pittsburgh. In practice, Carnegie was a pragmatist: Spencerian attachments aside, he rejected laissez-faire notions because of the necessity of government to modern economy as a source of steel contracts and for providing some minimal protection for workers.[89] Carnegie also effectively rejected the idea of "eugenic superiority," because of his belief that it was from the ranks of the poor that real leaders emerged—much as he had himself. By 1900, Carnegie declared himself a Progressive.

Of course, even the religiosity of the Rockefellers had made its compromises both with wealth and secular thought, transforming itself into an even higher "scientific" truth. In our case, "social-scientific" truth, emerging from and combining evangelical zeal with a worldly vision for constructing the kingdom of God on earth. According to Greenleaf, "scientism [assumes that] . . . genuine knowledge is only possible on the basis of matter of fact carefully observed, catalogued, or categorized in some way and, if possible, measured, quantified, and subsumed under a law or functional generality."[90] In this late nineteenth-century development were planted the seeds of modern social science.[91] It is unsurprising to note that the founders of American social science were often clergymen or otherwise steeped in religion.[92] The quest for personal salvation in Protestantism was transformed in the late nineteenth century into a social ethic. The kingdom of heaven was to be built and perfected on earth; God was immanent in all material forms, including social institutions, as T. H. Green had taught.[93] Evangelical zeal was, henceforth, to be transformed into earthly good works. The "social gospel" demanded the purging of sin in all corrupt national institutions and life—business, politics, state, church, and university. Leaders of this movement included the theologians Washington Gladden and Harry Emerson Fosdick, the philosophers William James and John Dewey, the scientists Asa Gray and Alfred North Whitehead, the political scientists Herbert Croly and Walter Lippmann, and the social scientists Thorstein Veblen, Herbert Ward, Richard T. Ely, John Bates Clark, and Woodrow Wilson.[94] McLoughlin argues that the "key concepts" of Progressivism were "relativism, pragmatism, historicism, cultural organicism, and creative intelligence," producing new values such as "efficiency, integration, systematization, regularization, and professionalization."[95] Social science, therefore, emerged as a rational enterprise for social engineering to modernize America, to deal with tumultuous internal change, and strengthen it for world leadership. Recall that "scientific giving" was the great innovation of the Big 3, a rational activity—an investment—with a view to securing certain kinds of social outcomes.

The architect of "scientific giving" was probably the Reverend Frederick T. Gates, a one-time Baptist clergyman and Rockefeller adviser.[96] It was Gates who helped modern philanthropy to "move charitable activities away from treating the symptoms of social problems toward . . . eliminating the underlying causes." According to David Rockefeller, this led to an "embrace [of] a scientific approach and to support the work of experts in many fields."[97] Giving became a systematic activity that also rationalized the structure of organizations that applied for Rockefeller funding. Gates eschewed "retail" philanthropy for "wholesale," top-down giving, because the former was chaotic and "subversive of discipline and effectiveness."[98] By giving to carefully scrutinized national organizations, Gates claimed that "Mr. Rockefeller's business sagacity was satisfied, and he came to have hardly less pleasure in the organization of his philanthropy than in the efficiency of his business."[99] Andrew Carnegie ran his own philanthropic foundations in much the way he had run his business empire—with hard-headed efficiency and dead-eyed focus: "I never like scattering my shot," he noted.[100] The effect of large foundation funds on university research, lamented Laski, was the *effective* control over the character, methods, and topics of research: " 'Dangerous' problems are not likely to be investigated, especially not by 'dangerous' men," citing a project not funded by a foundation because its "completion would be displeasing to Signor [Benito] Mussolini."[101] The mere existence of large funds influenced the development of research: "the foundations do not control," Laski counseled, "simply because, in the direct and simple sense of the word, there is no need for them to do so. They have only to indicate the immediate direction of their minds for the whole university world to discover that it always meant to gravitate swiftly to that angle of the intellectual compass."[102]

Ethnocentrism abroad was founded, of course, on a belief in "scientific" Anglo-Saxon superiority at home. Philanthropy aimed at the social uplift of other races, especially African Americans, through education. But their appointed leaders—in this case the General Education Board, an agency for several major philanthropies in the education field—were heavily influenced by racist beliefs. Gates himself withdrew his children from a mixed-race public school in Montclair, New Jersey, because black and immigrant children allegedly were "ill-mannered, filthy, and unsanitary." Blacks required vocational training only: "Latin, Greek and metaphysics form a kind of knowledge that I fear with our colored brethren tend even more than with us to puff up rather than build up," Gates believed.[103] Rockefeller-financed schools in the South accommodated racial segregation. As Wallace Buttrick, the executive secretary of the GEB, noted, "The Negro is an inferior race—the Anglo-Saxon is superior." Southern blacks were suited to "the menial positions, and [to] do the heavy work, at less wages, than the American white man" or immigrant.[104] Though neither Junior nor Senior supported such crude racist views, they were willing to kowtow to Southern segregationists; in the end, 90 percent of GEB funds were allotted to white Southern schools rather than their target group.[105] As Louis Harlan shows, northern philanthropists tacitly acquiesced in Southern blacks' disfranchisement and Jim Crow segregation in return for security for their investments in "industrial" education for blacks.[106] Indeed, reintegration of the post-Reconstruction South with northern industrial capital required a largely un- and semiskilled black agricultural workforce that would in turn "permit the Southern white laborer to perform the more expert labor, and to leave the fields, the mines, and the simpler trades for the Negro."[107] Therefore, agitation over racial equality merely created political instability and, consequently, uncertainty for northern investors. William H. Baldwin of the GEB wanted blacks to concentrate on laboring in the fields, shops, and mines, to aspire to what the existing Southern environment offered, the Tuskegee model of racialized education. Interestingly, in taking such a stance, northern philanthropists rejected and marginalized, through the power of the purse, the racial-equality educational strategies of northern missionary societies.[108] Despite some protests, such as at Fisk in 1925, Southern blacks were often muted in their criticism of racialized educational philanthropy for fear of losing even that support.[109]

The major foundations were also guilty of racialization, the most dire example being the Carnegie Corporation. Although more detail is provided in chapter 6, it is important to note that CC was especially supportive of racial segregation. In his in-depth study of philanthropy and Jim Crow, Philip Stanfield concludes that "the Carnegie Corporation was the most racially exclusive of the major foundations and was very supportive of white supremacy in apartheid societies. It dared not allow blacks any decision-making power in areas such as race-relations research and the development of black libraries. According to Carnegie Corporation protocol, black destiny was to be decided by whites only."[110]

Andrew Carnegie shared these views.[111] He championed the superiority of the "English-speaking peoples," calling for a "race alliance" of Britain, Australia, New Zealand, Canada, Ireland, and the United States, under the latter's leadership. Carnegie's attachment to social Darwinism and its mantra of "survival of the fittest" and echoes of the cult of manliness so common in Anglo-America at the time are of a piece with his calls for an Anglo-Saxon alliance.[112] Given their superior qualities, Anglo-Saxons were duty bound to export good government, the fruits of their industry, and their civilization to the four corners of the world. Andrew Carnegie, of course, famously opposed the American annexation of the Philippines after the Spanish-American War of 1898. His reasons for doing so, however, focused on the damage that would be done to American civilization by the inclusion of inferior breeds like the Filipinos, who did not even posses the advantage or grace of living in territories bordering the United States.[113]

CONCLUSION

Elitist, technocratic, utilitarian, and ethnocentric, the foundations' leaders presided over huge endowments that were aimed at social engineering. Their philosophy was generally practical, pragmatic, and utilitarian. The foundations were unconcerned with "ivory-tower" thinking for its own sake: they were deeply concerned that knowledge and expertise be mobilized. Their desired approach was through certified experts: social-scientific technocrats who "knew" and who would prescribe "solutions," ones usually directed at the relatively powerless whose subjective needs went unacknowledged. They claimed to want to address the underlying causes of social ills but failed to acknowledge—indeed, they could not—that the corporate capitalist system from which the foundations constructed their original endowments and the corporate investments from which the endowments continued to generate their income might have been significant contributory factors behind social problems. Instead, they were convinced that corporations served the national or global interest and that most problems stemmed from the individual—poor socialization, lack of education, problems of personality, family dysfunctionality, and the like. Ameliorative reform rather than radical change mark the foundations' approach to social issues.

The evidence presented above demonstrates the elitist, unrepresentative, and unaccountable character of the leadership groups that formed and ran the major philanthropic foundations. It also provides some insights as to their "worldview," the mindsets with which they acted on the nation and world. Their ethnocentrism and sense of social, national, and racial superiority provide an instructive underpinning for an understanding of their "internationalism." Theirs was an intensely "nationalist" internationalism, in the words of Sondra Herman,[114] an internationalism that promoted American power as the "last best hope of mankind," to paraphrase President Abraham Lincoln. America's anticolonial and anti-imperial past and its superior industrial and political systems marked it out as the most

progressive force in world affairs—a force for peace, prosperity, and freedom. America would eschew empire in favor of international organizations
representing the rights of small nations and big powers, peaceably resolving
international disputes and ensuring international security. Economically
and commercially, especially with the necessity of moving beyond their
domestic market and into the world trading system, philanthropic leaders, including the erstwhile protectionist Andrew Carnegie, grew increasingly attached to an open trading system within a multilateral framework
of international organizations. Rockefeller and Carnegie philanthropies
backed movements in the United States and elsewhere, especially Britain,
that supported first the League of Nations and, later, the United Nations,
the International Monetary Fund, and the World Bank. Within these and
other international organizations, the United States—usually in alliance
with Britain—was to exercise leadership. This represented a broadening out
of the appeals of Anglo-Saxonism to a wider range of countries, including the Scandinavian democracies, on which more will be noted in chapter
3. Ultimately, however, the major foundations were interested in building
American global hegemony. Building hegemony required not only the promotion of liberal internationalism at home but also the marginalization of
its principal opponent, American "isolationism." It is to this dual task that
our attention now turns.

3 | LAYING THE FOUNDATIONS OF GLOBALISM, 1930–1945

Social scientists are as much justified in making their skills and knowledge available for the conduct of the war as the natural scientist who works on gunsights.
—Joseph Willits

Promoting globalism, defeating isolationism, and winning World War II were key victories in the forging of the liberal-internationalist U.S. foreign policy Establishment.[1] Less well known is the role of major foundations in promoting the hegemony of globalism and undermining isolationism and in the more "hard-headed" Realist approaches to international affairs. In addition, foundations built and promoted effective international cooperation during the "isolationist" 1920s and 1930s as well as constructing and supporting formal and informal international organizations in and through which to promote American power in a "healthy international environment."[2] In combination, foundation-sponsored programs were influential in developing a Realist mindset, worldview, and knowledge base among strategic elites and more broadly in society.

The rise and diffusion of Realism and globalism within and through the academy merely brought universities more closely into line with forms of thought and practice about how power works in the real world that predominated within the American state, and that helped develop a set of ideas within which the two worlds could cooperate more fruitfully with each other, given an appropriate division of labor. Realism's and globalism's diffusion through university teaching helped cement the hegemony of these ideas within strategic minorities in American public opinion: the educated classes. In the division of labor between scholars and state officials, IR (and other) intellectuals/academics were mobilized behind hegemonic projects designed intellectually to penetrate the academy, "isolationist" strongholds in the Midwest, regional elites, as well as overseas elites, while the U.S. state employed "hard-power" strategies.

Realist knowledge and the IR discipline emerged at a time when "useful knowledge" was at a premium in the modernizing progressive university of the late nineteenth and early twentieth century. The logic of the private university in a competitive marketplace demanded the production of utilitarian forms of knowledge in order to generate income, professional accreditation, external research contracts, and stronger connections with corporations and the state. Additionally, the progressive university was increasingly dominated by men who saw the problems of the American state as their own and wanted to build a more powerful federal executive for domestic reform and world leadership. Nicholas Murray Butler, the president of Columbia University and head of an important CEIP division, exemplified the progressive university leader.[3]

The modern foundation mediated between the modern university and the state and between universities and big business.[4] The foundation organized crucial state agencies, international corporations, and the universities behind a hegemonic project of domestic federal-state building and U.S global expansion: Progressivism and imperialism went hand in hand.[5]

This chapter explores the roles of Carnegie and Rockefeller philanthropy in producing an influential, dominant Realist tradition in IR, but a Realism that took into account social, economic, and ideological factors in projecting national state power. It is difficult, however, to disentangle CC and RF's work in the complex area of promoting U.S. globalism as a political-economic-military project; undermining isolationism's politics, morality, economics, and worldview; and simultaneously assisting the rise of Realism. This process involved proliferating university IR courses and foreign area studies programs but much more as well, and it is important to see philanthropy's role in IR's and Realism's rise in a broader context that included university research and teaching, enhancing and facilitating elite foreign policy think tanks' advisory roles, building and amplifying the state's foreign policy research capacities, promoting public-opinion study and attentive public-opinion mobilization, and encouraging particular approaches and marginalizing others.

The foundations witnessed with obvious satisfaction and some anxiety the obvious decline of British and French global influence and played significant roles in raising American elites' awareness of the potential opportunities for their country to play a greatly expanded role in world affairs. Despite the failure to join the League of Nations, America's postwar isolationism, and economic protectionism during the 1930s, East Coast liberal internationalists actively built a dense network of think tanks, policy research institutes, publicity organizations, and so on to combat isolationism and build globalism. They constructed globalist counterhegemonic networks within an "isolationist" hegemony, using the networks to counter the "immorality" of aloofness, the economic "irresponsibility" of protectionism, and the "parochialism" and "backwardness" of "insularity" in the modern age of "high-tech" military capacities.[6] They mobilized to dilute neutrality legislation in the 1930s, promote freer trade, support the League of Nations, and further transform public opinion, the major political parties, the press, strategic elites, and intellectuals. They worked with state agencies most amenable to globalist thought, especially the State Department.

In addition, foundations played a strategic role in strengthening formal and informal international cooperation between its funded think tanks, scholars, and so on as well as in constructing new international organizations. By the 1920s, such groups believed the American elite was fit to lead the world: America was more advanced, democratic, and dynamic; opposed to moribund empires and atheistic communism; and a new way forward for a world of peace.[7] American internationalism, embedded in American-led international organizations, was that way forward.[8] By building state-oriented networks of scholars, think tanks, corporations, and labor unions, among others, the foundations believed they would generate a powerful domestic coalition for globalism, allied with like-minded internationalists in Britain, the British Empire, and Europe, which, in the long run, would lead to American hegemony. Network building as a socializing instrument did not, by itself, generate U.S. "hegemony," though it was a precondition of it. The flows of material incentives—grants, jobs, fellowships—integral to network building clearly played a role. However, both foundation network building and the rise of America to globalism were symbiotically connected to catalytic global events: the Japanese attack on Pearl Harbor in December 1941 was particularly significant, for example. Such catalytic events afforded precious opportunities to those forces best prepared to take advantage of the spaces opened up for "new" thinking, often considered "unthinkable" before the "crisis."

The scale of the task facing East Coast liberal internationalists required a comprehensive strategy that emphasized different things to different groups of people at different times. The banner of "internationalism" transmitted a range of messages, of which the main thrust was that America had global interests and, therefore, global responsibilities and obligations. A mature power needed to pull its weight and not live off others to underwrite their and the world's security.

This chapter examines three specific but interconnected foundation-led programs to promote Realism and globalism and undermine isolationism: their roles in university IR (and area studies) programs; in increasing the advisory capabilities of elite experts and the research capacities of the state; and in elite, attentive, and mass public-opinion formation and mobilization.

FOUNDATIONS AND UNIVERSITY IR (AND AREA STUDIES) COURSES AND PROGRAMS

Foundations played a key role in establishing IR and area studies as academic disciplines in the United States.[9] Below are considered two programs—one each at Yale and Princeton—that were highly significant in promoting globalism and developing Realism as the dominant tendency in IR.

THE ROCKEFELLER FOUNDATION AND THE YALE INSTITUTE OF INTERNATIONAL STUDIES

From the 1930s, the Rockefeller Foundation played a leading role in financing university programs of research in international affairs and in "non-Western" studies. Foundation officials were early to recognize the changing position of the United States in world affairs. This required, they believed, a new foreign policy, which in turn required trained experts who spoke foreign languages and knew the history, politics, and culture of societies that would enter the orbit of America's "national interest." University IR courses were important for educating future leaders of opinion expected to secure general acceptance of the United States in world affairs.[10]

The Yale Institute of International Studies (YIIS) represents an excellent example of early Rockefeller Foundation intervention. It was created in 1935 with a Rockefeller grant of $100,000 disbursed over five years.[11] From its inception, the YIIS focused upon "the subject of power in international relations"—an area neglected by American scholars.[12] It aimed to take a "realistic" view of world affairs, to be useful to makers of foreign policy, to produce scholarly but accessible publications, and to train academics for governmental service.[13] That it was later nicknamed "The Power School" by IR insiders is adequate testimony to Yale's successful institutionalization of *realpolitik*.[14] What decided the question within the foundation was that Yale had such senior academics as Frederick Dunn, Arnold Wolfers, and Samuel F. Bemis.[15] In addition to the initial $100,000 in 1935, the foundation provided a further $51,500 in 1941 (to run over three years) and $125,000 in 1944 (to run over five years), a total of $276,500.[16]

The *realpolitik* approaches of those who directed the YIIS (Nicholas Spykman, 1935–1940; and Frederick Dunn, from 1940 until after the war) were a source of obvious satisfaction to Rockefeller officials.[17] YIIS's annual report for 1942 stressed that the drafting of "abstract schemes of a new world order" and "ivory tower speculation" were *not* on the agenda. Instead, the YIIS focused upon "basic research" to fill conceptual gaps in current thinking and knowledge of international relations.[18] By 1944, the institute focused even more on issues "likely to cause the *most trouble*" for American foreign policy, such as Anglo-American and Western-Soviet relations.[19]

The memoranda and records of the YIIS bear out its Realism. One document reports the outcome of a conference in March 1945, which argued that the United States could no longer "take a free ride" in the conduct of European affairs. While Britain's international hegemony had effectively ended, it still constituted a key "bridgehead" to Western Europe. Consequently, Britain's continued survival was in America's national interest, to the point of war if necessary. Europe, the conference noted, had to be kept "in balance," and a new Napoleon or Hitler had to be prevented from dominating the continent. To avoid being dragged into another foreign war, America had to engage in the "dirty game of power politics." The conference recognized the dangers of Soviet expansionism while acknowledging the USSR's legitimate security concerns. Although the Soviets ought to be decisively checked territorially, it would be a mistake to oppose them by countering every movement for social reform. That would only convince Western liberals and radicals of the "reactionary" character of Anglo-American policy and "drive [them] . . . into the arms of the doctrinaire Bolsheviks." Finally, the memorandum argued that the American economy had become the major factor in global prosperity. Not only must future U.S. economic policies assist the regeneration of Europe (and so keep Britain and France "going concerns"), but they must also run the American economy "responsibly." American domestic prosperity would create a stable market for the world's products and thereby add to global security.[20] This imperialistic posture was endorsed by an internal foundation review of key books from the YIIS during the war.[21]

Despite its desire to be useful to government, the YIIS made a virtue of its "private" character. "The Place of University Research Agencies in International Relations," a 1943 memorandum written by Frederick Dunn for the foundation's officers, argued that private status gave more flexibility in research and an "opportunity to provide intellectual leadership." The institute could, for example, take up subjects of concern to the State Department that were also politically sensitive. Dunn argued that it was "dangerous" for a democracy if all its researchers were drawn into government service, as this tended to silence "able personnel" and diminish public discussion of important issues. Dunn argued that no one group of researchers, however "omniscient and benevolently inclined," could possibly approach issues from a variety of angles using different techniques and assumptions.[22]

However much the YIIS cherished its "independence," usefulness to government was its first priority. In August 1944, Dunn told Willits that the institute had set up a committee (with State Department representation) to consider how universities might "produce good decision-makers."[23] Two years earlier, the YIIS's annual report noted the first of several meetings with U.S. War Department officials concerning Near Eastern policy. "It was intended," the report stressed, "as a test of the possibility of quick mobilization of academic knowledge and its application to practical questions of policy." The 1941–1942 report further noted that numerous "foreign area courses" had been established at Yale, to increase the awareness of foreign societies; that the institute was sending information to the U.S. government "on demand"; and that YIIS graduates were performing valuable roles within several government departments, notably the State and War departments, the Board of Economic Warfare, and the Office of the Coordinator of Inter-American Affairs, led by Nelson Rockefeller.[24]

The War Department asked the Yale Institute to establish a School of Asiatic Studies for army staff officers, which it duly did in the summer of 1945. Meanwhile, the State Department and YIIS established a joint committee, with Dunn as chairman, to improve the training of foreign-service officers. The impact of such government connections was felt within the broader political science community by the formation of a "politico-military relations" panel by the American Political Science Association, under the chairmanship of Bernard Brodie (a YIIS member).[25] Even when the institute was, apparently, *not* being useful to government and therefore demonstrating its independence, it seemed to approach problems from a perspective not dissimilar to that of the State Department. One of the most telling examples appeared in its 1943 annual report, in a discussion of the importance of the Middle East to the United States. Security, the report noted, was not merely a military question: it also required a watchful eye on the peoples and resources that bordered strategic sea routes and military bases. The institute proposed an investigation of industrial development, the "rise of nationalism," and "race and population pressures as they affect the stability of these regions," with a view to early remedial action by the United States.[26] This was an early indication of the importance of national security–oriented area studies programs.[27]

The YIIS produced many books on the Far East, Anglo-American relations, and the place of Africa in American security policy. Over a half-century later, two stand out: William T. R. Fox's *The Superpowers: The United States, Britain, and the Soviet Union—Their Responsibility for Peace* (1944), which introduced the term "superpower" into the language;[28] and Nicholas J. Spykman's *America's Strategy in World Politics: The United States and the Balance of Power* (1942). According to the historian John Thompson, Spykman's study was the "most thorough analysis of America's strategic position made in these [war] years," the thrust of which was "that American interests demanded intervention in the war to restore the balance of power in Eurasia." (It was written before the Japanese attack on Pearl Harbor).[29] Spykman argued that the United States had to prepare a global strategy combining and integrating the key factors of power: military preparedness, economic vitality, political efficiency and mobilization, and ideological clarity. Spykman also abolished the distinctions between peacetime and war, as "total war is permanent war." Finally, and most profoundly, he argued that there is "no region of the globe [that] is too distant to be without strategic significance, too remote to be neglected in the calculations of power politics." Permanent war on a global scale: here is Yale's contribution to U.S. grand strategy.[30]

Both books received considerable praise and sold well. According to its publisher, Spykman's book, which sold almost ten thousand copies within three months, "may be considered one of the really influential books of our decade."[31] A foundation reviewer suggested that it sold well in Washington, D.C.,[32] and the foundation's social sciences director wrote that it was a "great" book that deserved "prayerful study." Olson and Groom argue that Spykman's book "held great appeal for Pentagon post-war planners."[33]

The influence of YIIS was also extended through the teaching of IR at the undergraduate and postgraduate levels, mainly through the establishment of an undergraduate major in IR in 1935. The IR major was built principally around the theme of national security and war. The course guide summarized it thus: "War as an instrument of national policy. Preparation for war in peacetime: mobilization of national resources. The conduct of war and its problems of social control. Military, economic, political, and propaganda instruments of war."[34]

During the 1940s, the U.S. Navy ran courses at Yale on war strategy and the "Foundations of National Power," coordinated by Princeton's Edward Mead Earle. This particular course was also offered at five other universities, including UCLA, Northwestern, Princeton, the University of North Carolina, and the University of Pennsylvania, indicating the further dissemination of this line of thought and enquiry across the United States. Inevitably, there was some student resistance to the attachment to "power," "force," and "war" in these programs at Yale, especially from students who saw IR as a means of Christian peace-building work. As Spykman reported to the Rockefeller Foundation in 1939, "the rather realistic approach to the subject at Yale sometimes shocked their [Christians'] youthful idealism but . . . did not deter them from recommending the treatment to others." As Paulo Ramos writes, "the conversion to realism was taking place."[35]

Student numbers in IR at Yale were modest before the war (seventeen in 1937–1938, rising to fifty-two in 1939–1940) but increased to eighty-eight in 1942–1943, stabilizing at about eighty after 1945. In total, Ramos estimates that approximately eight hundred students in total took the major in IR at Yale from 1935 to 1951.[36] Between 1935 and 1945, Yale graduated twenty-seven MA and doctoral candidates. Well-known IR alumni include Bernard C. Cohen, Lucian Pye, and William C. Olson.[37] Other alumni went on to join important U.S. foreign policy–related institutions such as the Council on Foreign Relations, the Foreign Policy Association, the Foreign Service, and the State Department.[38]

That the influence of YIIS reached much farther than the academic world was important to its foundation sponsors. Its work was respected by other foreign policy "influentials" and by policy makers. The State Department showed by their regular liaisons how important they believed its work to be. External advisers, such as Jacob Viner and Isaiah Bowman, continued to enthuse about the institute whenever the foundation asked for an assessment. Its research center and seminars attracted well-known academics, such as the political scientist Harold Lasswell, journalists such as Hanson Baldwin of the *New York Times*, and State Department–connected men such as Grayson Kirk, a member of the Council on Foreign Relations' War-Peace Studies Project. By 1945, the institute was broadcasting on the radio on the "problems of peace" prior to the San Francisco Conference, with the former undersecretary of state Summer Welles presiding.[39] With area studies funding from Rockefeller, Carnegie, and Ford foundations, the YIIS contributed significantly to the diffusion of the Realist paradigm and helped to generate a new "consensus of power" in the discipline of international relations.[40]

The institute's "independent" status helped legitimize its views. Specifically, there was little public acknowledgment of its continuous connections with either the foundation or with the state. It trained hundreds of undergraduates and dozens of graduate students for state service or academia—furthering the influence of its Realist approach. By 1948, YIIS began a journal, *World Politics*, and ran one of the most prestigious programs of postgraduate training in America.[41]

EDWARD MEAD EARLE, THE ACIS, AND THE PRINCETON SEMINAR

Earle[42] was a firm advocate of internationalism, receiving support from Rockefeller and Carnegie foundations for his work in the American Committee for International Studies (ACIS), of which he was research director from 1939,[43] and for a research seminar at Princeton (1937–1943). His approach to diplomacy and military history was practical, his main concern being to develop a more hard-headed and globalist—i.e., Realist—approach to American foreign affairs within the academy and polity. Although there is no necessary or automatic connection between Realism and globalism, Earle's interpretation of American national security requirements necessitated an activist foreign policy backed up by military force. Though a Realist, Earle showed an equal awareness of the domestic sources of U.S. foreign policy, including morality, trade, and defense of freedom. He was also free of the cynicism about human nature characteristic of postwar Realists, believing in the perfectibility of man and the educability of public opinion to back a muscular foreign policy.[44]

Earle dismissed the "divide" between domestic and international affairs, recommending social, economic, industrial, and educational reform in order better to prepare for military conflict. Earle suggested that the American people also needed to develop a "war mind." He recommended that the United States form a national security council to assess national strategic and security needs. Earle's definition of "national security" extended well beyond America's borders: "security" meant *intervening overseas to prevent the emergence of threats*—with the form of intervention varying with each specific circumstance.[45]

The mental preparation for war that Earle recommended was a significant element of the work of the Princeton seminar's participants. Alfred Vagts, for example, demanded that America's college students be properly "educated" to understand the "violence of the world" and be prepared for the "unremitting strain . . . of consistent military effort" demanded by the struggle against "totalitarianism." He insisted that colleges be transformed from "Ivory Towers into Watch Towers."[46]

Earle's aim, specifically in relation to the ACIS, was the conduct of "basic research" on the "interests, obligations, and opportunities of the United States" with regard to the postwar settlement. The term "basic research" was expansive enough to permit examination of how and on which terms the United States might participate in peacemaking and use its experience of federalism for global ends. As the war progressed, ACIS decided to conduct policy-oriented research, with a focus on four areas: the U.S. military position, the economic and social aspects of war preparation, U.S.–Western hemisphere relations, and studies of the "basic tendencies in present [*sic*] Germany, Japan and the U.S.S.R. and their implications for future United States relations."[47] The study of such global regions emphasizes the implicit and explicit belief that world affairs were American affairs and that the new technologies of warfare precluded an isolationist stance in foreign policy. The key issue to Earle and his collaborators was to construct a viable "grand strategy" that would maintain a balance of power, defend "vital interests," be supported by an appropriate military capability, and, significantly, retain the long-term support of the American taxpayer.[48]

Earle solicited the State Department as early as 1937 in regard to establishing a policy-oriented academic seminar aiming to produce "a grand strategy for the United States."[49] With a CC grant in February 1940 (of $86,500), Earle's research seminar established the relatively novel view (in America) that "military affairs are a legitimate and vital [academic] concern." Such studies, he argued, were "An Obligation of Scholarship." In a later memorandum, Earle argued that "national defence has always been a motive in American history and that war must be regarded as a fundamental social phenomenon." He urged, therefore, the study of "the role of military service in a democracy, the concept of hemispheric defence, our [military] position in the Far East . . . and military policy as a problem of legislation and administration." In late 1940 and in the spring of 1941, the CC provided $38,000 to Earle and the institute for his study of "United States Military Problems and Policy."[50]

Earle's seminar published reports ranging from isolationism (*Historical Origins of American Isolation*) to the promotion of Realism (*Geo-political Doctrines* and *Elements of Seapower and Balance of Power in Europe and the Far East*). Up to 1942, the seminar produced major studies on American naval power and was in the process of producing Albert K. Weinberg's *The Doctrine of Isolation in American History*. Such was the European (i.e., Realist) outlook and ethnic composition of Earle's seminar that one CC trustee, Arthur W. Page, referred to it as a "refugee colony."[51] To Earle, however, scholars from the more statist European tradition were an essential part of the reformation of American attitudes to international relations. Indeed, one of the seminar's most enduring products, *The Makers of Modern Strategy*, resulted from the synergy of American and European experts. As Earle's work gained academic recognition, the military services called him for consultation in Washington and also to make overseas inspection visits, specifically to military and naval bases associated with the "Destroyers-Bases Agreement" of 1940 between Britain and the United States.[52] Furthermore, Earle assisted Archibald MacLeish and William Donovan in the Office of the Coordinator of Information and simultaneously coordinated a program of fourteen lectures on the background to the European war for the U.S. Army's Training Division.[53]

Earle's seminar also had a significant influence on other universities' approach to military studies and IR, partly through an increased demand for lectures by seminar members and partly through provision of advice on establishing new courses. Albert Weinberg, for example, lectured on isolationism at Johns Hopkins University, Earle lectured at the University of California and at Princeton, and Herbert Rosinski gave the Lowell Lectures at Harvard.[54] An article by Earle, "National Defense and Political Science," inspired several leading universities to establish their own courses on war, power, and politics. *Time* magazine published Earle's "model syllabus" in military studies, spreading its reach.[55] In addition, the seminar distributed to universities and military academies two bibliographies—*Sea Power in the Pacific* (1942) and *Modern War—Its Social and Economic Aspects*. In 1942, seminar members published a book of lectures, *The Background of Our War*, for the War Department's army-orientation courses.[56] The academic

and military significance of the seminar was acknowledged by the reloca-
tion of the American Military Institute to Princeton and the appointment of
the seminar member Harvey de Weerd as editor of the AMI's journal, *Military Affairs*. The War Department also considered appointing the seminar
to the position of liaison between its "geopolitical" section and American
universities.[57]

The impact of Earle's *The Makers of Modern Strategy* was also far reach-
ing. William T. R. Fox declared it a classic in 1949, and Olson and Groom
argue it pioneered "strategic studies." In the 1970s, when interest in pre-
nuclear strategy increased, it was Earle's volume that scholars turned to;
the book was reissued in 1986.[58] Earle noted that the book had "put military studies on a respectable academic footing . . . [awakening] students of
politics to the fact that military strategy is an inherent part of statecraft and
can be ignored only at our dire peril."[59] Bernard Brodie was probably the
best-known individual product of the Princeton seminar. His *Sea Power in
the Machine Age* (1941) was widely adopted on university courses, his *Layman's Guide to Naval Strategy* (1942) sold over twenty thousand copies in its
first year, and his *The Absolute Weapon* (1946) effectively pioneered nuclear-
deterrence theory.[60]

Earle's work at the Institute for Advanced Study and ACIS represented
policy-oriented, hard-headed Realism. This is illustrated by its seminar program, its publications, and by the North Atlantic Conference. The work was
dubbed "indispensable" by Columbia University's Nathaniel Peffer in his
report to the CC. The research program of ACIS was having an effect right
across the academic discipline of international studies, as scholars who
participated in the Princeton seminar returned to their own institutions,
exercising "a certain invigorating influence in their own milieu."[61] Earle's
Princeton seminar placed at center stage national security orientations to
academic IR in the United States. According to Fox, by the late 1940s the
majority of American IR treatises and college course syllabi stressed "the
nature and operation of the state system . . . basic power factors . . . policies
of the great powers," an important shift from the prewar position.[62]

Enhancing the State's Research and Elite Think Tanks' Advisory Capacities

If Realism in theory and practice is focused on state power, then the Real-
ists/globalists in the United States in the 1930s and 1940s did their utmost

to enhance their state's capacities in various ways. Leading the effort was the Council on Foreign Relations (CFR), a think tank at the heart of the American foreign policy establishment.[63] Established in 1921 as an expert internationalist organization, by World War II the CFR had become the most authoritative American institution in its field, issuing the journal *Foreign Affairs*.[64] Its principal contribution to building the State Department was through the War-Peace Studies Project, which aimed at nothing less than the definition of American national interests, the development of blueprints for policy makers, and the provision of expert guidance on the nature of the postwar world and America's leadership role within it. The CFR suggested the War-Peace Studies Project to the State Department, as the former wanted to seize the historic opportunity to elevate America to "the premier power in the world." Given its politically sensitive character, the State Department recommended that the Rockefeller Foundation finance the effort.[65]

Between 1927 and 1945, the Rockefeller Foundation gave over $443,000 to the CFR for research that used the "study-group method," whereby group-based study among experts and practitioners resulted in authoritative publications. This method produced numerous books, including Allen W. Dulles and H. F. Armstrong's *Can We Be Neutral?* (1936).[66] The council's War-Peace Studies Project was funded from beginning (1939) to end (1945) by the Rockefeller Foundation, constituting a massive research effort that involved almost one hundred leading academics.[67] The project was divided into five study groups: economic and financial; political; armaments; territorial; and peace aims. Each group had a designated leader and a research secretary, and an overall steering committee allocated topics to each group, a member of which produced an initial statement of the problem, which, after protracted discussion, was written up and forwarded to President Roosevelt and the State Department. The project was connected with five cabinet-level departments and other official agencies. They held 362 meetings and issued almost seven hundred separate papers for official consumption.[68]

Given the scale of funding—$300,000 between 1939 and 1945—the foundation kept a very close eye on the CFR's value to foreign policy. Although the CFR easily rejected its most extravagant critics, even a cautious assessment must recognize its extraordinary closeness with the State Department. According to William P. Bundy, a CFR insider since the 1950s, the relationship between the council and the state was, during the war, the closest "any private organization [has enjoyed] at any time in American history."[69]

If its precise influence is difficult to determine, it is clear that the CFR's Economic and Financial Group developed the imperialistic "Grand Area" concept, which declared the whole world an "American national interest," a characterization shared by the State Department. In addition, the Territorial Group recommended that FDR declare Greenland a part of the Americas and therefore under the "protection" of the Monroe Doctrine. Finally, the CFR's groups were instrumental in drawing up memoranda that constituted the Moscow Agreement of 1943.[70] Isaiah Bowman argued that the CFR's work had filled vital gaps in thinking with regard to the Moscow Agreement. Council memoranda, he wrote, had "a blend of philosophy and action" that were most useful and without which the State Department would have been greatly impoverished during its preparations for Moscow.[71] Another referee endorsed this appreciation of the CFR. CFR groups, he suggested, had originated the agreement and had "made it possible for intellectual breezes from outside to blow through the State Department."[72] Finally, Leo Pasvolsky (special assistant to Secretary of State Cordell Hull) said that the CFR had not only initiated the Moscow process but had also played a vital role in "training and conditioning" people for official service more generally.[73]

The influence of the CFR's War-Peace Project also proved significant when the State Department established committees parallel to ones set up by the council and then gradually absorbed the latter into its own machinery. It was only in 1947 that the State Department established its own policy planning staff, a development prefigured by the War-Peace Studies Project. Reports on the role of the CFR's groups were uniformly upbeat.[74] State Department officials believed that the CFR men were to be trusted as expert, responsible, and discreet. It was on the basis of such reports that the foundation's president, Raymond Fosdick, wrote to the CFR that "the Rockefeller Foundation is very proud to have had a part in this significant project."[75]

In this way, the Rockefeller Foundation funded research that had far-reaching consequences for the United States. CFR men entered the State Department, helped define America's national interest, wrote memoranda, and exercised considerable influence, notably in the realm of contingency planning.[76] RF continued funding CFR because the State Department had neither the money nor machinery for long-term planning of its own. In so doing, RF violated one of its self-declared objects: to steer clear of policy making and politics in general. But the War-Peace Project was welcomed as a great experiment, "an exceptional opportunity to relate knowledge and action," according to one RF official.[77]

The three programs reviewed above were focused on state power: its centrality to international affairs and to war and peace making, as well as to its need for greater international knowledge-construction infrastructure, academically trained graduates, and university and think tank foreign policy expertise. In effect, the programs were organized, funded, and led by state intellectuals from the foundations, elite think tanks, and universities. Their approach, however, to the overall requirements of a new interventionist and anti-isolationist foreign policy was much broader than this. State intellectuals did not view state power in narrow terms or ignore the fact that "the state" operated within and was inextricably bound up with a specific social and political system with a history, myths, and culture rooted in popular sovereignty. On the contrary, state intellectuals viewed the U.S. state's global role and mission as founded upon shifting the main political parties, Congress, public opinion, and the press away from isolationism. There was no divide in their minds between promoting Realism, building state capacities, and mobilizing Americans for globalism. The next section of this chapter places the state-building programs discussed above into a broader context of mobilizing America behind globalism and against isolationism and pacifism. It begins with a program for the study of public opinion at Princeton and then examines the opinion-mobilizing activities of the Foreign Policy Association, the Institute of Pacific Relations, and the CFR's Regional Committees.

THE PRINCETON PUBLIC-OPINION STUDIES PROGRAM

Public opinion was, of course, of fundamental concern to those most interested in the construction of a new globalist consensus. The Rockefeller Foundation acted strategically to foster lines of study, teaching, research, and other activities that touched public opinion. Most significant was RF's funding of Princeton's Office of Public Opinion Research, led by Hadley Cantril. RF's president, Raymond B. Fosdick, argued that "nations fight not only on military, economic, and diplomatic fronts: they fight with words and pictures." It was with the impact of "words" that Cantril was principally concerned, particularly those used by American leaders regarding the war and the postwar world.[78] The foundation gave the office $90,000 over four years (1940–1943) to study public opinion and opinion trends; to experiment with new, research techniques; and to train a new generation of researchers. Of the total, $15,000 was allocated for the tabulation and analysis

of poll data collected over the previous five years by the American Institute of Public Opinion, the organization led by George Gallup.[79] A further
$5,000 was used to pay Gallup to ask questions about war issues on Cantril's
behalf.[80] Cantril, with his desire to discover "who believes what, how intensely, and why," was at the cutting edge of public-opinion research in the
United States. If his research could reveal, as he claimed, "basic [American]
values and attitudes," then he would be in a position to influence their "specific war attitudes."

Cantril studied opinion as influenced by "objective" characteristics such
as income, education, ethnicity, religion, region, and age to "learn why
opinion changes, [and] predict opinion trends."[81] Cantril passed a great deal
of information to President Roosevelt's office, to the Council of National
Defense, and military intelligence. "The practical leader," Cantril suggested,
"when confronted with a real problem, could avail himself of this information." He further commented that such information could be used to "guide
education" and to help government "predict the resistances they would
meet in formulating peace proposals; it would show what education and
propaganda is necessary . . . to get people to accept a 'just peace.'"[82] Indeed,
government officials suggested that Cantril regard some of his findings as
"'military secrets'" to be kept out of the public domain.

Cantril studied public attitudes toward Latin America, the impact of
presidential radio addresses, the popularity of a "Keep-Out-of-War" Party,
and the socioeconomic characteristics of isolationists and interventionists.
Briefly, the research showed that Americans interested in Latin America
were more likely to be anti-Nazi and pro-English. From this, Cantril ex-
trapolated how an hypothetical propagandist might use that knowledge
by building up a general anti-Nazi frame of reference that could then be
mobilized "to create specific opinions for specific action against Germany
in South America" or anywhere else. Finally, he added, to transform an attitude into an action required propaganda that would increase the "personal
significance, [the] . . . 'felt intensity'" of the Nazi threat.[83]

The research on presidential radio addresses showed that listening to the
president correlated positively with income and that listeners were mainly
interventionists (pro-Britain) because they believed they had more to lose
by a German victory. The research also showed that, following FDR's fireside
chat of December 29, 1940, the proportion of listeners favoring aid to Britain rose by 9 percent. More usefully, Cantril showed why that increase re-
verted, within four weeks, to its former level (because no presidential action

had followed to maintain momentum). Concluding that FDR's speeches did have "some influence," Cantril suggested that their influence might be increased among lower-income groups if the broadcasts were more widely advertised in advance.[84]

On the nature of a possible antiwar party, Cantril's research suggested that women would outnumber men by three to two and that young people from lower-income groups would be "particularly noticeable." Semiskilled and skilled workers would form over 40 percent of the party; farmers, 17 percent; employers, 13 percent; and professionals, 10 percent.[85] Socioeconomic class appeared to be a fundamental variable. Interventionists were mainly men from the middle- and upper-income sectors of American society, who had the most to lose in the case of a Nazi victory and would suffer least from the privations of a war economy. "In brief," Cantril concluded, "there is little conflict here between self-interest and sympathy [for Britain]."[86]

Such findings, based on "scientific" analysis, were of use to policy makers. By 1943, $50,000 had been paid by government agencies and departments to Cantril's office, not including unspecified amounts from the coordinator of inter-American affairs.[87] Certainly, the foundation official principally involved with this work, John Marshall, believed that Cantril had "won . . . rather unusual recognition in government circles."[88] The U.S. Army (section G-2) even went so far as to open an office at Princeton (within Cantril's own), a "Psychological Warfare Research Bureau."[89] By 1943, Cantril's office was cooperating with twenty-two government (and private) agencies.[90] The State Department was using Cantril (confidentially, so as not to publicly reveal its "worries") to study public attitudes toward a postwar settlement.[91] Cantril even received several appreciative letters from President Roosevelt.[92]

To highlight his utility, the Rockefeller official John Marshall told Cantril that government was interested in two things: "what is being said" by political leaders and "studies of the effect." Joseph Willits defended this argument when he wrote about the propaganda value of opinion polls. Although the foundation's policy was to shun propaganda, he argued that, for the duration, "all bets may be off on this subject; social scientists," he suggested, "are as much justified in making their skills and knowledge available for the conduct of the war as the natural scientist who works on gunsights."[93] Consequently, the foundation brought Cantril's research findings to the attention of overtly *political propaganda* organizations such as the interventionist Committee to Defend America by Aiding the Allies (CDAAA).[94] In practice, despite their prewar reservations, the Rockefeller Foundation funded studies to manipulate "mass sentiment" to ward off Nazi and Soviet threats.[95]

By 1939, when the isolationist-interventionist debates were at their most fierce, the foundations funded organizations to press the case for American belligerence and to crush the case for isolation and neutrality, such as the Committee to Defend America by Aiding the Allies and the Fight for Freedom. The prointerventionist and anti-isolationist CDAAA and FFF, which were in the main headed by leaders of the Council on Foreign Relations, reached out to numerous groups in American society, including organized labor and, for the first time, African Americans.[96] The warhawks organized black branches in Harlem and Chicago, alongside two chapters at historically black universities (Howard and Lincoln). Having few connections with the black masses, they sought to mobilize the leaders of black opinion— trade-union leaders (A. Philip Randolph), churchmen (Adam Clayton Powell), academics (Ralph Bunche), and newspaper editors.[97]

The CDAAA/FFF black-mobilization campaign linked the fight against Hitlerism with the struggle against domestic racial discrimination. The warhawks' leaders were highly critical of America's past record in racial matters and hoped to wean black Americans away from perceived "indifference" to Hitlerism or active support for isolationism and communism.[98] In addition, they saw continuing racial discrimination in the defense industries as divisive and inefficient, as it diminished maximum production efforts. It was in this area that FFF, in particular, made a significant contribution by supporting President Roosevelt' s executive order 8802 (in 1941) banning such discrimination. It is also clear that the warhawks recognized the importance attached to domestic U.S. race relations by the peoples of Asia and Africa and used the opportunities offered by the war to try to promote civil rights reforms.[99]

Foundation officials consistently checked the quality of the work of Cantril's office with independent external referees, including George Gallup, Edward Mead Earle, and Lester Markel and Arthur Hayes Sulzberger (both of the New York Times).[100] By producing "scientific" research findings, Cantril impressed policy makers eager to exploit his research and techniques. Many public agencies began to use his research techniques. Politicians and the attentive public were concerned with his finding that popular commitment to internationalism was superficial and that much work remained to be done. Mastering techniques to discover the mysteries of public opinion was fundamental to Cantril's utility. Once mastered, it was believed that such techniques could be used to alter radically the meaning of the term "the consent of the governed." Popular consent could then be "manufactured" or "engineered" more effectively.[101]

FOREIGN POLICY ASSOCIATION (FPA)

Formed in 1918, the FPA believed that the United States should play a larger part in the world than it had, making it incumbent on Americans to learn about foreign affairs.[102] It was concerned with educating public opinion from a liberal-internationalist perspective, and it won the support of Carnegie philanthropy from its earliest years.

By the late 1920s, the FPA developed a wide range of activities, including research and publications dealing with current and historical foreign policy matters, an active speaker's bureau, numerous local branches, a Washington bureau, luncheon discussion meetings attracting over forty thousand people annually, and a weekly fifteen-minute program on NBC radio entitled "The World Today."[103] It was thus an organization that aimed at influencing public opinion at one end and contributing to government policy at the other. By World War II, the FPA had seventeen local branches and a membership in excess of ten thousand.[104] It was also engaged in emergency war work for the U.S. government, especially in the State Department's postwar foreign policy planning efforts, and its president, General Frank McCoy, served as a consultant to the Office of the Coordinator of Information.[105]

In the late 1930s, the FPA developed a research department that, under the successive leadership of Edward Meade Earle, Raymond Leslie Buell, and Vera Micheles Dean, produced a fortnightly report that found its way into "the files of the majority of men seriously at work on foreign affairs, whether officials, editors, writers or professors."[106] From 1936, the FPA produced a large number of high-quality publications for popular consumption—its Headline Books series—which sold remarkably well. By 1942, there had been thirty such books published, selling 1,250,000 copies in total. The U.S. War Department bought 200,000 of the Headline Books for its orientation courses for the armed services in 1943.[107]

Although the college educated were the chief targets of the FPA's educational programs, other sections of the population did receive attention too, including organized labor, for which a special series of forums was arranged in 1942.[108] It also cast its eye on high school and college students and toward school teachers, in a sustained campaign lasting over two decades.

In 1943, the FPA received a $5,000 grant from CC to distribute its Headline Books to high school students. The previous year, 400,000 books had been sold to such students.[109] The CC's sister organization, the Carnegie Endowment for International Peace, helpfully distributed two thousand books to its high school international relations clubs across the country, and the boards of education of eight cities placed Headline Books on their recommended lists. During the same period, FPA produced and distributed maps, study guides, and bibliographies for students, teachers, and club leaders and organized teacher-student seminars and a college students' conference.[110] The material produced was written, according to a Carnegie Corporation report, in a style "readily understood by young people." Finally, the books were not merely sold as an end in themselves: special study kits were also distributed, consisting of suggestions for group projects, examination material, and additional literature.[111]

The FPA also used the NBC radio network to further its educational work, broadcasting a series of talks entitled "America Looks Abroad" to the United States, Canada, and parts of Europe and Latin America.[112] By 1943–1944, the association was cooperating with the University of Colorado and the Rocky Mountain Radio Council in broadcasting a weekly fifteen-minute program devoted to foreign affairs.[113] As an FPA memorandum pointed out, "to justify its existence, the Foreign Policy Association must not only demonstrate its capacity to do authoritative research, but establish its ability to put knowledge to work."[114] The producers of "The March of Time" films, which were shown in 11,000 cinemas globally, wrote that the FPA's "reports have been a *chief source of information* for us on these foreign stories and have been invaluable because of our confidence in them."[115]

It is impossible to know the impact of all these lectures, broadcasts, and discussion groups. Certainly, it was widely perceived to be a highly important organization, one praised by official policy makers and by the Carnegie Corporation, which provided the FPA with over $65,000 in the decade up to 1945 and another $136,000 between 1947 and 1949 alone.[116] Carnegie Corporation President Frederick Keppel wrote in 1938 that of all the attempts at adult education, "few, if any, have been so significant and so influential as the activities of the Foreign Policy Association." Carnegie's Charles Dollard wrote in 1942 that "the Corporation is proud to claim some small part in making possible the fine work you are doing."[117] Official policy makers also praised the work of the FPA as adding to the popular knowledge and understanding of foreign affairs in the United States and in promoting the United Nations.[118]

INSTITUTE OF PACIFIC RELATIONS (IPR)

The IPR was founded in 1925, in Honolulu, as an organization of nations with Pacific-area interests.[119] Its original members included the United States, China, Japan, Canada, and Britain. The IPR aimed to be "non-sectarian, non-controversial, and non-propagandist"[120] but was forced to disband by the early 1960s after a sustained McCarthyite campaign against it—for "losing" China.[121] The American Council, later known as the American Institute of Pacific Relations, was the most powerful of the national councils and exerted "a strong influence over the International IPR," according to Thomas.[122] The most prominent names associated with the AIPR were the Asia scholar Owen Lattimore; Edward C. Carter, who headed the American and International IPR; and Frederick Vanderbilt Field, the Vanderbilt family millionaire and convert to communism.

Carter was, by all accounts, a highly dynamic individual who strongly believed that the AIPR/IPR ought to discuss "current political questions," even though the IPR could pronounce no institutional policy. Carter was responsible for making the IPR's journals *Pacific Affairs* and *Far Eastern Survey* scholarly and respected publications. Carter also used his contacts in the philanthropic foundations to win funding for the AIPR.[123]

Owen Lattimore, who became editor of *Pacific Affairs* in 1933, believed that although the AIPR was free or "independent of any official connections," the other national councils—notably the British—were "establishment forces," given the presence among them of official foreign policy makers.[124] It is argued below, however, that the AIPR, though formally private, became connected with government and was, practically from its very formation, generously funded by the Carnegie Corporation, an important element within the *American* foreign policy establishment.[125] Of South-West Asia, for example, he took the "realistic" establishment view: the United States, he wrote in a confidential Council on Foreign Relations paper, could not allow its enemies to control that region, because "we secure from it huge amounts of raw materials and sell to it huge amounts of finished goods."[126] It was, moreover, because of Lattimore's identification as an "establishment" figure that he was persecuted in the 1950s, during the general anti-IPR campaign.[127]

The Carnegie Corporation's trustees valued the AIPR and provided generously for it. Up to 1932 alone, the corporation awarded $127,486 to its activities; between 1938 and 1945, this increased to $158,500; and in the years 1946 and 1947, when the AIPR received its final corporation grant, the sum rose still further to $175,000. In total, the CC gave the AIPR over $460,000.[128] Rockefeller invested $950,000 in IPR between 1929 and 1941.[129]

Public meetings, conferences, and a wartime program of popularly accessible publications constituted the bulk of the AIPR's domestic activity. Focused mainly on West Coast cities, the AIPR established libraries and study centers, conducted teacher-training seminars, and aided local clubs, colleges, churches, and U.S. military educational divisions in gaining knowledge of Pacific matters.[130] In San Francisco, the AIPR had 450 members, five full-time staff, and a teacher-training program on Pacific relations accredited by the local school board.[131] In Seattle, the AIPR conducted twenty public forums for adults, students, and their teachers and sponsored a high school essay contest. It also held an annual joint conference with the Canadian Institute of International Affairs.[132]

The AIPR also organized periodic two-day conferences across the United States, which were attended by local people and Far Eastern affairs experts. "For better or worse," Peffer argues, "the Institute has been the means of increasing consciousness of the Far East in the United States." In addition, Peffer credited the AIPR with having inspired the increased teaching of Pacific area studies and the establishment of Far Eastern departments in schools, colleges, and universities.[133]

Cooperation with like-minded internationalist organizations such as the FPA and CEIP also occurred on a regular basis. Joint seminars were organized by the AIPR and FPA for New York teachers and high school students throughout the war years, to promote discussion of Japan, issues on the world war as a whole, postwar questions, and matters relating to the United Nations. Such events attracted several hundred students and helped promote "international-mindedness and student leadership."[134] The CEIP not only funded aspects of the AIPR program—to the tune of $15,000—of providing bibliographic material to teachers and news stories to the press and the preparation of radio broadcasts but also cooperated with the institute in a range of educational activities.[135] In 1943 through 1945, the CEIP's "international centers" in San Francisco and Chicago jointly sponsored the AIPR's conferences on Far Eastern and general foreign policy matters.[136]

The AIPR also had a highly developed and internationally respected program of research and publication. Its *Economic Handbook of the Pacific Area* had become "the standard work on the subject," its fortnightly *Far Eastern Survey* was widely respected, and its quarterly *Pacific Affairs* was "a solid review," according to Peffer. The IPR's publication program, *The Inquiry*, ran to twenty-five short volumes, "the best available distillate of data pertaining to the Pacific," and it would be invaluable to peacemakers after the war.[137] For more popular consumption, the AIPR produced a series of pamphlets with titles such as *Japan and the Opium Menace*,[138] *Showdown at Singapore*, *Japan Strikes South*, and *China: America's Ally*. The U.S. Army alone had ordered ten thousand copies of each of the pamphlets "for use in its orientation courses."[139]

After the Japanese attack on Pearl Harbor, AIPR became an essential part of the administration's war effort. Its research program was increasingly "determined by Government needs," because the AIPR was the "only agency [with] considerable . . . information about the area."[140] As the Office of War Information, the Office of Strategic Services, and the armed forces increased their demand for the AIPR's research and knowledge, the corporation stepped up its support.[141] AIPR was an important educational force for internationalism in the United States and commanded foundations' financial support.

CFR's Regional Committees on Foreign Relations

Peffer's report noted that the CFR's membership was small but "chosen with a view to their strategically important position in their respective milieux." CC trustees had themselves formed that very opinion: between 1923 and 1932, CC contributed $382,230; between 1938 and 1945, it contributed a further $261,300, a total of $643,530.[142]

CC directly initiated the council's program of regional committees from 1938 onward. CC's aim was to improve "adult education" in foreign affairs, in a manner that would be "helpful" to the State Department. CC's presidential assistant, Charles Dollard, was from the very beginning conscious of the need to "get in touch with the State Department," before proceeding to officially contact the Council on Foreign Relations, the organization that would establish and run the committees. One foundation trustee, Arthur W. Page, suggested that President Frederick P. Keppel consult Secretary of

State Cornell Hull "and ask him if there is any way, within our proper and legitimate . . . [sphere] in which we can help him." The committees, everyone agreed, would be very useful in helping to "educate" regional public opinion, or at least that section of it that was made up of "opinion formers."[143]

The committees were, of course, conceived of in elitist terms by the council's leaders: they were to be made up of "leading individuals" who were to be "assisted to [reach] right decisions . . . [who] will in turn, through their influential positions, affect the opinion and action of the masses."[144] Although CC had always rejected the charge that it ever sponsored propaganda, one of the referees that it appointed to examine its proposals suggested that such "education of public opinion" would break the "monopoly of effective methods" utilized by the "dictatorial regimes." It would create, he concluded, "public support for an intelligent foreign policy."[145]

The aim of the original seven committees was to "aid in stimulating greater interest in foreign affairs on the part of community leaders in widely separated areas."[146] By 1944–1945, there were twenty committees with over nine hundred members.[147] According to Percy Bidwell, the organizing secretary of the committees, their principal function was to aid the formation of constructive local and regional leaders of opinion that would back a globalist foreign policy.[148] In terms of membership, one third of the committee men were in business, one of the most prominent being Charles E. Wilson, the president of General Motors. Sixteen percent were educators and 15 percent lawyers, and there was a smattering of trade-union leaders and farmers' representatives. There were also a number of congressmen and newspaper columnists and editors. Frank Capra and Walt Disney were two prominent members of the Los Angeles committee.[149]

Most of the committees had a lively program of regular meetings, organized study, and research and participated in a two-day annual national conference of all such bodies.[150] The New York Council used the committees as vehicles for its influence and for gathering public-opinion data from across the country. The CFR published, for a time, a summary of regional committee reports, "Some Regional Views on Our Foreign Policy," replacing them in 1945 with more specific surveys, "with a view to making the results available to the Department of State."[151] In 1944, Secretary of State Cordell Hull permitted State and Treasury Department members to visit the committees "as part of their official duties."[152]

Bidwell believed that the committees had become very influential in their localities.[153] More independent reports from local committee secretaries,

CFR men on speaking tours (such as Allen W. Dulles), and the State Department placed greater value on their work and effects. Even a postwar State Department assessment of the committees (in 1952) argued that they had played a vital role "in the forming and supporting of sound foreign policy."[154] Indeed, during the war, the State Department had consciously sought to "discreetly guide . . . [such private committees] in channels which seem to the Department to be useful and away from schemes which the Department feels are dangerous or utopian." The CFR's committees in particular were of great interest to official policy makers who wanted to manipulate their discussions and, indirectly, local public opinion. Assistant Secretary of State Hugh Wilson argued that the CFR ought to "send a man here [Washington] on current questions. This man could talk with the proper people in the State Department, preparing a memorandum on his own which would not be attributed to the Department, and circulated for the confidential information of the men on the selected [Committees on Foreign Relations] list." Of course, another official wrote, "we could [so] arrange [it] . . . that the men on the selected list would not be notified that this was State Department material."[155] As their original organizing secretary, Francis P. Miller, wrote in his memoirs, the committees were not only important "listening posts to sense the mood of the country" but also played "a unique role in preparing the nation for a bi-partisan foreign policy."[156] They were a fundamental part of the Carnegie Corporation's strategy for educating public opinion in the period immediately before the outbreak of World War II and during it.

The initiation of the committees' project by the Carnegie Corporation and its continued funding of it are highly significant in understanding its institutional culture and position within the foreign policy establishment. This culture was intensely political and "statist"; the corporation saw the problems of American foreign policy *as its own* and tried, within its "proper and legitimate" sphere of action, to solve them. Before proceeding, however, CC officials were careful to consult with the State Department, lest their initiatives be considered less than "helpful."

The construction and strengthening of regional elite opinion were vital aspects of America's rise to globalism, dovetailing with the CFR's and others' work in Washington, D.C., and with that of Earle at Princeton. It further undermines, therefore, Karl and Katz's view that the foundations were disinterested and nonpolitical. By mobilizing regional elites, the Carnegie Corporation and the CFR were attempting to generate a new internationalist

consensus by both challenging isolationism in its heartlands and by arm-
ing with knowledge and arguments its own internationalist allies. This was
a conscious attempt to mobilize bias behind a particular conception of
America's role in a new world order.

A REJECTED APPLICATION

The claim above is reinforced by the reception accorded a radically different
proposal by the Columbia University sociologist Robert Lynd, which was
rejected for funding by Carnegie philanthropy. Lynd's "A Proposed Study of
the Potentialities of Democratic Processes in a Period of Mobilization" was
to be conducted over a period of fifteen months in eight sections, costing
$233,000.[157] Lynd assumed that for America to wage a war against fascism,
it would need to mobilize its own people; the problem was that, left to the
state bureaucracy and its corporate allies, there would develop bellicose
militarism, undermining civil liberties. Democracy, Lynd argued, ought to
be a system in which humans can realize their full potential and satisfy
their needs, and if this tendency could be strengthened, people would fight
wars without resorting to chauvinistic propaganda. His study envisaged a
sociological survey of the social condition of the people, their basic physical
needs, their information requirements, and so on. Fighting a war against
fascism, therefore, would enhance democracy rather than diminishing
it.[158] This proposal, sent out to twenty-six referees, was rejected by just five
reviewers. Among its champions were Lynd's fellow Columbia University
professors Charles Beard and Philip Jessup.[159]

The voices of the critics, however, carried more weight with CC. The
most severe critic, Howard J. Savage, of the Carnegie Foundation for the Advancement of Teaching, was vituperative. Lynd and Savage approached the
problem of war mobilization and the nature of democracy from completely
opposing perspectives. Savage emphasized his military record and claimed
that Lynd's "sociological fuddy-duddy" could not possibly "prepare people
to kill others." Savage further argued that Lynd only concerned himself with
one threat to U.S. democracy, namely Nazism, and said nothing "of a communistic menace." Lynd's proposal, lambasted as the "nadir of stupidity," was
rejected by both Carnegie and Rockefeller foundations.[160]

Rejection of Lynd's proposal after Savage's ruthless critique is instructive as to the vision of democracy, national purpose, leadership, mass

mobilization, and war that was held by CC and RF. The latter were considered "tough minded," worldly, practical; Lynd, by contrast, was bookish, rhetorical, and a "do-gooder." Philanthropy's fertilizer was more appropriate for Yale, Earle, et al. than for Lynd. Lewis Coser's argument that foundations are the "gatekeepers of ideas" who fertilize and foster certain lines of research rather than others rings true.[161]

INTERNATIONAL NETWORKS, 1930S–1950S

The foundations' national and international network-building initiatives were integrated. The Big 3 foundations and their networks were involved in a self-conscious hegemonic project for globalism and against isolationism; their domestic activities were aimed at promoting the idea that America was dependent on and connected to the world and could no longer ignore world affairs. If America, the self-evident good country of the "chosen people,"[162] did not "nip" global threats in the bud, it would suffer economic hardships and threats of (or actual) military attack, and the forces of "evil" would dominate the globe.[163] Indeed, the overall U.S.-stated aim in the definitive Cold War justification, NSC-68, recognizes a desire "to foster a world environment in which the American system can flourish," to be achieved through containing the USSR, but it is also "*a policy we would probably pursue even if there were no Soviet threat . . .* [a] policy of attempting to develop a healthy international community" of U.S.-dominated organizations, such as the IMF, World Bank, NATO, the Marshall Plan, and so on.[164] As the world got smaller, interventionism made (common) sense.[165] It was seen by U.S. state and private elites that leadership of international organizations constituted "from an American vantage a desirable world order."[166] And in those world orders, international organizations were rarely permitted independent powers, and the U.S. always (and unsurprisingly) "sought to protect its interests." To Craig Murphy and Robert Cox, international organizations such as the International Labor Organization and the League of Nations represent the international institutional architecture for capitalist accumulation regimes.[167] Relatedly, James T. Shotwell, the Columbia University historian and Carnegie Endowment representative at the ILO, noted quite explicitly the procapitalist and anticommunist aims of the organization in an article entitled nothing less than "The International Labor Organization as an Alternative to Violent Revolution." In it, he argued that the Bolshevik revolution and political instability across Europe forced labor issues onto the Paris Peace Conference's agenda. Subsequently, peacemakers worked to "prove to the workers of the world that the principles of social justice might be established under the capitalist system."[168]

The foundations' international network building was as strategic as their national enterprises. As Rockefeller officials noted when selecting London-based colleges (such as the London School of Economics) for investment, that city's institutions were already part of a worldwide imperial network that offered significant advantages. Influencing the questions asked and methods of research engaged in at the heart of the British Empire meant multiplier effects across the globe.[169]

The major American foundations played key roles in generating several international organizations in and through which their ideas could be expressed and the *idea* of international governance could be normalized, especially after the U.S. Senate's nonratification of the League of Nations. Creating international forums for discussing labor conditions, trade, legal norms, war debts, reparations, war, and peace provided opportunities for U.S. elites to promote their own positions but also to try to cooperate in advancing non-nationalist, anticolonial, and noncommunist arguments. Despite the idealistic character of the declarations of American internationalists and of their more recent supporters,[170] this was a bid for hegemony. As Ikenberry notes, "hegemonic control emerges when foreign elites buy into the [potential] hegemon's vision of international order and accept it as their own."[171] Such persuasion is conducted by "direct contact with elites in these states, including contact via diplomatic channels, cultural exchanges, and foreign study."[172] He might have added private international organizations to that list. For American internationalists, building international organizations was for the purposes of what later became known as "track two" diplomacy, where state and other elites meet informally to air differences during protracted international negotiations between states.[173]

The foundations funded the long-term cooperative efforts of the American CFR with its British counterpart, the Royal Institute of International Affairs (RIIA, also known as Chatham House).[174] Founded as two branches of one Institute of International Affairs, the CFR and Chatham House became national organizations in the early 1920s. Nevertheless, their cooperation developed and became "special": they were champions of Anglo-American cooperation and, indeed, alliance, as the best way of combating "aggressors" and securing world peace. They established joint conferences and study groups from the 1920s right into the Cold War, informal and semiformal diplomacy that shadowed their official counterparts in their respective governments—for example, on naval matters, trade, war debts, postwar issues in the Pacific region, and so on. While they did not "resolve" problems, they created spaces within which policy-oriented elites were able frankly to air their grievances and indicate how much political room for maneuver their respective governments enjoyed. They also created and reinforced habits of Anglo-American cooperation and dialogue.[175] During World War II, when both organizations were heavily incorporated into their respective official foreign policy–making bureaucracies, the two groups' leaders together and with their respective governments planned the postwar international institutional architecture that became known as the Bretton Woods system: the International Monetary Fund (IMF), International Bank for Reconstruction and Development (IBRD, or World Bank), and the United Nations.[176] In regard to the latter, the role of the CFR as an organization and of Isaiah Bowman is well documented. It is clear that, for Bowman and the CFR, the United Nations was for the maintenance of national security, and international organization would be the route to avoiding "conventional forms of imperialism."[177] American power would be exercised through an American-led "international" system.

Building, and modeled, on that core cooperation between CFR and RIIA, there developed from the 1920s momentum behind an institutes-of-international-affairs "movement." Institutes developed in Australia, New Zealand, Canada, and South Africa as well as in Italy, Belgium, Holland, Germany, and France. Adapted to their own domestic conditions, these institutes received funding from the major American foundations,[178] because their general aims were similar to the foundations' own conception of international affairs at a time of increasing nationalist rivalries, economic autarchy, and military conflict: to increase international dialogue to avert war and economic depression and to build international habits of mind and activity.[179] As Dobell and Willmott conclude, the institutes represented the founding generation of a "transnational elite" that went on to play important roles in laying the foundations of the contemporary world order.[180]

Even more than that, however, foundation elites aimed at building international associations and networks of democratic countries as bulwarks against aggression and militarism. Their schemes are interesting, as they have, since the end of the Cold War, once again become fashionable. The recently U.S.-mooted "community/concert/league of democracies"[181] (and the less well-known but interesting "Anglosphere,"[182] which promotes the union of English-speaking peoples) had its 1930s and 1940s counterpart: Federal Union (FU). Championed by the *New York Times* journalist Clarence Streit and Chatham House's Lionel Curtis, Federal Union (between Britain and its imperial subjects, America, Canada, South Africa, Australia, New Zealand, and the Scandinavian nations) was conceived of as a union of democratic, peace-loving nations of "advanced" peoples, a 1930s version of democratic peace theory in action.[183] The racism inherent in Federal Union was clear to—and condemned by—contemporary observers as a "great blonde beast,"[184] especially as its founders intended to diminish the voting power of Indians and other people of color by using taxable capacity as the basis of representation in the federal assembly.[185] Taxable capacity was finally chosen after consideration of various disenfranchisement methods such as literacy tests, which were used in the Jim Crow deep South of the United States. Of course, despite high levels of sympathy among British and American elites, including Prime Minister Churchill, Federal Union never came about. Nevertheless, it provides an insight to what Anglo-American elites thought about the world and how they sought to act upon it. And the moving spirits behind the movement were part of the American foundations' far-flung but well-connected networks. This was at a time of crisis for the League of Nations, which had been powerless to prevent Nazi and other aggressions and during a time of exploration of various schemes for "world order." When wartime discussions began—within and between CFR-RIIA and their respective foreign offices—the core ideas/values of FU played an important role.[186] The leaders of the institutes-of-international-affairs movement and Federal Union overlapped, as did their funding sources. Together, they made more dense the elite international networks through which American foundation leaders sought to embed their values in the international system.[187]

American foundations were major supporters of international cooperation in informal, private associations. Such associations took the form of institutes of international affairs; the Institute of Pacific Relations, for discussions between the powers of the Pacific rim; supporting the social-justice aims of the International Labor Organization (ILO; Carnegie was particularly active in this respect);[188] and even building international legal institutions such as the Permanent Court of Justice (once again, a significant Carnegie-backed project). American philanthropy also supported the

International Studies Conference (ISC) of the League of Nations' International Institute for Intellectual Cooperation (IIIC), which, by 1945, had developed into the United Nations Educational, Scientific and Cultural Organization (UNESCO).[189] While James Shotwell of the Carnegie Endowment served as the American committee's chairman (1932–1943), the ISC and IIIC both received generous funding from the Rockefeller and Carnegie foundations.[190]

The foundations were themselves international organizations or, rather, national organizations with international reach. The CEIP, for example, had a European office in Paris as well as representation in Geneva (the headquarters of the League of Nations). The Rockefeller Foundation was internationally oriented from its earliest days, particularly in relation to its work on illness and disease but also in its work with the American churches at home and overseas.[191] The Carnegie Corporation, which was particularly active within "British" Africa, had offices clear across the continent.[192]

CONCLUSION

American philanthropy played a vital role in America's rise to globalism and in the concomitant rise of a Realist tradition as a dominant feature of American IR. The initiatives reviewed show that the Rockefeller and Carnegie foundations were engaged in a hegemonic project to assist the American state to enhance its institutional capacity and expertise in order better to project its power. The role of the American state in leading this effort—with the active participation and assistance of private elites such as the CFR, FPA, IPR, CEIP, and so on—was well understood. Yet that would never be enough: the universities would have to play their role, especially in producing more and better-trained graduates with methodological and theoretical approaches that lent themselves to adaptation in the world of policy making and implementation. Area studies and IR programs, therefore, with notions of state power, balance of power, vital interests, and the inevitability of war were funded at elite institutions such as Yale, Columbia, Princeton, and Johns Hopkins, as were prestigious research fellowships' programs, conferences, seminars and, later, professional societies: a networked infrastructure for building successful academic careers and for producing new generations of graduates and institutions to employ them. The professional networks, once established, became powers in their own right, generating specific types of knowledge; privileging specific method-ologies and theoretical frameworks; monopolizing access to research coun-cils, philanthropic and state funding, and policy makers; and policing the networks' ideological-intellectual boundaries.

Yet, the *realpolitik* favored by the state, philanthropy, and university IR leaders still represented only a partial aspect of the overall globalist project. The United States, as a democracy, featured a powerful Congress that all too frequently swayed to the winds of public opinion. State elites and their allies feared the power of American public opinion and sought better to un-derstand its laws of motion and, thereby, to intervene in public debates and mould elite, attentive and, indirectly, mass opinion. The Princeton public-opinion studies project, the CFR's regional committees, and the FPA's and IPR's meetings and conferences for college and high school students more than adequately demonstrate the seriousness of elite efforts to engineer the consent of the American people behind the globalist project. It is no co-incidence that belief in the veracity of state power in academic IR should develop at the same time as key elites came to believe that the United States was ready to assume the moral and political leadership of the world, hence justifying support of an increasingly dense national and international net-work of foundation-sponsored organizations and activities.

The next section of the book—chapters 4 to 7—considers in greater depth the influence of postwar area studies programs, which were used not only to encourage organized learning about the world that United States elites wished to lead but also better to intervene in that world in order to promote American power and combat its enemies. Chapter 4 explores the foundations' roles in promoting Americanism and combating anti-Americanism during the Cold War.

4

PROMOTING AMERICANISM, COMBATING ANTI-AMERICANISM, AND DEVELOPING A COLD WAR AMERICAN STUDIES NETWORK

American private enterprise . . . may strike out and save its position all over the world, or sit by and witness its own funeral. That responsibility is positive and vigorous leadership in the affairs of the world—political, social and economic. . . . As the largest producer, the largest source of capital, and the biggest contributors to the global mechanism, we must set the pace and assume the responsibility of the majority stockholder in this corporation known as the world. . . . Nor is this for a given term of office. This is a permanent responsibility.
—Leo D. Welch, Standard Oil (1946)

We have about 50 percent of the world's wealth but only 6.3 percent of its population. . . . In this situation, we cannot fail to be the object of envy and resentment. Our real task . . . is to devise a pattern of relationships which will permit us to maintain this position of disparity without positive detriment to our national security.
—George Kennan, Policy Planning Staff, State Department (1948)

There are indeed ideologies which Americans cannot tolerate . . . and there are political devices and points of view to which Americans must declare themselves eternally hostile.
—John W. Gardner, vice president, Carnegie Corporation (1948)

The United States emerged from World War II as the world's premier power.[1] It was militarily victorious, almost unscathed by a war fought thousands of miles from the mainland, and now enjoyed a massively expanded industrial capacity. It also possessed "pent up" capital looking for suitable investment outlets.[2] The United States had, as we have seen, also been developing the domestic infrastructure for globalism—greater knowledge of the world's most strategically important regions and countries. There was bipartisan support for a greater role for the United States in the world, especially through new international organizations such as the United Nations, International Monetary Fund, and the World Bank. The conditions were ripe for American hegemony.

Yet there were anxieties among U.S. elites. A reemergence of isolationist opinion, the lack of public commitment to permanent American global leadership, and the rising influence of communism and nationalism/neutralism, especially in Europe but also in Asia, threatened to take even greater portions of the world out of the circuits of the global capitalist system. It would be difficult to "sell" American global hegemony as a positive good despite the ability and willingness of American elites to take up the "responsibilities of power" to create a "healthy international environment" of market economies, which they believed to be the only way to thwart postwar political and economic crises of the kind that had scarred the 1930s.[3]

It was under such conditions that American elites sought to develop strategies for global hegemony. The construction of the "Soviet threat" as an existential struggle between freedom and slavery, civilization and barbarism[4]—effectively conflated in the public mind with communist and other leftist-nationalist movements with little linkage with the Soviet Union—became the principal justification for American and Western rearmament and expansion, under a "defensive" rhetoric.[5] Opposition to American hegemonic policies was attributed to communist influence or anti-Americanism, and combating both was seen as essential to a "healthy international environment" of open economies and societies.

Therefore, the ideologies that John W. Gardner in the epigraph claims are intolerable to "Americans" are frequently labeled "anti-Americanism" or "un-Americanism." American philanthropic foundations played key roles in combating "anti-Americanism."[6] On the positive front, the foundations promoted the most attractive aspects of American life, values, and institutions. More problematically, however, and especially during the Cold War, American foundations fought "anti-Americanism," as they defined it, by challenging those tendencies within the United States and globally that opposed "Americanism," for example, Third World anticolonial and European nationalist movements. In both sets of activities, the foundations were acting in accord with the expansionist objectives of the American state and the East Coast foreign policy Establishment.

With large-scale financial resources deployed through national and global networks, the foundations' struggles on behalf of *their* definition of anti-Americanism were highly influential. As this was an intensely political and ideological activity, it violated their oft-publicized nonpolitical and scientific mission.[7] Their more or less open collaboration with American state agencies further highlighted their effective and enthusiastic incorporation into the machinery of successive administrations.[8] State-private networks in American studies helped foster communities of scholars producing intellectual work and exchange; interpreters of U.S. culture, history, and values; and, ultimately, a positive environment for transatlantic diplomacy. Once a sustainable network of "native scholar-power" had been established, foundations and U.S. state agencies engaged in "partial withdrawal" and moved on to fresh territories.[9] More negatively, foundation and U.S. state funding aimed to undermine opposition to American power and policies, especially pacifism or neutralism (as between the superpowers), particularly among allied nations. As Robert Spiller notes, despite their "differing" aims, state and foundation programs "tended to supplement rather than conflict with each other."[10]

American philanthropy's leaders saw numerous threats to their globalist aspirations: Europeans' and others' envy and resentment of American power and ignorance or misunderstanding of the new superpower's society, culture, and politics. Opposition to U.S. foreign policy, therefore, was seen as based on emotion, ignorance, and nostalgia. The solution was cultural or public diplomacy targeted at strategic elites to persuade them that the United States was a force for good in the world, defending freedom and fighting tyranny; that its culture was deep and not shallow; that its material wealth was not the sole obsession of its culture; and that it had a serious interest in abstract ideas. In short, the aim was to show that U.S. power was not the naked expression of a dangerously superficial society, a volatile political system, or a hollow political elite.[11] American leadership was cultured, educated, rational, sober, and thoughtful. It could be trusted to use its power wisely in the interests of the world system, not purely in its own narrow national interests. This was a "soft-power" strategy to complement the global reach of America's postwar military might.[12]

This chapter considers the foundations' programs in promoting Americanism—especially through developing American studies programs at home—and combating anti-Americanism among European elites.[13] It considers the role of the Carnegie Corporation in injecting fresh vigor into

American studies programs at home, in the context of Cold War ideological competition; the role of the Ford Foundation in financing Henry Kissinger's Harvard Summer Seminar and the Salzburg Seminar in American Studies, targeted at European elites' anxieties about U.S. power; the role of the Rockefeller Foundation in developing American studies in Britain and the European Association for American Studies; and the role of Ford in furthering the clandestine anticommunist Congress for Cultural Freedom.

"Anti-Americanism" is a pejorative term; it is the anti-Semitism of the intellectuals to some, a psychological disorder to others, or a reaction to modernism sourced in envy and resentment of American wealth and power.[14] State and foundation officials routinely viewed (and view today) critiques of America or American policies through such lenses. Criticism of the United States is seen as rooted in prejudice or anxieties or felt inferiorities of the "anti-American"—not in American policies. In effect, seeing anti-Americanism this way *removes* "America" from anti-Americanism. Consequently, U.S. policies can continue unchanged, although greater efforts are required to allay irrational fears and improve understanding of American motives. Even opposition to America's war of aggression on Vietnam was characterized as "anti-Americanism" in foundation reports.[15] Here, then, is tacit acceptance that some level or other of "anti-Americanism"—whether based on resentment and envy or on rational opposition—is inevitable *and a cost worth bearing*, because a change of policy would undermine or contradict a core U.S. interest or objective.

SELLING AMERICANISM AT HOME

This section considers some of the ways in which the Carnegie Corporation promoted American studies at home, in the context of America's rise to globalism after 1945 and its increasingly conflictual relationship with the Soviet bloc.[16] The evidence shows how deep were the concerns of foundation officials and trustees regarding the nature of the cultural, ideological, and value-based Cold War. They were particularly concerned that America's students lacked conviction in America's heritage, in what America stood for, and how that might hinder the rising superpower in aggressively facing down the challenges of European dissent, Third World nationalism, and Soviet power.[17]

CC actively promoted the teaching and study of "American Civilization" and values in colleges and universities across the country. A corporation report of 1950, written by Vice President John Gardner, noted that students were being educated in "a moral vacuum," in which values were being learned in rote fashion, lacking the conviction needed to engage in superpower competition.[18] Gardner aimed to use Carnegie funds to explore how college students could be made more conscious of their national values, as they "may have to defend [them] tenaciously . . . [given future] ideological, economic, and perhaps military conflict. . . . Wisdom of policy, economic vigor, and military might can carry us far, but no one doubts that in the ultimate test we shall have to seek our strength in the hearts and minds of the American people."[19] It is clear that because the corporation lamented inadequate levels of *appreciation* and felt intensity of American values, it chose to approve university American studies programs most likely to lead to an appreciation of U.S. civilization—arts and humanities—and shied away from the more critical social-scientific disciplines. One of the problems Gardner noted was the tendency in American education to promote overly rationalist and positivistic ways of understanding values; values were things to be learned through "value neutrality," not lived. In fact, "non-rational considerations are much closer to the heart of the issue" than rational, reasoned, and knowledge-based ones.[20] In this regard, Gardner overlooked the fact that Carnegie had championed the *virtues* of rational, positivistic social-science methods for decades.

Gardner conceded that promoting a narrow idea of "America" would play into the McCarthyites' hands. "We must insist that the term 'Americanism' does not achieve its greatest utility as a cloak for one's own prejudices. We must assert that irresponsible [i.e., McCarthyite] use of the term 'un-American' is intolerable," as it divides Americans and "leaves them confused as to the identity of their *true* enemies." Controversially, Gardner was convinced "there are indeed ideologies which *Americans cannot tolerate*, and that there are *political devices and points of view* to which Americans must declare themselves *eternally hostile*."[21] The only criticism Gardner received for this conclusion, as head of a "liberal" philanthropic organization, was from the preeminent student of attitude formation Gordon W. Allport, for whom "the red flag of danger" went up; he enquired whether there really are "thoughts that we can't have as Americans?" Allport suggested to Gardner that he alter the wording, acknowledging that Gardner was indeed "on the side of the angels."[22] Gardner reformulated his conclusion thus: "There are indeed ideologies which are incompatible with the system of values we would like to think of as American." Gardner claimed that he certainly had *not* meant that America "go in for some kind of thought control,"[23] yet the implication is quite clear and was even so to a "friend" of the corporation.

Gardner's report called for a renewed belief that, despite the complexities of the large-scale forces that seem to determine the lives of individuals, people could take control of their own destinies: "those societies which have in fact influenced or changed the course of history have been supported by the conviction that their own efforts were effective in bringing about a scheme of things in which they believed."[24] Carnegie wanted to ensure that, in America's rise to global economic power and military reach, it would help in any way it could.

Between 1949 and 1958, the corporation invested over $900,000 in developing American studies in the United States, including courses in "American civilization" and a vibrant American Studies Association.[25] The purpose was simple: to teach America to be more self-conscious, to "Know thyself ," to understand its past achievements and glory in them, and, most importantly, to be prepared to make the ultimate sacrifice in their defense. This was, it was hoped, to be achieved by sponsoring the writing of popularly accessible histories of the United States by distinguished historians; the program was decidedly *not* for the promotion of "fundamental historical research" or for a broader understanding of the "mysteries of historical scholarship." Rather, it "will *always* be to illuminate one or other facet of American Civilization."[26] At all times, however, it was the contribution to meeting the "*present historical crisis*" by the study and teaching of American studies that was the litmus test for funding by Carnegie.[27] After a decade of the Cold War, the Carnegie Corporation concluded that its almost $1 million investment had created some excellent American studies programs at Brown University, Barnard College, the University of Pennsylvania, and Colgate and was supporting preexisting high-quality programs at Amherst and Princeton. Those universities also featured strong student governance, bringing to life the civic virtues associated with Americanism and its educational curriculum.[28]

Carnegie, therefore, was fighting un-Americanism at home as an effective part of the Truman anticommunist campaign; the fears of disloyalty in the nation and federal government had their counterpart in the academy, in the concern over the mental and emotional fitness of America's youth to take up the struggle against enemies domestic and foreign.[29] Far from being above the fray of ideological and political turmoil, Carnegie and the other foundations were completely immersed in the principal currents of Cold War politics.

This was further demonstrated once McCarthyites in Congress charged the foundations with un-Americanism. The foundations' arguments in their defense are instructive: they denied being anti-American, un-American, or pro-Marxist, stating categorically that they never awarded grants to known communists. That is, they were of the same anticommunist mindset as most of America's political elite in the 1950s—they just used more subtle methods. Dean Rusk, the president of the Rockefeller Foundation, stated: "Our foundations refrain as a matter of policy from making grants to known Communists," for two reasons. First, such grants violate "the clearly expressed public policies of the United States," and second, because of "the increasing assaults by Communism upon science and scholarship."[30] These remarks were made without a hint of self-doubt or irony. In relation to "repentant Communists," Rusk was more understanding though , naturally. "One questions . . . [their] . . . political naivete, and . . . willingness to submit their minds and spirits to totalitarian discipline." Rusk also denied that any of the Rockefeller Foundation's activities could be described as "political" or as "propaganda."[31] In denying their support for left-wing projects, the foundations were reaffirming their ideological commitments to Americanism, the U.S. government, and free enterprise—all objectively considered to be "good things." Valuable enough, of course, to be worthy of export.

HENRY KISSINGER'S HARVARD UNIVERSITY INTERNATIONAL SUMMER SEMINAR

As Lucas argues, Kissinger's Harvard Seminar illustrates the degree to which the United States' hegemonic project integrated culture, the academy, and American foreign policy, tightening the core elements of a state-private network to wage a cold war.[32] The advantage of such state-private networks was that official policy objectives could be advanced by purportedly unofficial means.[33] American foundations were ideal institutional mechanisms for promoting Americanism and combating anti-Americanism.

The Harvard University International Summer Seminar was originally formed by Harvard's William Y. Elliott, a CIA consultant and Kissinger's doctoral supervisor, with its initial funding ($15,000) coming from the CIA, in 1951.[34] Kissinger became the linchpin of the seminar, developing its ideological rationale and recruiting the participants. By 1953, Kissinger had obtained financial support from the Farfield Foundation, a conduit for CIA finances. In 1954, the Ford Foundation began its sponsorship of the seminar, the beginning of a long relationship.[35] Thus public and private finances were inextricably bound up in the origins of Kissinger's seminar, fully exemplifying the state-private network concept.

The aim of the Harvard University International Summer Seminar, Kissinger argued, was "to create a spiritual link between the younger generation of Europe and American values," as Europeans were frustrated with the collapse of "traditional values" and the rise of what appeared to be an unsympathetic United States, "a bewildering spectacle of economic prosperity and seeming misunderstanding of European problems."[36] It is clear from Kissinger's Harvard activities and, perhaps, from his own immigrant experiences of assimilating U.S. values that he appreciated the need to go beyond "facts" about America to a far deeper, more mystical underlying unity between Americans and Europeans. Negative European attitudes opened the way for "neutralism" and communism. The seminar would "assist in counteracting these tendencies, by giving inwardly alive, intelligent young Europeans an opportunity to study the deeper meaning of U.S. democracy." The program, however, would fail if it were merely one of "dogmatic indoctrination"; therefore, it had to be focused around *persuading* Europeans that Americans were genuinely concerned with "abstract problems" and not just "material prosperity." The program was to be a forum for "*disagreement and criticism*," with a view to *demonstrating* that "self-reliance is a *possibility* despite the complexity of the present age and that the assumption of *personal responsibility* is more meaningful than unquestioning submission to an apparatus." Like communists, democrats needed to display "the strength of their convictions."[37] The rationale of the program is not dissimilar to the Carnegie Corporation's emphasis on the role of individuals in taking control of their own destiny. This was a program designed to empower strategic elites to dare to challenge the status quo of reflexive anti-Americanism.

The Harvard Seminar was no blunt-edged attempt at indoctrination: the deeper abstract and philosophical meaning of life in American democracy animated the program by examining the concept of freedom, "the striving for self-realization in art against the felt pressure of convention, the quest for a reconciliation of rationalism, personal responsibility and dogmatism in religion." The seminar aimed to produce no "absolute solutions" to policy and social problems but to generate an "*elucidation of fundamental issues*," making "social problems . . . *challenges for normative concepts*."[38]

THE ROLE OF THE FORD FOUNDATION

Given the leadership of Ford in the early 1950s—men such as Paul Hoffman, John J. McCloy, and Shepard Stone (all connected with the State Department or CIA)—the foundation provided a perfect source for privately financing the Harvard Seminar.[39] Between 1954 and 1959, Ford awarded $170,000 to the seminar, bringing together potential leaders from across Europe and Asia and familiarizing them with American leaders, values, and institutions. In all, between 1954 and 1971, Ford contributed millions of dollars to the efforts of Kissinger and others to improve transatlantic relations.[40] For instance, the 1954 group of forty participants, aged between thirty-five and forty years (a group that often sought refuge in "a narrow nationalism," according to Kissinger),[41] included a German diplomat, a British member of parliament, a French journalist, a Korean lecturer, and a Filipino lawyer, among others. Numbers were kept low enough to enable seminar leaders "to pay personal attention to each participant." The success of the program depended "to a large extent on its selection process." The seminar received around seven hundred European applications annually; final selection was based on recommendations by American and European elites: the contributors to Kissinger's journal, *Confluence*; seminar alumni; "Harvard faculty with European connections"; and the recommendations of international societies such as the English-Speaking Union and various institutes of world affairs. Asians tended to be selected based on recommendations by the U.S. Information Service, Harvard alumni clubs, and university appointees.[42] All recommendations were assessed for shortlisting by Kissinger, his assistant, and by a national of the applicant's country of origin, interviewed in Europe by a trusted representative.[43] The final decision was made at Harvard.

Seminar members were "prolific" writers and speakers upon return to their homes, spreading the Harvard Seminar's message far and wide. State Department and Institute of International Education representatives, who had observed the seminar at close quarters, also endorsed its importance.[44] In 1956, Ford reported that the seminar was producing a number of positive effects on participants and for the United States in general. For example, the seminar seemed to be an excellent forum in which to "correct false impressions of the United States, notably among Asian visitors"; it attracted "influential or potentially influential people" from strategic areas; its effects were felt beyond Harvard, as "responsible" press comments suggested; that other

U.S. universities were influenced by the seminar through the participation of faculty and dissemination of seminar publications; and the seminar "helps to develop understanding and a sense of common purpose between Americans and influential foreigners and among the foreigners themselves," some of whom had set up seminar alumni clubs, including a regional seminar in India. *Ford funded many of the alumni meetings and circulated seminar literature to all seminar alumni, helping to sustain the network.*[45]

The seminar was skillfully devised to provide a range of contacts with American life over a period of two months: seminars on politics, economics, philosophy, art, American democracy, and discussions on "America's role in relation to other countries of the world"; evening lectures by outsiders and Harvard faculty, including a robust defense of the McCarthyite investigating committees by James Burnham; *foreigners' presentations on their own nations' problems*; and visits to American business organizations, labor unions, newspapers, and baseball games, as well as to local families' homes. Weaved into a complex program aimed at appreciating America's role in the world were numerous meetings devoted to such seemingly irrelevant topics as "the nature of the poetic," French theater, the German novel after World War II, and the revival of religious art in France.[46] Yet herein lay part of the strength of the seminar, which was designed to illustrate the fabric and depth of American life, and the meetings on these latter-mentioned topics helped to achieve the seminar's objective of overcoming "national prejudices."

Genuine *engagement* between participants and seminar leaders provided a sense of *ownership* among the visitors.[47] Kissinger outlined the detailed program to the Ford Foundation, showing the way in which the political scientist Earl Latham had led a discussion of the pluralistic character of the American political system and how the MIT economist Charles P. Kindleberger had examined economic conditions in the world system. In detailed discussions, issues such as communist China, neutrality, and world communism had been thoroughly aired.

Social occasions were explicitly arranged to "encourage the establishment of personal friendships with Americans," thereby creating emotional bonds between elites.[48] The social program, Kissinger claimed, led to a greater appreciation of American society than any formal lecture courses. For Kissinger, the program's most "decisive" impact was the "attitudes engendered in the minds" of participants in "*the crucible of informal conversations.*" It was noted, for example, that "Seminar members found that an evening's conversation with an American couple and their friends resulted in a

more profound appreciation of the American society than months of reading prior to coming here."[49]

Through the intensity and close contact over eight weeks, seminar members discovered "a wealth of channels toward general international understanding." In these ways, the Harvard Seminar, Kissinger concluded, "provided them with a unique opportunity to assess the qualities of the nation
which bears the heaviest burden of responsibility in the Western World. . . .
Each of them has carried away a deeper insight into what they had previously distrusted in America—an insight often resulting in elimination of
their initial disturbance."[50] Working in the Widener Library at Harvard,
participating in challenging discussions, and enjoying the performances of
the Boston Symphony Orchestra *dispelled participants' initial ideas about
the shallowness of American culture.*[51] In short, Kissinger declared the seminar an unqualified success, because it engendered among elite Europeans
and Asians empathy, understanding, and appreciation of American society,
its elite, and its "burden of responsibility" to the West.

Participants' evaluations of the seminar were overwhelmingly positive.
Kissinger passed on to the Ford Foundation hundreds of letters from participants as evidence of the seminar's effectiveness. Participants reported
that the seminar was "exciting, informative, and remarkable for *candour*";
that it was "forming an [international] elite which is so badly needed" in
building world unity; that understanding gained helped to *challenge* any
"false accusation thrown against the American people"; that the seminar
exhibited little of the stereotypical American "conformism"; and that "your
method of recruiting [American] speakers who are *critical and who tell us
the worst as well as the best is far more disarming and successful than any sort
of traditional propaganda.*" Alain Clement, a journalist with *Le Monde*—a
leading neutralist newspaper (i.e., supportive a concept of an independent
Europe wedded to neither superpower)—returned a convert to American
culture, Harvard, and Henry Kissinger.[52] Kissinger thought that the seminar, despite his own growing responsibilities with the U.S. State Department, National Security Council, U.S. Arms Control and Disarmament
Agency, and the RAND Corporation was so effective and important that he
would continue to organize it.[53] Important alumni of the seminar include
such leaders as Japan's Yasuhiro Nakasone (1953), France's Giscard d'Estaing
(1954), and Malaysia's Mahathir Mohammed (1968).[54] In form and content,
the Harvard Seminar differed radically from the public diplomacy of the
post-1989 and post-9/11 periods.[55] It provided to seminar members "a sense

of actively participating rather than . . . merely being recipients."[56] The seminar, however, was just one part of an impressive array of public diplomacy
operations at the time.

"The Faint Odor of Cultural Imperialism": The Salzburg Seminar in American Studies

The Salzburg Seminar in American Studies[57] was, in effect, the overseas
counterpart of the Harvard Seminar:[58] it was targeted at European men and
women at the cusp of leadership positions in their own society and was run
on the basis of *candid exchange, criticism, and intellectual engagement*—a
"Marshall Plan of the Mind."[59] It began in 1947 as a cooperative venture
between the Geneva International Student Service and the Harvard Student
Council to improve Europeans' understanding of American society. By the
late 1960s, 6,500 fellows had attended courses at the seminar's castle, Schloss
Leopoldskron.[60]

The aim of the seminar was simple: to improve transatlantic understanding (because even highly educated Europeans regarded the United States in
"a distorted and negative light")[61] through "*dialogue* between people who
count and who are going to count." According to the president of Columbia University, the seminar was designed to have its "greatest effect upon
men . . . who must be counted upon by the public opinion–forming groups
in their respective countries."[62] It was further noted for highlighting the
"*unvarnished facts* about the United States" and for exploring transatlantic
issues "with *candour and in depth*." If a "true" picture were to be painted, "it
is not always flattering." Great emphasis was placed on critical engagement
among participants and American seminar faculty, the flavor of which is
captured by key terms recurring through every report on the seminar:
problems to "hammer out" between faculty and participants, "candour
tempered by tolerance," "seeking together," "finding together," avoiding
propaganda.[63] It was the concept of a "two-way avenue of learning" that
motivated the seminar's organizers, and this was to bear fruit.[64] This was
evidenced by a Czech fellow's comment in 1967: "*Your propaganda is the
best propaganda, because it is not propaganda at all*."[65] On the basis of that
"nonpropagandistic" propaganda, European elites were to spread their understanding far and wide through their organizations, newspapers, books,
and lectures.[66] As Salzburg officers argued in 1960, "in Europe, more than
in America, public opinion is molded by a relatively small number of peo-

ple. They disseminate their *reoriented* ideas on American life through their newspapers and periodicals, schools and universities, trade unions . . . "[67]

An analysis of Salzburg Seminar fellows by occupation (1951–1959) reveals its success in recruiting emerging elites: of the 2,878 participants, there were 718 graduate students; 564 teachers/academics; 376 journalists, editors, and writers; 343 government officials and civil servants; 260 lawyers; and sixty union leaders. Fellows were drawn from a range of countries: the best represented were Germany (585), Italy (478), and France (411), all pivotal continental states.[68]

In their grant applications, Salzburg officers consistently differentiated their (American) ideas, methods, and outlook from those of their European fellows. Europeans were elitist in attitude, Americans more egalitarian. Europeans were constantly impressed by American openness, in contrast to their own reticence. For example, even the open-access character of the library facilities and resources at Salzburg (ten thousand books, one hundred periodicals, a wide range of newspapers) was reportedly "a source of amazement to Europeans unused to such 'open' procedures and is, again, an experience for them with a basic American characteristic."[69]

The Ford Foundation began financial support for the seminar in 1955 and covered 20 percent of its financial costs for the next twenty years—funding totaling almost $1 million. The State Department and the Fulbright program furnished much of the rest. The Fulbright program was inaugurated in 1946 to increase mutual international understanding through the exchange of scholars across the world. Ford believed that the Salzburg Seminar was "one of the most effective of all American Studies programmes," affording opportunities further to connect East and West European leaders, as attested by State Department officials.[70] The seminar's board of directors included Harvard's Dean (and later national security adviser to the Kennedy and Johnson administrations and Ford Foundation president) McGeorge Bundy, Emilio G. Collado of Standard Oil, and MIT's Walt Rostow.[71]

In operation, the seminar's schedule was intense. Run over four weeks (thrice a year), it featured morning lectures, afternoon small-group work, and evening discussions and private reading in its well-stocked library. The "seemingly informal" aspects of the program, as organizers put it, were fundamental:

> The continual extra-curricular discussion among Fellows, faculty, and staff, all of whom live under the same roof throughout the session; the

recreational activities in which everyone participates; in fact, the actual teaching method itself—the constant opportunity for questions during lectures and the close association with faculty which differs so radically from the European method, all give impressions in the understanding of America as a working democracy and, as such, are as important as the actual subject matters taught.[72]

The specific effects of the Salzburg Seminar are difficult to gauge. An internal Ford report surprised its own author as to the seminar's effectiveness over a period of two decades. The sociologist Daniel Bell lauded the seminar as educating and bonding together European intellectuals and for launching the careers of several young scholars, such as Ralf Dahrendorf (the author, most famously, of *Class and Class Conflict in Industrial Society* in 1959 and director of the London School of Economics from 1974 to 1984) and Michel Crozier (the author of *The Bureaucratic Phenomenon* in 1964). For Bell, Salzburg alumni were immediately distinguishable at the Congress for Cultural Freedom seminars he had directed during 1956–1957.[73] The seminar's president, Dexter Perkins, noted the spontaneous formation of alumni clubs—"Salzburg Circles"—that held reunions to "discuss American society," at their own expense. He also noted that alumni had a "conception of the United States that is more sympathetic—or, at least, more objective." The seminar also inspired the formation of the European Association for American Studies after the former's 1954 conference of American civilization academics, a significant multiplier effect of the Salzburg initiative. The aim of EAAS was to "continue the work begun by the Seminar-sponsored conference."[74]

THE BAAS AND EAAS CONFERENCES

The study of American subjects in the educational systems of other countries strengthens the basis for a better understanding of American life and institutions on the part of those elements of the population that shape public opinion and give direction to national policy— through educators, students, intellectuals, serious writers.

—J. Manuel Espinosa, Bureau of Educational and Cultural Affairs, State Department (1961)

The major American philanthropies were always international in their orientation and internationalist by conviction.[75] Not only did this entail general sponsorship of worldwide educational and research programs, but it also featured a number of overt attempts to promote the study and appreciation of the United States abroad. Two ways that such appreciation was promoted are briefly explored below.

The relationship between Britain and the United States has often been described as "special," especially given the two countries' cooperation during World War II, but also because of shared cultural, linguistic, and political traditions. Indeed, promotion of American studies by the British Board of Education, Ministry of Information, and the Foreign Office began in earnest in 1941, when it was clear that American power would surpass Britain's and that the latter would need better to understand the former. Prior to the war, the Carnegie Endowment had tried to promote interest in American affairs in the United Kingdom. That such interest in the United States was driven largely by changing political conditions is evidenced by the fact that the British state had also promoted greater study of France, when alliance with that country looked most likely to aid the war against Germany, and greater knowledge of the Soviet Union after July 1941, when the latter became a British ally.[76] In addition to the wartime alliance, Britain played a key role in American Cold War global strategy: she had a vast, though declining, empire replete with military, naval, and air bases, which the United States lacked; was a willing ally in the struggle against communism/nationalism; and could deploy military forces with some rapidity. The cementing of this relationship—at the level of cultural and educational exchange—was established U.S. policy. The foundations were keen to strengthen Anglo-American relations, particularly in the period up to and following the Suez crisis of 1956, which starkly revealed the global power shifts away from European empires and toward the United States, and, in Britain's case, after the Labor Party's conference decision of 1960 unilaterally to dispense with Britain's nuclear weapons, causing concomitant alarm among champions of the "special relationship."[77]

The Rockefeller Foundation funded the initial conferences that evolved into the British Association for American Studies (BAAS). In developing BAAS, RF was acting in concert with state agencies, specifically the Fulbright Commission, the U.S. Information Agency, and the U.S. embassy in London. That is, the American studies projects in Britain—at Oxford and Cambridge, Nottingham, and Manchester, and elsewhere—were considered significant elements of American foreign cultural policy. Indeed, Fulbright's Richard P. Taylor noted that the latter and the foundation were

BAAS's "twin godfather[s]," so vital had their contribution been to its for-mation and growth.[78] According to Frank Thistlethwaite of St. John's Col-lege, Cambridge, the initiative for the initial meetings had been Taylor's.[79]

The origins of BAAS lie in a series of four Fulbright- and Rockefeller-funded "missionary conferences," as they called them, from 1952 to 1955, which brought together—for up to five weeks—a number of academics, schoolteachers, and others interested in the United States.[80] The confer-ences featured numerous prominent American speakers, including Barry Bingham, the publisher-editor of the *Louisville Courier-Journal*, an ardent Anglophile, supporter of U.S. intervention into World War II, and a leading member of the Fight for Freedom, a hawkish prowar organization led by the Council on Foreign Relations.[81] Bingham, who resided in halls during the conference, "became the chief man on the American side; astonishingly kind and cooperative; completely ungrand." The most prominent academic at the same 1955 conference was the historian Richard Hofstadter. Other prominent American academics included C. Van Woodward (Johns Hop-kins, Yale), William T. R. Fox (Yale), and Alfred Kazin.[82]

The aims of the Fulbright conferences were to "counteract the lack of information" in Britain regarding the United States and "to correct mis-information and misunderstanding," bring together British and American scholars, promote the teaching of American subjects in British schools and universities, and create a network of *independent* scholars "*spontane-ously* organizing themselves into a corpus capable of carrying on the work of these conferences, as a response to an indigenous demand rather than through super-imposition, e.g. the window-dressing of support from some American foundation" (emphasis added)! Unpacking that set of aims is beyond the scope of this chapter, but it is clear that neither Fulbright nor Rockefeller were really interested in a completely independent or sponta-neously established association—the supplying of "information" and the correcting of "misinformation" are loaded with unquestioned assumptions and meanings. As a "patriotic" organization that opposed the left inside and outside the United States, Rockefeller was not amenable, especially during the McCarthy era, to funding any association that might challenge the sta-tus and role in the world of the United States. The state-controlled Ful-bright Commission was institutionally bound to anticommunism, broadly defined as it was in the 1950s. The original conferences, therefore, were part of a plan to promote pro-American and to combat anti-American think-ing in the world.[83] Indeed, the original recommendation for the Fulbright conferences came from the State Department,[84] impressed as they were by the results of the Salzburg seminar.

The effects of the conferences were generally viewed positively by the Fulbright Commission. While many delegates just enjoyed the esprit de corps and the social aspects of the gatherings, others saw additional benefits. A headmaster from Wales noted that he had a vastly "increased understanding of the American people." A history master, David Kintoul, from Fettes College, Edinburgh (former British Prime Minister Tony Blair's alma mater), was most impressed and was "eager to continue the studies well begun." There were also a number of comments that would have warmed hearts in the State Department: an English teacher from Penzance felt the conference built a "proper bond for [Anglo-American] security in the future." A teacher from Dorchester thought that "I cannot imagine any better way (short of shipping large numbers of us over to the States) of promoting Anglo-American relations." Finally, a history teacher from West Lothian wrote that "the professors enabled me to acquire a more soundly-based and sympathetic understanding of the development of the United States and of its present position in world affairs."[85]

Inspired by the success of the conferences, Thistlethwaite and a number of other prominent Americanists, such as H. C. Allen, Marcus Cunliffe, Dennis Welland, Max Beloff, William Brock, and Herbert Nicholas,[86] considered ways of creating a permanent academic association to promote the study of the United States in British universities, hold an annual conference, produce an index of American research materials available in Britain, and launch their own academic journal. Its proposed program required further financial aid, which the founders hoped would be supplied by the Rockefeller Foundation.[87] A memorandum to that effect by the Fulbright Commission's Richard Taylor, produced in 1955, hoped that such ideas would "spark your [British Americanists'] imagination." Taylor indicated in this memorandum that "assurances have been received from at least one American Foundation that it would be interested in assisting financially such an Association or Council. It is imperative, if advantage is to be taken of this concrete interest, that such an Association should be formed forthwith with the appropriate active incorporation, officers both honorary and at the working level."[88] Taylor was the executive secretary of the ad hoc committee of what became BAAS, an officer of the Fulbright Commission, a representative of the American state, and a close confidant of the Rockefeller Foundation. His "advice" and suggestions, therefore, carried great weight in the formative stages of BAAS and in extending American plans to promote the study and understanding of the United States in Britain.[89] BAAS was duly formed on May 12, 1955.[90]

Further advice was offered by E. F. D'Arms of the Rockefeller Foundation, who had been involved in establishing the German Association for American Studies and the Salzburg Seminar, directly to Thistlethwaite, as to the future activities of the fledgling BAAS. D'Arms feared that a BAAS journal might prove difficult to launch, "given the difficulties which all journals face these days." BAAS went on to form the *Journal of American Studies* in 1967. Additionally, D'Arms recommended that BAAS liaise with its American counterpart—the foundation-funded Association for American Studies—regarding setting up an information service for British scholars to find out about research opportunities and visits to the United States.[91] D'Arms, in addition to proffering advice, was also extending and strengthening the foundations' own American studies organizational network. Without Rockefeller's financial support, it was recognized that "it is doubtful if the Conferences could ever have made the contribution [to bringing together British Americanists and initiating BAAS] at all."[92]

In addition to Rockefeller and Fulbright funding, BAAS also received funding directly from the U.S. Information Agency (USIA) for its catalogue of UK-based American research material. USIA provided $20,000 for the purpose to hire researchers and pay for travel expenses, a secretary, and office materials.[93] Given the ambitious plans of BAAS officers, however, further funds or gifts were required for possible new premises (the Commonwealth Fund offered some rooms rent free in Harkness House in London), new advisory services to British academics, and new publications—possibly a journal. Thistlethwaite noted that BAAS had already gained one hundred members, including seventy-four academics and twenty-four technical college teachers and school teachers. Thistlethwaite asked for more money from Rockefeller to hold different types of conferences—a week-long one for academics and researchers and another for a broader audience interested more generally in the United States—and for secretarial expenses. BAAS wanted, "in these formative stages [when] we are inhibited by lack of funds," funding over several years to "put us on our feet."[94] At a later meeting between Thistlethwaite and D'Arms in New York, while the former was a visiting professor in the American civilization program at the University of Pennsylvania, Thistlethwaite suggested that BAAS become a "gatekeeper" for the numerous British academics wishing to apply for Rockefeller funding.[95]

In its formal bid for Rockefeller funds, BAAS outlined its mission to "transform the knowledge of scholars, educators and informed laymen in Britain about American history, literature and institutions." One year into its life, BAAS had acquired 117 members. It had the advantage, it claimed, in spreading knowledge and understanding of the United States over the Fulbright Commission and the English-Speaking Union, as, unlike the former, "we are independent of the government," and, as unlike the latter, BAAS is not a society for "propaganda," the implication being that such factors made the others appear suspicious to British eyes. Believing that the way to spread knowledge was to *begin at the top*, an approach directly in line with Rockefeller thinking, BAAS would start by firmly establishing American studies as a legitimate and respectable academic discipline in the universities, causing ripple effects to be felt at the level of examinations at secondary schools, public schools, and sixth-form colleges. "Only by exerting this kind of influence will a new generation of British people grow up with a sensible understanding of American affairs," BAAS argued. British Americanists also needed research funding for visits to the United States, particularly for the purposes of pursuing doctoral and other graduate training. "Without such a [Rockefeller] grant, we are in danger of being ineffective. And our collapse," BAAS threatened, "coming at this particular moment, would set American Studies back a generation." Underlying BAAS concerns, of course, was the Suez crisis, which caused a deep rift in Anglo-American relations in 1956. In all, BAAS asked for a total of $150,500 over a five-year period,[96] to which Rockefeller agreed in 1957, much to the delight of Gaines and the Fulbright Commission.[97]

Overall, the Rockefeller Foundation and the Fulbright Commission contributed strongly to the formation of a vibrant and energetic BAAS, which promotes American studies as a university discipline; publishes an academic journal, among other publications, of high standing; and holds an annual conference. Its "pump-priming" sponsorship—especially the fellowship program—built the future of American studies by funding young scholars, some of whom became leaders in the field.[98] Whether it achieved the aims originally attributed to the initiative is very difficult to tell; that it cemented Anglo-American relations at a particularly difficult time in the Cold War is clear from the reports of the conferences and from the BAAS *Bulletin*.[99]

During the 1960s, the Ford Foundation—through the American Council of Learned Societies (ACLS)—built on the work of the Rockefeller Foundation and the U.S. Information Agency during the previous decade. The objectives of American studies' promotion were noted to be "in constructing . . . [a world] . . . in which it will be possible to live at all," according to an internal report for the Ford Foundation.[100] In other words, American studies was seen squarely within the struggle against the Soviet Union's apparent existential threat to American civilization. The latter had provided $331,000 for American studies in Britain from 1956 through 1969.[101] Ford allotted $5.6 million for American studies in Europe and the Pacific region, of which $1.1 million was invested in Britain. Of the 201 scholars who received fellowships, Britain was awarded forty-nine, closely followed by Germany's forty and Japan's thirty-six.[102] In particular, the University of Manchester played the role of "nursery" for British Americanists. Manchester supplied trained scholars who went on to head up departments at Sussex, East Anglia, and Hull. In the wake of these developments, American studies grew at the London School of Economics and the universities of St. Andrews, Glasgow, and Edinburgh. The U.S. embassy in London, which had also contributed to the formation of BAAS, invested $74,700 to found the Institute of U.S. Studies in London and funded eleven chairs and lectureships and almost forty book grants across the United Kingdom. Additionally, the Fulbright program financed almost six hundred scholars annually to cross the Atlantic.[103] The overall effect was to "create a highly trained elite group of educators and researchers . . . [aware] . . . of the realities of American institutions and life which provides . . . a basis for intellectual discourse and understanding."[104] This was welcome news to the U.S. embassy in London: its cultural attaché (perhaps somewhat unrealistically) noted the existence of "a close parallel between knowledge of the United States on the part of the citizen and his overall approval of American foreign policy." This was as welcome to the Ford Foundation, whose internal memoranda conceded the political character of their motivation in funding the program:[105] "Despite the faint odor of cultural imperialism," Ford's Howard Swearer noted, "it was quite proper given the circumstances to promote American studies."[106]

At the Pan-European level, the Rockefeller Foundation provided vital funding to the European Association for American Studies (EAAS), which was founded at the foundations-funded Salzburg Seminar in American Studies in 1954. The role of EAAS was to coordinate the promotion of American studies in Europe, especially since the formation of the German,

British, and other associations.[107] The immediate result of Rockefeller funding of EAAS was the conference decisions of 1957: for European scholars
to focus research on "transatlantic influences and comparative studies of
the two continents." Further, EAAS, with specific research monies from
Rockefeller, agreed to encourage scholars to research "The American Image in Europe," subdivided into "the political image of America in different
European countries . . . the impact of American educational theories in
Europe . . . and the activities in Europe of American writers" after World
War I. The Rockefeller Foundation noted that the proposed $20,000 grant
would provide leverage against more "traditional" scholars in Europe, who
tended to suggest to younger scholars projects that were "unimaginative
and traditional in character."[108]

The effect of EAAS, according to Fulbright's Robert Spiller, was to provide the smaller European countries—Switzerland, Benelux, and the Scandinavian nations—"an outlet for their interest in American Studies which
they otherwise would not have," which helped "the American cause [in Eu-
rope] as a whole."[109]

The promotion of American studies in the United States and abroad was
aimed at promoting the active support of American values at home and
an understanding and respect for American culture abroad. It was an attempt to export the foundations' domestic values to the world and led to the
construction of a global network of American studies scholars, institutes,
and associations. BAAS and EAAS were two such important aspects of the
network, both encouraged and financially aided in their formative stages
by collaboration between private American foundations and the American
state. Although there were numerous student demonstrations in the 1960s
at Ford/ACLS-funded institutions, two things are noteworthy: student interest in American subjects or study in the United States did not diminish,
and no violent attacks were carried out on foundation-funded institutes,
in sharp contrast to U.S. government facilities abroad. This underlines the
advantages of promoting initiatives through apparently private, nonpolitical foundations, despite their ongoing collaboration with the American
state.[110] *In combination, however, the foundations and the American state
built enduring networks that, at their strongest, created a positive environment for transatlantic diplomacy and, at crisis points, helped weather storms
that might have become far more violent had the networks not existed. But,
through good times and bad, their networks endure, attracting scholars and
resources, marginalizing other voices and agendas, and producing prestigious*

knowledge and symbolic capital. Marcus Cunliffe, a pioneer of American studies in Britain, agreed that British Americanists had said little new or original about the United States and mainly sought to "explain and justify ... American experience ... within the framework of ideas and assumptions set by Americans themselves." Of course, Americanists had also rebutted "misconceptions which flourish on left and right," which was healthy. [111] *The networks, originally a means to other goals, become an end in themselves, generating outcomes that are rarely, if ever, publicly stated.* To be sure, networks cannot prevent a crisis—such as the Suez crisis of 1956—but they can assist the process of "normalization" in the postcrisis period.

COMBATING ANTI-AMERICANISM ABROAD

The foundations actively supported organizations and pursued policies that combated anti-Americanism on a global scale during the Cold War, defining as anti-American practically any foreign criticism of the United States. This section explores one example of how the foundations combated what they perceived as anti-Americanism. In so doing, it becomes clear that the "anti-American" and pro-American aspects of foundations' global roles represented two faces of the central aim of promoting U.S. power and undermining nationalism and/or leftism.

THE FORD FOUNDATION AND THE CONGRESS FOR CULTURAL FREEDOM

Combating anti-Americanism and fighting communism were very closely related, given the breadth of definition of both concepts, in the eyes of the Ford Foundation and of the U.S. Department of State and other state agencies. In fact, it is clear that communism represented the most stark version of anti-Americanism—a coherent worldview that challenged the free market, private property, limited government, and individualism. It should occasion little surprise, then, that Ford took a favorable view of one of the most notorious CIA programs—the Congress for Cultural Freedom (CCF),[112] seen by its founders as "the cultural-intellectual equivalent to the political economy of the European Recovery Program (ERP) and the security framework of NATO."[113] CCF received important support from Ford's board of trustees, which was packed with former CIA and OSS members, in addition to Marshall Planners and members of the U.S. High Commission in Germany, including John J. McCloy, for instance. The relationship with the CIA, CCF, and numerous other opponents of communism and anti-Americanism was close, enduring, and smooth.[114] The only "disagreements" were over whether Ford should act as a conduit for CIA funds and over ways in which Ford could continue to fund CCF but not be publicly seen to be supporting a CIA initiative.[115]

CCF's worldview was dominated by positivistic empiricism, rationalism, technocratic modernism, and a general opposition to "totalizing" philosophies (i.e., Marxism, but also laissez-faire liberalism). The CCF represented a form of intellectual rationalization of the political economy of the Marshall Plan and the New Deal/Fair Deal of Roosevelt and Truman.[116] It also shared the worldview, broadly, of the Ford Foundation.

CCF's anticommunism lost its edge, according to Scott-Smith, after the death of Stalin in 1953, and it found its new mission in promoting the benefits and advantages of Western freedom, pluralism, and social democracy. They championed revolution-free welfare capitalism and the rise of the classless society. As with Ford's economists in Indonesia (see chapter 5), CCF stalwarts promoted variations of Keynesian economic management. In Europe, this line of thought led directly to "end of ideology" thinking from a trio of American social scientists—Daniel Bell, Seymour Martin Lipset, and Edward Shils.[117]

The political impact in Britain of the CCF was felt primarily in the politics of the Labor Party, which, to many American observers, had too powerful a left-wing, anti-American element at all levels.[118] Opposition to U.S. foreign policy, the siting of U.S. military and air bases on British soil, and the Party Conference's decision in 1960 that Britain should unilaterally disarm its nuclear weapons were indicative of Labor's "anti-Americanism." Therefore, CCF fostered the *right wing* of the Labor Party and movement—including Hugh Gaitskell, Denis Healey, R. H. S. Crossman, Tony Crosland, and Roy Jenkins. CCF's Milan Conference of 1955 provided these Labor leaders—all MPs, and Gaitskell set to became Labor's leader later the same year—a chance to build alliances with European "moderate" socialists and even with the "reformist wing of the US Democratic Party as represented by . . . such luminaries as J. K. Galbraith and Arthur Schlesinger Jnr." The aim, according to Scott-Smith, was to strengthen the reformist left and maintain their "Atlantic alignment." Healey was a leading Bilderberger in the 1950s and 1960s.[119] In 1961, of course, Gaitskell was able to reverse the "unilateral nuclear disarmament" decision.

A key player in the Ford Foundation, CCF, and European labor politics was Shepard Stone.[120] It was Stone with whom Denis Healey conducted the preliminary negotiations, at a Bilderberg meeting in 1954, that led to Ford's funding the new London-based Institute of Strategic Studies. Ford provided $150,000 over three years to the new think tank, which supported the Atlantic Alliance and boosted right-wing Labor Party ideas favoring nuclear weapons and the American-led North Atlantic Treaty Organization (NATO).[121] It therefore provided intellectual and political support to opposing the left-wing, "anti-American" forces in the labor movement.

Although the CCF was exposed as a CIA front in 1967, the Ford Foundation continued to support the organization. Some prominent former supporters—such as the French sociologist Raymond Aron and the labor theoretician W. Arthur Lewis—were unwilling to have anything more to do with CCF unless it changed its name, address, and funding sources. According to Aron, the anti-Soviet role of CCF was no longer necessary. CCF supporters agreed that "its functions in the Western world need new definition." Francis X. Sutton noted that "anti-Americanism is now an important intellectual phenomenon in Western Europe. An American-financed organization cannot readily cope with this phenomenon; either it is actively pro-American or it bends unnaturally and awkwardly to be 'fair.'" The Sutton memorandum noted that CCF publications, especially *Encounter*, had been not been "sufficiently critical of the United States," especially over American policy in Vietnam. Sutton concluded that CCF was an absolute necessity in dealing with "problems of irresponsibility [among intellectuals] and decay of purpose," despite "a certain tension" in Ford's supporting semisecret activity.[122] Sutton recommended an award of $4.65 million to a revamped, internationally funded CCF.[123] In fact, trustees voted $7 million to the CCF's successor, the International Association for Cultural Freedom, for 1967–1971,[124] based on the same networks that had been constructed by the CCF and headed by Shepard Stone.

CONCLUSION

Anti-Americanism is neither a Cold War nor a post–Cold War phenomenon. As William Appleman Williams long ago noted, the United States has been fighting cold wars, mainly on an anti-American rhetorical basis, against all sorts of enemies, from left and right, from nationalist to communist to conservative. The Cold War did not begin in 1917 (or end, for that matter, in 1989–1991); it must be understood as "an ongoing confrontation between modern Western capitalism and its domestic and international critics." The reason, according to Williams, that observers have mistaken America's confrontations with the Soviet Union and Communist China for "the real cold war is that they were the first large nations to be successfully organized by the critics of capitalism."[125] The United States has defined all opponents of its expansionism as anti- or un-American.

The foundations have reflected similar views, both at home and abroad. They promoted American studies networks to strengthen Americans' emotional attachment to core values and denied funding to those they believed undermined Americanism—a right-of-center liberalism that promoted managed change and opposed anything to its left and right. Globally, the major foundations constructed networks of American studies scholars and associations, especially in Cold War Europe. Their promotion of pro-U.S. modernizing economists in Indonesia, Nigeria, and Chile (and in other parts of the world—see chapters 5–7) significantly affected those countries' economic and political development. More clandestinely, the foundations backed the CIA-supported Congress for Cultural Freedom to combat anti-Americanism and procommunist forces.

Taken together, U.S. foundations' American studies programs were a powerful means by which global elites' "anti-American" prejudices were addressed through initiatives that *directly* touched thousands—probably tens of thousands—of men and women. Indirectly, Ford's public diplomacy struggle against "anti-Americanism" affected millions of students, academics, journalists, and newspaper and magazine readers.[126] The Kissinger and Salzburg seminars were integrated, coherent, focused, well-organized, profoundly engaging, authentic educational programs designed for two-way exchange and learning—and they were, thereby, not seen as condescending propaganda or even *any* kind of propaganda. The programs at Harvard and Salzburg *created enduring nuclei of scholars and other opinion formers, networked with American institutions and faculty and with one another, functioning effectively long after the short seminars were over*—what Spiller called "native scholar-power." The message of the seminars was not only in the spoken and written word; it was in the very texture of the whole experience: members *lived* Americanism when they criticized and debated race relations or foreign policy.

The Harvard and Salzburg seminars were successful for one other reason: they were directed at elites whose national and world orientations were not *fundamentally* antagonistic to the aims of American power. After all, most Europeans were products of a colonial culture constructed over centuries. As "postcolonial" powers, their worldview transformed into a neocolonial "developmentalism," to redefine or, rather, recalibrate their relationship with the Third World. Their problems with the United States broadly sprang from resentment at their own nations' fall from global grace alongside America's ascendance as well as from a fear of the consequences of American power in the nuclear age. That is, overall, despite their skepticism, they were not beyond persuasion by a sophisticated elite diplomacy set in prestigious Harvard Yard or an eighteenth-century European castle to lend a patina of antiquity to the United States and significant gravity to the proceedings. They were susceptible to the exercise of "soft power" precisely because European elites had a vested interest in the world system, the management of which had passed largely into American hands after World War II.

The Harvard and Salzburg programs supplemented and supported at the level of substate and private elite leadership what states were trying to achieve in this period: alliance formation as a way to greater Western penetration of the Third World, during a period of rising anticolonial nationalism and global competition with communism. Indeed, the programs were integrated into the objectives of the State Department, which worked with Harvard and Salzburg "intimately but unofficially."[127] Ford Foundation funding helped construct the infrastructure—the institutional settings, organizations, professional societies, conferences and seminars, alumni networks, publications—that enabled the formation and endurance of elite networks that influenced the climate of intellectual and popular opinion in an era of emerging American global leadership.[128] Ford claimed to be acting nonpolitically, nonideologically, and independently of the state. Yet its outlook, as demonstrated by its own archival records, shows that Ford operated with a rather formal notion of "independence," behind which lay a philosophy saturated with Gramsci's concept of "state spiritedness." In practice, the Ford Foundation was a strategic part of an elite state-private network that united key elements of a Cold War coalition—a historic bloc—behind an imperial hegemonic project.

Of course, the foundations did not always succeed in attaining their goals in regard to Americanizing the world or even neutralizing all anti-American sentiment. Yet their influence should not be underestimated. Their resources were strategically targeted, in coordination with American state-led initiatives, over a long period of time and helped generate modernizing elites and cadres of Americanists who tended, at the very least, to take sympathetic views of America's global role. In addition, by targeting funds at particular groups of scholars, the foundations were effectively depriving other academics, with other perspectives, of resources. The foundations engaged in a clear mobilization of bias whose outcomes tended to favor pro-American outcomes, under the public guise of funding "scientific" academic research and teaching. Anti-Americanism was, in part, the global "enemy," around which at least some of the efforts of the American state and of foundations cohered in order to promote, strengthen, and defend American global power. The following chapter explores the Ford Foundation's overt and covert activities—and their explosive effects—in undermining, combating, and, ultimately, replacing leftist nationalism in Sukarno's Indonesia in the 1950s and 1960s.

5 | THE FORD FOUNDATION IN INDONESIA AND THE ASIAN STUDIES NETWORK

U.S. interest in Southeast Asia rests largely on economic and strategic factors.[1] American foreign policy makers became particularly concerned during World War II that Japan's imperial expansion threatened American (and, more generally, Western) interests. Indeed, the Roosevelt administration—several months before the attacks on Pearl Harbor—declared that it would wage war on Japan should the latter threaten Indochina, Indonesia (at the time known as the Dutch East Indies), or Malaya.[2] Southeast Asia was a rich source of mineral resources (the source of most of the world's rubber, tin, rice, and tungsten, for example) and an important market for finished goods. It was also highly compatible with the American economy[3] and seen as being significant to American security as the Panama and Suez canals.[4] After 1945 and the emergence of newly independent countries—India, Pakistan, and Indonesia, for example—American planners were additionally anxious about the growing influence of both communism and "neutralism" or "independence" as sources of foreign policy of the new states, movements in which Indonesia had taken a leading role by the mid-1950s.[5] Yet American elites found woeful their own knowledge of Asian history, languages, and cultures. Without such knowledge—developed in a manner at once useful to scholars and to policy makers and referred to in militaristic terms as a way to "attack" a problem across a range of "fronts"[6]—it was feared that America would be unable to influence the development of Asia, leaving the way clear for communist control.[7] This had occurred in China in 1949 with Mao's successful revolution, and the war in Korea suggested that the threat remained grave.[8]

That is the broad context for this chapter's focus on Indonesia, which was seen as a key asset economically and strategically.[9] It was also one of the world's most populous countries, a leader of the Non-Aligned Movement, which aimed to steer a path between the superpowers, and it sustained the largest communist party and movement—numbering some fifteen million people—outside the Soviet Union and China.[10] American elites wished to ensure that Indonesia entered the American orbit; was open to economic, financial, and commercial relations with the West; and was aligned against the communist powers in international politics. As a consequence, an American state-private network developed to "study" Indonesia in order better to intervene in its affairs and influence its political and economic development. In the long run, despite great anxieties in the 1950s and 1960s, Indonesia was politically and economically transformed and integrated into the American/Western orbit. This chapter explores the traumatic processes by which this occurred, focusing on the role, in close collaboration with agencies of the American state, of the Ford Foundation.

Despite the importance of the Ford Foundation in the reconstruction of the postcolonial Indonesian state and society, there is no detailed empirical examination of its programs in that country. There is a single journalistic article—whose conclusions were hotly contested outside the scholarly realm—which makes controversial claims about the "imperial" role of Ford in Indonesia.[11] Beyond that, there is only passing recognition, even though Chalmers and Hadiz argue that the impact of Ford-trained Indonesian economists in the late 1960s "fundamentally transformed the economy . . . [such that] by most criteria remarkable economic progress has taken place . . . creating a favorable investment climate for capitalist development."[12] Even Bresnan's *Managing Indonesia*, a virtual Ford insider account of that country's post-Sukarno economic and political transformation, omits discussion of the foundation's transformative role, emphasizing instead the Indonesian economists' autonomy.[13] In stark contrast, however, in an internal Ford memorandum Bresnan wrote in 1970, he observed that "this elite [was] drawn from the economics faculties in which the [Ford] Foundation had invested so heavily."[14] George McTurnan Kahin's recent memoir also holds back a great deal of information about the foundation's role in that country, despite Kahin's complaint that other scholars had "consciously or unconsciously swept under the rug" too much that was significant in political and economic outcomes in that country.[15]

This chapter uses newly researched Ford Foundation archival sources to consider Ford's roles in Indonesia and to adjudicate between competing claims about the functions of American philanthropy. On one side, neo-Gramscians claim that U.S. foundations represent a hegemonic force in American society and a force for promoting U.S. hegemony globally, especially during the Cold War.[16] Gramscians would therefore expect to find, in the case of the Ford Foundation's roles in Indonesia, strong evidence of private "ruling-class" organizations among those promoting policy-oriented scholars, academic, and intellectual networks for a major reorientation of the Indonesian academy, economy, and society, as *part* of the process of undermining and eliminating an anti-American regime. They would expect to find strong evidence of Ford's penetration of Indonesian elites as part of their attempts to prepare a counterhegemonic movement against the established government of Indonesia.

Conversely, it is argued by foundation insiders and a number of scholars that U.S. foundations are relatively benign forces for U.S. and overseas development and that they are organizations that are authentically nonpolitical and aim at the betterment and "humanization" of society and the world.[17] Indeed, the Ford Foundation is regarded by many of its trustees as exuding "an aura of respectable honor."[18] Karl and Katz (and others), therefore, would expect to find, in the case of Ford's role in Indonesia, disinterested, nonpolitical, and nonideological grant-making and investment initiatives that were independent of the American state; that is, they would expect to find evidence to confirm the Ford Foundation's own *publicly stated* claims about its role.

This chapter tests these rival claims against documentary evidence drawn from the comprehensive archival records of the Ford Foundation, including key trustees' oral histories, official correspondence, field-office reports, internal memoranda, grant files, and minutes of trustees' and executive and other committee meetings. Ford archival sources furnish evidence of their funded programs, projects, and network construction in the U.S. academy and in Indonesia (in this case) and the extensive liaison between the American and Indonesian university systems, including doctoral training and fellowship programs. In addition, Ford archives yield evidence of the foundation's connections with agencies of the American foreign policy apparatus—including the State Department, the Central Intelligence Agency, and the Economic Cooperation Administration, among others. The chapter focuses on two particular Ford-funded programs—University of California–Berkeley's interconnections with the Economics Faculty at the University of Indonesia and the Cornell Modern Indonesia Project—to provide concrete cases from which conclusions may be drawn in regard to the rival claims made by neo-Gramscians and their critics.

THE ASIAN STUDIES NETWORK

In general, Ford followed a set format in its overseas operations: first, strengthen or develop a U.S.-based area studies capacity in the region of interest by investing large resources at elite American universities; second, and almost in tandem, develop relevant institutions in the "target" nation or region; third, bring the two parts of the emerging network together; and fourth and overall, ensure that the entire program fits with the broad objectives of the American state. Being a private, nonstate independent organization assisted Ford enormously in winning acceptance from potentially hostile governments overseas.

Assistant Secretary of State for Far Eastern Affairs Dean Rusk clearly signaled a U.S. state interest in the Far East and the need for official and unofficial provision of education and training to the peoples of the region.[19] This aligned with President Truman's Point Four program of promoting American technical knowledge and cultural attributes as a strategy for Third World development. Ford acted on that injunction with specific reference to Indonesia (and Asia more generally) by commissioning an extensive survey of existing Asian studies programs in U.S. universities and embarking on a program of major investment in the new "discipline." Through the Modern Indonesia Project at Cornell and the connection between economists at the University of Indonesia and at UC–Berkeley, as well as through important programs at MIT and Harvard, Ford established a tightly knit academic network oriented toward the production of scholars dedicated to policy-related work in Indonesian political and economic development. The network included Indonesian and American government officials and agencies. Ford's operations became known as a "private Point Four program,"[20] championed by Paul Hoffman, who had headed up Marshall Plan aid to Europe through the Economic Cooperation Administration (ECA).[21]

The Ford Foundation's interest in Asia and Asian studies began early and was specifically focused by two profound developments: the successful communist revolution in China in 1949 and the outbreak of the Korean War in 1950. Also significant were concerns over the character of Indonesia's

political leadership, the "communist threat" to Japan, and nationalist resistance to French rule in Indo-China. In short, Cold War ideological and
military competition and, equally importantly, nationalist threats to American economic interests in the region drove the Ford Foundation's interest
in Asia. Their concerns manifested themselves in large-scale investments
in practical and policy-oriented research programs as well as in "basic research" designed to generate the basis of longer-term useful knowledge.

The utilitarian nature of Ford's interest in Asian studies was manifested
from the moment that the foundation commissioned Stanford University
to conduct a confidential survey of educational provision in that area at U.S.
universities in 1951.[22] Rowan Gaither noted that Ford wanted to develop
knowledge of "critical foreign areas" and to present such knowledge to "decision-makers and the public," fearing that U.S. foreign policy would "be
inadequate unless our knowledge . . . —political, economic and social—is
increased, utilized and disseminated."[23] The original grant awarded totaled
$35,000.

Documents associated with the Asian studies survey are replete with a
definite understanding of the political power of *mobilized* knowledge. In
one memorandum, Dyke Brown, a key Ford official, suggested that the idea
was "to mobilize Western resources of knowledge with respect to Asia . . .
[because] . . . Asia is critical in world developments" and because "the Soviet Union has capitalized on Asia's revolutionary convulsions to the dis-
advantage of the West." The memorandum went on to argue that "time is
short and our existing knowledge must be applied effectively and with dispatch." As the existing expertise in the United States on Asia was scattered
across the country, Ford pressed for "an integrated approach . . . to enlist
the cooperation of individuals and institutions in a plan to mobilize the
materials, knowledge, and talent available." Further on, the memo again
noted the "need . . . for mobilizing scattered and inadequate resources . . . to
[meet] the demands of a rapidly changing cold-war world." This could best
be done by constructing networks of highly motivated American scholars[24]
in strong departments and institutions undertaking research on Asia and
linked with relevant individuals and groups in Asia. Knowledge development and mobilization, in an integrated and planned manner, Ford recognized, lay at the heart of its mission both to aid U.S. foreign policy makers
and in the "struggle for the minds of men in Asia." One of the aims of the
Asian studies project was to promote better understanding of "Western ideals" in Asia, which could only occur through studies of the "Asian mind";

hence, studies were proposed that would research "Patterns of Thinking . . . [and] . . . Radicalism and Conservatism in Modern Asia."[25]

Ford's own extensive connections with Washington, D.C., policy makers were reinforced by those of Stanford University. For instance, Stanford's proposed study of "Strategy and Tactics of Soviet Political Policies Toward Asia" aroused great interest in the Central Intelligence Agency, the U.S. Air Force, and the State Department, with the latter keen that Robert North, a historian at Stanford, who was among the originators of the proposal, work there on the project.[26] Indeed, the proposal received State Department advice at an early stage, focused as it was on assisting official policy.[27] Additionally, there were numerous scholars serving the American state, such as the historian William L. Langer (CIA), or very close to state officials, such as Clyde Kluckohn (Harvard's Russian Research Center), to advise Ford on how to develop its strategy and research programs and on the precise character of its liaison with state officials, to maximize benefits for both parties. This was scholarship in the service of the American state, privately financed but located entirely within the mindset of officialdom.

The Ford-commissioned survey of Asian studies showed significant strength at certain institutions—such as Cornell, Harvard, Yale, Johns Hopkins, and California—but a general picture of unsystematic subject coverage. The report recommended the immediate reconstruction and strengthening of key centers of Asian studies, which the Ford Foundation's trustees vigorously supported. Ford's International Training and Research division (ITR) was the principal source of area studies funding to U.S. universities, spending approximately $52 million from 1951–1961 to "increase American understanding of the unfamiliar areas of the world . . . [and] . . . to increase the number of Americans with special competence in these areas." Additionally, ITR invested almost $29 million on university graduate programs in foreign affairs for professional engineers, educators, lawyers, and so on. In just ten years, ITR funded sixteen universities that constructed thirty-three foreign-area training and research programs.[28] From 1951 to 1966, ITR expended $258,444,169 on area studies, language development, strengthening professional fields, and the administration of foreign academics.[29] In Indonesia, Ford spent $1.8 million on developing English-language teaching facilities alone, from 1951 to 1956, and helped establish ten English-language centers for training 1,500 secondary-school teachers. Indonesia later adopted English as its second language. The foundation also invested over $1 million in Indonesian technical educational facilities.[30] Between 1951 and 1962, Ford invested $10.1 million in technical assistance programs in Indonesia.[31]

Ford, alongside the Rockefeller Foundation, constructed Southeast Asia studies programs at American universities. For example, in 1957, Ford funded a China studies center at Harvard with a grant of $300,000, in addition granting $125,000 for training teachers in East Asian studies. At the same time, Ford awarded $579,000 to Cornell, of which $300,000 was allocated for Southeast Asia studies, $75,000 for China studies, and $204,000 for field-training facilities in the Chinese language. On the latter grant, Ford reported that "the universities concerned and the State Department concur in the recommendation that this grant be made."[32] Such foreign-areas training could often best be done in the United States, because of superior facilities and because many countries were "sensitive to being the object of foreign study."[33]

Additionally, Ford considered it vital to help create an Asian studies community by providing, from 1954, hundreds of thousands of dollars for an Association for Asian Studies (AAS) that would hold annual conferences and construct a forum where scholars could meet "government and business officials active in these fields whose recommendations can influence university and government programs." By 1965, the AAS boasted three thousand members, a quarterly newsletter, and a prestigious review, the *Journal of Asian Studies*.[34]

Ford Foundation officials wanted to produce "power" through "separate generating plants": strengthening extant centers, developing new ones better tailored to current needs, and linking them to one another and to their overseas "cousin" institutions. In addition, however, the networks would include government agencies and public-opinion experts. "Such . . . [mechanisms] would enable the Asian specialist to be used for the major purposes of the national interest." In short, networks as power technology.[35]

Cornell Modern Indonesia Project (MIP)

Ford allocated $224,000 to the Modern Indonesia Project (MIP) at Cornell University in 1954. In particular, Ford was keen to construct a social science wing within Indonesian studies at Cornell, with a special focus on field-based research and study. The political-ideological and Cold War character of the neutral and academic-sounding Modern Indonesia Project (MIP) is indicated by its original name: "Techniques of Soviet Indoctrination and

Control in Indonesia."[36] It was a program of surveillance (albeit academic) and study of the power structures, political movements, and decision makers in Indonesia, especially at the level of the village—where the majority of Indonesians lived. Elite and mass-based research was fundamental to this project, which was based on consultations with the CIA and State Department. Over the next decade, MIP produced numerous books, papers, articles, and reports. Those publications were circulated within the Indonesian and American scholarly communities, to official foreign policy makers in both countries, and to a broader public through the American press. In addition, MIP researchers were in contact with official U.S. foreign policy makers about their experiences in Indonesia. Most importantly, the Modern Indonesia Project—and other Ford-sponsored research initiatives in Indonesia and the United States—*fostered, constructed, developed, and consolidated a nascent modernizing knowledge network* that was articulated with the national state apparatus, American academia, and the general anticommunist objectives of U.S. foreign policy.

It was the job of Professor George McT. Kahin,[37] the director of Cornell's Southeast Asia program and a man close to key Indonesian academics like Sumitro and Djokosotono at the University of Indonesia, to operationalize Ford's plans,[38] which had previously been approved by the CIA.[39] His first worry was that the project, as it stood, as "a study of Communist movements . . . *per se* would arouse Indonesian suspicions" and jeopardize future work in the country. He was also concerned with a directive he had received from Ford's Swayzee "*not* to identify the Indonesia Study as a Ford Foundation project."[40] In addition, Kahin pointed out that a direct study of communism in Indonesia—to which he referred as "the problem" or main focus of the programme—would miss the essential fact that communist strategy was to "work within and capture . . . key positions in existing mass organizations."[41] The foundation accepted Kahin's concerns and suggested "that even those obsessed with the importance of Indonesian communism could understand it better within the context of the whole range of that country's political life."[42] Kahin then outlined an eight-part project encompassing detailed studies of central government, parliament, local government, labor and youth organizations, Islamic parties, the two major communist parties, the Socialist Party, and the Chinese community in Indonesia. *In each and every part of these studies, the central concern was to collect data on communists and their opponents and to evaluate their role, strength, and influence.* This was practical endorsement by Kahin that communism was *the* central problem of Indonesia—precisely the point of Paul Langer's initial aims, as endorsed by the Ford Foundation, for the project.[43]

In the study of central government, special attention was proposed for the influence of the Communist Party (KPI), especially in key ministries such as Internal Affairs, Labor, and Foreign Affairs and in the President's Cabinet Secretariat. This would be coordinated with the local government study, "again with close attention to the role of the Communists . . . [especially] in areas where Communist strength was most important."[44] Among labor organizations, special place was given to the Estates Workers Union and the unions of oil-field workers. Serious attention was proposed for Islamic parties, especially "the important left wing (Religious Socialist) of the Masjumi, rivals of the Communists." Research on the Chinese community focused on their relationship to the state, PKI, and international communism.[45]

Kahin planned to put the separate studies under the leadership of highly motivated academics working with graduate students with linguistic skills and area studies and disciplinary expertise, whom he would coordinate, mentor, and assist.[46] It was clear to Kahin, as an experienced "participant-observer," that special care was needed in selecting appropriate scholars: expertise alone was not the only consideration; it was equally important that researchers develop "rapport" with Indonesians and gain their confidence. This was most pointedly emphasized in the study of the Chinese community. Kahin suggested that the study be led by a man who would spend two years in Indonesia, because of the "sensitivity of the Indonesian Chinese to any probing in the political sphere." In his first year, the scholar should conduct a "general sociological survey"—assisted by a research student interested in the Chinese family—

> and only thereafter come to grips with the more strictly political questions. The first year could serve the dual purpose of winning him the sort of confidence he would need in order to get answers to questions of a political nature and at the same time give him an over-all understanding of Chinese society in Indonesia which would be extremely helpful in undertaking the more political study during the second year.

Kahin's scholarly skills, it is clear, served both scholarly and political ends,[47] a dilemma central to much policy-oriented research.

Kahin's first report to the Ford Foundation—covering the initial fifteen months of the Indonesia research program—provides a flavor of its direct and indirect effects. It shows, at its broadest level, the success of MIP in developing collaborative relationships with important elements of the Indonesian state—including the national police force—and with faculty of the University of Indonesia and Indonesian graduate students. In addition, MIP developed a number of spinoff research projects and even provided small-scale funding for other field researchers whose interests dovetailed with theirs. Finally, the Cornell MIP had direct effects on police training and local politics.

At the suggestion of Ford officials, Kahin had allocated the bulk of the Indonesian field research to local scholars, as Western academics were often regarded with "suspicion." The effects were twofold: first, this helped develop better-trained and experienced Indonesian social scientists and created *a stronger indigenous social-scientific community, doubling its original size.* Its second and equally important effect was *political*: it helped close "the appallingly wide gap between the small Western-educated elite and the masses of the peasantry."[48] Both processes were to have long-term effects on Indonesian society and politics.

To a certain extent, the University of Indonesia (UI) became a client of the Cornell program. From its financial resources, MIP subsidized five "substantial projects" at UI, the largest being "a study of the socio-political organization and articulation of twenty-three Javanese and thirty Sumatran villages." Both MIP and UI, however, maintained the fiction that costs would be shared equally between them, as it made "sponsorship of these projects . . . politically much more acceptable if outside money is not seen as being dominant." Kahin's report makes clear, however, that the Indonesians are "relying upon the Cornell Modern Indonesia Project to finance all or nearly all of this research."[49] These arrangements were endorsed by all appropriate UI officials, including its president, Djohan; the dean of the faculty of law and social science, Professor Djokosutono; and the dean of the faculty of economics, Sumitro.[50]

Kahin's report outlined all the projects being undertaken with Ford funding. It reads like a thorough series of surveys of power in Indonesia. One study focused on the "social, economic, educational, and political background of the Indonesian elite," especially the "political and military elites." This was in addition to the large-scale economic and sociopolitical program called the "Village Research Project," which proposed to collect "data . . . relating to the power structure, decision making, development of political consensus, influence and prestige rankings, and attitudes towards the outside world." Interestingly, the methodology of this research project formed the subject of a guidebook, authored by Kahin, that was subsequently made compulsory on courses of research and study at the National Police Academy. Indeed, the head of the national police, General Sukanto, and Dean Djokosutono of UI were "both strongly of the opinion that an effective police inspector must have a good knowledge of the power structure and political articulation of the village."[51] The report also outlined another form of direct intervention in the politics of Indonesia by MIP: its sponsorship of joint projects with the National Islamic Students' Organization on "Modernist Islam" and its history and contemporary role.[52] Finally, a "Student Attitude Survey" aimed systematically to examine the "outlooks of [high school and UI] students towards the world outside, in particular, Indonesia's relationship with the principal world powers."[53]

The production of published work, based on Ford's grants to MIP, is impressive. A *Bibliography of Grant-Related Materials* shows that, over a period of ten years, MIP published *at least* forty-four books, chapters, and articles. Cornell's position as the premier university program in Indonesian studies was advanced and consolidated by those publications. The research output covered most of the areas originally planned. The Indonesia project was—in 1960—adjudged by the Ford program officer A. Doak Barnett to have been "extremely productive."[54]

The *Bibliography* and other internal Ford memoranda demonstrate the multifaceted character of the MIP's interventions in Indonesian political and academic life as well as its semisecret manner. This is shown by the way in which Kahin mobilized willing Indonesian researchers—friendly to the United States—to undertake research informed by "insider" knowledge. In a letter to Clarence Thurber (FF), Kahin took credit for A. K. Pringgodigdo's study of the presidency, the author having been the director of President Sukarno's cabinet. Kahin claimed that he had expended much effort in getting Indonesians to "undertake research and writing on important aspects of the political processes in their country on their own and without any indication of relationship to Cornell . . . [and without] any indication that their work was anything but completely independent and quite outside the aegis of an American institution." Cornell's role was also deliberately not mentioned by the author in the preface to the book.[55]

Cornell's influence within the United States was directly enhanced by Ford grants: it became the premier American center for the training and supply of junior faculty in Southeast Asian studies.[56] Its Ford funding was renewed beyond its original three years—up until 1962.[57] In Indonesia, it is clear that MIP mobilized and consolidated key U.S.-oriented social scientists at UI, such as Sumitro; encouraged indigenous research; generated a vast knowledge base on Indonesia's political, economic, and social systems; and articulated Western-oriented elites with the mass of Indonesians in the countryside. *Cornell helped foster and strengthen a strategically placed academic-political elite that was increasingly frustrated with the Indonesian government's nonaligned, independent, anti-Western, and pro-leftist orientation* and suspicion of foreign aid, loans, and financial institutions. To Ford, the role of the Cornell initiative was, in the neutral public language they normally chose to adopt, to conduct "systematic inquiry which will be useful to the growth of the new economy," an economy oriented to capitalist-modernization strategies.[58] Behind the scenes, however, and sparking a debate within Ford as to the efficacy of conducting "intelligence operations,"[59] Ford officials had cleared the Cornell project with CIA Director Allen Dulles and the State Department; after all, the projects would yield knowledge "of vital importance to the United States."[60] Despite denying that the Indonesia program was "an intelligence operation," Langer noted, "I personally believe that the Kahin project will probably come up with findings which will prove, in the long run, much more valuable than most of the day-by-day work the [U.S.] government does."[61] It was also hoped that Ford-funded research might contribute "to the formulation of a sound policy on the part of the U.S."[62] Cornell, however, represented only one prong of Ford's Indonesian intervention.

Berkeley and the University of Indonesia's Faculty of Economics

This Ford program was one of its most controversial initiatives, generating public criticism and a flurry of concern within the foundation. An article by David Ransom in the left-wing magazine *Ramparts*, in 1970, claimed that Ford, along with the Rockefeller Foundation and the American state, had consciously used its Indonesia programs to train anti-Sukarno economists and social scientists, cadres of leaders who would run Indonesia once Sukharno "got out." The "expose" generated some concern within Ford, leading to the compilation of documents rebutting the claims. This section considers Ransom's claims and Ford's stated aims and programs to determine the degree to which Ford constructed an "anti-Sukarno" elite in Indonesia.

FORD'S AIMS

Ford funded this program with grants of $2.5 million, from 1956 to 1962, to assist the economic development of Indonesia. It aimed to do this, in part, by disbursing funds "to develop a faculty of economics and of a staff of related experts consisting of [Indonesian] citizens" and by constructing "an enhanced body of scientific knowledge and understanding of Indonesian institutions" at the University of California–Berkeley.[63] Ford officials felt that the "almost total lack of trained economists" hampered both Indonesian development and American competence and knowledge of that society's dynamics and institutions. Consequently, Ford wanted to build collaboration between Berkeley economists and UI faculty, in addition to providing doctoral fellowships to Indonesians at Berkeley, MIT, and Cornell. Ford planning documents show that foundation officials and trustees fully recognized that Ford-trained Indonesian economists would "be of great influence in the shaping of Indonesia's economic institutions in the future." Indeed, it was acknowledged that, by 1958, "the project has become increasingly associated with the internal development of Indonesia."[64] Although Ford's projects were justified in terms of increasing knowledge and understanding, it is clear that this knowledge was to be put to particular uses—for the "development" of leadership cadres that would be well placed "*no matter what turn the political crisis may take.*"[65]

RANSOM'S CLAIMS

Ransom's claims about Ford's ambitions and activities in Indonesia are simple: Ford sought to replace the old Dutch colonial elite with a pliable, U.S.-oriented Indonesian elite. In short, Ford represented the new American imperium in world affairs. In this view, Sukarno was far too anti-American, left wing, and procommunist to be a vehicle for American interests; instead, the U.S. preferred the upper-class leaders of the Socialist Party of Indonesia (SPI), especially Sumitro and Soedjatmoko, both of whom favored opening up Indonesia to foreign corporations. In 1957, Sumitro fled to Singapore after an SPI and Islamic rebel army-organized uprising, of which he was a leading figure, failed to dislodge Sukarno. After Sukarno, however, Sumi-tro was elevated to minister of trade in what Ransom calls the "modernist restoration," which was achieved not with U.S. troops but within "the hal-lowed private institutions of [U.S.] academia and philanthropy." Most con-troversially, Ransom claims that Ford's head of international training and research programs, John Howard, told him in an interview that "Ford felt it was training the guys who would be leading the country when Sukharno got out." Finally, Ransom claims that two leading American academics who objected to Ford's programs had protested and resigned.[66]

EVIDENCE: TRAINING THE "BEAUTIFUL BERKELEY BOYS"

The University of California–Berkeley/University of Indonesia program of cooperation in economics, business administration, and related social sciences began in July 1956 and continued until 1962. The initial grant for $500,000 was split between the two universities, with Berkeley receiving $300,000. UI was to spend the grant on fellowships to Indonesians to study at U.S. universities, principally Berkeley, Yale, and Cornell, and on improv-ing its research facilities in economics. Sumitro, the dean of UI's faculty of economics, emphasized Indonesia's need for educated and skilled research-ers with doctorates—in a nation with just fifteen Ph.D.s for a population of eighty million people.[67]

From Berkeley's perspective, the project aimed at "research, education, training and related activities designed to strengthen the Indonesian econ-omy, to enhance the standards of Indonesian administration, and to im-prove the scientific study and understanding of Indonesian society."[68] Such objectives were in line with the Ford Foundation's own ideas and those of leading Indonesian economists, such as Sumitro.[69] It was a program that sought radically to reorganize the Indonesian institutions' internal admin-istration and develop university "advisory and consultative services" to in-dustry and government. Berkeley agreed to provide several "faculty col-laborators" in general economics and fiscal affairs, industrial and business economics, agricultural economics and rural sociology, and social econom-ics and general sociology. In the collaborative process, Berkeley would gain further field-study experience and comparative analytical understanding and strengthen its specialized knowledge of Indonesian economy and so-ciety. In turn, UI would receive funding for its economics and social sci-ence programs; even more, U.S. assistance would "permit the university structure of Indonesia to play a more stimulating role in rendering service to the developing economy and society."[70] The head of Berkeley's group in Jakarta was Professor Leonard A. Doyle.[71]

The project appeared to work successfully, in general, and was renewed in 1958 for a further two years. By 1959–1960, there were twenty-one UI graduate students on Berkeley-managed programs in the United States: sixteen at Berkeley, two at Stanford, two at UCLA, and one at Columbia. A further ten students arrived in the summer of 1960. The annual report for 1959–1960 stated that the quality of Indonesian students' research and writing skills, based on expert field-staff supervision, was greatly improved.[72]

In addition, the research, dissemination, and advisory activities of Berkeley economists had yielded results. Several research papers and articles had been published on Indonesian monetary problems, the economics of the labor movement, kerosene distribution, entrepreneurship, and the problems of economic policy.[73] Berkeley staff presented research papers at other Indonesian universities, to government officials, and to members of the business community and served as consultants to insurance firms, government, and businesses. They also developed Indonesian case-study material to aid teaching in business and public administration.[74]

The reorganization and reform of the Indonesian university also, on the whole, progressed according to plan, though less rapidly than hoped. Ironically, Ford's plans for teaching and examinations were to end the Indonesian system of "free study" in favor of "guided study."[75] There was resistance from some non-U.S. trained Indonesian faculty, ex-colonial Dutch academics, and student-veterans of the anticolonial revolutionary army. There had, however, been great improvements in the rationalization of enrollment requirements and the scheduling of courses and written examinations. Despite resistance, changes had successfully, if slowly, been made, and reforms were expected to accelerate as more and more American-trained faculty returned.[76] Sumitro's own assumptions about the role of economics in development mirrored those within the Ford Foundation: economics was a science based on value-free facts, research, and logic and was oriented to policy and action.[77]

It is clear that Ford's programs at UI were consciously designed to Americanize the institution through a program of "modernization."[78] In a context that took fully into account the balance of political forces in Indonesia, including the strengths and weaknesses of the president, the army, and the communists and general attitudes to the United States, Ford reports refer constantly to the Indonesian state's attempts to "indoctrinate educators with appropriate political principles," by introducing "Eastern Socialist teachers," sending students to the Soviet Union, and by creating a climate within which U.S.-trained Indonesians had to "go to some pains to show freedom from influence by American training." Conversely, Ford's Americanizing programs are referred to as "progressive," "influential," and self-evidently "good" and "moderate."[79] In a 1961 status report on foundation programs, Ford referred to as evidence of "moderation" that the Indonesian government voiced support for private enterprise.[80] Returning Ford fellows were referred to as influential and "self-assertive . . . beginning to influence their institutions along good lines"; indeed, their demands were considered "encouragingly critical" of the Indonesian status quo. Returning Ford fellows were making "demands for change and progress"; as a body, they were "a small but potentially strategic body of qualified, trained leadership in education," without which Indonesia would be the worse.[81] Without Ford funding, Bresnan claims that there would have been no "economic miracle" in Indonesia.[82]

Of the two dozen returned Ford fellows, twenty-two had "loyally" returned to join the faculty at UI, "filling key positions," including the chairs of the economics department and business department, director of the Institute for Social and Economic Research, and so on. Their influence was felt across the university system, because they were assisting other universities as well as the Indonesian state. Indeed, because of their activities, the latter was considering establishing a governmental training facility for managers.[83] The influence of Ford-funded economists was nationwide: Sumitro was not only populating the major universities across Indonesia with his and Berkeley's graduates but was developing affiliates along the lines of his own faculty's affiliations with Berkeley. The faculty of economics at UI became a significant influential hub.[84]

The effect of American field staff at UI was felt at all levels of the institution, from teaching and research to administration and outside consultancies. Ford's American scholars were members of an informal "committee-group," set up by the chairman of the faculty of economics, Widjojo—a Ford fellow—to "discuss problems and offer advice" on academic, intellectual, and administrative matters.[85] Overall, the UI-Berkeley collaboration was declared "a clear success."[86]

In response to Ransom's claims of Ford's imperial aims and programs in Indonesia, the foundation created a confidential dossier replete with arguments directly to challenge Ransom in the U.S. press, should the "story" break. In practice, the story did not get very much publicity, and the dossier remained for internal use only. Ford's internal rebuttals argued that Ransom was laughably "off the mark"; that all they had really been interested in doing was to "prepare *teachers*, not government officials" at UI; and that their programs were nonpolitical and educational only. Ford merely wanted to help bring newly independent Indonesia "more nearly up to date in education, administration and agriculture."[87] All they had done was to train Indonesians in "modern economics of a kind practiced in international economic circles in most parts of the world" in order to create "'technocrats'... apolitical civil servants."[88] Yet, in even their own Ransom-rebuttal dossier, Ford acknowledges their support of the view that "the *political* future of Indonesia demanded attention to *economic soundness*,"[89] with "soundness" referring mainly to promarket and foreign investment–friendly economic policies.[90] Ford denied that they had consciously created the leaders who would take over when Sukarno got out. In fact, John Howard claimed that he had been misquoted by Ransom—that what he said was that "*as things turned out*," Ford's trained economists were "called to serve in the government" after Sukarno; they had not set out to create them.[91]

Yet, the evidence of the Berkeley program, as well as that of the Cornell Modern Indonesia Project, both justified in Cold War terms and in terms of Indonesia's strategic and economic value to the United States, undermines Ford's defense. Ford was not interested in only teaching matters in any case, according to their own records. Research, training a new generation of Indonesian scholars, boosting American expertise on Indonesian society and politics, gathering direct intelligence on Indonesian peasants' loyalties and attitudes, and so on were at the core of Ford's programs—in addition to keeping the U.S. State Department fully informed of all initiatives. These are not nonpolitical programs; they helped achieve U.S. State Department goals by articulating academia and officialdom, by reforming Indonesian universities, and by promoting broadly pro–free market economics teaching and research. An early Ford-commissioned report noted the importance of bringing Indonesia "into the orbit of the democratic states."[92] An even earlier report—prior to any Ford investment in Indonesia—noted that Indonesia's "loss to the free world would be a serious blow" and that Ford could assist by developing "leadership in depth" by educating a new generation of leaders to solve Indonesia's political problems.[93] As the evidence above has shown, Ford's role in Indonesia was not entirely about neutrally assisting a developing nation: its mineral and population resources and strategic location were of paramount interest, and its internal ideologies and politics were an object of surveillance. Pulling Indonesia into "the democratic orbit" was an openly stated goal that required covert and overt U.S. assistance against Dutch colonials and communist "saboteurs." And a "sound economy" required U.S.-trained economists, the most potent form of U.S. (nonmilitary) intervention. From Ford's point of view, "sound economics," by definition, meant free markets, the predominance of the price mechanism, and an economy open to foreign investment, loans, and trade;[94] indeed, these were considered the bases of successful "democracy building" and political freedom.

Ransom's article claimed that so clear were Ford's imperialistic aims and programs in Indonesia that two Berkeley academics, Leonard Doyle (the first field chairman) and Ralph Anspach (a graduate student), resigned in protest. Anspach, according to Ransom, claimed, "I had the feeling that in the last analysis I was supposed to be a part of this American policy of empire . . . bringing in American science, and attitudes, and culture . . . winning over countries—doing this with an awful lot of cocktails and high pay."[95] These claims are not addressed in Ford's Ransom-rebuttal dossier; nor is there any evidence of attempts independently by Ford to contact Anspach for his version of events, in contrast to contacts with scholars friendly to the foundation.

Professor Leonard Doyle, described by Ransom as an "essentially conservative business professor" who wrote a paper on "Reducing the Barriers to Private Foreign Investment in Underdeveloped Countries," based on his research in Indonesia, experienced problems relating to Ford's representative in Jakarta, Michael Harris.[96] Doyle informed Ransom that "I was not as convinced of Sumitro's position as the Ford Foundation representative was, and, in retrospect, probably the CIA," which resulted in Doyle's refusal to hire pro-Sumitro professors. As Sumitro was part of the political and military opposition—which had official CIA and State Department military and financial support[97]—Doyle wanted to avoid California's getting "involved in what essentially was becoming a rebellion against the government—whatever sympathy you might have with the rebel cause and the rebel objectives."[98] On the other hand, Ford internal documents suggest that the problem with Doyle was that he was difficult to work with and that he failed to "establish good working relationships with either Sumitro or his principal lieutenants."[99] Again, Doyle was not approached by Ford to verify the account he provided to Ransom.[100] Another relevant reference to Doyle in Ford papers relates to Doyle's *contemporaneous* complaints about Ford's programs and aims in Indonesia. For example, Harris wrote in January 1958 that Doyle had openly expressed disquiet about Ford programs, declared them "a dismal failure," and called on UC to discontinue their involvement. Harris reported that Doyle thought "that California had been an unwitting tool of State Department and [Ford] Foundation foreign policy objectives which he believed to be completely unsound. . . . Apparently he was not able or did not desire to conceal his views" from anyone, including UI faculty.[101] Yet in a dossier claiming to present a clear picture of Ford's programs, no provision was made to contact Doyle for his perspective.

Ford's Ransom-rebuttal dossier also criticized, as radically undermining Ransom's claims, the "fact" that he "lumps together" Ford with Rockefeller, USAID, the State Department, American corporations, and so on, implying that Ford wanted to "set the stage for the imposition on Indonesia of western economics," when in reality each of the organizations had different aims and methods.[102] The evidence cited above, however, supports the idea that Ford did wish to shift Indonesia out of the orbit of the "socialist/Soviet bloc" and—economically, politically, ideologically, and militarily—into the Western world. Although those organizations were separate, Ford went to great lengths to ensure that their programs were in line with official U.S. foreign policy. Ford's pluralistic defense does not stand up to close scrutiny, despite Ransom's journalistic hyperbole.

FORD AND THE TRANSITION FROM SUKARNO TO SUHARTO

Imposing change from outside may be putting it too strongly. The foundation targeted its financial resources to foster, construct, and sustain elite power-knowledge networks that were, in the main, already disposed to American development strategies, in an environment where funding was scarce and need was great. Thereby, Ford effectively financed certain disciplines, specific lines of enquiry as opposed to others,[103] and consolidated and sustained a pro-American counterhegemony within the Indonesian educational system that, in turn, was networked with several political parties, student organizations, Islamic groups, the national police, and the army. The aim was clearly to "win" Indonesia as a great prize—economically and strategically—for the West. Ford wanted political and economic change in Indonesia: from Sukarno's "radical society: anti-democratic, anti-capitalistic, and probably even anti-socialistic" to one that practiced "moderate" economic policies. As Widjojo was approvingly quoted in one Ford report, the Ford econo-mists were taking a long-term view to *"build for the future."* Bresnan ap-provingly quotes Widjojo's inaugural address at UI, emphasizing the neces-sity in economic policy of "efficiency, rationality, consistency, clear choices among alternatives, and attention to prices and material incentives."[104] Ford itself concluded that the most effective role it had played in Indonesia was in the *"building of nuclei of Indonesian cadre with institutional cohesiveness and durability . . . [and the] association of Indonesian and foreign supporting institutions which continues after the conclusion of substantial training pro-grams."*[105] Bresnan notes, in 1993, that the technocrats' "years at Berkeley and other (largely) American universities . . . gave them great confidence in their professional ability to set the nation on the path to economic growth; this alone *tended to set them apart from the others [nationalists], to bind them closely together as a kind of secular brotherhood, earning them the sobriquet 'Berkeley mafia.' "*[106]

This section considers Ford's attitudes to the changes that took place in Indonesia from the time it became untenable for Ford to stay in Jakarta (1965) to the time of their return (in 1967), the appointment of Ford-trained economists to Suharto's military regime, the role of the Ford-funded Har-vard Development Advisory Service team, and the overall changes that oc-curred in Indonesia after the military takeover.

Ford's office in Jakarta, which first opened in 1953, closed "in the face of growing Communist agitation" in 1965 and reopened in early 1967, when Sukarno was replaced by a *"moderate* military elite," according to a Ford re-port (emphasis added). This "moderate" military regime, claimed the Ford report, "lent its support to a group of Western-trained intellectuals who were brought . . . into key policy positions at the cabinet and sub-cabinet levels." In fact, the report concluded, "this elite [was] drawn from the eco-nomics faculties in which the Foundation had invested so heavily."[107] The latter economists were therefore, by definition, moderate.

According to Peter Dale Scott, some of the long-term recipients of Ford Foundation funding—including student groups—were deeply involved with the Indonesian military, whose self-image had increasingly developed to encompass a leading political role in national affairs.[108] In particular, groups that had played a role in the failed CIA-sponsored rebellion of 1958 were mobilized, in the 1960s, by the Army's "civic action" programs. The right-wing Islamic Masjumi party and its allied Socialist Party of Indonesia, led by Sumitro, were also backed by the CIA, to the tune of several million dollars.[109] Some SPI intellectuals and their associates in the army were also in close contact with Guy Pauker, an academic at Berkeley and RAND consultant: Pauker was openly advocating that the army take "full responsibility" for Indonesia's future, take on the PKI, and "strike, sweep their house clean."[110] Pauker, a vehement anticommunist, was among the scholars who taught army officers at Seskoad counterinsurgency, economics, and administration.[111] In an article of 1967, Pauker hailed the students who had led protests in Jakarta and noted Sukarno's closure of the University of Indonesia after staunch student opposition to his administration.[112] Scott suggests that the army began "to operate virtually as a para-state, independent of Sukarno's government." "This training programme was entrusted to officers and civilians close to the PSI. U.S. officials have confirmed that the civilians, who themselves were in a training program funded by the Ford Foundation, became involved in what the (then) U.S. military attaché called 'contingency planning' to prevent a PKI take-over." Interestingly, in light of such close collaboration with Ford scholars, the Indonesian Army's Territorial Organization had developed an infrastructure that included close liaisons with religious and cultural organizations, youth groups, trade union and peasant organizations, and local and regional political parties— organizations and groups remarkably similar to those studied by George Kahin's Cornell-UI group. Indeed, one leading Cornell group alumnus— Selosoemardjan—was closely involved in the liaison.[113] Scott concludes that "these political liaisons with civilian groups provided the structure for the ruthless suppression of the PKI in 1965, including the bloodbath."[114]

How did this "moderate military elite" rise to power in Indonesia, according to Ford's own internal reports? Suharto's accession to power followed an "attempted Communist coup" on September 30, 1965, a claim that remains contested.[115] Another Ford report on Indonesia, summarizing developments from 1953 to 1969, does not mention the violence associated with the military takeover, though it contains numerous references to the shortcomings of the Sukarno period. For example, the period is referred to as one of "political hooliganism," "threats and abuses," "abusive rejection of [Western] assistance," as leaving "scars" from "a long period of political repression," as "marked by destructive influences," an "almost uninterrupted state of instability," and with "inherent administrative weakness."[116] The one reference to the coup in this particular Ford report merely notes that "the coup was staged and put down" ninety days after Ford's offices closed in Jakarta: "Within eight weeks," however, "the new government and the Foundation formalized a new assistance project. . . . Important matters . . . were being given attention in Indonesia."[117] The massacre of hundreds of thousands of "communists" did not warrant even a footnote.

Perhaps Ford merely wanted to move on with business and not dwell on the past. This argument is undermined by the numerous and constant references to the Sukarno period, as noted above. On returning to Ford's reopened office in Jakarta, Miller noted that it was "my privilege . . . witnessing the shaping of affairs under General Suharto's New Order, seeing the impressive achievements."[118] Miller, however, had returned to Jakarta in April 1966—a year before the Ford office reopened. His commentary on what he observed there is instructive.

Miller noted in a letter to New York, which was passed on to McGeorge Bundy, Ford's president, that "Indonesia is vastly different"; the people "now feel that they are masters of their own souls . . . the country is . . . violently anti-communistic. . . . There is an atmosphere of sustained holiday-spirit and exhilaration over the change; and a virtual worship of the young people who have been forcing all elements against the Sukarno clique and regime." Miller was "struck . . . [by] the virtual hilarity over the liquidation of several hundred thousand fellow-countrymen (the estimate given me by more than one credible Indonesian was 400,000)." Indonesians, in Miller's experience, had never before known "as much freedom in critical judgments of Sukarno and his policies." Suharto, conversely, was enjoying "extraordinarily solid and enthusiastic popular support."[119]

There is neither the merest hint of criticism nor condemnation of the killing of four hundred thousand "communists." Miller provides only a picture of happiness and freedom previously unseen; Ford can do business with the New Order, as Miller rapidly reports in the rest of his letter. Although some—including the former U.S. ambassador to Indonesia, Howard P. Jones—estimate that one million leftists were massacred, the figure of 450,000 to 500,000 is accepted by the Suharto regime. In addition, almost 1.5 million leftists were imprisoned after the annihilation of the Indonesian Communist Party (PKI).[120] A leading role in the anticommunist massacre was played by students of the University of Indonesia, using the campus as their base, as Miller noted. One of Ford's Indonesian economists, Soedjadtmoko, told Miller that Ford's investment at UI "had really paid off in the past few months."[121] "I'm enjoying the trip. Hope all's well in New York," is how Miller's letter to head office ended, echoing the views of the American government.[122] Bresnan, conversely, claims that "informed opinion" was unaware of the scale of killing, despite Miller's contemporaneous report and close relationship with Bresnan.[123]

Despite later protestations about Ford's nonpolitical role in Indonesia, Miller was frank in his support of the new regime and proud of Ford's role in creating leading economist cadres that were informally advising General Suharto. Indeed, Miller, in a report that was copied to McGeorge Bundy, urged the necessity of U.S. government aid to Indonesia. He argued that *the regime needed strengthening to prevent the reemergence of Sukarno*; therefore, "some tactfully conveyed encouragement to them [Indonesians] might be crucial at this stage . . . any efforts of our Government now to establish contact, informally and at any appropriate place, inside or outside Indonesia, might well be worthwhile."[124]

Indonesia faced a grave economic crisis: inflation over 600 percent, growing external debt (over $2.3 billion), and inadequate export earnings. The new military regime believed that technocratic solutions were called for; they recruited Ford-trained economists, led by Widjojo Nitisastro (Berkeley), "heirs to the American tradition of thinking on economic development."[125] The other four members of the original five-man team of economic and financial experts were Mohammad Sadli (MIT), Subroto (Harvard; UI), Ali Wardhana (Berkeley), and Emil Salim (Berkeley). This was the same group of economists who had attended and lectured the armed forces at Seskoad, the Army's staff college, on economic development and reform. Suharto was impressed by their intellectual "clarity . . . [and] unanimity . . . and their pragmatic sense." They were later joined by Sumitro, "the mentor of them all," who was asked to return from exile by Suharto.[126] Foreign loans soon flowed in, as did overseas investment, especially following the drafting of a Foreign Investment Law in 1967. Once again, Ford-funded economists, working alongside Ford-sponsored American economists—this time from Harvard's Development Advisory Service—played a critical role. Ford supplied over $2 million to Harvard's DAS from 1968 to the mid-1970s to assist the National Development Planning Agency (also known as BAPPENAS), which was chaired by Widjojo.[127] Together, the economists worked out a "rational, encouraging and enlightened policy . . . to attract domestic and foreign economic participation and investment."[128] Although Ford declared the DAS-BAPPENAS project a success, along with the soundness of the New Order's market-led economic policies, there were grave reservations in Indonesia about the political impact of "modernization." For example,

Widjojo noted in 1973 that there was increasing public opposition to over-reliance on "the market system," "foreign investment/aid/advice," and to the "power and positions in the hands of the old economic group," i.e., the technocrats.[129] A Ford report in 1978 declared that despite "massive foreign investment" based on "concessions," very few new jobs had been created. In addition, the armed forces "remain massively involved in illegal tax collection, smuggling and commercial activities." And the technocrats were proving to be very poor state managers.[130] Yet the same basic charges had been leveled since as early as 1968,[131] and, despite them, Ford funds continued to pour into Indonesia, largely because the pro-American Suharto's middle-class constituency of big business, Moslem landlords, intellectuals, and students expected and received economic benefits from the New Order.[132]

CONCLUSION

The Ford Foundation, guided by leading businessmen and state officials was, from its very inception, at the heart of the postwar U.S. foreign policy establishment. Its leaders were anticommunist supporters of U.S. hegemony in world affairs. To be sure, the foundation's functions in the American-led world order differed from those of the state, but their objectives were the same: to penetrate foreign societies, economies, and polities and draw them into the American orbit—and away from nationalistic/leftist philosophies and alliances.[133] Ford constructed a series of networks—based around power-knowledge—that mobilized and integrated academics in the United States and Indonesia armed with theories of capitalist economic development. Ford's resources were also vital in generating specific lines of economic and political research, to the exclusion of others, thereby mobilizing bias. Even more than this, Ford acted in a semicovert manner to penetrate the Indonesian academy and to reform some of its flagship institutions, especially the University of Indonesia. The long-term effect of such programs and reforms was to create cadres of intellectuals, opposed to the Indonesian administration, who planned for the eventual demise of Sukharno and the opening up of the Indonesian economy to foreign investment, international loans, and friendship with the United States.

Ford's initiatives, however, were not one sided or imposed on unwilling Indonesian academics: they were welcomed with open arms by Western-educated, pro-American economists and even by the Sukarno administration. The former, however, were more fully aware of the full range of formal and informal activities that were being conducted under the banner of "research"—into the village power structure, students' attitudes, political elite backgrounds, and other studies. The latter appeared, on the whole, to accept Ford's public image of nonpolitical, nonideological, and unofficial aid agency.

Was Ford part of an American hegemonic strategy? Certainly, two American professors from the UI-Berkeley program thought so and duly resigned, citing opposition to Ford's "American policy of empire." The American "empire," as Huntington put it, was less wedded to territorial *acquisition* than to territorial *penetration*. Ford intervened in and intellectually penetrated Indonesia principally because of its economic resources and strategic position as well as its political-ideological attraction to communism and socialism and desire to carve out a specifically Indonesian path to development. American policy makers and Ford officials frequently justified their interest with reference to the Soviet and/or Chinese "threat," the Korean War, and general decolonization processes, projecting an image of *defensive* action. Though such defensiveness may have been justified, it was not the only motivating factor, as references to Indonesia as a "great prize" attest. Indonesia had much to offer American capital in terms of cheap labor, a large internal market, and its very favorable climate for foreign investment. Ultimately, therefore, the evidence strongly supports a Gramscian analysis of the roles of the Ford Foundation in Indonesia, severely undermining the orthodox views of Karl and Katz. Ford constructed in Indonesia an effective counterhegemonic bloc of politically and militarily well-connected intellectuals who looked to the United States and international financial institutions for their country's economic modernization and progress, greatly assisting its transformation into a "model pupil of globalization." In this project, Ford's initiatives dovetailed with and complemented those of the American state.

The next chapter turns to a continent generally neglected by the United States but that, as a result of its strategic and economic value, particularly to the resurrection of Western Europe after World War II, came into the consciousness of the American state and, therefore, the major American foundations: Africa.

6 | FORD, ROCKEFELLER, AND CARNEGIE IN NIGERIA AND THE AFRICAN STUDIES NETWORK

Nigeria is an oasis of democratic development in an arid desert of authoritarian-inclined African states.
—Arnold Rivkin (1962)

The African continent has provided the laboratory for research in almost every discipline and the multitude of problems connected with development . . .
—L. Gray Cowan

Unlike Indonesia, Nigeria was purportedly viewed by U.S. policy makers as *neither* a *direct* American strategic interest nor a vital economic asset.[1] Yet it was to U.S. officials "the most important country in Africa," providing America with "an excellent opportunity . . . to demonstrate to the newly-independent African nations that the best way to achieve their economic and political aspirations lies in . . . cooperating with the Free World."[2] Like Indonesia and Chile (see chapter 7), Nigeria was seen as a "laboratory" for "modernization" theory and particularly for the role of economic "planning" to avoid inflation and exchange controls as the key to building a thriving free-market economy within a politically stable democratic polity. The optimism characteristic of modernization theory and applied liberally in the 1960s, the allegedly inevitable linear progression through stages to full "development," was evident in both official U.S. aid and in philanthropic foundations' activities in Nigeria.[3] Indeed, there was great overlap in the thrust of the programs between official and private agencies, which shared evaluations of the significance of Africa in general and Nigeria in particular. Yet the level of knowledge about Africa and Nigeria, as exemplified by the title of a key book by one such planner—*Planning Without Facts*—was so low among U.S. officials and (many but not all of) their university and foundation-funded advisers that "planning" frequently turned out to be based on superficial generalizations, prejudice, and blind faith in the "rational" methods of the social sciences. Yet within a few years, Nigeria descended into a bloody civil war, which surprised (most) American experts, demonstrating both the latter's ignorance of Nigerian society and ethnic politics and that American planners had exacerbated the tensions of Nigeria through enriching a "new class" of "gatekeepers" that benefitted enormously and disproportionately from Western aid and markets.[4] In the long run, American aid and modernization strategies delivered little by way of benefits to the mass of Nigerians but did a great deal to build and maintain pro-American elite networks, mindsets, and agendas—and an economy and polity increasingly undermined by corruption, deep indebtedness, and inequality.

African studies in the United States developed in tandem with American elites' increasing interest in Africa. Their interest being largely instrumental in character, Africanists saw Africa as a laboratory for theories of development and modernization, much as missionaries had seen it as a source of converts to the truths of Christianity. Africa was to be studied, observed, dug up for archaeological evidence, its peoples' voices recorded for evidence of its cultural and social development, its thought patterns analyzed, and its peoples' responses to modernity and rapid change assessed by behavioral scientists. Then lessons would be drawn up and applied by policy makers, university builders, and military strategists. If the study of Africa was an overseas "project," the African Studies Association (ASA) was its professional vanguard: small, self-perpetuating, closely knit, well funded, and well connected with state agencies. As modernization theory unraveled under the weight of problems ignored (or unseen, being beyond the theory) in Africa and Nigeria, so the ASA's elite (white) leadership faced a rebellion from below from its own membership, who were outraged by the association's elitist character, its racially exclusionary practices, its involvement with America's intelligence agencies, its refusal to condemn apartheid in South Africa, and its failure to consider the educational needs of African Americans. The 1969 Montreal "uprising" and walkout of ASA members— some white but mainly black—against their leaders led to a split in the association, the effects of which have lasted decades. The lack of consultation by

Carnegie and Ford—and the ASA—of Africans about African development and the almost complete absence of black American Africanists in the leadership of the ASA and its powerful committees were of a piece, a remarkable demonstration of a mindset whose foreign policy fully reflected its domestic attitudes. These "secular missionaries," who had failed to see what was going on in their own association, confidently believed that they could solve the problem of poverty and development in Africa. Their failure, however, obscures a great "success": the construction of domestic and foreign elite cadres that continued to function after the "crisis" and that, after some hand-wringing and reform, form the basis of the foundations' continuing programs: the network as both means and end of foundations' activities.

Africa's Significance to the United States

Though Nigeria and Africa more generally were not necessarily of decisive importance to the U.S. economy or private American investors, there was clear recognition of *Africa's* economic and strategic significance to both the United States and Europe. The latter, it will be remembered, was the object of American attention through the Marshall Plan and NATO, which included significant efforts at encouraging greater intra–Western European cooperation. The restoration and preservation of a strong Western European bloc as market and strategic ally in the Cold War was an American vital interest. The restoration of Europe's lines of communication with its former African colonies was fundamental. Africa was also, of course, of especial importance to African Americans, and though this was recognized by some Africanists it was hardly acted upon, and then only for a short-lived period in the 1970s, by either American policy makers or the major foundations. The latter's racist attitudes on the intellectual capacities of African Americans were broached in chapter 2; they were magnified in the postcolonial settings of Africa. In a Carnegie Corporation–funded volume, Rupert Emerson, an African Studies Association stalwart who unselfconsciously writes of the relatively recent "discovery" and "rediscovery" of a mysterious Africa, notes that American policy makers only took Africa seriously once strategic interests were threatened during World War II. Africa is significant because America cannot ignore a continent that covers a fifth of the world's surface, would be a fundamental loss if it entered the Soviet bloc, and was of great economic significance to NATO allies.[5] Africa was vital to Europe. It is rich in industrial diamonds, columbium (used in the

aerospace industries), cobalt, chromium, and beryllium; a significant producer of tin, manganese, copper and antimony; its uranium (in Congo and
South Africa) was fundamental to the atomic age; the discovery of oil in
Libya and Algeria elevated their importance; and its agricultural produce
includes coffee, cocoa, cotton, and vegetable oils.[6]

Africa's "backward" character, however—as a result of colonialists'
"failure . . . to bring their African wards" up to the levels of "the imperial
centers"—had created an incendiary problem that, according to Chester
Bowles, created an "ominous revolutionary situation" threatening the "free
world."[7] Emerson was very conscious of the threat of Africa's slide into the
chaos caused by Algeria's "terrorism" against French rule, the Mau Mau rising in Kenya, and the "troubled affairs of the Congo."[8]

As ever, the "solution" to the "problem" of Africa lay in elite top-down
modernization. As Emerson noted, French and British colonial rule created
at least the embryonic bases of new African leadership elites familiar with
the modern West and normally speakers of an "alien" language, in contrast to the "masses," whose mindsets are more traditional. That "Western-
educated and in many respects Western-orientated elite" would win the day
in Africa, though not without conflict.[9] It was Emerson's view that Africa's
future leaders must be educated in the United States to effect the greatest
intellectual transformation.[10] Acculturation of an African elite had political and economic consequences, including expanded markets for Western
consumer products.[11]

Emerson does not label as anti-American African voices that question
America's motives. He is clear that America must be active in Africa but
aware that his country's anticolonial credentials were severely undermined
by alliances with the colonial powers, its tepid attitude to revolution, and
the treatment of America's twenty million black "citizens." As Vice President Richard Nixon pointed out after his visit to Africa in 1957, "we cannot
talk equality to the peoples of Africa and Asia and practice inequality in the
United States."[12] The linkage of America's policies toward Africa and Asia
with her domestic racial order, particularly in the deep South, was by the
1950s and 1960s accepted by the liberal Establishment, though not necessarily consistently acted upon at home.[13] In consequence, the racial question—
of the relationship between white and black Africanists and their respective
access to resources—was to cause a major schism in the 1960s politics of
African studies. Indeed, it could hardly have been otherwise, given the history of enslavement and Jim Crow racial discrimination.[14]

It is against this backdrop that the major foundations' activities must be viewed. Africa's significance was of great consequence to the Carnegie Corporation, as part of its remit included the British colonies and dominions. Carnegie acted as a significant catalyst for the development of African higher education in "British" Africa, bringing into close cooperation U.S. aid agencies, Ford and Rockefeller foundations, the State Department, major American investors, and the British Colonial Office. Nevertheless, and instructively, Carnegie's interest in the erstwhile British Empire focused disproportionately on the whites of South Africa and white colonial educators across the rest of the (British) African continent. Beyond Africa, Carnegie focused on Australia, New Zealand, and Canada, an important indicator of a continued Anglo-Saxonism. Africa's development needs only became urgent once Ghana became independent in 1957 and Vice President Richard Nixon had declared the significance of Africa for America. Rockefeller philanthropic interest in Africa preceded that of Carnegie but focused, in its earliest days, on public health, tropical diseases, and scientific research. As Donald Fisher and Richard Brown have noted, the imperial character of such programs was evidenced by their motivation to rid the world of diseases that negatively impacted the lives and health of colonialists, soldiers, and missionaries.[15] Although Rockefeller supported educational exchanges with Africa in the 1920s, it was not until the rise of independent Africa that Rockefeller took an active interest in its political and economic development.[16] Ford, emerging during the Cold War, was the most overtly "political" in its approach, despite maintaining a formal veneer of scientific objectivity. Ford collaborated with U.S. state agencies and engaged in active institution-building programs, including economic planning units, such as at the University of Ife, and behavioral sciences at the University of Ibadan, both in Nigeria. Ford also funded in large part institutes of African studies in Ghana and Nigeria in a bid to construct stronger senses of national identity in newly independent states.

The foundations also contributed millions of dollars to build African studies either as a separate "discipline" or to the study and research of African issues within existing disciplines in the U.S. academy. In addition, the foundations, especially Carnegie, were instrumental in founding the African Studies Association in 1957 and later making the ASA their main conduit for grant making in the fledgling discipline. Within a decade, however, the ASA was to be challenged for its racism and elitism in excluding black Americans and concentrating resources at a few elite institutions.

Nevertheless, the foundations' activities, in collaboration with one another and numerous other key agencies in African institution building, travel scholarships, research fellowships, and the funding of major new programs and study centers in African studies in the United States, created active and prolific networks of scholars, investors, philanthropists, and policy makers that proved broadly enduring and influential. Although publicly intended to alleviate poverty and "underdevelopment" and inaugurate economic growth and prosperity, the programs' achievements fell short. American foundations' programs that purportedly steered a middle course between the demands of African nationalists for rapid progress and the elitism of British colonials who were more interested in creating an African elite in their own image ultimately created networks that were elitist in outlook and composition and contributed little to national development or removing inequality. The construction of elitist and pro-American/Western networks were the foundations' most enduring achievement.[17]

AFRICA IN FOUNDATIONS' THINKING

Africa in the thinking of American foundations in the 1950s was still loaded with colonial images—backward, barbaric, violent, and stagnant. It needed help as it "awakened" from its long "sleep" and became "restless" and self-conscious. This view skipped over and absolved from responsibility colonial rule and at the same time credited colonialism as the source of the African "dawn." At one level, of course, such developments were inevitable, though largely a by-product of liberal-elitist colonial education—welcomed by some, feared by others, perhaps the majority of colonial administrators. At another level, it is clear that colonial authorities fostered development of native elites for functional purposes: to aid colonial rule. But extractive states were interested primarily in raw materials, mineral wealth, and commodities and provided few if any services to their subject peoples. They had little need of extensive administrative apparatuses and therefore of anything more than a tiny minority of educated Africans. But an Oxford education did foster Western-oriented elites, which the American foundations would work further to nurture and develop, as Emerson noted above.

However, to men like Alan Pifer, the image of the African and of Africa was bleak, though with a few glimmers of hope, as befits missionaries of modernization. Before he visited Africa, he informed his trustees, "I assumed the people would all be very much alike and the terrain an endless jungle."[18] This echoed the views of a key Carnegie-funded scholar who headed up an African development research center at MIT, Arnold Rivkin. For Rivkin, Joseph Conrad's *Heart of Darkness* and Andre Gide's journals provided the framework for making sense of Africa. Rivkin had noted that Conrad's Africa of the 1890s, which Gide considered "the other side of hell" in the late 1920s, was still very much present in 1950, when Rivkin first visited.[19] Rivkin's trip to Madagascar is symbolic of the American interest in Africa expressed also by the Carnegie Corporation. As part of his duties under the Marshall Plan, he visited Madagascar to secure for the United States strategic stockpile raw materials, such as large flake graphite and phlogophite mica.[20] This "lost frontier," according to Rivkin, needed to be rediscovered, understood, and, ultimately, controlled. Rivkin was encouraged to find in Madagascar "a small but growing elite of [colonially] educated Malagasy . . . hovering between traditional and modern society, [who] were soon to lead an independent state." Understanding this "vital transitional group" would provide "an insight into what was to happen in Africa later."[21] Of course, the terminology of the 1950s and 1960s had embedded within it more subtle but clear traces of colonial-era racism: "backward peoples" "struggling" toward "modernity" and "development" bore all the hallmarks of Western superiority in all areas of life and suggested that these were difficulties that could only be borne with American expertise. That, at least, was the ideology. Strategic raw materials and the like, needed for America's military competition with the Soviet Union and global hegemony, played their role more or less explicitly in this vision.

In a private memorandum to Carnegie's John Gardner, in the wake of Ghana's independence in March 1957, Pifer was decidedly unromantic about the significance of Africa to America's global well-being:

(1) as a geographical area four times the size of the U.S. producing minerals and primary agricultural products of great importance to America and (2) as the home of nearly 200 million people, most of them colored, who, unless we are very careful, may take sides against the West. . . . We are going, therefore, to need every bit of expert knowledge we can possibly muster about all parts of the African continent.[22]

In 1954, Pifer stated that Carnegie's interest in Africa was primarily motivated by a desire to strengthen "the western democratic part of the world" despite the fact that most Africans still lived under colonial rule.

At a State Department conference in 1955, Pifer and other foundation officials listened to a number of official statements that were described by Pifer as "generally good" and that consisted of the department's policy toward Africa: to keep the continent "free of inimical influences" but friendly to the United States; to ensure Africa's "political, economic, and social evolution" in America's image; guarantee "U.S. access to resources"; "safeguard any strategic needs"; "increase U.S. commercial, industrial, and cultural activities"; and to "consolidate our cultural and moral position with respect to Africans."[23] It is difficult to tell the difference between the approaches of Carnegie and of the State Department to Africa, despite the former's declared independence of the latter.

It is clear, given the character of American interest in Africa, that Africans' role in "development" would be subordinated to the higher strategic goals of American and Western power. This is further evidenced by the very careful way in which British colonial sensitivities were dealt with by Carnegie officials. Not only were British experts preferred for advice on African development, but they were even sympathized with in regard to the "burdens" of colonial responsibility: "No longer must London be expected to produce all the ideas for these areas,"[24] even if Africa was "a British sphere of influence."[25]

Tellingly, Africans were rarely, if ever, in the 1950s consulted on development options for their own continent. For example, at the most significant conference on African development—which laid out the blueprint for the development of higher education and related issues in West Africa for a decade or more—organized by Carnegie in 1958 but involving Melvin Fox and John Howard of the Ford Foundation, representatives of the British colonial authorities and American government agencies, and several Africanists including Vernon McKay (Johns Hopkins University, prior to which he was at the Africa desk at the State Department), there was not a single African invited or involved. Indeed, the participants did not even have to hand any information on African assessments of African needs and priorities. Murphy, a sympathetic authorized chronicler of Carnegie in Africa, notes that such a state of affairs was "not unusual for the time," because it was "commonly felt in American and British circles that Africans had not yet become sophisticated in this area, that they were inexperienced, and that their identification of needs might be either uninformed or politically biased, or both."[26] In other words, Africans were not yet adequately trained experts on their own societies and thus likely to be politically prejudiced, in contrast to objective colonial authorities, corporate investors, philanthropists, and modernizers of U.S. aid agencies. This would change in the 1960s when, as Murphy notes, Africans had been adequately trained and gained appropriate "experience and judgement."[27] As Rupert Emerson noted above, Americans had definitely lost some of their anticolonial vigor by the 1950s, though at the same time they lamented their own ignorance of Africa and planned to tackle the problem through massive investment in African studies in the United States.

BUILDING AN AFRICAN STUDIES NETWORK

Foundation and state elites lacked expertise in or significant experience of Africa. It is instructive to observe, therefore, the strategies pursued by foundations to construct such expertise, because it tells us a great deal about their underlying elitist and racial assumptions. Despite the existence of a number of African American scholars of Africa in several historically black colleges and the severe lack of expertise in the vast majority of mainly white elite universities, the foundations elected to begin constructing African studies at the latter institutions, largely marginalizing extant programs of research and teaching. In part, at least, this stemmed from the foundation leaders' own backgrounds in elite universities and in part from their ideas about "excellence" and the sort of men and institutions that could be expected to produce it. In part, too, this stemmed from an underlying suspicion of the political views of many scholars at historically black colleges who had long been critics of America's racial order and supporters of African nationalism. This point is driven home further by the financial support given to some black American scholars who either expressed opposition to African independence movements or were relatively well connected, and therefore trusted, by state and other elites. That said, it is also the case that racialized foundation funding was partly the effective result of their focus of attention on university graduate programs in building expertise on Africa, at a time when historically black colleges focused on undergraduate education. Nevertheless, even in this matter, foundations did support undergraduate programs at some mainly white elite universities, while giving inadequate recognition to black universities that ran graduate programs, such as Howard. For all the recognition among liberal elites, especially in the foreign policy field, that emerging Asia and Africa were watching how America's racial disorders and pathologies were playing out and that America needed to put its own house in order if it were to win hearts and minds among people of color in the world, the relative liberals who ran the foundations permitted, encouraged, and funded a virtually segregated program of research and teaching in African studies for over two decades. The consequences of this were dire: a major revolt against the African studies "establishment" in the 1960s and a "permanent" split in the African studies community.[28]

The importance of Africa and African studies to American foundations may be indicated by the levels of funding provided from the late 1950s to the late 1960s. The Ford Foundation alone spent $164 million on African development programs between the early 1950s and 1974, particularly in the social sciences, and a further $18 million on research and training programs. Of the $25 million that Ford contributed to Nigerian universities, one third was invested at the University of Ibadan. Rockefeller Foundation contributed a further $9 million to Ibadan between 1963 and 1972. Carnegie, meanwhile, expended $10 million at African universities, particularly, though not exclusively, in the field of teacher education.[29]

The Ford Foundation was the largest single benefactor of African studies programs in the United States. Of its over $34 million investment in African studies, $16.4 million went to Columbia University alone; $8.5 million went to Chicago, $6.3 million to Yale, and $3 million to Johns Hopkins. Foundation funds also went in large quantities to programs at Northwestern, Boston, Indiana, Wisconsin, UCLA, Harvard, Stanford, Michigan, and Wisconsin.[30] By the mid-1960s, twenty-two institutions offered programs of study of Africa, an increase of thirteen since 1957. In addition, thirteen colleges offered three or more courses whose primary focus was Africa.[31] By the 1990s, many of the original programs in African studies funded by the foundations and federal government were designated National Resource Centers in African Studies, though they were joined also by Howard, Tuskegee, and Lincoln universities, among others.[32] At the founding of African studies in its modern form, however, Howard University was seen in a highly negative light by those who went on to "found" the field. In a report to the Ford Foundation in 1958, L. Gray Cowan, Carl Rosberg, Lloyd Fallers, and Cornelis W. de Kiewiet noted the weakness of all extant major universities in their national survey of the field. For example, they noted the predominance of anthropology and lack of political science, history, and economics of Africa at Northwestern; the very low standards and prestige of Boston University's graduate programs; California's nonexistent program; and Harvard's unwillingness to develop African studies unless the foundations *guaranteed* fifteen years of funding. Howard, on the other hand, which had run an African studies program since 1950—at both the undergraduate and graduate levels—was dismissed as an institution, along with its Africanist program. Despite being the nation's largest black university, Howard's claim to have a "special interest in Africa" was denied. Howard's raison d'être, the survey committee claimed, as a "Negro university is slowly disappearing," while its Africanists, "while competent in their field . . . did not appear to us to have any very strong drive nor were they particularly concerned with new fields, such as African History," although Howard's course in African history was noted, along with its courses in African art and on the economic and social impacts of the West on the continent. Black universities, it was concluded, had "no prior claim" to African studies: "While, undoubtedly, they are doing . . . some excellent work, it would appear that it could equally be done at any other university." The wafer-thin logic of this line of reasoning was contradicted by other reports written by Ford officials in awarding admittedly small grants to Howard in the mid-1950s. Even Ford's reports, however, bore the mark of racial assumptions when they justified grants to Howard on the basis that its programs were no longer based on "emotional or political bias."[33]

A Ford report by one of its Africa representatives noted in 1970 that Ford's International Training and Research Division had signally failed to "recognize the special interests in Africa among black Americans" and provided no "meaningful support for development of a single major African Studies Program among the black colleges."[34] Interestingly, however, LeMelle (who was African American) credited Ford with the ability to right past mistakes, even on strategies that were "correct" and effective in other regards in "discovering" Africa and in making manifest the "restless African continent['s]" unanticipated complexities.[35] The challenge that was Africa was urgent, however, and Ford had answered the call and trained "a generation of Africanists" by 1970, many housed in over sixty university centers, including twenty major centers. By 1970, faculty numbers exceeded five hundred in African studies proper, and an even larger number had received "an exposure to Africa" during graduate training. Research produced was considered to be of high quality and large in quantity, with 1,422 research projects registered between 1965 and 1969. The African past was being "reconstructed" as "essential for understanding 'contemporary' Africa."[36] Without the support of the Ford Foundation, African studies, it was claimed, would not have achieved "academic legitimacy" or its breadth and depth of development. Indeed, echoing the ideas of Harold Laski, cited earlier, LeMelle argues that Ford was responsible for providing the "constructive criticism" that "reoriented" Africanists to pay increasing attention to "development problems such as urban planning, land economics, development administration, demography . . . political stability and national integration" and to problem solving rather than general and basic social science.[37]

The African Studies Association

The African Studies Association (ASA) received over $630,000 from the foundations from its founding in 1957 to the late 1960s.[38] The ASA was founded in March 1957, with a grant of $6,500 from the Carnegie Corporation, at the strong suggestion of Alan Pifer, because he felt that the study of Africa needed to be promoted by a professional society independent of governmental influence, in strong contrast to the African-American Institute.[39] Yet, Pifer would have been aware of numerous discussions between foundation heads of the necessity of "closer link[s] between research activities and output of the U.S. with the decision-making process in the State Department," which directly challenged the notion of both the political objectivity of the foundations and of some of their funded organizations.[40] Instructively, the thirty-six founding members of ASA, selected by an ad hoc committee that had been meeting sporadically with Pifer for two years, and the constitutional arrangements they developed and endorsed contributed to the split in the organization a decade or so later. According to Gwendolen Carter, a leading light in ASA's conception, birth, and growth, "fears of McCarthyism or of CIA infiltration" led the founders to create a College of Fellows that would act as gatekeepers of the organization and as nominators and electors of its officers, including president, vice president, and the members of the eight-person board of directors. Such control of ASA led directly to charges of "elitism and autocracy" and also served effectively as the principal mechanism of white elite control over the association. Fears of McCarthyism, however understandable, were also an effective method of racial and political exclusion—of *predominantly* black Africanists who operated as scholar-activists in historically black colleges, had nailed their colors to the mast of pan-Africanism, and had directly linked the plight of Africa to the condition and treatment of black Americans. Challenging mainstream approaches, black American Africanists felt duty bound to use their knowledge to make scholarly advances *and* political arguments. This made them "suspicious" and "un-American" to American elites and brought them attention from the Federal Bureau of Investigation.[41] E. Franklin Frazier of Howard University, who, by the late 1950s, was seen as more "objective" and less "biased" and "emotional" about Africa, was the sole African American at the ASA's founding meeting, though St. Clair Drake had been invited but was unable to attend.[42] As Gershenhorn argues, the foundations opposed funding any scholars challenging continued European domination of Africa or the State Department's Cold War stance.[43] Thus Lincoln University, Kwame Nkrumah's and Nnamdi Azikewe's alma mater, headed by the prominent African American scholar Horace Mann Bond, and cast as "suspect in British colonial eyes," received no funding for its Institute for the Study of African Affairs, formed in 1950.[44]

With additional "core funding" of $100,000 from the Ford Foundation in 1961, supplemented by $150,000,[45] the ASA grew rapidly; by the mid-1960s, it had 1,700 members; its working committees encompassed a wide range of fields—archaeology, archives/libraries, fine arts and humanities, government and academic research, languages and linguistics, literature, oral data, publications, research liaison, undergraduate and high school education, and Washington liaison.[46] The ASA was later characterized by a Ford Foundation report as "a strategy of directed development"—"a sizable general support grant combined with the skills of astute academic politicians and sound economic management" helped greatly in "institution-building," according to Pearl T. Robinson. Its "close-knit network" of leaders was both the source of the ASA's success and its "Achilles heel."[47]

Although founded to be independent of the American state, it is clear that the ASA was anxious to be helpful to American governmental agendas. Such interest extended to collaboration with the U.S. Army, which, in the wake of uprisings in Congo, Algeria, and Kenya, was interested in the dynamics of African societies.

In 1964, the U.S. Army presented to the National Academy of Science (NAS) a proposal for "a center for basic research in social psychology, sociology, and ethnology and humanistic science on Africa." This was one prong of a program of three research centers that would also focus on Latin America and the Oceanic South Pacific. The primary focus was to bring to bear the whole range of the social sciences, as well as industrial and civil engineering and agricultural expertise, for "research on problems of military interest." In addition, universities selected for the Army programs were expected to have already established "liaisons or other base connections in the appropriate foreign areas *to facilitate ready entrance of scientific personnel into the university and civil life of the countries and cultures of major concern*" (emphasis added). Extant centers of African studies earmarked as essential by the U.S. Army were precisely the ones built up by the big foundations: Northwestern, UCLA, Indiana, Johns Hopkins, Wisconsin, Boston, and Columbia—represented at the meeting by the leading lights of the ASA, including Gwendolen Carter (Northwestern), Gus Liebenow (Indiana), Philip Curtin (Wisconsin), Al Castagno (Boston), Vernon McKay and Robert Lystad (JHU), James Coleman and Benjamin Thomas (UCLA), and L. Gray Cowan (Columbia).[48]

The proposals were then presented to representatives of Africa research centers in February 1965, at a conference at Northwestern University. There were participants from all the major university programs and from the U.S. Army (Lynn Baker), State Department (Robert Baum), and the National Academy of Science–National Research Council (Glen Finch). Noting the necessity of additional funding to assist the research of Africanists and increased interest among "public agencies" for "knowledge covering the whole range of human behavior and environment in Africa," the meeting decided to form a committee of Africanists to consider proposals. Northwestern was tasked with seeking an initial research development contract worth $100,000 from the U.S. Army.[49]

The principal concerns expressed by Africanist scholars about the U.S. Army's proposals were pragmatic and summed up by James Coleman of UCLA's African studies program. He noted that social scientists had worked long and hard for recognition of their potential contributions to public policy and were, therefore, "extraordinarily reluctant to respond negatively" when approached by "a responsible research agency of the Federal Government." Social scientists had concerns, of course, about collaborating with the government, but that did not "reflect an ideological hostility," because there was no "doubt that the goals of those agencies reflect the moral purposes and national goals of our society, and, consequently, such a relationship does not—certainly need not—contaminate or corrupt the purity of objective scholarship." However, there were severe problems of perception of American social scientists in Africa: most Africans regarded American scholars as government agents. Indeed, "the notion of a scholar being independent of his government is *difficult for all but the most educated Africans to comprehend*" (emphasis added). The issue, then, was to develop and maintain an "image of scholarly independence and objectivity . . . if social scientists are going to maintain access and their credibility" in Africa (or anywhere else). Coleman counseled against a "*direct* relationship between the Department of the Army and formally constituted African programs in American universities," in favor of funds administered by the NAS or the National Science Foundation and in consultation with the ASA (emphasis in original).[50] Clearly, this would establish a certain distance between the U.S. Army and Africanists, but it would remain the case that the purposes of army funding and the basis for evaluating the funding program would be research useful to the American military's goals in Africa. The army was setting the conditions and context for research with social scientists eager for public recognition.

The U.S. Army's program was clearly part of the abortive "Project Camelot" (most famously known for its focus on Chile and more generally across Latin America), a program aimed at the causes of "internal war" and rebellion. French-Canada, Nigeria, and India were also selected by the Department of Defense for *behavioral* research toward "increasing our capability to anticipate social breakdown and to suggest remedies."[51] The role of social science was to study societies' social and behavioral dynamics and produce useful knowledge. A memorandum by NAS's Wilton Dillon noted the army project's Camelot connections and provided greater detail on the precise aims of army research funding. Lynn Baker's memo, attached to Dillon's, baldly stated that the army would fund "basic research" in social and human sciences "in support of counter-insurgency and limited war operations." The role of the several new research centers would be to "review, interpret, and evaluate existing data" and train "young scientists . . . in the gathering of new data and the creation of new knowledge from field research." The "Research Objectives" were to encourage "research in potential crisis areas," emphasizing data collection and analysis "in understanding and handling the early stages of insurgency, including search for indicators of impending unrest and revolution and indicators of progress in specific insurgency situations." The army was also interested in "youth and student participation in societal change and stability."[52]

Leading American Africanists—such as Vernon McKay—supported the concept and its goals and welcomed the "useful side effects of the Project Camelot incident," i.e., greater attention among relevant agencies of the "problems existing in the relationship between government agencies and the academic community." A plethora of committees had resulted from

Camelot's "downfall," including the NAS's Advisory Committee on Government Programs in the Behavioral Sciences and renewed efforts by agencies such as the Bureau of Research and Intelligence of the State Department. Yet Africanists worried that they would still be seen as CIA agents in Africa and face greater obstacles for research clearance from the authorities.[53] However, it remained the case that many, though not all, Africanists were willing to produce "basic research" funded by the military, in the belief that working on "impractical" topics could be profoundly valuable.[54] In the aftermath of Project Camelot, however, Carnegie refused to serve as a financial conduit for U.S. Army funds to Africanists conducting oral-history research on nationalist movements, including Mau Mau in Kenya,[55] although the Ford Foundation provided funding for the Oral Data Collection project of the ASA's Research Liaison Committee (RLC). The Department of Defense used other means to mobilize Africanists' expertise for possible future military operations. This was highlighted by Pierre L. van den Berghe's exposure of one such proposal to contribute to a DoD project entitled "The Impact of Tribalism on the National Security Aspects of Nation Building in the Congo." This project, directly following the demise of Camelot, aimed to provide military planners information on "'social tension, civil unrest, violence, and insurgency' in the Congo so that 'military policy decisions can be made more accurately . . . especially for counter-insurgency operations,'" citing a previous U.S. military intervention in the Congo in 1964 as precedent.[56]

REBELLION IN MONTREAL, 1969

Serving U.S. Army research plans—and becoming embroiled in Project Camelot's acrimonious demise—was in part the cause of the rebellion by mainly black ASA members against its leaders. Though it culminated at the ASA's annual convention in Montreal in 1969, the problems had been simmering for several years. The problems stemmed from the oligarchical character of the ASA and its powerful committees, which had become increasingly linked with "the key priority-setting and grant-making institutions in the African Studies field," according to Pearl T. Robinson.[57] ASA board members and committee chairmen, such as Gwendolen Carter (chair of the Languages and Linguistics Committee), acted as gatekeepers for funding in their respective areas: Carter's committee acted as an advisory panel to the National Defense Education Act's administrators in the field of African languages, channeling funds to specific institutions and programs.[58] More subtly but very effectively, ASA board members dominated the Joint Committee on African Studies, a body of research scholars appointed by the SSRC and ACLS; the Joint Committee administered and disbursed research grants and planned future research in the humanities and social sciences. Robinson argues that such activities initially "lent prestige and legitimacy" to the ASA; later, they were its "Achilles heel."[59] Continuing the Greek-tragedy theme, "just when the prestige of the Association was at its highest point, a dramatic showdown" with members centered on the claim that the ASA's influence was built on "the wheeling and dealing of academic politics and of [ASA leaders] pursuing their goals by cultivating their connections with the government and foundations."[60] A protest begun in 1968 by a black caucus of ASA members demanding greater black participation in ASA affairs transformed in 1969 to a full-scale rebellion—racial and ideological—against the association, temporarily halting the Montreal convention. While black members complained of their exclusion from ASA leadership roles, racist research agendas, and the complete lack of attention to domestic race questions, others—so-called Young Turks—condemned ASA for its "conservative bias" in favor of established power in Africa.[61] Too late in the day, the ASA agreed to reform, prompting a mass walkout by black members, who set up the African Heritage Studies Association (AHSA) under the leadership of John Henrik Clarke. The "old guard" were in a "state of shock";[62] even a year later, the then-president of ASA, Gray Cowan, could not refer to the rebellion in Montreal other than as "events at the meeting."[63]

The ASA reformed itself. It ended its exclusive arrangements with the large African studies programs at major universities, foundations, and government agencies; operated an open, single-category membership policy; had greater *African* representation on its board; and condemned the racist and colonial policies of South Africa, Portugal, and Rhodesia. Nevertheless, the ASA lost its exclusivity and, therefore, some considerable credibility as America's only Africanist organization. Yet it proved able to recover some lost ground, based on its Ford Foundation–sponsored Research Liaison Committee (RLC), originally formed in 1967 to manage and improve ASA relations with Africa-based scholars in the wake of Project Camelot and other claims by Africans of being exploited by American graduate students and scholars![64] But Ford took some of the blame for the ASA's failings. Robinson noted that Ford had endorsed the ASA's exclusive practices and its connections with government-agency research agendas. The foundation "demonstrated a certain lack of sensitivity to issues which ultimately proved to be critical," Robinson argued. It is important not only to build institutions, Robinson opined: "even more important in terms of long-range developments are the policies and outputs which will result from the new creation."[65] Carnegie's response to the events at Montreal was neutral, though nothing was said about their own responsibility in encouraging the formation of an oligarchic ASA.[66]

In the spirit of "reform," Ford adopted a three-pronged "attack" on the problem of racial exclusion in the field of African studies: it limited its funding for the AHSA, financed a number of Afro-American studies programs at "strategic centers," and offered fellowships to black Americans to conduct field research in Africa and the Middle East. While these were welcome initiatives, Ford's approach was elitist in application and displayed many of the same insensitivities and racial assumptions that had come to cause such a rupture in the Africanist community in Montreal. President McGeorge Bundy's view seemed to weigh heavily on Ford officials' minds: in speaking about the possible effects of new Afro-American programs of study, Bundy warned that "there is a box here that is being opened and out of it will come pain and trouble."[67]

Funding to AHSA—a radical Africanist organization for scholars of "African" descent—was limited to its annual conference of 1970. Ford awarded $10,000 to cover costs of travel for overseas speakers.[68] While the AHSA's executive committee prepared a funding proposal to the Ford Foundation, there is little in the records after 1970 to suggest that Ford assisted the organization. According to the rationale for the Middle East and Africa Fellowship Program for Black Americans (MEAFP; see below), *neither* the white-dominated ASA nor the African-only AHSA were "perceived to be neutral," and both were part of the "state of profound confrontation" in "American black/white Africanist relations."[69] Despite that, however, Ford Foundation annual reports for 1970, 1974, and 1975 show that $165,000, $90,600, and $50,500 (totaling just over $300,000) was voted in each of those years, respectively, to the *African Studies Association*. Ford simply was not interested in funding to anywhere near that level an organization such as AHSA, which aimed "to counterbalance . . . Eurocentric" perspectives on Africa and African Americans by "redressing traditional misconceptions" by being "Afro-centrically relevant" and building appropriate networks between all people of African descent.[70] Despite its non-neutrality in evaluating the disbursement of grants, the ASA remained the favored Africanist organization.

To address the issue of increasing demand in the colleges and universities for black studies and Afro-American studies, Ford decided to try to influence the long-term development of the subject area. Believing that "properly conceived" courses were necessary, they targeted "pace-setting programs under way at strategic locations" such as Yale and Howard. Yale was to receive $184,000 to establish an undergraduate program; Howard received $143,567 to set up a new department of Afro-American Studies. Howard was seen as the source of almost half of America's black leaders. Ford understood that it had fallen behind the times on this matter, as hundreds of colleges had hastily established Afro-American programs. But, as ever, Ford would steer America toward "orderly development . . . by helping a few strategic institutions get off on the right foot." Anxious to avoid developing "model" programs with immediate effects, Ford-sponsored programs, it was expected, "may set some standards of quality by which other institutions can measure and eventually revise their own offerings."[71]

The Middle East and Africa Fellowship Program (MEAFP) for black Americans received almost $1 million from Ford funds over a period from 1969 to 1980. The aim was to improve black representation in development-related agencies, train more blacks from historically black colleges in the South, and try to "heal" the split in the Africanist community. The program failed on all counts, according to a Ford-sponsored report, although it constructed a new "black fellowship network" of funded scholars to rival the "white fellowship network" that most black and some white Africanists had protested about.[72]

Of the historically black colleges, just two (Atlanta and Howard) offered graduate programs in African studies and therefore fell within the remit of the MEAFP initiative. Ford had wrongly assumed that most black Africanist students were registered at black colleges; in fact, most blacks in the field were at the major white universities and African studies programs. The consequences of this assumption, however, were clear: in 1971–1972, all fifteen fellowships awarded went to students from elite universities, with Harvard winning four, Stanford three, NYU and Columbia two each, and the remainder shared by Yale, Chicago, Northwestern, and Michigan State. Research topics included economic planning in Nigeria, Nigerian political development, Egyptian manpower problems, the Africanization of

Nigerian universities, the impact of religion on economic behavior, and the state in the Congo.[73] That is, research topics remained in line with the "needs" of African development. By 1979, 79 percent of all fellowships had been awarded to black students in the major universities, while 44 percent came from just four universities: Columbia, Harvard, Stanford, and UCLA. Only two fellowships were awarded to students from black colleges.[74] Further, black fellows complained that white scholars continued to dominate funding sources, such as the equivalent and much larger fellowship program funded by Ford through the SSRC; failed to respect black scholars' research competence; and appeared to be "racist" in their analysis of Africa. Craig Howard, reporting confidentially to Ford, noted that the "underlying causes of the earlier friction [made manifest at Montreal in 1969] appear to remain" a decade later.[75]

Craig Howard's report also highlighted the role of black selection panels—drawn from elite universities—in channeling fellowships to students in their own disciplines studying at elite institutions. Applicants from such institutions were better advised on application and interview processes and often used their advisor's connections with selection-panel members to influence outcomes subtly; they were part of a "fellowship network," while faculty at small black colleges were not. Pearl T. Robinson, for example, who had been a MEAFP fellow, later became a selection panelist. Outside that network, black and white applicants were disadvantaged. Black fellowship applicants to the SSRC's program in the same field, however, were severely disadvantaged, with a less than 10 percent chance of success between 1976 and 1979. On the other hand, the Ford program had produced sixty-four black Africanist Ph.D.s in ten years.[76] The program was discontinued in 1980, because the Ford Foundation assumed, wrongly, according to Howard, that blacks could now compete in the SSRC program. In fact, of the thirteen MEAFP fellows—some of them among the strongest of candidates—who applied to the SSRC between 1976 and 1979, only one was successful; this outcome was likely to perpetuate patterns of black marginalization in African studies. Howard called on Ford to be even handed—either retain the MEAFP or cut the SSRC's funding for such programs too, or face the fact that Ford was reestablishing "the control point of future access to the field in the hands of one aspect of a continuing conflict [which] would aggravate both the tension and the inbalance [sic] in the field."[77]

While most black fellows went on to teach mainly at state universities, just two joined elite universities such as Indiana and Michigan, four were

faculty at black colleges, and several joined important policy-oriented organizations. For example, Randall Robinson, as director of TransAfrica, mobilized black public opinion on Rhodesian issues, while other fellows went
onto consultancies with the State Department, World Bank, and the United
Nations.[78] The major results of the program seemed to have been significant, but not necessarily in ways foreseen by Ford: there was an increase
in the cadre of black Africanists attached to mainly elite white universities, welded into an effective network, who went on to join "mainstream"
organizations. Network building and, through networks, incorporation remains, therefore, a key outcome of foundation programs.

PROGRAMS IN NIGERIA

Although domestic squabbles are supposed by some to stop at "the water's
edge," it is clear that the racial, elitist, and imperial mentalities evident in
African Studies were reproduced in the encounter with Africa itself. The
Cold War contextualized the origins of large-scale American interest in Africa,[79] and its end signaled a cooling of federal and foundation interest in
the continent, but the post-9/11 war on terror has again revived interest in
Africa's Muslim populations in particular.[80] The networks established by
federal and foundation funds were extended to Africa, with the relations
between American researchers and African institutions experiencing the
difficulties between rich and poor and between the representatives of
the powerful west and north and dependent south. This inevitably skewed
the development of the African university to be more closely attuned to the
concerns of American foundations—and if American academics skewed
their research toward well-funded foundation programs, how much greater
was the pressure to do so on African scholars and institutions with few, if
any, alternatives?[81]

Wallerstein notes that American anthropologists acted as "secular missionaries" in Africa, assigning themselves "the role of counselor and advisor
to African institutions, overtly and covertly, explicitly and implicitly, invited or uninvited." Of course, their intentions were sincere and good; their
effects, however, could be explosive, as was shown at the Montreal meetings
of the ASA in 1969 and also by events in Africa itself.[82]

Carnegie led the charge into Africa, given its long-standing interest in
the British colonies. With a mindset not unlike the paternalistic British Fa-
bians at the turn of the twentieth century, Alan Pifer lamented the lack of

known facts about Africa and wanted to generate a greater knowledge base of its problems and needs, as a first step toward investing in the continent. Inevitably, the Carnegie view was that education held the key to development, and most of their efforts, as well as of those they mobilized, such as Ford and various U.S. agencies, were directed to developing a system of colleges and universities that would mass produce men and women qualified to "develop" Africa. *Without any African input at the planning stage*, Carnegie officials, British colonial experts, and others met to determine the future directions of African higher education, especially focusing their attention on Nigeria, which by the late 1950s was preparing for independence from Britain.[83]

American foundations, despite being separate organizations, did have an informal "plan" for Nigeria, a plan that was coherent and integrated, leaving a lot less to chance than the Development Plan for Nigeria they promoted (with full participation of the Nigerian state). Part of the foundations' plan involved intervening in Nigerian education, especially in building the University of Ibadan, Nigeria's only university.[84] The Carnegie Corporation–funded Ashby Commission on Nigerian education recommended in 1960 a university in each region of the country as the basis for modernization. The Ashby Commission's report was accepted by the Nigerian federal government. According to Ashby, the commission advocated an "evolutionary, not a revolutionary programme" for Nigerian universities that "must be built upon the past and must not be discontinuous with it."[85] The Nigerian federal government accepted and implemented every one of the commission's recommendations, including establishing, with Carnegie funds ($225,000), a Bureau for External Aid, which leveraged in $30 million of aid from the U.S. Department of Education to Nigerian universities over the following decade. At a cost to Carnegie of around $87,000, the Ashby Commission yielded over $80 million dollars in foreign aid to Nigerian higher education. Murphy concludes that Carnegie-inspired processes were "pivotal" to Nigerian educational development in the 1960s.[86] Several new universities sprang up, though Ibadan retained its central role as the intellectual "engine" of the entire Nigerian university system, which became increasingly oriented to serving development and nation building in independent Nigeria. Ibadan also, therefore, became embroiled in Nigerian politics through its increasing involvement and identification with the Nigerian federal government. In consequence, it was dragged into national-ethnic politics, losing Ibo ethnic staff during the 1967–1970 civil war.

Ojetunji Aboyade (himself a Cambridge Ph.D.) noted the Anglocentrism of the political and academic elite that dominated Nigeria after independence.[87] He also charged that elite with causing the ills of Nigeria—"the traumatic civil war, the total lack of commitment, dedication and patriotism on the part of the general populace, the false sense of values and the almost total neglect of a search for authentic Nigerian scholarship."[88] The implantation of Western values in Nigeria created an influential neocolonial mindset inimical to the interests of a newly independent nation, permitting the "continued exploitation of our human and material resources by the new form of imperialist international arrangements."[89]

The University of Ibadan, founded in 1948 as a college of the University of London, had its first Nigerian vice chancellor, Kenneth O. Dike, in 1960. An anthropologist, Dike had taught at Northwestern University and therefore associated with the founding lights of the African Studies Association, and he had been one of three Nigerian members of the Ashby Commission. It was under Dike's leadership that Ibadan established "close rapport with government and . . . high policy-making circles."[90] That process owed much to American foundations' preoccupation with encouraging Nigerian universities to act as manpower creators for development. As Adeleye notes, funding from international sources (Ford, Rockefeller, and Carnegie, as well as UNESCO and the World Health Organization) occurred on a vast scale—for capital projects, new faculties and departments, postgraduate training, and visiting professors.[91] It was only massive American foundation funding, which Dike so assiduously pursued, that "made the rapid expansion . . . possible at Ibadan."[92] The problem was that associating with the Nigerian "power elite," which was riven by ethnic political party competition and rivalries, politicized Ibadan's own faculty, hardening ethnic consciousness when appointments and promotions were made, insinuating—rightly or wrongly—that ethnicity had been the reason for appointment rather than merit. The corrupt party politics of independent Nigeria—the seeds of which were planted in the late-colonial era and then nourished with external aid after independence—mired Nigeria's premier university in the brutal politics that led to civil war. Many Ibadan academics were involved in the secessionist movement that directly led to the outbreak of the civil war in 1967.[93]

Between 1958 and 1973, Ford granted $4.75 million to Ibadan for a wide range of specific and general projects including, uniquely, a General Development Grant of almost $3 million.[94] Although smaller than the Rockefeller Foundation grants totaling almost $9 million, the decision to invest in Ibadan's goal of becoming the premier university in West Africa was made by the two American foundations, without any consultation with the Nigerian government. Thus, Ibadan's goals conflicted with the increasingly regional character of Nigerian politics and brought opposition from the country's president, Nnamdi Zikiwe. Once again, American foundations acted in a manner that did not fully appreciate national-regional ethnopolitical dynamics, drawing criticism from academics appointed to evaluate their grants to Ibadan.[95] Nonetheless, by 1973, Ibadan was a mixture of British, American, and Nigerian in terms of its identity and was a lot more integrated into the Western Region of the country.

From the mid-1960s, the programs funded at Ibadan by the Ford Foundation included economic planning–capacity building at the Nigerian Institute of Economic and Social Research, an Institute of African Studies, and a Behavioral Sciences Research Unit. The latter, for example, was considered essential as part of studying the "psychological reactions of the African populations . . . in the light of rapid social and cultural changes."[96] Specific research projects included Nigerian students' attitudes, criminal homicides, ecology of criminal delinquency, and family and social-class dynamics.[97] In addition, the unit trained anthropologists, sociologists, psychologists, and social workers in understanding and dealing with processes of integration and disintegration in rural villages, as well as "the problems of adaptation and motivation among industrial workers."[98] Rapidly changing societies like Nigeria were increasingly prone to social breakdown—increasing numbers of psychiatric patients, prostitution, juvenile delinquency, drug addiction. All such outcomes led to a drain on human resources; studying the causes of breakdown and means of adapting individuals and communities to change were considered central "to the question of achieving orderly social and economic development." Failure to study such matters scientifically also means that development resources are often wasted, as the reactions of people in villages who are targets of development programs are little understood or engender "popular resistance to the changes involved," impeding industrial "takeoff." The *extreme conservatism* of rural farm workers slows economic development in agriculture and limits the conditions for industrialization. It was considered vital that work be done to understand how to engineer a *"change in attitude"* among rural populations, particularly the youth, "in order to allow them to contribute to the evolution of a new socio-economic structure."[99] The author of the document—a grant application to Ford—was Professor Tom Lambo, a Nigerian connected with Northwestern University. There are certainly echoes of the kind of studies commended by Project Camelot under the sponsorship of leading American Africanists, including Northwestern's Gwendolen Carter.

CC and Ford were, of course, also interested in economic development and planning. Ford-funded planning, however, was not quite social democratic or European leftist planning, let alone in any sense socialistic. Planning under Ford's auspices was principally oriented toward the creation of a strong market economy that was open to international trade, finance, and investment and to accepting voluminous foreign aid from the West in general and from the United States in particular.[100] Labeled a "unique nation" in Africa, Nigeria was earmarked by Arnold Rivkin, the director of MIT's Project on African Economic and Political Development, and, more significantly, the Kennedy administration to be an economically strong and politically stable ally of the West, integrated into the global capitalist order. According to Rivkin, Nigeria was committed to "a pluralistic and democratic internal structure and system which gives priority to economic development as a means of building internal political cohesion."[101] Hence, the Kennedy administration pledged $225 million to aid the plan even before it was approved by the Nigerian federal and regional governments. In his report to President Kennedy, Rivkin, who had headed up the special mission to Nigeria in May 1961, noted that Nigeria's plan would be well conceived and pervaded with a "sense of social justice."[102]

The "moderate," i.e., generally pro-Western and Pro-British, Nigerian political elite, which had formed with reluctant British colonial support and encouragement and under conditions of widespread anticommunism in the public and private sectors, was the principal ally of the United States and Britain.[103] It was that "new Nigerian elite" that was to benefit most from independence and trade, investment opportunities, government contracts, and aid that followed.[104] "Moderately" nationalistic but pro-Western and corrupt, this new elite signed technical, aid, and defense pacts with Britain; took a cool line with the Soviet bloc; and legislated against the employment of known "communists" in the Nigerian civil service, despite the shortage of educated and trained manpower in the country and the consequent overreliance on foreign advisers and consultants.[105] Yet it was this class that was to ensure that the benefits of a market economy be spread to "a growing segment of Nigerian society," as Rivkin argued.[106]

One key adviser was Wolfgang Stolper, a German-born American economist trained under Joseph Alois Schumpeter, an associate of Rivkin's center on Africa at MIT, and proudly known as a "Mason boy," after his long association with founder of Harvard's Development Advisory Service, Edward Mason.[107] Stolper was funded by the Ford Foundation, seconded to the Ministry of Economic Development as head of its Economic Planning Unit, and tasked to draw up Nigeria's First National Economic Plan. Stolper, with more than a hint of imperial hubris, admitted he knew nothing about Nigeria or Africa but noted that one could have *too much* knowledge and experience. Indeed, he felt that "breadth of experience is a much overrated commodity . . . as much a source of error as of wisdom."[108] As he notes in his rather candid diary of the nearly one and a half years he spent in Nigeria, he had nothing to prove in that country: his reputation as an economist was secure, thanks to his work during the decade leading up to 1960, which had focused on the economy of East Germany; his main claim to fame was his co-authorship, with the Nobel laureate Paul Samuelson, of the Stolper-Samuelson theorem. Celebrating his ignorance of Africa and Nigeria, he authored the book *Planning Without Facts*, in which he tells the official story of his ideas and role in Nigeria. Sober, rational, disinterested, and scientifically rigorous as his case in *Planning Without Facts* reads, the diary of his African adventure somewhat undermines his claims to objectivity and rationality. The diary's extensive character and its candid entries outlining his racist stereotyping of Nigerians also challenge his claims to be working unearthly hours to write up "his" plan for Nigeria while combating all kinds of unreasonable opposition and enduring widespread laziness among support staff.[109]

Ultimately, the benefits to Nigeria of Stolper's economic plan are ambiguous if not elusive. According to Aboyade, Nigeria's postindependence rates of growth were poorer than they might have been had there been improvements in economic organization and rationalization. Social and income inequality had also reached dire proportions.[110] Aboyade was also certain that the Nigerian government had made an error in not inviting Nigerian economists to develop the plan, especially as they chose American economists—Stolper and Lyle Hansen—with no experience in national planning to draw upon.[111] Despite this, Stolper (and, to a lesser extent, Hansen, who had served Harvard's DAS in Pakistan) "provided the basic intellectual framework of the Plan," generating "tremendous heat" in Nigeria.[112]

To Stolper, freedom of the individual was fundamental to a successful economy. In addition, "the only valid investment criterion is economic profitability." Elaborating on this, he argued that economic profitability was a generally applicable principle; anyone who wanted to consider "social" aspects in investment criteria was guilty of "manifest economic nonsense."[113] Stolper favored short-term benefit over long-term investment, free movement of capital, unhindered repatriation of profits by foreign corporations, and complete opposition to nationalization. Despite this, his self-image—as expressed in his private diary—was as a "nation builder," the inventor of its future, and a member of the Nigerian civil service.[114] Despite his constant criticisms of corruption among the political and business elite, he fully accepted that it was possible for corrupt ministers, such as Festus, the minister of finance, to be "patriotic" servants of their country.[115] In effect, Stolper (along with Ford and the U.S. State Department) was willing for political reasons to accept the corruption of the Nigerian political elite so long as the country remained anticommunist, pro-American, and open for business. And the colonial-era, British-educated elite—academic and political—was happy to cooperate.[116]

According to the Ibadan University economist Ojetunji Aboyade, Stolper's plan was ill suited to the needs of Nigeria and was at heart a neoliberal project that fetishized the market mechanism, profit maximization, and an export-oriented economy. He also criticized Stolper for not having drawn up anything approaching a plan—which implies a reasonable degree of state ownership and control—because he proposed privatization at every turn. Stolper was opposed to the state in general and had a technocratic, elitist mentality. Stolper also falsely believed that Nigeria's comparative advantage in primary commodity exports would, eventually, allow it to "develop" a strong economy; instead, the dependence to an extraordinary degree of commodities on the world market meant inherent economic instability and insecurity for the country's mainly agricultural population.[117]

Aboyade's critique of Stolper extended to the Nigerian federal government, which Aboyade believed lacked courage and conviction, let alone social mission and conscience. The plan, he noted, had "no soul," no underlying philosophy worthy of national sacrifices. The plan was to achieve and maintain the growth of the highest possible living standards, without defining precisely what that meant in practice or how that might be achieved. In the long run, according to the plan, the Nigerian economy was to achieve

Rostowian "takeoff" by 1980; i.e., it would no longer be reliant on aid in the form of foreign loans.[118]

Obliquely, Aboyade's critique is quite progressive, even though he is caught up in a contradictory position. As a relatively progressive nationalist, he wants to promote growth, social justice, and national development for improving living standards. He supports a strong role for the state in that process. He even led the Economic Planning Unit, once the plan was in place; taught at Ibadan University's economics department; and helped nurture a national elite. Yet the political elite of which he was critical was developed and nurtured by British colonials and supported by American aid. Its nationalism was always skewed toward reliance on the West for defense, trade, ideology, and legitimacy. The elite's anticommunism meant shying away from authentic social and economic planning, state ownership, and strong regulation of currency and capital flows. The elite's widely acknowledged corruption, which encompassed the channeling of funds toward personal and ethnic-group gain, thus fueling ethnic tensions and rivalries, made what planning there occurred even more unlikely to yield tangible results for Nigeria's people. In short, Aboyade was expecting a pipe dream: a corrupt, foreign-oriented elite that would develop Nigeria for the Nigerians. Indeed, he notes his disappointment that "an opportunist political party game to consolidate economic class interests" had stunted "progressive dynamic leadership." Power in Nigeria, inefficient as it was, operated merely to distribute the economic spoils to "political insiders." Foreign economists and others—and here he is referring to the likes of Stolper, Rivkin, Ford, USAID, and the World Bank—play upon Nigerian leaders' vanities by lauding the country as "a giant with considerable stabilizing force in the turbulent politics of Africa," when a giant can just as easily be "a congenital idiot."[119] Yet Nigeria's leaders were hailed as effective, nonideological "pragmatists," fertile ground for American economists who claimed to eschew ideology for rational, nonideological, theory-free thought. Aboyade was caught in a trap: he worked at an institution heavily reliant on American foundation funding, for a state that was completely open to the West, and with a political elite that was content to act as an intermediary between foreign powers and corporations and economic opportunities in Nigeria.[120] He was unable successfully to challenge the dominant order, even though his ideas were plainly social democratic rather than owing anything to Marxism. Indeed, his participation might be seen as legitimizing that very order; he is therefore an example of incorporation into the Establishment. As

Stolper noted in his diary, newly educated Nigerians were "captured by the system [and] likely to become part of the Establishment."[121]

Wayne Nafziger's excellent and thorough analysis of Nigeria's slide into civil war places the blame squarely with an ethnic "settlement" at independence that was dominated by self-interested elites whose main aim was to maintain a system of spoils from which they benefitted most and who had no interest in poverty alleviation or general prosperity.[122] In effect, the Nigerian elite fostered by the British colonialists for postindependence rule and lauded by Emerson, Pifer, Rivkin, and Stolper was the heart of the problem that led to the coups d'état of 1966 and the bloody civil war of 1967–1970. American authorities had noted as early as 1951 that many Nigerian elites were so ambitious for "political prestige and monetary gain" that they could be controlled by appointment to high office and the powers of patronage that afforded.[123] Indeed, Rivkin informed the House Committee on Foreign Affairs in 1961 that Nigeria "is a society very responsive to economic incentives."[124] It was that system that Ford, Rockefeller, and Carnegie operated within and therefore legitimized when they continued to invest funds, despite their knowledge of widespread corruption and political opportunism—and furthermore by promoting Nigeria as "an oasis of rationality in a sea of unreason," as Stolper wrote in his diary.[125] Of course, the Nigerian elite was favored because it was anticommunist and open for business: despite "independence," almost 92 percent of Nigeria's exports were primary products in 1965, and almost all its trade was with the capitalist West, while foreign banks and businesses benefitted disproportionately from the relaxed investment and tax regime. The Nigerian political class benefitted from "rake-offs," as Nafziger notes.[126] The political class with which Ford et al. did business was, according to Sklar, "the primary force that creates economic opportunity and determines the pattern of social stratification," a process well recognized by Stolper's diary notes on the subject.[127] The Nigerian political class—and Ford—backed Stolper because their economic preferences for Nigeria served well the interests of the business-oriented political elite and aligned with the "private enterprise" and anti–income redistribution preferences of Stolper's economic philosophy.[128]

It is clear that American foundations, without actually understanding the long-term significance of Nigerian dynamics, ended up pursuing a course of action, across several sectors, that exacerbated ethnic tensions, tolerated political and business corruption, and generated a form of market economy that sharpened inequalities across ethnic groups and social classes. According to Green, the Nigerian Plan authored by Stolper was "basically a proposal for growth within the existing economic and socio-political structure; it is *not* a call for development through structural change," as well as being utterly unrealistic in its "stated growth goals."[129] Indeed, Green argues that *Ghana's* economic plan was more attuned to rapid economic development, not Nigeria's, openly naming Arnold Rivkin as making "unsubstantiated judgments" unencumbered by a knowledge of economics. To Green, the problem in Nigeria lay at the door of its politi-cal class, "operating an oligarchy behind—a now badly-cracked—façade of parliamentary democracy."[130] Ghana's government, on the other hand, was more mass based "and responsive to mass aspirations." This was known during the life of the plan to professional economists other than those fa-vored by the Ford Foundation, MIT, and the U.S. state. Their policies played an indirect role in Nigeria's slide into civil war.[131]

CONCLUSION

The evidence above shows clear continuity of the foundations' domestic and foreign strategies—a smoothly continuous approach to African studies at home and to Africa itself—undergirded by elitist, racial, and imperial assumptions. A globally hegemonic mindset is revealed in the foundations' funding strategies, with a state-private network central to its realization. Retaining Nigeria in the Western camp and contributing to European re-covery and strength took priority over poverty alleviation or improving mass living standards. Equally, it is clear that the Nigerian political class fully supported this approach principally because they were its main ben-eficiaries. That political class—a class-based ethnopolitical settlement in a federated political system with clearly demarcated (but always contested) lines of regional and central revenue raising and collection—was con-sciously fostered by the colonialists in the 1950s (and, in the case of tribal chiefs who predominated in the Northern Region, much earlier, and then by U.S. interests both official and private).[132] Given the strategic and ideo-logical interest in Africa, the foundations' knowledge requirements were skewed toward information for influence and control rather than the lofty goals of "development." Or rather, the components of "development" that favored some degree of social progress—greater levels of equality, welfare, and the like, which would affect most immediately mass living standards and life chances—were easily postponed or jettisoned, while core goals of "development," such as the maintenance of a pro–free market "moderniz-ing" elite, regardless of its levels of corruption and violence, were advanced. In the writing of Nigeria's national development plan, Stolper—with full support of the Nigerian political class—dismissed social considerations as "economic nonsense."

The outcomes of foundation funding—and other Western funding—were that Nigeria remained in the Western camp because its pro-American politi-cal and knowledge networks, despite failure adequately to develop the coun-try, proved resilient. Despite their failure to achieve the ends for which it was claimed they were established, foundation networks continued to form the basis of Nigerian planning and educational development: networks as ends but also as means to unstated ends.

Similarly, at home, Africanist networks remained very strong and useful, as they created legitimate knowledge of the kind of Africa that U.S. strategic interests wanted and needed to produce, while ignoring other realities in Africa and other knowledge creators on Africa in the United States. U.S. strategic interests wanted an Africa that was dependent, backward, helpless, and devoid of initiative and ideas. Only with foreign—mainly American—intervention would Nigeria and Nigerians achieve their full potential and achieve "takeoff," in Rostowian terms.

A Gramscian perspective on the role and influence of the major foun-dations is, therefore, upheld: they were engaged in developing and imple-menting a hegemonic project involving the state, corporations, and intellec-tual elites fostered by the major foundations. There is little evidence of the foundations as part of an independent "third sector" beyond big business and the American state and outside politics and ideology. Knowledge is not neutral—it is thoroughly immersed in the struggle to define the world in particular ways that serve specific interests and not others. That is why the foundations were so particular about the kinds of people and institu-tions they chose to support or to consign to the margins. Indeed, this was precisely the case in regard to foundation activities in Indonesia, as shown in chapter 5, and was the case in what is hubristically known as Uncle Sam's "backyard," specifically Chile, which is the subject of the next chapter.

7 | THE MAJOR FOUNDATIONS, LATIN AMERICAN STUDIES, AND CHILE IN THE COLD WAR

Jakarta is Coming
—Graffiti across Chile before the military coup (1973)

The Foundation has a structure and interests, symbolized by the people it picks for trustees and officers, that suggest there would, in the long run at least, be limits on our freedom to opt for overly leftist values and objectives, to support scholarship that would show how power and wealth is controlled in a given society or what social patterns are perpetuated by, for example, the operations of a multinational corporation or the foreign assistance programs of the Agency for International Development.
—John Farrell, Ford Foundation

There could hardly be a more clear-cut example of a strategy by the United States to transform another country's political economy than that of Chile after the military coup of 1973.[1] The effect of a *self-conscious* American state strategy, with sustained support from the Ford and Rockefeller foundations, to transplant into Chile an economic ideology of free-market competition surpassed the strategists' own expectations: a country that was thoroughly statist, with a decades-old welfare state and recognized as the intellectual epicenter for Latin American "structuralist/dependency" thought, was transformed into a "laboratory" for neoliberal experimentation on a radical scale. The Department of Economics of the University of Chicago, led by Ted Schultz, Arnold Harberger, Milton Friedman, and the less direct influence of Frederick von Hayek, was the vehicle for the *secular missionaries* effecting the transformation; the private Pontifical

Catholic University of Chile (CU) was chosen as the bridgehead into Chile and, from there, to challenging the rest of Latin America's attachment to the ideas and policy implications of "structuralism"—particularly the thought of Raul Prebisch and the UN Economic Commission for Latin America (ECLA, or CEPAL, its Spanish acronym). The International Cooperation Administration (ICA and, later, as USAID) was the initial inspiration and principal financier; Ford and Rockefeller supplied substantial additional research funds (well over a million dollars) from the mid-1950s to the *late* 1970s (in the case of Ford). The result: the economists trained at Catholic University, with other right-wing Chileans, developed a secret plan in 1972 for a postcoup economic strategy, overwhelmingly supported the military coup, joined the Pinochet government, and provided technocratic expertise for the brutal regime. The stated aim of ICA/USAID, Chicago, Ford, and Rockefeller—and the "Chicago Boys" created by these programs—was Chilean economic and social development: instead, Chileans' freedoms were curtailed, democracy destroyed, and human rights violated. Chilean society became more unequal, and its economy became deeply indebted to international banks.[2]

There is, however, another aspect of this matter that requires exploration if one is fully to understand the effect of American foundations on Chile: the fact that, alongside funding free-market economics thinking, they also funded the economists of the "center" and "left" who championed ECLA's ideas. ECLA's "statism" was less an article of faith in "socialism," even less Marxism, than it was the institutionalization of a policy adopted to meet the demands of the economic crisis of the 1930s, which generated statist responses the world over. ECLA fully recognized the necessity of developing a strong private sector alongside an interventionist state. This was to have an important bearing on U.S. foundations' economics programs in Chile.

The long-term consequences of the American foundations' Chilean "experiment" were interesting: the construction of cadres of "opposition" economists who would later become "governing" economists—in cases of funding for both "left" and "right." Free-market economists constituted a new intellectual/professional viewpoint previously missing in Latin America/Chile. The funding of centrist/leftist (i.e., statist) economists, in the long run, maintained and developed cadres who would eventually replace the Chicago boys in Chile, once political democracy was restored in the 1990s. The key point is that both schools of economists favored by American foundations were part of a spectrum of economic beliefs featuring important overlaps: only the most extreme elements of the Chicago boys rejected the state in its entirety, and hardly any of the funded "statist" economists rejected the market or a significant role for private capital. Additionally, and highly significantly, *the foundations were interested in promoting the most technocratically-minded leftist/centrist economists and consistently promoted the virtues of "apolitical" research and scholarship.* This, then, is the "pluralism" that the foundations sought to promote in Chile/Latin America: a predominantly free market–oriented capitalism versus a more state-driven capitalism. Both sets of economic ideas, however, were championed by technocratic economists, expert cadres trained in broadly the same analytical frameworks and methodologies.[3] The military coup and regime, however, was to have important unintended consequences. For the first time, leftist and centrist Chilean scholars became unmoored from political patronage—their political parties were dissolved and "their" state dismantled, forcing them into collaborating with scholars of differing political tendencies just to survive. Consequently, when they "returned" to Chile, they were more overtly apolitical and more self-consciously technocratic in outlook. Pinochet's economists, who had always championed a technocratic approach, now were "opposed" by technocrats of the "left" and "center." This, too, was significant and linked with U.S. foundation largesse: many of the exiled Chilean social scientists were "housed" in research institutes that were funded by international agencies, including the leading American philanthropies.[4] Beyond that left-center-right spectrum lay Cuba, backed by world communism: that was "beyond the pale," as would be expected.

Along with the strength of dependency theory and policies in Latin America, the Cuban revolution, combined with the activities of Che Guevara, inspired in American elite circles a fear of the expansion of communist power even further into America's "backyard." It forms the essential backdrop to any understanding of the era and the mindsets of the American foreign policy establishment. Pluralism, then, was a concept that could not include certain political forces and tendencies—its underlying base was a capitalistic economy with an "appropriate" mix of state and private initiative but with complete opposition to Cuban-style socialist expropriation of the means of production. The other related point is that American foundations were "forced" to sponsor "statist" economics because of the general consensus, including within the business communities and, especially in Chile, around the necessity of the state's role in industrialization strategies.[5]

Hence, Ford and Rockefeller foundations backed both major universities in Santiago—Catholic and the University of Chile—in a self-conscious strategy of *complementarity* in institutional development.

By the late 1980s and 1990s, of course, many leftists the world over had abandoned as untenable many of their ideological/political attachments to statism and embraced a watered-down version of market economics, particularly in the conditions of globalization. This helps explain the rightward shift to privatization of President Fernando Henrique Cardoso in Brazil, a former left-of-center *dependista*. In short, the ideological spectrum of beliefs in regard to economic policy and strategy had narrowed from the 1970s to choices between variations of market capitalism, with an "enabling" state rather than an interventionist one. The long-term consequences of foundation-sponsored economics in Chile and Latin America more generally, conditioned by changing political circumstances, economic and financial crises, and the onset of globalization, were significantly to marginalize socialist options and narrow the range of economic strategies to choices between capitalist market strategies.[6] U.S. foundations sustained a strong, largely centrist, internationally connected counterhegemonic intellectual-political network in Chile that gradually came to accept the neoliberal model, with a social dimension, by the late 1980s.[7]

LATIN AMERICA AND THE UNITED STATES

Latin America was, and is, an area considered part of the United States' "sphere of influence"; indeed, it is often referred to as its "backyard." The Monroe Doctrine openly declared the principle of "America for the Americans" (under U.S. leadership) in 1823, supplemented by the Roosevelt Corollary in 1904: the right of the United States to intervene to protect civilization and stop barbarism.[8]

U.S. interest in Latin America waxed and waned according to developments internal to those states as well as with interest shown by European powers in expanding their influence.[9] Consequently, interest intensified whenever nationalist forces gained ground, leading to numerous U.S. military interventions to support threatened regimes or to replace unfriendly governments with those more congenial to American interests.[10] With the drive to war in Europe in the late 1930s, the United States took measures to counter the possible growth of Nazi influence. Although the onset of the

Cold War saw Latin America as relatively stable and "unthreatened" by world communism, left-nationalist developments in Guatemala and the revolution in Cuba of 1959 caused waves of panic about the regional spread of communistic revolution throughout the region.[11] The Kennedy-Johnson administrations viewed the Cuban revolution as a political threat to American interests, a source of subversion, "sabotage[,] and terror," according to Undersecretary of State George Ball.[12] It was America's aim to strengthen Latin American states' capacity to withstand communist subversion. President Kennedy's Alliance for Progress increased the rates of aid to Latin America to support "development" with social justice—although it had little effect other than to support and encourage friendly regimes and leaders. The same point was made in 1962 by one who thought the Alliance for Progress may herald a new age of American support for radical reform and social justice but who also feared the contradiction of the principles of the Monroe Doctrine (opposition to "un-American" policies) and the alliance.[13]

In addition to perceived security interests, the United States had significant economic, commercial, and financial interests in the region. When President Dwight Eisenhower toured Latin America in 1960, his delegation boasted about the over $9 billion invested by American corporations in the region and the over $4 billion of government loans and grants between 1945 and 1960.[14] In 1880, the value of U.S. direct investments in Latin America had totaled a mere $100 million, growing to $1.7 billion by 1914. At that point, Britain's foreign investments in the region stood at $3.7 billion.[15] By 1929, at $3.5 billion, the United States was the largest foreign investor in Latin America, with a 40 percent share.[16] Until the late 1950s, 30 percent of U.S. capital flows abroad were destined for Latin America.[17] According to the U.S. Department of the Interior, Latin American exports to the United States accounted for significant proportions of strategic raw materials identified as essential. For example, 99 percent of America's bauxite, 36 percent of its manganese ore, copper (60 percent), iron ore (43 percent), lead ore (31 percent), zinc ore (35 percent), and crude petroleum (31 percent) came from Latin American sources.[18] Overall, 20 percent of U.S. overseas earnings from direct investments derived from Latin America.[19]

Chile was heavily dependent on U.S. corporations for investment, on the American state for economic aid, and on the major international financial institutions—upon which the United States exercised significant influence—for financing development and trade and for maintaining economic operations. By 1970, for example, U.S. direct investments totaled just over

$1 billion, out of total foreign investment of around $1.6 billion. Over 50 percent of such private investment was in the mining industries, the rest principally in the manufacture of consumer goods aimed largely at those with the capacity to pay, i.e., the Chilean middle and upper middle classes. In some areas, including iron, steel, and metal products; tobacco; automobile assembly; and pharmaceuticals, U.S. corporations controlled over 60 percent of the assets. Copper, the sale of which produced most of Chile's foreign exchange, was 80 percent U.S.-controlled.[20] In combination, Chile's industrial and trading dependence on the United States was very significant, leaving her economy vulnerable to external manipulation and sanctions. Add to that the leverage of the U.S. government in the World Bank, the International Monetary Fund, and the Inter-American Development Bank, and political developments in Chile not to the liking of American administrations could be approached by a variety of measures. When President Nixon ordered the CIA to "make the [Chilean] economy scream" in the wake of the election to president of Salvador Allende in September 1970, it is to some of the potential levers of power above that he was referring.[21] As Petras and Morley argue, "the externally linked enclave [of Chilean industry and mining] in effect was a 'hostage' of the metropolitan countries."[22]

THE DEVELOPMENT OF LATIN AMERICAN STUDIES IN THE UNITED STATES

Scholarly interest in Latin America has shadowed that of the American state and economic interests and, indeed, has historically expressed itself as being in general support of U.S. aims in the region. According to Helen Delpar, U.S. state interest in the region created a demand for expertise on its economics, politics, and culture. The instrumental character of much of this interest, however, clearly shaped the features of Latin American studies.[23] Mark Berger suggests that Latin American studies "has been intimately connected to US expansion in Latin America and the rest of the world" and "facilitated the creation and maintenance of the institutions, organizations, inter-state relations, and politico-economic structures that reinforce and underpin the US hegemonic position in the Americas."[24]

Driven principally by concerns internal to the United States, the rise and development of Latin American studies has been sporadic and unsystematic, depending on federal and foundation funding levels.[25] Interestingly, however, the Latin American Studies Association (LASA), founded in

1965 in the wake of the exposure of "Project Camelot," was an organization critical of close academic-state links and associations.[26] Equally interesting is that LASA's first president was Kalman Silvert, who shortly thereafter joined the Ford Foundation as its Latin America program adviser. Silvert, a sociologist, was deeply involved in the foundation's programs in Chile and in the post–military coup handwringing that Santiago field officers engaged in. Silvert represents an "extreme liberal" position on the military coup and the role of the Ford Foundation as an American organization in Chile. Later in this chapter, a detailed analysis is conducted on the extremely difficult position such liberals found themselves in after September 11, 1973, and how they charted a way forward that was to yield results once the military regime permitted a transition to political democracy.

Americans' interest in the lands to the south, whether they called it Spanish America, Hispanic America or, from the middle of the nineteenth century, Latin America, began early.[27] Only in the twentieth century, with the rise of the modern university, did a specialized field of Latin American studies—focused on history, anthropology, and geography—appear. By the end of the century, Latin American studies was an established discipline. In particular, the period from the 1930s to the late 1970s witnessed the strongest growth of the discipline. Delpar shows how closely academic interest in the region followed such external "threats," indirectly indicating the symbiotic relationship between knowledge and power.[28]

Helen Delpar provides compelling evidence of the conscious build-up by the federal government and private foundations of Latin American studies from the late 1950s. Under the 1958 National Defense Education Act (NDEA), the federal government undertook to provide up to 50 percent of the costs of language-based area studies centers. By the mid-1960s, NDEA funds to the tune of over $300,000 sustained several centers of Latin American studies, including at UCLA, Texas, Tulane, Florida, and Columbia. Other federal sources included the Fulbright-Hayes Act, National Endowment for the Humanities, National Science Foundation, USAID, and the Department of Defense. The funds were for a variety of purposes, including graduate language training, research travel, doctoral and postdoctoral fellowships, and conferences across the humanities and social sciences.[29]

Although the Carnegie Corporation was most active in Latin American studies in the 1950s, it gave way to the far larger Ford Foundation by the 1960s. Nevertheless, CC granted almost $500,000 to fund research and training at Cornell and to ACLS-SSRC to improve research on Latin

America. The Joint Committee on Latin American Studies was formed at the request of ACLS-SSRC in 1959 to advance field research, assisting fifty-five individuals over a five-year period. Network building was a key concern of the Joint Committee—both among Latin Americanists in the United States and between them and their counterparts in the region. Sponsoring a survey of the field by Carl Spaeth, of Stanford's law school, Ford granted $1 million in 1962 to build academic networks lubricated by faculty interchange between selected institutions, including UC-Berkeley and Los Angeles, Harvard, Columbia, Texas, and Minnesota. In 1963, a further $1.5 million went to fund postdoctoral researchers, additional research materials at the Library of Congress, training library specialists, and Latin American studies programs generally and at Cornell, which received $550,000. Millions more were invested by Ford in other Latin American programs at Florida, Texas, Stanford, Tulane, and Wisconsin, as well as at the Brookings Institution and the Joint Committee. The latter received, between 1963 and 1971, $1.3 million, making it the "primary Foundation vehicle for channeling assistance" to Latin American studies.[30] Inevitably, Latin Americanists developed a journal for their field, *Latin American Research Review* (*LARR*), and a national organization, the Latin American Studies Association (LASA), with full Ford Foundation support—$40,000 and $100,000, respectively.[31]

The theme—expanded knowledge networks for expanding power—is continued in a later report. Report 000100 of the Ford Foundation gives a very good summary of the core aims of the foundation in its social science programs in regard to Latin America and is worth quoting at length. There are strong echoes of the same concerns as expressed in the case of Africa and African studies. A memorandum by Reynold E. Carlson, a professor of economics at Vanderbilt and Johns Hopkins universities, Ford's associate director of Latin American programs, and U.S. ambassador to Columbia (1966–1969), provides a hard-nosed reading of Ford's core concerns.[32] He shows the scale of Ford's support for the social sciences in Latin America from 1960–1966: 25 percent (just over $13m of almost $53m) of all Ford funding in the region went to social sciences between 1960 and 1965; of that, 37 percent ($4.75m) was allocated to economics. He shows that several centers of excellence had been funded across the region, in several countries, including the Getulio Vargas Foundation and the faculty of economics at the University of São Paolo, in Brazil (both also funded by USAID), and the universities of Buenos Aires, Cordoba, and Tucuman, in Argentina.[33] However, he laments the dearth of sociologists and political scientists, as opposed to economists, in Latin America. The problem, he argues, is that "sociologists are suspect characters at best," adding that in the regional context, they also tend to work within a "Marxist frame of reference," making them "doubly suspect." Yet "social development" is the "new frontier," constituting the increasing integration and participation of all classes in national life, especially as Latin America moves from a "traditional agrarian, hierarchical, oligarchic, and paternalistic society into one which is urban, industrial, contractual, and, hopefully, democratic." How can Ford "participate in the process and perhaps to a small degree accelerate the transition," particularly its *direction* and *rate of change*"? Carlson also asked how the process might proceed in an "orderly and evolutionary" manner, with sufficient flexibility to "accommodate the stresses and strains being generated."[34] Transitions generate "tension points" that, unless "identified at an early stage . . . will be compounded, generate heat and create situations which *cannot be resolved within the existing political and legal institutions*" (emphasis added). The role of the sociologist of development is fourfold: identify "tension points"; "isolate the factors contributing" to them; devise methods "to eradicate, or at least substantially alleviate, these tensions"; and develop a sense of the costs of such alleviation strategies. "The task of a social scientist is not to offer normative judgments but to indicate the available solutions and to alert the decision-makers of their respective costs."[35] This is a classic statement of social scientists as apolitical technocrats and is riddled with American assumptions about what constitutes a "good," "democratic" society—one without suspect Marxists, revolutionary upheavals, and unmanaged, disorderly change. In the final part of his memorandum, Carlson suggested that American social scientists needed to collaborate more with their Latin American counterparts, because "points of tension are not always amenable to quantitative analysis," leading to misidentification of tension points and their sources, as well as of alternative solutions to tension resolution. Even "basic research" was fundamentally focused on the tasks identified above: the lack of adequate social statistics—on population, urbanization, and agrarian reform, for example—meant grave problems in diagnosing social ills with significant political effects.[36]

Given the focus of Project Camelot on Chile, Carlson's report shows how closely aligned was Ford's thinking with official U.S. state thinking—first, a state-private shared approach to social science as an aid to preserving and advancing American "national" interests, and second, the conversion of social scientists into sources of intelligence ahead of possible future military or other interventions to ensure that societal problems were resolved within the "existing political and legal" order, in which the United States had strong and well-established vested interests.

Inevitably, however, given the crises of American society and power in the 1960s, there were severe tensions and disturbances to the knowledge networks established by the American state and foundations. This had been the case with both African and Asian studies. LASA was born in 1965 with the alarm bells of Project Camelot ringing in its ears. Still, Latin Americanists, especially those associated most closely with the "establishment," were, in the main, fairly conservative: they had been appropriately critical of the Cuban revolution's trajectory after 1959 and sought ways to oppose communist expansion through channeling foreign aid for capitalistic economic development. It fell to the likes of William Appleman Williams and C. Wright Mills, radical academics from outside Latin American studies, to write the books that inspired the younger, radical generation of scholars to challenge LASA's elitism, its proximity to the U.S. government, and its failure adequately to challenge American intervention in the Dominican Republic and the blockade against Allende's Chile.[37] New organizations—including the North American Congress on Latin America—were formed to protest against LASA and condemn America's domination of the region. They did not receive Ford funding.[38]

PROGRAMS IN CHILE

According to Valdes's fascinating account of the Chicago boys, the Ford Foundation exhibited *naïveté, ignorance,* and *neutrality* in their programs of funding Chilean social science. This is despite his examination of some of the rich archives available at Ford and Rockefeller. Valdes's attention is largely on the University of Chicago's Department of Economics and the reports to ICA that its stalwarts submitted. However, my reading of foundation documents challenges Valdes's and suggests that he appears to accept at face value what the foundation representatives themselves suggested about their roles in Chile.[39]

As noted earlier, U.S. state strategy was to undermine and replace dependency theory. Dependistas—of various tendencies—promoted nationalistic capitalist economic-development strategies based on state-led industrialization, high tariffs on imports, import substitution, welfare states, and so on.[40] The practical implementation of this theory meant restrictions on U.S.

trade with Latin America and Chile, high taxes on foreign investment, occasional nationalization of foreign investment, fixed exchange rates, and laws restricting the repatriation of multinational corporation profits.

ECLA championed dependista thought, which had been developed by Raul Prebisch, a former central banker from Argentina who headed ECLA from 1951. In order to undermine ECLA, seen as too left wing by the American state, the United States engaged in a two-pronged strategy: first, through the Organization of American States and second, through funding free-market economics via the ICA-inspired University of Chicago–Catholic University of Chile linkage.[41] Both RF and FF backed the ICA/USAID program for many years. RF and FF also backed economics at the University of Chile, which was more attached to dependista schools of thought and supplied economists to various governments of the center and left, including Eduardo Frei in the mid-to-late 1960s and Allende in the early 1970s. However, it is important to note that the economics faculties of both universities were not monolithic—each featured economists (both faculty and students) from other schools of thought.

Ford was itself the subject of some political controversy in Chile, provoking a strike by the "Marxist teachers' union" at its oldest "normal" school in 1969, because the Ford grant required a foundation representative on the school's reform project board. In addition, Ford had become overly identified with the Christian Democratic Party and administration of Frei (1964–1970) and with the institutions most associated with that party and regime, such as the Catholic University, the Barnechea Center, and the National Research Council (CONICIT).[42] In his report on the activities of Ford's Santiago office in 1970, Peter Bell also noted the "moderate" character of the Frei administration and its worthy attempts at "far-reaching economic and social change," despite its failure to deliver on most of its promises. As "our office was understandably attracted to the liberal, technocratic, and reformist approach of the Christian Democratic Government . . . we provided grant support" for its reform programs in education and agriculture and in regional and urban planning.[43] This, of course, rather stretched Ford's stated policy of remaining nonpolitical. It was in line, however, with official but covert U.S. support, via the CIA and other state agencies, for Frei's presidential election campaign in 1964.[44]

The meaning of "political" for Ford requires some clarification. While *policy-oriented research* was supported by large grants, Ford tried to steer away from openly *party-political* activity by social scientists. Policy-oriented research was defined as nonpolitical and technocratic: it could and would form the basis of policy-related advice to official policy makers. However, electoral activity, partisanship, and ideological warfare with opponents in or beyond the academy was treated with some suspicion, particularly from the left but also, later, from the right. Ford wanted, in effect, to transplant into Chile an "American" model of the policy-oriented social scientist: one who could serve any mainstream political party or administration by providing "objective" advice based on certified professional expertise that eschewed ideology and politics. The implication was that objective, impartial, and scientific knowledge was possible, desirable, superior, and the only basis of developing a modern state, polity, society, and economy. Party politics, on the other hand, was motivated by power and hence corrupt and divisive, a source of instability. At the heart of this analysis lay the experience of the United States itself in the late nineteenth and early twentieth centuries, when American elites were themselves involved in a "search for order," an end to partisan struggles, "pork-barrel" politics, and the "tyranny of the majority." It is in this narrowly defined sense that Ford and other American foundations claimed to be nonpolitical. Hence, their hopes and plans for a "pluralist" and professionalized Chilean social-scientific community were not seen as in any way "political"—the exercise of influence to affect outcomes. They were seen as "technical" adjustments and developments necessitated by the objective requirements of "modernization."

Ford funding for projects in Chile totaled $22.5 million between 1960 and 1970, according to Peter Bell. By 1970, Ford was funding "approximately half of all Chileans now studying for their doctorates in the United States."[45] Some $3 million had been granted *directly* to the (private) Catholic University and $3.3 million *directly* to the (state) University of Chile.[46] In addition, there was a $10 million *convenio*, or collaboration, between the University of California and the University of Chile, principally in the hard sciences and engineering.[47] Bell conceded that Ford had granted no funds to the "Communist-led State Technical University," despite its having twice the number of students as the private Catholic University.[48] Other Ford officials also acknowledged that the foundation had created few, if any, fellowship opportunities for Marxist or communist scholars.[49] This is, of course, quite instructive of Ford's intentions of building the basis of complementarity, under the guise of pluralism, of academic institutions and outlooks in Chile, specifically Santiago, which Bell refers to as "the Geneva of Latin America," given its concentration of international organizations' regional offices.[50]

The objectives of Ford in Chile in the field of economics are discernable from the vast quantities of reports, memoranda, and correspondence generated by Ford officers in Santiago and New York. The archives constitute a remarkably clear record of Ford's aims and strategy in the field of economics' development—focused on building networked, complementary institutions in Santiago, the hub of a regional network serving the whole of Latin America—educating economists, training students and faculty, and reproducing the "model" across the region. Alongside these strategies developed the language of pluralism, which was also subject to a very specific meaning for Ford officers. In this case, "pluralism" was not meant to be harshly competitive and selfish but to generate scholarly debate and discussion among social scientists, especially economists, who might disagree on the role of the state or the market in economic policy but who could debate the issues and agree to disagree. That is, pluralist debate was to be based on a common foundation of theoretical, methodological, and analytical techniques and professional development, which unified the experts despite their differences of political opinion. Economics was a science beyond politics and ideology, and modern scholars of that science had to operate accordingly. Ford's pluralism, then, was a truncated pluralism: it was not as competitive as the theory would suggest. The second point is that it excluded Marxists and communists: the pluralist spectrum, for Ford, included principally the Chicago boys on the right and "mainstream" dependistas on the left. This constituted an attenuated pluralism that drew boundaries on the kinds of economics and economic development that was desirable: fundamentally capitalistic, with a debate about the roles of states and markets.

The Chicago boys, of course, ended up advising Pinochet's military regime—an unintended consequence of Ford's promotion of pluralism in Chile. To the left (and center), Ford scholars were variously persecuted—dismissed from their posts, exiled, and marginalized by the military regime. Ford's investments in economists—on right, left, and center—were, however, protected by the foundation in various ways. Ford continued to fund economics at Catholic University for four years after the military coup. Ford also developed programs to rescue its investments and "rehouse" them until better days, when military repression waned. Importantly, however, it should be noted that the foundation did not accept that it was generating two mutually exclusive wings of economics—always stressing the political-ideological overlaps between students and staff.

Behind this entire technocratic agenda lay a profound assumption: that the findings and discoveries of rational social science, especially economics with a mathematical base, were universally applicable, everywhere, all the time. This approach allowed for some level of pragmatic refinement to suit local conditions, but the general model held true. Economics was scientific, its findings were laws, and there could be little fundamental argument. This clearly also reflected a general assumption about the kind of economy that was "normal"—an open economy producing what it did best, reflecting "comparative advantage," promoting relatively free trade and reciprocity. This was the official version of what the General Agreement on Tariffs and Trade (GATT) stood for: equality of nations in an open world system.[51]

The next section outlines the development and impact of the Chicago boys and the role of American foundations. It then explores the foundations' *complementary* support for dependista economics and its effects. Both programs strongly reflect the foundations' main, usually unstated, preoccupations: constructing powerful technocratic networks that endure over time and have an effect on national economic policy and the promotion, through such networks, of American hegemony. As Peter Bell, Ford's Santiago representative noted in 1970, in the case of grants to agricultural development, despite a $1.5m expenditure, there had been "a proliferation of effort" and "a welter of interchange" but little development.[52]

However, Ford was a "thinking organization" that permitted (some) room for discussion and debate. As Osvaldo Sunkel, the dependista economist, noted at a Ford Foundation "soul-searching" conference in December 1973, in the wake of the military coup in Chile, the Vietnam War, the Watergate scandal, and the general failure of the development agenda: "When an imperialist power begins to have difficulty, it begins to study itself."[53] This aspect of Ford will be explored, as it had consequences for its programs for Chilean scholars marginalized by the Pinochet regime.

THE CHICAGO BOYS

The sense of belonging to a "small beleaguered minority" frequently results in the creation of inward-looking close-knit groupings that can become almost fanatical or cultish in form and self-immersed in a group norm. That is the way the "Chicago boys" and their Chicago mentors, credited with transforming Chile in the 1970s into a laboratory for neoliberal experimentation, are frequently seen and, indeed, saw themselves.[54] This was also certainly the case for the "Berkeley boys" at the University of Indonesia. The latter—operating as an "alien" group committed to free markets and privatization in an environment of statism and opposition to free-enterprise capitalism—developed an almost caste-like mentality that sustained them during the 1950s and 1960s, until the rise of Suharto. Even under Suharto, however, the Berkeley boys remained very close and generally failed to renew their group's membership with new blood, so powerful were their in-group ties.

As the general outlines of the story of the Chicago boys is well known, their construction and influence will be described only briefly and principally with a view to demonstrating a larger point not often made: that the foundations were instrumental in fostering technocratic economists of both left and right in Chile from which, in the long run, developed a general consensus on economic strategies in the era of neoliberal globalization.

The Chicago boys' construction was a key project of the American state and the major foundations. Valdes argues that central to the plan was the dislodging of the hegemony of dependista thought in Chile and, by extension, the whole of Latin America, by the creation of an "organic intellectual elite" linked with the Chilean entrepreneurial class, which had been incorporated into the statist coalition alongside organized labor and justified by Prebischian economic theory. The "project" was initiated by Albion Patterson, the head of the ICA in Latin America. Rejected by the economists of the University of Chile,[55] Patterson persuaded Catholic University to sign a contract with University of Chicago economists, to train over several years the best Chilean students up to the doctoral level. After training at Chicago, graduates would return to Catholic and build its own Chicago-oriented economics. Chicago also sent several professors to Santiago to advise on and conduct research on the Chilean economy.[56]

Between 1956 and 1964, ICA/USAID granted over $800,000 to the Catholic-Chicago program, principally to finance Chicago economists stationed in Santiago and pay the tuition and maintenance costs of Chilean graduate students at Chicago.[57] By 1963, of the thirteen full-time economists at Catholic, twelve had been Chicago trained.[58] Their training was intensive and personal: Ted Schultz, Milton Friedman, and Arnold Harberger, among others, took deep interest in their students' welfare, families, and intellectual development. Students on the program were, unusually, given desk space to work and a weekly seminar to discuss the latest research on Chilean economic problems and solutions. Harberger invited students to his home. Graduate students were retained as research assistants so they would learn at first hand the problems of the Chilean economy and the "right" way to think about solving them, i.e., through market solutions. As one of their number said: trained in Chicago meant "correct knowledge [to] make correct decisions." Chile was a "laboratory" for studying under-development—especially in studying the sources and solutions to inflation, issues related to money supply, and problems of agriculture, exchange rates, trade controls, and so on. Despite admissions by some Chicago economists that they "knew nothing" about Chile, their zeal for promoting free-market solutions to economic problems was unlimited.[59]

Despite the general image of an exclusive link between Catholic and Chicago, however, Valdes points out that there were outliers: not all Catholic University students went to Chicago (a few went to Columbia and Harvard, for example). He also points out that some Chicago boys were also based at the University of Chile, rather than at Catholic. Hence, from the earliest days of the program, the effort to transplant a specific economic ideology through training cadres of Chilean neoliberal economists was broader than is often appreciated.[60]

A point that Valdes does not develop relates to the purposive role of American foundations. In Valdes's account, the foundations are "present" in the background rather than conscious actors in their own right. This is consistent with his view that the foundations were largely ignorant of what ICA/USAID were doing, i.e., combating ECLA's statist ideas. The foundations' records do not bear out this interpretation. The Rockefeller Foundation, for example, granted $500,000 to Catholic University economics programs from 1956. At the same time, RF awarded $1 million to economics programs at the University of Chile. More is written on the latter program below.

The key concept that unified Chicago economists, the ICA, and private foundations was "human capital development," which was thought to be the key to economic development. The idea was simple: investment in people generated returns, because educated people created wealth and solved problems. The idea was hardly new, of course, but it coincided with the interests of Chicago economists and ICA administrators, who wanted to marginalize dependency theory from Latin America as one basis of resurrecting market economies there, and with the interests of the major foundations, which already believed in the importance of education in transforming developing societies. The consequence was the production of cadres of neoliberal Chilean economists who owed more loyalty to their Chicago mentors than their compatriots—including economists—at Catholic University and looked more to the logics of the International Monetary Fund than to nationalist economic strategies. Their economic ideas elicited hostility from their fellow economists in Santiago, further alienating the Chicago boys and accentuating their "autonomy from internal interest groups," as Valdes puts it. The Chicago boys clung even more to their "economic science," their truth, and alma mater. When Pinochet came to power, the Chicago boys took their opportunity to transform the economy and ignore everything else. Their time had come.[61]

By 1963, the Chicago boys had wrested control of economics at Catholic University, preventing the recruitment of economists of other traditions to "balance" their influence. Dean Chana was replaced by Sergio de Castro, the virtually unchallenged leader of the Chicago boys, along with Carlos Massad. Massad, a Christian Democrat, returned to work at the University of Chile, indicating that the Chicago program transferred economic techniques that were capable of adaptation and use regardless of an individual's party preferences. The University of Chile saw the Chicago boys as essential to continued foundation funding and backed them to the hilt. The Ford Foundation obliged by backing plans to transform the economics department at Catholic into a training center for the whole region. Even further, Arnold Harberger won acceptance for his plan of spreading the Chicago boys' influence through sending them to a regional network of free-market economics training facilities. Hence, the programs expanded to include the Cuyo Project, in Argentina, and the University del Valle, in Colombia.

Valdes shows that American foundations exercised "enormous influence" on the development of economics in Chile. For example, Ford and Rockefeller were jointly responsible for increasing the number of economists in Chile from 121 in 1960 to 727 by 1970. Relatedly, the number of institutes of economics in Chile increased from four in 1960 to ten a decade later.[62] The economists in question were also better trained than previously, particularly in quantitative techniques. Ford had granted $552,000 to Catholic University economists and $1.3 million to their counterparts at the University of Chile.

Valdes draws two conclusions that I challenge here: first, that Ford "had no perception" that there was a battle being waged by ICA/Chicago against ECLA's ideas, and second, that Ford was *ideologically neutral* in its approach to funding economics in Chile, hence the funding pattern above. On the first point, Valdes acknowledges Ford officials' awareness of the ideological bias of the Chicago boys but that they expressed no opposition. That conclusion emphasizes Valdes's relatively narrow idea of "ideology." Valdes sets up left/dependista economics *against* right/neoliberal economics and sees only ideological neutrality in foundations that backed both horses. Instructively, he acknowledges that combating Marxism was a key objective in Latin America and, therefore, Ford was reticent to confront the Chicago program when it was generating rational analytical techniques that challenged Marxian approaches. Additionally, Valdes does not mention the role of the *Rockefeller Foundation* in this matter. RF records show that officials met with Albion Patterson, head of the U.S. Operations Mission in Chile, in October 1956, to discuss the Chicago–Catholic University economics program. At one meeting, Patterson pointed out the advantages of linking the universities: Chicago, he suggested, "is on the one hand strongly theoretical in its approach, *and on policy lines it is a vigorous proponent of the virtues of the market price system as against state socialism.* AWP feels that this is a point of view which badly needs emphasis in Chile" (emphasis added). When Patterson pointed up his "fear" that "the people trained under the Chicago–Catholic University program may be drawn off into business instead of staying on at the University in teaching and research," the RF official replied that he "had already discussed the problem with T. W. Schultz [the head of economics] at Chicago" and that RF would complement ICA's program by providing research funding for Chicago returnees.[63] In fact, at the meeting with Ted Schultz, RF officials had felt that RF would have liked to be even more involved in the Chicago-Catholic program, but the ICA had already "so well worked out" the arrangements. RF looked for "big returns" on its research funding.[64] As if to drive home the point, Schultz denied a desire to "sell" any ideology but reiterated to RF officials that the principal problem in Latin America was "the indiscriminate intervention of governments . . . and their tendency to rank the inflationary problem below that of economic growth."[65]

Ahead of the meetings described above, RF officials had received the first report by Chicago on the collaborative program. The contents of the report are clear: Chicago was organizing the development of a research community that would also educate the broader citizenry, through publications ranging from working papers and journal articles to a "Series on Popular Economics Education" on topics close to neoliberals' hearts: "money and inflation . . . the economics of price control," among others. The report noted that the program's advisory committee, which included Joseph Grunwald, director of the Institute of Economics at the University of Chile, and Jose A. Mayobre, ECLA's Chile representative, had "thought well of the plan."[66] If the point had not already been made that Chicago was going to be engaged in a serious program of shifting attitudes through policy-relevant research that would inevitably draw it into political controversy, the report spelled out the "dilemma": Chilean economic problems required "impartial research" but at the same time were politically controversial. Catholic's economists, therefore, had to tread a fine line between "highly relevant economic research" and the production of "political tracts." The solution was to focus on impartial "fact-finding" to produce usable data from which economic discussion in Chile could proceed.[67] In sum, the aim of engaging in a political battle of economic ideas could hardly have been more clearly advanced, while the RF officials' response was to support the program by agreeing to recommend complementary funding to build Catholic University's economics department.

In addition, the economists at the University of Chile—the dependistas—were not as radical as Valdes implies. In combination and in a broader context, the programs at Catholic and the University of Chile were *complementary*, not competitive, and were seen as such by Ford. Indeed, that so many University of Chile economists entered the *Frei* administration—one favored by Ford, the CIA, and the Catholic Church and that was overtly *reformist and opposed to the left*—is direct evidence that there was no fundamental ideological divide between the two schools of economic thought.[68]

Furthermore, Valdes suggests that Ford was naïve in its assessment of pluralism at Catholic. However, Ford and Rockefeller saw pluralism in the fact of relatively separate and autonomous sets of economists at different institutions, which they constantly sought to bring together and build effective relationships between. The principal barrier to their effective unity as economists was their degree of partisanship—their attachment to specific rival political parties. Much later, after the military coup, the problem of partisanship was "solved."

The ascent of the Chicago boys to the pinnacle of their influence, however, did not end with their effective takeover of the faculty of economics at Catholic. They had still to persuade the Chilean business community of their credibility and become what the ICA program intended them to be: the business class's intellectuals. This they did by their ability to hold their own during student unrest in the late 1960s, when the rest of the university

system was paralyzed by protests. In addition, the increasing political polarization of Chilean society under the Frei administration forced into one
camp practically all forces opposed to state intervention, including elements of the Christian Democratic Party. With Allende's election and the
failure of constitutional attempts to unseat him, the previously alien ideas
of the Chicago boys came to sound increasingly realistic to Chilean entre-
preneurs: political crisis brought with it clarity. The Chicago boys were being taken seriously by the very community their economic theories placed
in the vanguard of a free economy. Hence, they engaged in open political
propaganda through the mass media and conspired behind closed doors to
develop secret plans for economic change under a military government. As
Arnold Harberger noted in September 1970, there was serious talk among
Chilean elites of a military coup as the only way to stop Allende's "Marxist"
plans. The Chicago boys were central figures during the entire period as
well as planners of the military's future economic thinking and policies.[69]

DEPENDISTA ECONOMICS AND THE FOUNDATIONS

As noted earlier, Ford and Rockefeller granted more funding to economics
at the University of Chile than they did to Catholic University, undermining the idea that the Chicago boys were their sole interest in that country.
Narrowly conceived complementarity and pluralism were the buzzwords
within the foundations in regard to economics at Santiago's foremost academic institutions. Additionally, foundation records show that from the
mid-1950s, economics at the University of Chile (UC) was developing along
technocratic lines too—attempting in teaching and research to provide a
"sound" basis for "independent" judgment. In contrast to the general view
that UC economists were opposed to capitalism per se, the department's
members conducted research not only for government consumption but
also on a contractual basis for several large multinational and other private
corporations, including the Ford Motor Company.[70] Finally, and most instructively, the character of economics at UC was described as approximat-
ing the production of research at the U.S. National Bureau of Economic
Research (NBER), precisely what Chicago's Ted Schultz claimed was oc-
curring at Catholic University's economics initiatives.[71] The head of the faculty of economics at UC, Luis Escobar, was appointed Pinochet's finance
minister (1984–1985); he had served as President Alessandri's minister of
economy from 1961 to 1963.[72] What follows is the presentation of evidence

from the foundations' records demonstrating overlaps in the technocratic orientation of the two major sets of economists in Santiago.

One of the key figures in economics at UC was Joseph Grunwald, an American economist who was the director of the Institute of Economic Research. The institute was highly valued by the Rockefeller Foundation for its "academic and practical" research in areas such as "the productivity of the Chilean economy," the greater Santiago area's labor force's characteristics, the historic influence of foreign corporations on Chilean economic development, and the impact of Chile's expensive and complex social-security system on its economic progress.[73] Such data were of considerable use to Chilean government planners and in "contributing realism to the training of Latin American economists."[74] Three allocations were made to economics at UC by Rockefeller, totaling over $250,000 between 1957 and 1961.

Grunwald emphasized the technocratic and "objective" character of the institute's work by citing specific examples of the effects on public policy and opinion of its study of the government's anti-inflation program of 1956, an issue that raised the political temperature, given its possible effects on the employment levels in the country. In conditions in which no one had any empirical data, politicians and the press were opining on the threat of mass unemployment. The institute's labor-force survey produced the first statistics on the level of actual unemployment, and its findings were viewed favorably and reported across the press. Echoing the dilemma pointed up by Ted Schultz, economic research, Grunwald argued, necessarily has "political implications" but must be done for the good of society and public debate,[75] a position in line with foundations' thinking—so long as such implications did not question the fundamental power structures of market societies. Grunwald's institute also produced popular economics publications and broadcasts to "enlighten public opinion."[76]

Grunwald introduced neoclassical economics to students at UC, covering the ideas of Paul Samuelson and George Stigler, for example, along with other quantitative economists, such as Wassily Leontief and Leon Walras. He also covered the thought of Keynes, John Hicks, and Roy Harrod. Marx was not among the theorists considered in Grunwald's teaching. Grunwald's assistant director, Carlos Massad, trained at Chicago, underlining further the overlaps between UC and Catholic University economists.[77] Interestingly, Ford's William Carmichael noted that although "all of the [Ford] Foundation's programs have a very conservative political orientation . . . those associated with them feel that education in the fields of economics and administration in the University of Chile is under the control of leftist elements." This, despite that, by 1965, Carlos Massad, a Christian Democrat, was director of the institute.[78]

To some extent, of course, there were political differences between UC and Catholic University—the latter was more conservative, the former more centrist. And given the politicized character of the Chilean academy, such differences were accentuated by academics themselves, particularly as they sought party patronage as routes to greater income and government posts. However, Ford reports, particularly those by the U.S. economist John Strasma, who later became a Santiago-based program officer with the Ford Foundation, suggest that UC's economists willingly served administrations of the center (Frei), center-right (Ibanez), and left (Allende) and that their leftist image was much exaggerated, as was the "reactionary" image of Catholic University economists. Ford granted to UC economics $450,000 in 1961, while Rockefeller chipped in with another $150,000 in the same year, to establish the Graduate School in Economics (ESCOLATINA) to serve the needs of Latin America as a whole. Strasma stressed that UC's Institute of Economics was "clearly the most pluralistic" group of economists in Santiago, a mixture of socialists, liberals, and conservatives as well as several " 'apolitical' technicians."[79] Of course, there were ECLA economists like Osvaldo Sunkel and Pedro Vuskovic who taught at UC, but their economics were not necessarily exclusively "Marxist."[80]

Grunwald helped create at UC a close-knit network of economists in a position to "absorb" Ford's new grants from 1962 when the Institute of Economic Research and the Graduate School in Economics were merged. This was done "to develop a scientifically oriented teaching program in economics; to evolve, refine and promote sound and objective analysis and solution techniques for the problems" of economic development.[81] According to Strasma, the program was successful because of the "Foundation's decisive assistance," creating 162 highly trained economists from across the region who, upon graduation, had taken up roles as teachers or policy makers in their respective countries. But Strasma remained dissatisfied: he wanted to deepen and expand the program by attracting even more students and making ESCOLATINA "an action center" for high-level research and, even more, the center of a network that would "exercise a guiding influence in both organizational aspects and the design of teaching and research programs in the other Latin American faculties of economics via its members' direct participation in seminary and advisory activities in other faculties."

Strasma's mission, fully shared by Ford, included plans to bring to Chile economists from "advanced countries" to work with the emerging cadres of UC graduates to "provide a scientific and authentic picture of the Continent's real problems and, with this nucleus . . . to create a scientific atmosphere that will be adequate for analyzing Latin American realities."[82]

A list of research projects underway at ESCOLATINA in 1965 provides evidence of technocratic work of direct use to the Chilean government and private corporations. Projects include studies of demand for products such as tractors, chemicals, newsprint, paper, and milk concentrates; the transportation system; population distribution patterns; productivity rates across economic regions; input-output analyses of manufacturing industries; quantification approaches to the demand for money; patterns of income, consumption, and savings' rates in Chile; and so on. There is nothing there suggesting particularly radical economic analyses or methods nor a specific political agenda over and above that implied by a market system with a strong state sector.[83] It reflects precisely what was promised at the time a Ford grant of $500,000 was awarded—a program of research focusing on "quantifying" Chile as an aid to economic development in "both the public and private sectors."[84]

The teaching curriculum also betrays little that may be defined as politically radical per se, even if there are hints that UC economists were interested in the socioeconomic aspects of development. For example, in 1962, the curriculum consisted of a staple of economic principles, social accounting, agricultural economics, statistical inference, economic theory, fiscal policy, and mathematical economics. By 1962, of course, Carlos Massad had been promoted to director of ESCOLATINA. On the staff, for example, was the economist Alvaro Bardon, who, from 1976 to 1981, served as the president of the central bank during the Pinochet regime, while Carlos Clavel, Herta Castro, and James Locke were graduates of the Chicago program.[85] Other economists, among the twenty-seven named in a report, were educated at Stanford (Hector Assael), Kiel (David Alaluf), Iowa State (Ivan Bello, Kurt Ullrich), Harvard (Juan Braun, Carlos Hurtado, Teresa Jeanneret, Roberto Maldonado), Yale (Mario Cortes, Luis Federici, Carlos Sepulveda), MIT (Eduardo Garcia), LSE (Arturo Israel, Ivan Yanez), and Duke (Ricardo Lagos).[86] Another report indicates the funding sources for overseas study periods of faculty members: of the eighteen faculty for whom information was indicated, seven had received scholarships from the

Rockefeller Foundation, five from USAID, and one from the Fulbright program.[87] The predominantly U.S.-educated and U.S.-funded faculty members set up teaching programs that resembled U.S. graduate schools and invited their former professors to ESCOLATINA. Among visiting professors were faculty from Harvard, Vanderbilt, and Chicago (Arnold Harberger, 1966) as well as from the RAND Corporation (Delbert Fitchett, 1966).[88]

A survey of economics students at UC in 1967 confirms the argument. For example, 73 percent of students felt the curriculum was too "theoretically orientated, and all but one were unhappy about it." Students felt that not only did the curriculum fail to reflect anything of the "reality in the outside world" but also that the there was a "deficiency in the theoretical analysis presented." While 73 percent felt that the programs were "ideological," only 5 percent argued they were Marxist in orientation, and an overwhelming 95 percent who thought the programs were ideological thought that they were dominated by persuasions that were "Capitalists" or "Neo-Liberal." Ninety-five percent of students felt that the program should be oriented to training students to become " 'agents of change' rather than to 'maintain the system.' " Challenging what sounds like a technocratic approach, 65 percent of students wanted an education that reflected "Knowledge of Latin American Reality" rather than "the training of a 'Professional technically efficient [sic].' "[89] Students seemed to want more radical economics teaching at ESCOLATINA than the faculty members were able or willing to provide.[90]

A memo by Strasma in 1972 bemoaned the lack of books and journals on "socialist economic studies." By 1972, of course, ESCOLATINA's program was operating under differing conditions, notably the leftist Allende government of popular unity and, therefore, paying a lot more attention to "socialist" economics and, especially, postrevolutionary Cuba. More attention was also being paid to dependency theory in the context of greater interest in "autonomous development" and development for "the essential interests of the workers."[91] At this point, Chilean academics' political polarization was becoming ever sharper, as UC faculty left for government posts or for Catholic University. Even then, however, according to Strasma, who doubled as a Ford program officer and faculty member at ESCOLATINA, when the curriculum "came under the control of economists with a solid grounding in Marx and a commitment to an economic policy program along the lines of the campaign program of President Allende," teaching was "predominantly socialistic but not overly dogmatic." Most significantly, the curriculum, under the direction of Ricardo Lagos, sought to instill "rationality in economic policy as well as a new global explanation of Latin American economic problems."[92]

Ford officials stressed to ESCOLATINA staff an "outward-looking orientation, i.e., of searching for ways to strengthen relationships between the Faculty and other institutions engaged in or concerned with teaching and research in economics and administration." The aim was to use Ford's "bargaining power to insist that future support be contingent on progress being made toward the objective of a more rational and cohesive integration of efforts in the social sciences in the University of Chile and in the greater community of which it is a part." Not only is this a clear indication of Ford's desire to engineer specific changes in the institutional complex of economics research and teaching; it also shows a conscious plan to deploy Ford's financial power to that end. The memorandum cited above also shows that Ford was conscious that Rockefeller and the U.S. government were also considering supporting UC's work in public administration "in an effort to build a strong 'international center' of teaching and research in the social sciences." Rockefeller awarded $200,000 for 1965–1966 to aid economic research at Catholic and UC and, in general, to strengthen Santiago's claims to be an "international center."[93]

Such an ambition—an outward-looking "constellation of social science institutes"—continued into the 1970s, despite deep political splits within the academy.[94] It was Strasma's view that teaching at ESCOLATINA was not "rigidly sectarian nor wedded to any one variety of contemporary socialist doctrines" and would contribute to the intellectual mix in Santiago's menu of programs. ESCOLATINA was producing graduates of high quality across Latin America and for regional organizations.[95] Still, Chilean academic polarization caused headaches for Ford staff members. Peter Bell, the head of the Santiago office, was doubtful over the general leftward drift of economists and others at UC and posed some difficult questions, which affected Ford's work in Chile. For example, he asked to what extent Ford was "willing and able to recognize pluralism within a generally Marxist orientation" and what degree of strain Ford could bear in choosing between grant proposals of that kind. A debate ensued among Ford staff about the ideological and, therefore, nonrational character of the teaching curriculum.[96] One report, based on conversations with ESCOLATINA's leadership—Donald Castillo (director), Carlos Romeo, and Alberto Tassara—noted that the Santiago office of Ford had granted no funds to ESCOLATINA since

Allende's election victory. In part, this was attributable to the departure of several senior figures for high government posts. Pedro Vuskovic, for example, as minister for the economy, "was the architect of the regime's offensive against banking and industrial monopolies in Chile." Remaining faculty, largely "openly Marxist . . . evidently does not struggle hard against the tendency for political criteria to overshadow scientific standards, but does attempt to compensate by structuring the courses so that the individual student gains as wide an exposure as possible to various currents of economic thought." In contrast, economics at Catholic University was seen by Ford's Santiago's office as "stronger overall" than ESCOLATINA's, given the former's greater competence in "econometrics and neo-classical economic theory."[97] Yet other reports suggested that ESCOLATINA, by 1973, had weathered the storm of defections of staff, recruited more experienced faculty, and offered the most pluralistic of economics faculties anywhere in Latin America, teaching everything, including classical, neoclassical, Marxist, and dependency theories. ESCOLATINA comprised equal numbers of pro- and anti-Allende economists, epitomizing the crisis in Chile as the military coup approached.[98] The crisis in Chile—in politics, economy, and the academy—was reflected by increasing anxieties within the Ford Foundation. The military closed ESCOLATINA in 1973, leaving Latin America dominated by "economists and planners with technocratic and conservative outlooks,"[99] groups that would continue to receive Ford support for several years after the military coup.

AFTER THE SEPTEMBER 11, 1973, MILITARY COUP

"Schizophrenic" was the word used by some Ford officials to characterize what happened to its social scientists after the coup: right-wing economists at Catholic joined or otherwise supported the military junta; other elements suffered heavily at the hands of the military authorities.

Numerous Chicago boys joined the military junta, including their leader, Sergio de Castro, as well as Jorge Cauas, Miguel Kast, Sergio de la Cuadra, Alvaro Bardon, and Pablo Baraona. They served Pinochet as ministers of finance (Cauas, Castro, Hernan Buchi, de la Cuadra), ministers of economy (Baraona, Bardon), and budget directors (Juan Carlos Mendes, Martin Costabal). Other neoliberal economists from Catholic University took positions in ODEPLAN, the national planning office, including Rodrigo Mujica and Ernesto Silva, as did Miguel Kast, before he was appointed minister of planning in 1978. Jorge Cauas, for example, promulgated "shock treatment" to build an economy centered on freer trade and export promotion, a new "Chilean economic model."[100] Government spending was drastically reduced, unemployment rose, and living standards fell. The relationship between the Chicago boys and the military, of course, was strong even before the coup: recall that Sergio de Castro had been the principal author of the secret economic plan of 1972, known as "the Brick," because of its size and weight. He was ably assisted in that enterprise by Juan Carlos Mendez. None of this was unknown to Ford officers in Santiago and New York. It did cause them some concern, although they chose to continue disbursing funds to Catholic University economists until 1977, when Ford adjudged that conditions in Chile no longer were conducive to independent university research under conditions of pluralism. Interestingly, their assessment followed that of Catholic University "centrist" economists at CEPLAN, the Ford-funded center for planning research, led by Alejandro Foxley. CE-PLAN—composed almost entirely of Christian Democrats who had supported President Eduardo Frei (1964–1970)—decided in 1976 that their position at Catholic was increasingly precarious and, after consultations with Ford, set up an independent research center, CIEPLAN, to continue their work. In many ways, CEPLAN/CIEPLAN personified the "objective" technocratic style Ford favored: critical of Allende and Pinochet and firmly attached to a center ground that had all but disappeared in Chile by 1970. Continued Ford funding throughout the Pinochet years led Foxley (a Wisconsin Ph.D. in economics) to serve the first postmilitary government of President Patricio Aylwin, as minister of finance (1990–1994).

Ford was aware before the coup that Catholic University economics had lost key staff from 1970 onward and thus looked increasingly like their "Chicago" image. The only full-time economist who supported the Allende administration, Eduardo Garcia, left Catholic to join the government's economic advisory commission, while a part-time economist of the left, Osvaldo Sunkel, left to join FLACSO, because of his increasing ideological marginalization. This, according to Ford, seriously eroded the "pluralism" of economics at Catholic, leaving the department uniformly opposed to the Allende administration.[101] Despite Ford's expressed concerns, there was no thought given to cutting the institute's funding (it had been awarded $252,000 in 1972). After the coup and in conjunction with the increasingly difficult atmosphere within Catholic University and further departures

from the institute to positions in government, Ford reconsidered that position. According to Jeffrey Puryear, there were strong doubts as to whether
the institute "will continue to assume a critical role vis-à-vis government
policy,"[102] yet, as late as August 1975, over a year later, Ford was granting
additional funding ($6,000) to the institute, although with a specific in-
struction that the grants "may be expended only for charitable, scientific,
literary, or educational purposes."[103] Valdes was not entirely wrong, then,
to consider Ford officials naïve. Indeed, it was not until 1978 that the grant
of $252,000 was finally "closed," when all funds had been expended *and an
additional ten graduate fellowships funded* "to compensate for our decision
not to continue large-scale assistance to the program."[104]

Ford also continued financial support to Catholic's neoliberal agricultural economists. The latter were reportedly "euphoric" at news of the
military coup: two department members—Juan Carlos Mendez and Rodrigo Mujica, "had participated in the preparation of an economic plan
which was subsequently adopted by the Junta." A Ford report also noted
that "the initial impulse of several of the staff members was to lend their
personal and professional support, formally and informally, to governmental policy-making and administrative functions."[105] There was no thought
among the economists about the levels of repression and "losses of lives"
that occurred after the coup, just the opportunities to influence policy. As a
Ford report put it, the agricultural economists "are taking a definitely constructive attitude."[106]

Despite knowledge of the role of several Catholic University economists
in precoup economic planning for military rule, Ford officials took what
may only be described as an avuncular, indulgent line: Norman Collins of
Ford expressed "strong concern . . . about the dangers . . . of their becoming
involved, as university professors [but not in their 'individual capacity'], in
policy-making and advisory activities." Collins continued, "it appeared to
me that the group had not given sufficient attention to the difficulty, even
impossibility, of maintaining their position as independent analysts and
critics of policies and programs they would be designing and implementing." Collins believed that his warnings changed the economists' behavior
and that "the prospects appear reasonably bright that the Department of
Agricultural Economics can continue to offer a high-quality graduate program," and he recommended that a further $26,000 be transferred to the
department.[107] Another report argued that Catholic University economists

were still leaving for government and not being replaced, which was "clearly symptomatic of the current government's vision of the social role of the university: an institution fully integrated into and at the service of government." Later, the same report argues that the department "might end up becoming a vassal of government" with no "freedom of thought and independence of criticism." As early as November 1973, then, almost the entire staff of the department had been "drawn into assisting their colleagues who have taken full-time or advisory positions in government." The relationship between the Department of Agricultural Economics and the Chilean state constituted the subsidization of the state by the university, as the latter had to continue to pay the salaries of academics whose governmental posts were yet to be formalized and, thereafter, pay the differential between the government and academic incomes. The military regime was also funding increasing numbers of its staff to study economics in the department, as they envisaged being in power "for quite a while," according to Professor Fernando Martinez, the director of the graduate program. At the same time, replacement economists being sought by the department were uniformly right wing, with thought for neither "disciplinary nor ideological breadth."[108]

Yet in March 1974, Peter Bell wrote to Fernandez about the necessity to ensure that the department maintain its "academic independence from government [and] a reasonable degree of pluralism among staff and students."[109] Further recommendations for making grant payments were made in March 1974 and every quarter until 1977, despite the fact that each report noted the department's domination by the military regime.[110] Ford's attachment to its academic-institutional investments was evidently very strong. But, as Puryear noted in 1978, the foundation "learned something of the limits of outside assistance in counterbalancing institutional and national problems."[111]

CENTER FOR NATIONAL PLANNING STUDIES (CEPLAN)

CEPLAN was founded in 1968 at Catholic University, funded by Ford. However, CEPLAN's director, Alejandro Foxley, had already been associated with Ford through the MIT-ODEPLAN project, funded to the tune of $440,000.[112] From the time Allende was installed as president, CEPLAN economists generally sought to play an "intellectual" role "among professionals and scholars" to produce future policy recommendations. They were critical of both Allende's statism, particularly of his income-redistribution programs,[113] and of the Chicago boys' neoliberalism. Key members of CEPLAN included Oscar Munoz (Ph.D., Yale) and Ricardo Ffrench-Davis (PhD., Chicago). This group was especially strong at using quantitative data from government sources to evaluate past policies and in projecting "future alternatives." Their work, as opposed to that of the other economists at Catholic University, was "founded in Chilean reality."[114]

According to John Strasma, CEPLAN's members were uniformly linked with the Christian Democratic Party and were generally very good economists "experienced in government" with "quantitative skills in social sciences." Foxley openly declared that any attempt at broadening the political affiliations of CEPLAN members would be "pernicious" and likely to "sabotage productivity."[115] In that regard, Foxley in no way differed from other groups of economists on the right or left. Of all the groups funded by Ford, CEPLAN*istas* came closest to Ford's ideal: "moderate" and technocratic.[116]

Immediately after the military coup, CEPLAN seemed little affected, despite the fears of one of its members, Oscar Munoz, that he might be dismissed for being of the "independent left" though critical of Allende—and the torture of one of its researchers.[117] CEPLAN members continued their work but dropped projects on income redistribution and trade unions in the copper industry. CEPLAN was also "more discreet in the use of its language, and perhaps in the selection of topics which it treats . . . [to] diffuse [*sic*] some of the political sensitivity of its research in domestic circles." CEPLAN also focused on "technical issues . . . and [placed] less emphasis on issues like labor participation."[118] Nevertheless, Foxley adjudged that the situation at Catholic was deteriorating, as right wingers gradually took control of the upper echelons of the university administration and narrowed room for independent thought. In early 1976, CEPLAN members, forbidden to teach in graduate programs, began discussions about its future with Ford, the UN Development Program, and the International Labor Organization. In mid-1976, CEPLAN was dissolved and, with a Ford grant of $265,000, established CIEPLAN, a new independent research center, with a promise of continued future funding.[119] CEPLAN had built an international reputation for excellence based on Ford-funded research, publications, doctoral training, and professional exchange programs. As a result, the group's professionalism had improved, and their theoretical and methodological techniques had sharpened. They had been extraordinarily productive for a small group (totaling never more than twelve), producing thirty-eight research papers and four books by April 1974. At that date, there were a further twenty-one projects underway, promising seven books and many more articles. According to Puryear, CEPLAN was a highly productive, well-organized, and "closely-knit group," a center of attraction for the whole region.[120]

University of Chile Economists

The coup's immediate consequences for Chile's left-wing and (later) centrist economists were dire: mass dismissal, arrest, exile, and stigmatization. Peter Bell estimated that the military regime would force out of the universities by the end of 1973 around 10 percent of students and faculty for political reasons. At the University of Chile, forty-four of forty-seven members of the Department of Political Economy had already been dismissed or suspended. Around "one-third of the Marxist population [of the universities] will have been removed" by the initial wave of repression, Bell added, while the remainder "will be circumscribed in what they teach, research, and publish. . . . The universities will be more technical than scientific, more technocratic than critical."[121] As Nita Manitzas, a Ford official in Santiago, put it: "our agricultural economists are sitting in the Junta and the sociologists are getting wiped out in the stadium."[122] Despite the great faith placed in social science, no one appeared to predict a military coup. Chile was thought to be immune to such an outcome, except by the military, the business community, and its collaborators among the neoliberal economists at Catholic University. Ford's Peter Bell had also suggested that a military coup was out of the question.

Shock within the Ford Foundation led to a serious bout of soul searching, the contours of which are instructive. The contrast with Ford reactions to the even bloodier military takeover in Indonesia in the 1960s, described as a "moderate military regime" by Ford officials, is stark. In Chile, there was expressed deep concern for human-rights violations and the extirpation of civil liberties. Officials even suggested that President McGeorge Bundy use his contacts to ask for Secretary of State Kissinger's direct intervention in some cases. This simply did not happen in Indonesia in 1965–1966, a country that was described, it will be recalled, as being in a holiday mood following Sukarno's ousting from office. What led to the deep sense of loss in Chile following the coup? And to what did the soul searching lead?

Ford's sense of loss requires some context. An important aspect of it was captured by Osvaldo Sunkel's wry comment that "when an imperialist power begins to have difficulty, it begins to study itself." The United States at the end of 1973 was experiencing "difficulties": the oil crisis, the debacle in Vietnam in general and as pointed up by the Pentagon Papers, and corruption at the very pinnacle of power exposed by the Watergate scandal and subsequent resignation of President Richard Nixon—not to mention a welter of domestic social crises and protests that led to a sense of a "crisis of democracy" and a breakdown of law and order. Additionally, the 1970s brought to an end the optimism of the 1960s as the "development decade" and the hopes pinned on the Alliance for Progress. Poverty, hunger, and social inequality persisted, despite expensive aid programs and huge loans. American liberals motivated to improve the world—to using American power for "good"—were reeling from the realization that their programs had hardly dented the surface of global problems and, even more, that American power might not be so "good" after all.

In such a context, Ford officials in Latin America, who had seen a recent military coup in Brazil followed by severe repression, were reasonably optimistic about Chile's prospects. Chile's democracy was resilient and deeply embedded. More foundation money was invested in Chile, per capita, than in any other country outside the United States.[123] Conditions for "success"—meaning a modern, developed, technocratic state—were good. Ford officials described Chile as at a stage of development "comparable to the Rostowian stage of 'take-off.' "[124] The coup, thus, was a shock. *It broke apart networks built over two decades of foundation investment.* Intellectual freedom—the very cornerstone of independent, critical inquiry—had been crushed in Chile. And it was *intellectual freedom* in particular that Ford chose to focus on in its responses to the coup: defining the conditions for research and teaching freedom as the basis of whether or not to invest any further funds in extant institutions *or* in new groupings that were being formed. Yet Ford chose to continue funding economics programs at Catholic University, despite the involvement of many economists there in precoup economic planning and the *general* support there for the military coup and regime. Ford stressed—as ever—the necessity of apolitical, technocratic research. In the long run, Ford and other American foundations were successful in generating the kind of technocratic outlook that they associated with a modern state. Crisis proved to be a fundamentally important condition of that success.

HUMAN RIGHTS OR PROTECTING VALUABLE HUMAN ASSETS?

An internal report by Ford shows that after the military coup, foundation officials chose to focus on "preserving" the "valuable human resources" of which their knowledge networks were constructed.[125] Naturally, Ford wanted, during the brutal coup and its repressive aftermath, in which thousands were arrested (approximately 13,000) or killed (approximately 2,700),[126] to focus on the academic community it had helped build and thereby preserve "valuable skills."[127] But, according to Puryear, Ford excluded assistance to "confirmed political militants."[128] At the University of Chile alone, at least two thousand academic staff (22 percent of the total) were dismissed.[129] Ford chose to grant $500,000 to several of its previously funded organizations to help "rescue" scholars it had funded or who worked in "program-related fields."[130] The aim was to ensure internal and external refugee scholars' "productive employment" through travel grants, fellowships, or salary-support supplements. The foundation was in "network-preservation" mode. CLACSO, for example, relocated 650 Chilean intellectuals by the autumn of 1974, and LASA and WUS resettled 227 academics in Canada, the United States, and Britain. The report declared that Ford "achieved most of its objectives":[131] the network was saved, bringing "great honor on the Foundation."[132]

Yet according to Ford's Richard Dye, the tougher decisions were still to be taken concerning the regime in Chile and Ford's relationship to it, as well as whether to continue operating in the country. Dye argued that the situation in Chile was so repressive, even by March 1974, that it bordered on "the totalitarian," with a regime "called by history to eradicate the influence of dangerous and subversive intellectual currents embodied in 'foreign ideologies' and the 'social sciences.'" There was a "sustained and comprehensive process underway to purge Chilean institutions of any independent thinking and capacity for autonomous action" directed not just at Marxists but "all the social sciences (except interestingly enough, *economics and administration*) and groups of left-center and center persuasion as well as the left." At Catholic University, teaching and research in economics was prevented from criticizing the "capitalist–free enterprise model" and needed to stress its "technocratic" credentials.[133]

Kalman Silvert defined Chile as a "totalitarian" state "in which the individual stands naked before the power of the state, unprotected": no press freedom, the constitution cast aside, no political parties or civil government,

intellectual freedom crushed, trade-union leaders "killed, imprisoned, ter-
rorized. . . . Fright appears to have become an instrument of governmental
policy." Silvert argued that "*it is impossible to follow a legal life in contemporary Chile*," and "the Foundation *must not be subversive of the regimes within
which it operates*," he concluded, heavily implying Ford's withdrawal from
the country.[134] Despite this, Dye argued that Ford should remain in Chile to
conduct what he called "option-broadening programs," "maintain . . . major
Foundation grantees," and to "preserve the Chilean intellectual tradition
and the recruitment and training of the next generation of intellectuals,"
whether in or outside Chile, "in a private center" or "safe havens."[135] Puryear
drew the same conclusion: despite massive repression, "the Foundation's
extensive record of past activity argued against a sudden withdrawal," and
there remained " 'space' . . . for activities . . . that were *pluralistic* in nature."[136]
That, indeed, was the position taken by foundation officials.[137]

One consequence of the coup—which sits somewhat at odds with the
very practical nature of Ford's immediate responses—was questioning
within the foundation itself of the entire paradigm of Rostowian modernization theory. In December 1973, Ford Program Officer Nita Manitzas attacked the "wantonly optimistic" theories that mere American "technical
know-how" and economic growth would generate economic development
and liberty.[138] Such economic determinism, she argued, led to massive investment by Ford in university-based economics throughout Latin America.
"The transferability of North American wisdom and technique," Manitzas
argued, "was an article of faith running through much of the Foundation's
program," including blind faith in assisting "apolitical" planners and the
like. Development was one long unbroken story of success: this was wrong,
Manitzas contended: "Development" did not adequately feed, house, educate, or clothe people; indeed, "development" exacerbated extant inequalities and began to polarize societies, eroding the "political middle," as had
happened in Chile. The foundation's backing of economics and other social
sciences resulted in "schizophrenic" outcomes: the backing of technocratic
economists capable of joining a brutal military regime while turning a blind
eye to state violence, alongside a more critical set of sociologists. In the
future, Ford needed to take account of this history, Manitzas concluded. By
any measure, this was a remarkable critique of the foundation's programs
over two decades across Latin America, if not the world. Yet, it exemplifies
the very depth of the crisis within the foundation. Even so, Manitzas was an
outlier, a critical and largely ignored keeper of the foundation's conscience.

Kalman Silvert agreed: the foundation had believed that "economics is 'infrastructural,' the basis of all," a value-free science at the heart of development and modernization. The coup in Chile and Ford's subsequent conference on Chile, Silvert argued, forced Ford to accept that knowledge was not value free. But this begged another question: if knowledge is not value free, what should Ford's values be, and how should they be expressed? Silvert argued that Ford should travel from problem solving to problem "finding"—Ford should in future listen more to locals in defining the problem in the first place and then "turn to helping others 'find' the solutions." This was a significant reconceptualization of the nature of Ford's "intervention" in Latin America.[139] *In combination with Manitzas's arguments above, it indicates a desire on the part of some Ford officers even more deeply and profoundly to intervene in Latin American life.*

At the postcoup Ford conference at which the above arguments were aired, the Socialist Party's Ricardo Lagos, the former head of economics at the University of Chile, argued for Ford funding to a wider range of organizations, including those without an institutional base because of the military repression. The alternative was that "much of social science in LA [Latin America] may die," bringing the discussion back to practicalities: what was Ford going to do in postcoup Chile? And this raises an interesting distinction not noted in this book at an earlier stage: *that a difference appears between elements of Ford's own officials—not trustees/officers or New York versus field office, but between trained social scientists and those in more overtly bureaucratic roles.* Those of social-scientific backgrounds tended to see the coup and its aftermath far more as an existential problem, invested with far greater meaning and import, while those who may be seen as more "bureaucratic" in orientation tended to see the issue in more practical terms. In the end, though, both Manitzas and Silvert, the social scientists, for all their existential probing, were practical enough to see that ultimately decisions were necessary—they wanted radically to shift the focus, however, to permit local people (though they did not say who those locals might be, and where trained, and in which social-scientific traditions) to take the lead. As Silvert noted, although "you cannot live without a definition of policy," the question remains: " 'who defines the problems?' How do we test, express, establish priorities?" Ford was wrong, he argued, to think that creating "technical men" would solve problems. The fact is that "men create reality, not the other way around. It is an error to let the ten problems defined on the Op-Ed page of the *New York Times* determine what we define as problems." At the same time, he critiqued the navel gazing underway at Ford: it was too attached to the past. Perhaps the structure and limits on Ford, as noted at the very head of this chapter, were real after all: *there were limits on Ford's internal liberalism that could not cope with the logical extension of some of the arguments advanced by Silvert and Manitzas—a radical shift in power away from Ford as an American organization to one more or less completely in the hands of "locals"*: Ford as enabling authentic, locally led development.

Ricardo Lagos offered a diagnosis of how Chile had reached its crisis point, arguing that social scientists were themselves to blame, indulging in "ideological debate," identifying their institutions with political parties, hollowing out pluralism, and leaving academics vulnerable. The coup had forced a change and brought greater clarity: "In Chile, many social scientists are now trying to join up with people to whom they were previously opposed, in order to save the disciplines." The issue was, to Lagos, "how to maintain certain persons (leftists) who are not politicized but who want to remain in Chile."[140] Osvaldo Sunkel also noted that research does not stop with the closing of an institution—it could continue anywhere, just as academic refugees from Europe had managed in the 1930s. Peter Bell summed it up: they were no longer "institution building" but trying to maintain "social science in and of itself."[141] As William Carmichael noted at the end of one conference session, Ford investments in Latin American social science were historically so strong that they would, of themselves, generate new outcomes in regard to postcoup Chile. *There were indeed grounds for optimism, even as military repression gained force.*[142]

In the concluding session of the OLAC conference, Lagos made a plea for Ford to focus on its core mission: "Ford's business is ideas," he noted. Ford should fund work that leads to theoretical insights that, in the long run, will "resolve the problems of the poor." Latin American social scientists had, for example, developed dependency theory and should continue to be funded to create "new explanatory concepts and paradigms rather than frittering away limited resources on problems like rural poverty."[143] "*The creation of a scientific community . . . could be an end in itself for the Foundation*," one Ford official (Peter Cleaves) argued.[144]

Ultimately, Ford's strategy for postcoup Chile contained elements of all three viewpoints advanced, though not in equal measure. The "bureaucratic" perspective of Dye, Bell, and Carmichael, dovetailing with Lagos, Sunkel, and, incidentally, Foxley's preferences, predominated: Ford programs continued in Chile to protect "their" intellectual assets for future use. The social scientists—Silvert and Manitzas—successfully initiated a deeper analysis of what Ford stood for and should do. And, as Cleaves is cited above as saying, in the end Ford was all about building and maintaining knowledge networks—indeed, it was "an end in itself for the Foundation."

Nita Manitzas provides a summary of Ford's programs for independent and refugee scholars after 1976 when, in addition to the $265,000 granted to CIEPLAN, Ford allotted $343,000 to preserving a measure of "critical, constructive, intellectual 'space' and dialogue in a stringently authoritarian setting."[145] Manitzas argues that Ford's main concerns were to prevent a "lost generation" of scholars by preserving the scholars most closely associated with Ford in the past who might develop alternative paths for future development. This was no charitable exercise, she argued: funded scholars and groups had to conform to "international standards" of research and demonstrate "relevance" to the "realities and trajectory of the Southern Cone."[146] $206,000 flowed to Chilean researchers to those ends, collectively helping to "strengthen the infrastructure for the local social science community."[147] The fact that Ford funding was used to leverage other organizations' support demonstrated the "multiplier effect" of the foundation's work. To Manitzas, research quality by 1980 was "far better than it was before the rash of military coups" in Chile, Argentina, and Uruguay, but this was mainly attributable to the fact that only the hardiest, most committed, and patriotic of social scientists were still active.[148]

Another report, by Elizabeth Fox (assisted by Manitzas), stressed that private research centers were trying to develop ways of "bringing together . . . economic efficiency . . . with social equality,"[149] an early indication of the rejection of Chile's historical statism and the embrace of a sort of "social" neoliberalism.[150] That Chilean scholars were unusually susceptible to external influences was also noted: they suffered from "excessive dependence . . . on international financing . . . [because] the staff . . . must constantly be 'selling' projects in order to survive."[151] It was not only Ford, however, that was funding research in Chile: the American Enterprise Institute was donating funds to the Corporacion de Estudios Publicos, which was directed by Pinochet's daughter, to justify "a new technified democracy." CIEPLAN, however, operated on a "dissident model," or what Silva calls a "dissident technocracy,"[152] networking with MIT and others to disseminate inside and outside Chile research critical of the military's economic policies.[153] Indeed, CIEPLAN was extraordinarily productive: by 1980, Foxley's organization had produced a series of thirty-two essays, twenty-three technical notes, twenty-one short articles, nine books, and a number of articles in the press. They had held numerous seminars in specific policy areas including education, health, housing, military doctrine, inflation, and unemployment. CIEPLAN members were on the advisory boards of CLACSO, the American SSRC, and the Woodrow Wilson International Center for Scholars, among others. CIEPLAN was actively trying to address the military regime's claim that the economy would fall apart should there be a return to civilian government. CIEPLAN implicitly accepted the basic thrust of the military's formulation, however, and worked to show "how this [economic] disequilibrium can be managed in the short and mid-term."[154] According to the economist and CIEPLAN member Patricio Meller, the organization attempted to moderate popular demands for a return to state intervention in favor of incrementalism and gradualism. Chile had had enough radical experimentation—from Frei's revolution in freedom through Allende's socialism and Pinochet's shock therapy—and required stable, technocratic governance. Writing in 2007, Meller claimed that CIEPLAN adopted a new approach—"growth with equity"—a variation of the Anglo-American "third way."[155] After the first postmilitary administration took power in 1990, CIEPLAN supplied the Aylwin government with its minister of finance (Foxley), minister of labor (Rene Cortazar), budget director (Pablo Arellano), and research director of the central bank (Ffrench-Davis), among others.[156] CIEPLAN recognized the significance of adapting Chile to the new environment of globalization.[157] Much later, as president of Chile, Ricardo Lagos adopted the same approach to economic policy.[158]

In addition to CIEPLAN, Ford funded umbrella organizations, such as the Academy of Christian Humanism (affiliated with the Catholic Church), FLACSO, and VECTOR (Centre for Economic and Social Studies). Those organizations sheltered scholars who had been forced out of the universities. FLACSO's work in Santiago was provided $383,000 by Ford from 1974 to 1978. The problem, however, with FLACSO was that its projects were rather amorphous, unfocused, and eclectic and therefore unlikely to get much funding from international sources, which wanted to sponsor "empirical 'problem-solving' projects."[159] The Academy of Christian Humanism (ACH), established by the Catholic Church in 1975, was an umbrella organization under which marginalized scholars could gather with a degree of protection. VECTOR was the secular equivalent of ACH, sponsoring workshops, seminars, and lectures and publishing working papers and a monthly bulletin. It also focused on the organized-labor movement in Chile. VECTOR, ACH, FLACSO, and CIEPLAN, among others, were divided by political party and religious affiliation but united by opposition to the military, leading them increasingly to organize joint activities.[160] Such groupings were fundamental, according to Chilean scholars, in establishing "the communicational, ideological, cultural, and, in part, political infrastructure that enabled later . . . a whole civil society [to spring] up again with relative force. . . . Without those ten years of work, the resurgence [of civil society] would probably have been much weaker, narrower, and slower."[161] With strong international networks as well, Puryear notes that Chile's "dissident intellectuals remained firmly connected to the global academic mainstream."[162]

Ford's postcoup programs—in conjunction with numerous other international agencies—were ultimately successful: they helped to sustain a strong, vibrant, intellectual infrastructure that combined party, nonparty, and church-based umbrella organizations and active research centers producing "realistic" analyses and critiques of Chilean economy, society, and government. Ford supplied an average of $800,000 per year to Chilean research and other groups throughout the 1980s.[163] The elimination of much of the "hard" left and the driving underground or dispersal abroad of most of its leaders by the military regime meant the silencing of Marxist voices in the dialogues within the new or reconstituted knowledge networks Ford and others had sustained throughout the 1970s and 1980s.[164] As Osvaldo Sunkel noted in 1993, "the political spectrum . . . now tends to converge towards central positions [and thereby] attenuate, moderate and reduce controversies, to avoid addressing them."[165] Indeed, these networks—usually headed by Christian Democrats—nurtured and incubated a "moderate" counter-hegemonic bloc against military rule that was pragmatic enough to "realize" that much of the military's economic program could not and should not be reversed,[166] nor should the military be prosecuted for human-rights violations that included thousands of killings, torture on a grand scale, and hundreds of thousands imprisoned and exiled.[167] Ford's programs not only created "spaces of liberty"; they also created the spaces within which Chilean thinkers transformed their own self-concepts and concepts of political rule.[168] They used the spaces financed by foreign agencies to engage in radical self-criticism, talked across political parties for the first time, and integrated former politicians with strong academic inclinations and educational backgrounds.[169] Ricardo Lagos established the Party for Democracy in 1987 while remaining chair of VECTOR, and Alejandro Foxley became even more active in the Christian Democratic Party.[170] It was in the crucible of intellectual "realistic" ferment, in the heat of a military regime, that Chile developed a "democratic" Socialist Party that rejected revolution and embraced "representative democracy," making possible "a unified opposition" movement.[171] Without such infrastructural support in those critical years, built upon decades of previous investment in Chilean "human capital," it is highly unlikely that Chileans would have been able to mobilize and win against the military in the 1989 plebiscite and garner strong support from the international community, particularly the major financial institutions of the neoliberal "Washington consensus."[172]

CONCLUSION

Ford's programs in Chile were ultimately profoundly successful: they generated networks of scholars linked with political and state organizations and affected the course of Chilean political and economic development. To be sure, Ford was not at all supportive of Pinochet's military regime—but the foundation was, at least in part (along with the Rockefeller Foundation and ICA/USAID), responsible for the creation of a community of neoliberal economists who were ready with a radical economic plan to root out statism and install the free market as an institution and as a discipline in all areas of life. This is a point upon which Ford officials remained almost completely silent, even when soul searching after the military coup; they did not accept their own responsibility in creating the knowledge communities that put their expertise to use in such radical ways and without regard for human-rights violations. They preferred to view economics as a set of analytic and methodological techniques rather than as an overtly ideological and political force for radical change. Indeed, it may be said that Ford and other American agencies were hardly disturbed by the advent of free-market economics per se: they objected to the complete silence of the neoliberals on the social effects of economic policies (much as they worried about the economic inefficiencies of Allende's social policies). Yet they seemed more disturbed by Allende than Pinochet: leftist economists received no funding at the University of Chile after 1970, even though Catholic University's Chicago boys continued to receive funding four years after the military coup, for which they had actively prepared in advance. According to Huneeus, the economic policies and repressive actions of the Pinochet regime were complementary, the latter making considerably easier the implementation of the former.[173] In creating a network of centrist research and semipolitical organizations during the Pinochet years, Ford generated the basis of the transformation of a diverse and divided set of academic and political exiles into a powerful centrist force for Chilean reform. Once again, their pre- and postcoup investments overlapped and reinforced one another, creating an opposition cadre of scholars for political and technocratic rule in the 1990s. Three decades of investing in Chilean universities finally paid dividends, as that country's social scientists and its political class came to accept the "Washington consensus" under conditions of globalization and market discipline.[174]

In his book on Chile's intellectual communities, Jeffrey Puryear fully recognizes the power of networks as a technology of (democratic) change. His conclusion is especially noteworthy, particularly from the perspective of the central argument about network power—as an end in itself and as the means of attaining ends otherwise not publicly stated by American philanthropy—advanced in the current study. Puryear argues that it is vital that funding bodies establish "*networks even when their precise impact cannot be determined in advance.*" Such networks—composed of well-trained scholars, "institutions, standards, colleagues, debate, and international contacts"—were "a stock of high-level human resources" for the time when "democracy returned." "Sustained investment in creating a stock of talented social scientists can qualitatively change a country's political culture and its political technocracy."[175]

AMERICAN POWER AND THE MAJOR FOUNDATIONS IN THE POST–COLD WAR ERA

When the Cold War ended, so did the United States' principal rationale for its global role, its "military-industrial complex," and a large number of its national security policies. The "Soviet threat," the existence of an expansionist and aggressive communism orchestrated from Moscow and threatening world peace and American national existence and security, was no more. American power, which this study suggests *had its own expansionist and hegemonic purposes*, required a new rationale for continued global engagement. This was particularly important because of insistent demands for a "peace dividend" after the Cold War—"payback" for sacrifices made to retain a massive military budget to fight the Red Threat: social programs to tackle domestic poverty, health care, educational underachievement, spiraling inner-city crime, falling living standards, and increasing social and economic polarization.[1]

One aspect of a new rationale for U.S. power came in the form of *promoting democracy*, which, especially after the terror attacks of 9/11, *objectively* "unified" liberal internationalists, conservative nationalists, and neoconservatives. While democracy promotion is an old idea, it gained new impetus in the form of scientifically established "truth": democratic peace theory (DPT). This represented a fundamental rhetorical shift in the rationales of U.S. national security: the United States was now promoting democracy as the principal source of global security and peace. Critically, at the same time, DPT encouraged the identification of zones of the world that were anti- or nondemocratic and their categorization as *threats*: nondemocracies were by definition more warlike, unstable, likely to back terror groups, and to threaten the world by acquiring weapons of mass destruction (WMD).

The world was now divided between *zones of peace* and *zones of turmoil*, the latter requiring pacification through democratization.

DPT effectively contained in it the logic of capitalist globalization, interpreted as it was as the promotion of "*market* democracies." DPT, then, was reshaping the contours of the global political order and justifying capitalist globalization: open societies and open markets went hand in hand. However, just as there were "rogue" states threatening the global peace, so were there those excluded from the benefits of capitalist globalization—unable to compete in the market—who were sources of disorder and political instability. They required action from the United States/West, and the role of leading state and interstate agencies, foundations, and other nonstate actors was to *humanize globalization's harsher aspects*, much as the Big 3 had been doing for almost a century at home and in the Third World. This was a form of *social* neoliberalism[2] not dissimilar to the post-Pinochet regime in Chile in the 1990s.

After 9/11, these tendencies sharpened: DPT became even more overtly a source of unity in the U.S. foreign policy establishment, which almost unanimously backed the "Global War on Terror" against "Islamofascism," as some called it.[3] 9/11 also revived interest in area studies but in a new form, one shot through with interest in *Islamic* area studies and the need for greater understanding of the religion, its adherents, their languages, and the causes and methods of religious "extremism." The 2003 U.S.-led war on Iraq and the continuing war in Afghanistan sharpened the demand for scholarly knowledge of these countries, cultures, and languages.

The war on terror—of which the 2003 Iraq war and subsequent U.S.-led military occupation of the country are part—did not go (quite) according to plan during the George W. Bush administrations (2001–2009): critical voices grew on the issue of *coercive* regime change and democracy promotion, the war's *ultimate* (though mainly post-facto) rationale, along with Iraq's nonexistent WMD. There was also much public and opposition party clamor on America's rising global unpopularity, greatly amplified by exposés of human-rights violations in U.S.-run detention camps, including Guantanamo Bay (Cuba), Abu Ghraib prison (Iraq), and Bagram Air Base (Afghanistan). In that context, the foundations backed (mildly) "critical" inquiries better to represent the Establishment: the Princeton Project on National Security, for example. They would continue the war on terror but broaden the range of security threats faced by the United States to include global pandemics and climate change, develop strategies to more effectively combat "anti-Americanism," and secure the United States/West *better* than Bush. In many respects, President Barack Obama's Democratic administration (2009–) and its national security strategy (2010) embody the continuation of the war on terror *without* Bush.

The big American foundations, as ever, backed the general "resetting" of American foreign policy, as they see the world and America's role in it from the same perspective: they backed capitalist globalization strategies; indeed, they were drivers of globalization itself. The world continued to require active American leadership—a Soviet-free world was one of turmoil and instability requiring continued intervention both humanitarian and military. It was also an opportunity *to remake the world more closely to conform to America's self-image*. In addition, of course, new powers were emerging requiring integration and accommodation into the U.S.-led global order—China, for example, and India. Despite dramatic shifts in the global distribution of power, therefore, the major foundations' mission hardly altered: they remained committed to a U.S.-led global order with institutions that have embedded within them values and interests congenial to the United States.

This chapter reflects the changed world and programs of the foundations. It explores their roles in promoting and consolidating two overarching and complementary frameworks of American power in the post–Cold War world: an economic order signified by capitalist globalization and a growing recognition of the necessity of various amelioration strategies, including forums to hear the voices of globalization's critics, and a political/security order characterized by an upsurge in U.S.-led democratization. The chapter then examines the radical upsurge in "anti-Americanism" in the wake of the U.S.-led war on Iraq and growing anxiety about America's global role. It also examines the foundations' roles in renewed attempts to combat anti-Americanism and develop "new" concepts for American power that might make it more acceptable to the world. There will be a special focus on the activities of the German Marshall Fund of the United States (GMFUS) and of the Princeton Project on National Security (PPNS), both significantly reliant on funding from the Big 3 foundations. Finally, and very briefly, the chapter considers the role of the major foundations in the development of Islamic subjects that witnessed growth after 9/11, despite the relative decline in area studies funding after 1991. The evidence indicates the degree to which Islamic "area" studies reflect state imperatives. This is not to say that they have no life of their own; it is to argue that the dominant changes therein tend to reflect the broad interests of the U.S. state and elite foundations for the reasons argued throughout this book: there is no duping of individual scholars involved or required. Rather, objective structures of financial power and intellectual legitimacy offering large grants for major programs of policy-relevant research and study are practically irresistible for scholars and their institutions. As a result, *the kinds of problems identified* and the more or less broad *manner of their treatment* tend to reflect the dominant elites' thinking, within the kinds of institutions that the foundations and U.S. state have backed for the past century.

Globalization and Global Civil Society

The historical experience of the Big 3 foundations of building national and international networks finds its contemporary expression in the hectic bid to create a global order that *suits, extends, and defends* globalizing capitalism.[4] As Thomas Friedman argues, the world today is characterized by "integration and webs" as well as by an unequal distribution of benefits. Effective globalization requires global institutional architecture as well as supportive global civil society, for the same reasons that an industrializing and "nationalizing" America one hundred years ago required a national civil society—a series of densely networked publics composed of strategic minorities—to provide its social base. The Big 3 foundations, among other newer American foundations, are at the very heart of these developments today. They are actively supporting existing international organizations and promoting new organizations more suited to global conditions. The overall strategy remains unchanged, even as programs and personnel change: Americanized or American-led globalization remains the aim. It is also clear, however, that American foundations are not alone in this venture, though they remain the most significant actors.

American philanthropy tops the world league, although foundations are now a feature of practically every continent. Since 1987, the number of foundations in the United States has grown from 28,000 to about fifty thousand. The new foundations hold some of the enormous growth in wealth in the 1990s. Their assets expanded from $115 billion in 1987 to over $300 billion, and their international giving topped $3 billion in 2002. Record increases in international giving were recorded from the mid-1990s, which is attributable to the rise of new fortunes, especially Bill Gates's Microsoft Corporation, as witnessed by the formation of the Bill and Melinda Gates Foundation.[5] The terrorist attacks of September 11, 2001, however, dealt a temporary blow to the trend, although they focused greater attention among foundations on the global sources of domestic problems.[6]

Increasingly, European, Japanese, and Australian foundations are engaging in international activities. There are over sixty thousand foundations currently operating in the "old fifteen" EU states. In Italy, of the over three thousand foundations surveyed by the European Foundation Centre (EFC), half were founded after 1999. Over 40 percent of German foundations were set up in the decade up to 2004. Their combined assets total over £100 billion, with the Wellcome Trust topping the league, with assets of £10 billion. Increasingly, European foundations are engaging in cross-border and global activities, with 30 percent already doing so and 68 percent expressing an interest in doing so in the future. Further legal reforms to simplify and incentivize international philanthropy are the subject of reform campaigns backed by the major foundation networks. The EFC's Europe in the World initiative—to project European philanthropic and political-cultural influence onto a global stage—is driving increased linkages between European foundations and international organizations (Organization for Economic Cooperation and Development, UN Development Program), corporations, and an array of global networks such as the Transatlantic Community Foundation Network and Network of European Foundations for Innovative Cooperation. The world is dense with foundations, foundation networks, and networks of networks.[7]

In the era of America's *rise* to globalism, the foundations constructed and promoted, at home and abroad, *liberal-internationalist* versions of Americanism. In the era of *globalization*, they promote a "transnational" Americanism that backs the neoliberal project but seeks to blunt its harsher edges.[8] The foundations today are *replicating* their historical strategies at home and abroad; they seek to protect the existing system of power by engaging in activities to ameliorate the negative consequences of that very system of which they are both a central component and beneficiary.[9] As a "Break-out session [on] Globalization" at a meeting of the International Network for Strategic Philanthropy (INSP) concluded, "foundations' portfolios have benefited from globalization."[10] At the beginning of the twentieth century, the foundations targeted the alleviation of domestic poverty and the slum—brought on by urbanization and capitalist industrialization; today they focus on the worldwide social fallout of neoliberal globalization.[11]

The IMF and the World Bank are widely considered, along with the U.S. Treasury, to be the motors of neoliberal globalization.[12] Founded at Bretton Woods in 1944–1945 with full support from the Rockefeller/Carnegie foundations, they continue to garner sustenance from East Coast philanthropy. As is shown below, the World Bank has received grants from the Ford Foundation, and David Rockefeller has been a consistent IMF stalwart.[13]

As was historically the case when American foundations often carried out programs that the state would not or could not, it is also the case today— given the dramatic loss of state legitimacy associated with Reaganomics and Thatcherism—that nonstate actors are scurrying to perform key functions. Offsetting the fallout of increasing gaps between rich and poor has become a key foundation task, especially by backing "pivotal institutions that can shape behaviour away from risk factors and *dangerous directions* [i.e., anti-Americanism and anti-globalization protests]," according to the Carnegie Corporation.[14] Part of the solution is seen to lie in "promoting democracy, market reform and the creation of civil institutions,"[15] that is, in the neoliberal project itself. Carnegie actively promoted, during the 1990s, "Partnerships for Global Development," headed by prestigious academics and politicians, that promoted liberalization of markets as a core concern. Contrary to Peet et al., neoliberal globalization's foundation backers do not see a wide gulf between neoliberalism and its critics: by their social amelioration policies, they hope and claim to promote the market *and* social justice.[16]

The Rockefeller Foundation declared in 1985 that the reduction of social inequality lay at the heart of its economic developmental concerns. In 1999, the incoming president of RF, a former vice chancellor of the University of Sussex, Gordon Conway, stressed that the foundation had two priorities: "first, to understand the processes of change spurred by globalization and second, to find ways that the poor and excluded will not be left out." Inherent in foundations' attitudes is the taken-for-granted neoliberal character of globalization.[17] Therefore, it is unsurprising that the third of what some may call an "unholy trinity," the Ford Foundation, granted the Hudson Institute, a conservative think tank, $150,000 to assist "economists and officials of Estonia, Latvia, and Lithuania [to] develop plans to transform their economies and integrate them into the world economy."[18] To examine the consequences of market reforms, Rockefeller administered a project, at a cost of

$150,000, toward "an exploration on trade liberalization and its impacts on poor farmers."[19]

American foundations support the key engines of globalization. For example, Ford awarded a grant of $400,000 to the World Bank to fund the latter's "Consultative Group to Assist the Poorest to develop the capacity of microfinance institutions and improve member donor practices in supporting microfinance."[20] Microfinance is a strategy for lifting into the marketplace those too poor to get loans from mainstream commercial banks. The Ford Foundation claims some credit for the development of microcredit in Bangladesh, the forerunner of the Grameen banking system. Critics argue that Grameen has hardly dented poverty, increased poor-family indebtedness, and played into the hands of corporate investors.[21] In 1999, RF granted $800,000 to the World Bank's Economic Development Institute for economic growth acceleration strategies.[22] Further Ford grants were made in 2003 to institutions that try to build interconnections between large Western corporations and small enterprises in the Third World.[23] During the 1990s, the head of the Rockefeller family—David Rockefeller—offered unconditional support for the IMF's global programs, without which the world would return to the economic crises of the 1930s and the threat of global economic and military conflicts.[24] A Rockefeller grant of $250,000 aimed to finance "strategic workshops and meetings among Asian government officials, academics and civil society groups on the governance of the World Trade Organization."[25]

American foundations are globalizing forces in their own right, too,[26] consciously strengthening global knowledge networks between universities, think tanks, government agencies, and philanthropies.[27] The International Network for Strategic Philanthropy (INSP), set up by the German Bertelsmann Foundation—with U.S. foundations' support—encourages the global spread of philanthropy. The (American) Philanthropy Initiative, Inc., aims to ensure the "strategic and systematic investment of private philanthropic resources to address complex, interconnected manifestations of chronic underdevelopment." RF has backed several initiatives to train a new generation of global givers. Similar programs are run by the Ford, Hewlett, Kellogg, and Charles Stewart Mott foundations. Even philanthropy-strengthening groups have access to a network of support groups such as the Council on Foundations and the European Foundation Center. Global givers are further networked with regional and national philanthropies such as the Asia Pacific Philanthropy Consortium and to international networks and associations such as the World Economic Forum, which, in turn, has its own global social-investors program.[28]

In that context, the grants information that follows is the tip of a very large iceberg. The Ford Foundation granted $400,000 to the Academy for the Development of Philanthropy in Poland (ADPP)—which grew out of a USAID project—to strengthen foundations locally. A Ford grant of $220,000 supports efforts to link Polish and Belarusian NGOs. Relatedly, Ford awarded $500,000 to the Brazilian Association of NGOs to help organize the World Social Forum (WSF), a body developing "alternatives to current patterns of globalization."[29]

The Ford Foundation is an enthusiastic though controversial supporter of the World Social Forum (WSF). Indeed, private corporate and philanthropic funders are the second-largest donors to the WSF, acting as a brake on WSF's critique of capitalist globalization. FF has invested well over $1,000,000 directly in WSF to help it organize events and globally to disseminate its message.[30] At its third annual meeting, WSF attracted one hundred thousand delegates from 156 countries—feminists, trades unionists, and so on. According to Michael Edwards, the director of the Ford Foundation's Governance and Civil Society unit, WSF changed the "terms of the debate about globalization. . . . There's [now] an inescapable public debate about the role of corporations and the distribution of globalization's benefits . . . largely due to the WSF crew."[31] WSF, with the FF's and others' sponsorship, promotes critiques of some of the "negative side effects of market liberalization: growing economic disparity, the privatization of health care and environmental degradation." The ultimate aim, according to Ford's Edwards, is a "global civil society," the influence of which would bear comparison to the effects of the Bretton Woods system formed during World War II.[32] WSF aims to construct "an alternative development model and to construct a new form of globalization."[33] A Carnegie Corporation grant of $25,000 assists "dialogue on globalization between representatives of the World Economic Forum and the World Social Forum."[34] A Ford grant of $500,000 to the London School of Economics aims to help scholars explore "the depth of global governance and its accountability to a polity," another reformist measure promoted by all three major U.S. foundations.[35]

The WSF, however, is the subject of much criticism. For example, MumbaiResistance argues that WSF is funded by Western agencies "to mitigate the disastrous projects of development cooperation and structural adjustment programmes" they have themselves organized.[36] They claim WSF's sponsors have co-opted antiglobalization forces and channeled them away from "direct and militant confrontation . . . into discussions and debates that are often sterile, and mostly unfocused and aimless." Some participants at WSF meetings complain that they are expected mostly to "listen" to WSF leaders rather than to participate; the aim was "putting a human face on globalization." The World Bank refers to the WSF as "a maturing social movement," and the bank's officials have been granted observer status at WSF meetings. WSF's supporters include Brazil's President Lula, the head of the Workers' Party and a proponent of IMF policies and U.S. free-trade agreements and opponent of peasants' land struggles. WSF acts, ultimately, to blunt the harsher edges of capitalist globalization.[37] The 2004 organizers of WSF meetings, in Mumbai, India, refused Ford's donations because of Ford's role in India's Green Revolution, which created and exacerbated the problems of poor farmers.[38]

WSF meetings in Nairobi, Kenya, in 2007 attracted similar criticism from African organizations. According to one source, the meetings were dominated by mainly "white North[ern]" NGOs, while southern voices were underrepresented. The meetings were also sponsored by large corporations with exclusive rights at WSF. Indeed, WSF meetings had the feel of a "trade fair," while poor attendees were forced to take direct action merely to gain entrance to meetings. The atmosphere was decidedly apolitical, and there was little in the proceedings to suggest that politics is principally about struggles between "the haves and the have-nots."[39]

A recent academic study of the Nairobi WSF concludes that WSF operates less like the leading force behind a counterhegemonic project opposed to neoliberalism and more like a source of entertainment—a "court jester" rather than a "postmodern" prince. In developing ever closer links with organizations at the very heart of neoliberal globalization, WSF has been co-opted by the very forces it was established to displace.[40] Gramscians argue that the major states, global corporations, philanthropies, and other forces are a "nascent historic bloc" that develop policy and "propagate the ideology of globalization" even within organizations that are promoted as alternatives to it.[41]

Attention now turns to the intellectual underpinnings of the political counterpart to corporate globalization—the promotion of *market* democracies by the United States in the post-Soviet era.

Democratic Peace Theory: A New Rationale for American Power

"Democratic peace" is the underlying theoretical basis of the foreign and national security policies of President Barack Obama (as it was of his defeated Republican rival, Senator John McCain). Democratic president Bill Clinton championed "democratic enlargement" and "democratic engagement" in the 1990s, and promoting freedom and democracy was pivotal to the Bush Doctrine.[42]

This section demonstrates the significance of foundation-funded knowledge networks to the rise of DPT from a relatively obscure theory of social science to a broadly accepted basis of national policy. Of course, no claim is made suggesting that foundation networks alone translated such ideas into policy; the intellectual space opened up by the end of the Cold War played a key role, as did 9/11, in such developments. But in an uncertain post–Cold War world, the social-scientific "certainties" promised by DPT proved decisive. The fact that there was support for DPT from across the political spectrum made its adoption more likely. Without DPT—which could operate either unilaterally or multilaterally, peacefully or coercively—U.S. foreign policy might not have a concept that could cohere its identity or supply it a "value-free," "scientific" post–Soviet era rationale. From the intellectual straitjacket of Cold War containment mentalities, in which almost anything could be justified if it diminished Soviet influence, DPT offered a scientifically proven and easily comprehended "law" of international behavior.

Development of Democratic Peace Theory

Democratic peace theory provides democracy promotion with intellectual legitimacy; it has gained widespread acceptance in the academic community and spawned a productive "research program."[43] Going even further, Jack Levy (in his Carnegie Corporation–funded study) calls DPT the only "empirical law" of international relations.[44]

Below are explored the origins, development, and rise to scientific law and established political practice of DPT, initially by the Ford (and, later, MacArthur) Foundation–funded scholar Michael Doyle, in the 1980s, which led to significant theoretical reorientations among liberal internationalist scholars in the American political scientific and international relations

(IR) community as well as to the "democratic engagement" orientations of the second Clinton administration (1997–2001). The second, though overlapping, line of development encompasses the work of Larry Diamond, the Hoover Institution scholar closely associated with the Democrats' Progressive Policy Institute, the "democratic enlargement" agenda of the first Clinton administration, and the Council of the Community of Democracies.

Though traceable back to Immanuel Kant, it was Michael Doyle in three articles in 1983 and 1986 who placed the issue firmly back on the academic agenda. This was in part done with funding from the Ford Foundation from 1979 to 1982.[45] Ford allotted $409,735, for a three-year period, to the overall project, "Support for Research on the Future of the International Economic Order,"[46] of which $90,000 was granted to Doyle and Miles Kahler, for a three-year study on global North-South economic relations. The project included an examination of the influence of ideology on international economic relations. Doyle was also interested in testing "a number of theories of foreign policy that posit regular connections between state and society, interest and ideology, tradition and contemporary response, and systemic position and economic strategy." The project emphasized the increasing levels of economic differentiation among Third World states. When the more developed Third World states—"the Kenyas, Ivory Coasts, and Taiwans"—liberalized, they would begin to form a "party of liberty."[47] The seeds of Doyle's subsequent work on the "liberal peace" are present in his Ford-funded project. The "party of liberty" on the world stage has reappeared as the Concert of Democracies. Of course, there are other important sources of Doyle's ideas on DPT and of their subsequent impact. For example, it is vital to recognize that Doyle's initial overt foray into DPT was "serendipitous"—the need to address a student meeting at short notice. It is also evident, however, that bringing the ideas to publication required space and time, for which Doyle graciously expressed his appreciation to the Ford Foundation. For his later work on the matter, Doyle acknowledges his debt to the MacArthur Foundation.[48]

Ahead of Doyle's 1983 article, however, President Ronald Reagan had declared the inherently "peaceful" character of "liberal foreign policies" in a speech in London in 1982 and, later, established the National Endowment for Democracy (NED) to promote democracy. The birth or modern rebirth of "liberal peace theory" in its sophisticated sense was Doyle's work, yet it also coincided with the Reagan administration's aggressive anticommunism, providing an ominous warning about the uses of academic theories by policy makers, as Doyle himself had cautioned.[49] Of course, Doyle's DPT contained an appreciation of the "liberal peace" as well as a critique of "liberal imperialism." Successive American presidents have taken aspects of DPT and used them for purposes unintended by its original authors. Undeniably, however, Doyle's theory was located within a broadly liberal framework that emphasized the idea that free markets were also sources of world peace, echoing Reagan's economic liberalism.[50]

LARRY DIAMOND AND THE CLINTON ADMINISTRATION

Diamond, a liberal hawk, is a key figure in the migration of DPT from academia to policy makers. An academic at Stanford, he has co-edited NED's *Journal of Democracy* since 1990, was closely associated with the Progressive Policy Institute (PPI) of the Democratic Party, and contributed an important study on democracy promotion to a Carnegie Commission in 1995. A leading member of the Council of the Community of Democracies, Diamond served the Bush administration in Iraq as a senior adviser to the Coalition Provisional Authority (January to April 2004).

Diamond introduced DPT to the PPI and the Clinton administration. Diamond's PPI Policy Report, *An American Foreign Policy for Democracy*, enunciated the basic principles of DPT and *extended* the peace thesis to argue that democracies are more reliable as trading partners, offer more stable "climates for investment [and] honor international treaties." Welcoming the end of the Cold War, Diamond urged the United States to seize the opportunity "*to reshape the world*" and transform attachment to global "order and stability" into openness to reshaping national sovereignty to enable American interventions abroad. Diamond emphasized America's "*scope to shape the political character of the entire world for generations to come.*"[51] Linking idealism with realism, Diamond claims that America's own security is protected by democratizing other nations, providing a strategically compelling reason to make democracy America's mission. Indeed, Diamond argues that democracy promotion offered a viable alternative to President George H. W. Bush's "New World Order," which, Diamond argues, was obsessed "with order, stability, and 'balance of power'—often at the expense of freedom and self-determination." Finally, Diamond argued that the United States should form a new "association of democratic nations" to mobilize rapid "action on behalf of democracy."[52]

Diamond's unique contribution was to introduce DPT to Clintonite thinking. The PPI helped harness academic ideas to Clinton, as shown by Clinton's speech in December 1991, which paraphrased Diamond's report. For example, Clinton noted President Bush's attachment to "political stability . . . over a coherent policy of promoting freedom, democracy and economic growth." Democracy does not merely reflect our "deepest values . . . [it] is vital to our national interests." But even more than Diamond, Clinton stressed the dangers of the "new security environment" in which to build on "freedom's victory in the Cold War."[53]

Clinton more sharply "securitized" DPT, dividing the world into democratic and autocratic zones, the latter being a new threat to the former.[54] As Buger and Villumsen argue, "creating the certainty of democratic peace . . . increased the uncertainty about the relations between democratic and non-democratic states . . . thinking in terms of a zone of democratic peace also created a vision of a 'zone of turmoil.' "[55] Clinton's national security adviser, Tony Lake, noted in 1993 that Americans should now "*visualize our security mission as promoting the enlargement of the 'blue areas' [of the world] of market democracies.*"[56] Lake, who proclaimed Clinton's foreign policy as "pragmatic neo-Wilsonianism,"[57] overtly promoted enlargement as "*the successor to a doctrine of containment,*" the substitution of a defensive concept for an active and expansionist one.[58] In the same securitizing vein, Deputy Secretary of State Strobe Talbot noted that America operated in "the new geopolitics: *defending* democracy in the post–cold war era."[59] To Joseph Kruzel, DPT provided a preemptive strategy for national security, eliminating threats "by turning a country into a democracy."[60]

Note, however, that DPT needed additional ballast if its potential of global transformation was fully to be exploited by U.S. national security managers. As Smith notes,[61] democratic transition theory also had a role to play, and Diamond merged the two approaches. The net effect is to argue with "certainty" that not only does democracy guarantee peace but that it is also straightforward for states to transition toward it rapidly. Diamond's theoretical synthesis is exemplified in his work for Carnegie's Commission on Preventing Deadly Conflict. In *Promoting Democracy in the 1990s*, Diamond suggested that democratic transitions need not be hamstrung by historic or "societal pre-conditions." He argued that "the precarious balance of political and social forces in many newly democratic and transitional countries" provided "international actors . . . real scope to influence the course of political development." Using the language of security, Diamond suggested that democratic states prioritize democratic transitions in countries of "importance . . . to their own security and to regional and global security," selecting countries for transition that could "serve as a . . . 'beachhead' for democratic development."[62]

The Clinton administrations worked actively to construct a "Community of Democracies" along the lines indicated in Diamond's PPI Report. Championed by Secretary of State Madeleine Albright, a Council for the Community of Democracies (CCD) was founded in 2000, in Warsaw. The CCD's formation may be viewed as the continuation of a process of dividing the world into zones of democratic peace, of transition/turbulence, and the rest—and of increasingly hardening the boundaries as a precursor to greater pressure on some powers to democratize. The CCD was especially interested in engaging with nations that were in danger of backsliding on democracy during the "turbulent transition" that had been identified by Mansfield and Snyder.[63] As a result, CCD developed a number of regional groupings of democracies and a Democracy Caucus at the United Nations. It is very much an American enterprise funded from numerous sources, including the U.S. Department of State and the Rockefeller Foundation.[64]

The coincidence of the Cold War's end with the rise of Bill Clinton's presidential ambitions presented an opportunity for DPT—via scholar-activists like Diamond—to go straight from opposition platforms to policy-making circles. In its migration from academia to the state, however, DPT became militarized: words like "threat," "national security," "zones of peace," and "zones of turmoil" became increasingly associated with "peace" theory. DPT was transformed into political technology, establishing "certainty" among policy makers looking for fresh orientations and a higher moral purpose for American power.[65]

HARVARD AND THE DEMOCRATIC PEACE

If Diamond was a critical link to the Clinton administration at its formative stage, Harvard's Belfer Center for Science and International Affairs was crucial to DPT's "maturation" and legitimacy. Belfer's policy-oriented journal, *International Security*, despite (or perhaps in defense of) its realist leanings, played a key role in elaborating DPT by publishing a series of articles, followed by a "reader" in 1996. Specializing in policy-relevant articles,[66]

Maliniak et al. note that *International Security* is one of the twelve leading journals in the field and that security-studies specialists are the keenest of IR scholars "to engage the policy community," with 30 to 60 percent of articles addressing policy issues, in contrast with 10 to 20 percent of such articles in other IR journals. *International Security* has consistently been among the top five most cited IR journals.[67]

The 1996 "reader" was partly funded by support from the Carnegie Corporation,[68] and the Belfer Center has long received support from the Ford Foundation.[69] Belfer, part of the Kennedy School of Government, funded by the Kennedy family, turned its attention to the "lessons of Vietnam" in the late 1960s, examining the misuses of history and historical analogies by national security managers.[70] Belfer continues to enjoy linkages with the major foundations. For instance, David Hamburg, a former president of CC, is a member of Belfer's International Council. In 1997, the Carnegie Corporation granted $700,000 to the Belfer Center for work on "new concepts of international security and formulating policy recommendations." CC emphasized the work of the center in identifying the "*conditions favorable to the 'democratic peace' hypothesis . . .* whether U.S. foreign policy should seek to promote democracy . . . [and] the hypothesis that many democratizing states undergo a volatile transition in which they tend to be relatively more likely to engage in war."[71] The center's advisers and fellows also include Robert Zoellick, president of the World Bank and former deputy secretary of state; William Perry, Clinton's secretary of defense; Paul Volcker, chairman of the Federal Reserve Board (1979–1987); the historian Niall Ferguson; and General John Abizaid, commander of U.S. Central Command. More recently, Paula Dobriansky, the Bush administration's undersecretary of state for democracy and global affairs, joined Belfer as a senior fellow. With over one hundred scholars and practitioners from the worlds of business, government, and the military, Belfer is a university-based think tank; its principal aim is to "advance policy-relevant knowledge."[72]

Promoting democracy occupied a key place in the pages of *International Security* in the 1990s, especially because President Clinton "was an explicit believer in the democratic peace hypothesis."[73] The complementarity of theory and practice were made clear in *Debating the Democratic Peace*: "the question of the democratic peace also has practical significance. If democracies never go to war with one another, then the best prescription for international peace may be to encourage the spread of democracy. . . . The spread of democracy would reduce the likelihood of threats to the United States and expand the democratic zone of peace." However, the editors warn, the theory, if wrong, could lead the United States into "major wars and years of occupation."[74]

It was also in *International Security* that Snyder and Mansfield strengthened DPT and dampened the Clinton administration's ardor for democracy promotion.[75] Deputy Secretary of State Strobe Talbott indicated his familiarity with debates in *International Security* over the democratic peace and specifically of Mansfield and Snyder's article.[76] In their article, Mansfield and Snyder noted that democratizing states are more likely to go to war than mature democracies, especially in the first decade, because old elites mobilize nationalist appeals to compete in the democratic regime, which, in turn, reinforces new elites' own nationalistic rhetoric, making it even more difficult to control newly mobilized publics. Should the fledgling democracy collapse, the returned autocracy is likely to wage war. The lack of durable stabilizing institutions in new democracies make it difficult to form stable coalitions and policy coherence. Mansfield and Snyder suggest that the West help promote pluralism through long-term engagement, minimizing the "dangers of the turbulent transition."[77] Their article was originally published in *Foreign Affairs* (May–June 1995) before its publication in *International Security* in its summer 1995 issue. This may well have been its principal route to the Clinton administration, which, as we know, switched from democracy promotion to democratic engagement in the late 1990s.

In a number of subsequent writings, Mansfield and Snyder developed their arguments along the above lines. They published *From Voting to Violence* in 2000, funded in part by the Ford and Carnegie foundations, and *Electing to Fight* in 2005, supported by Hoover and Belfer. In these and other works, Mansfield and Snyder argued for concrete steps to encourage the development of the rule of law, a neutral civil service, civil rights, and professional media *ahead* of the holding of elections in would-be democracies.[78] The emphasis had shifted from immediate democracy to the building of the institutional bases of *stability*. In 2005, criticizing the Bush administration's crude interpretation of the possibilities of DPT, Mansfield and Snyder implicitly complimented the Clinton administration's nuanced approach.[79] The authors argued that for democracy to succeed, it was necessary that such states go through *sequenced* development of the preconditional bases of democracy. This is arguably the more nuanced approach pursued by the Obama administration.[80] Mansfield and Snyder's work has not rejected DPT; more accurately, they have developed it along "realist" lines so as to make its implementation more effective.[81]

Clearly, DPT became influential only after the Cold War—principally with the Clinton administration—and only after it had been legitimized by policy-oriented elite knowledge institutions. In the process of moving from academic theory to foreign policy, however, the "peace" theory was "securitized."

Further to the political-ideological right, Francis Fukuyama's championing of DPT[82] had also set in train a movement among neoconservatives more militantly and aggressively to pursue DPT to its "logical" conclusion: forcible regime change. Interestingly, groups such as the Project for a New American Century (PNAC) were actively engaged with Clinton's Pentagon by 2000, and Fukuyama became prominent in the Princeton Project on National Security, headed by John Ikenberry and Anne-Marie Slaughter, as well as Tony Lake and George Shultz, on which more below.

The evidence above shows the influence of DPT. Conceptually, from Clinton to the neoconservatives, there occurred a change in the way the purposes and justifications of American power were thought about. America's liberal values and its national security interests were unified by DPT. Symbolically, DPT legitimized American preponderance in a world made dangerous by rogue and terrorist states that were undemocratic and brutal, harbored terrorists, and threatened the peace. Intervening against such regimes further secured America's self-image as a good state—all while maintaining powerful armed forces and military budgets at near Cold War levels and heading off demands for a "peace dividend." The instrumental influence of DPT is seen in the Clinton era and, perhaps, most clearly, in the post-9/11 Bush Doctrine and the war on Iraq that followed.

However, in practice, the processes by which DPT became so dominant in policy circles were neither straightforward nor predestined to succeed. DPT was initially ignored. Later, its influence ebbed and flowed. It had its triumphalists, more sophisticated supporters, and critics, especially among realists, and there were competing paradigms. Its influence relied on a combination of unforeseen events and shocks as well as powerful networks that both promoted and refined the theory. Jentleson shows it took a specific mindset—that of a former policy planner and college professor, Tony Lake, as opposed to the lawyerly secretary of state, Warren Christopher—to concretize Clinton's espousal of "almost pure Kantianism" in his 1994 State of the Union address.[83] Yet, it has continued to exert influence regardless of the party in power.[84]

COMBATING ANTI-AMERICANISM IN THE BUSH ERA

The militarily aggressive Bush era, rationalized as promoting democracy and freedom, witnessed a spectacular increase in levels of anti-American-ism on a worldwide scale, particularly in the wake of the 2003 Iraq war, which acted as a catalyst that brought to the surface general anxieties about American power, including U.S.-led globalization.[85] American power was seen as disreputable and unjust across wide swathes of global opinion. While the Bush administration made renewed attempts to rebrand Amer-ica through various initiatives, private foundations set to work to reform public diplomacy more effectively to alter global perceptions of American power. The section below examines the attitudes and activities of the Ger-man Marshall Fund of the United States (GMF), a relatively new operat-ing foundation that received funding from Ford and Carnegie to combat anti-Americanism and develop transatlantic dialogue. The point is that Ford, Carnegie, and Rockefeller foundations were willing to fund elite "fire-fighting" activities as well as grander plans to develop "alternatives" to the Bush doctrine.

The GMF's [86] funders include Ford and Rockefeller philanthropies, the CFR, NATO, and US AID.[87] GMF's programs are essentially focused around two *complementary* goals: promoting transatlantic cooperation and combating anti-Americanism in Europe, by building collaborations between U.S. and European elites, including academics, journalists, policy makers, business leaders, think tanks, and philanthropies. Its projects are designed to develop "innovative solutions" to transatlantic problems, "an opportunity for American voices to be heard in Europe and for European voices to be heard in America, and for both Americans and Europeans to be heard throughout other world regions." GMF locates itself at the center of numerous global networks that include universities, mass media, the U.S. Congress and Senate, the European Union, industrialists' organizations such as the Confederation of Indian Industry, and George Soros's Open Society Institute.[88]

In 2003, GMF engaged in a wide range of activities to build transatlantic cooperation. GMF financed a survey of *Transatlantic Trends* across seven

European countries and the United States. In June, GMF organized a symposium of twenty-eight American and European think tanks, shadowing the official U.S.-EU summit. The symposium analyzed diverging attitudes toward the Middle East and on global trade and examined "the prospects for resolving the tensions" between the power blocs. Presentations of the findings and recommendations were made at the U.S. Capitol by U.S. Congressman Doug Bereuter; Pat Cox, president of the European Parliament; Marc Grossman, undersecretary of state for political affairs; and George Papandreou, Greece's foreign minister. Continuing the examination of European-American divergent-opinion consideration, GMF arranged a special "Strategic Discussion with Henry Kissinger" for emerging German leaders.[89] Finally, GMF launched the Trade and Poverty Forum (TPF) in February 2003, with the aim of developing U.S.-European and Third World leaders' dialogue on those matters. Its first report, "Restoring Trust in the WTO: The Challenge for Cancun," was followed up by "attention to how to respond to the breakdown of trade negotiations in Cancun, and how to advance broad development goals." The TPF consists of six delegations from the United States (headed by Robert Rubin, former secretary of the treasury),[90] Japan, India, Brazil, South Africa, and Europe. The TPF wants to "focus on rebuilding the confidence of developing countries in the importance of world trade for their economic well-being" and to "educate the press and public about the importance of US-EU leadership on trade and development matters."[91]

An important part of GMF's work since 2000 has been its annual meetings of "Emerging Foreign Policy Leaders" at Lake Como, Italy. This program is conducted in partnership with the Bertelsmann Foundation and the Center for Applied Policy Research. Over thirty U.S.-EU leaders—"from a range of professions, from the private sector and media to government and think tanks"—examined the causes of transatlantic division, the Israeli-Palestinian conflict, "the future of international organizations such as the UN and NATO; economic and financial interdependence; and what steps can be taken to renew and rebuild transatlantic relations."[92]

The GMF has a significant research fellowships initiative. In 2003, Britisher Mark Leonard was awarded a fellowship to travel in the United States. Leonard was director of Prime Minister Tony Blair's think tank, the Foreign Policy Centre, and the editor of a book, *Re-Ordering the World*, a call for a new "liberal imperialism" in the wake of 9/11. Leonard asserted that "[Osama] Bin Laden is an aftershock of the mistakes made after 1989" by presidents George H. W. Bush and Bill Clinton and by Prime Minister John

Major,[93] an echo of the perspectives shared by the Bush administration and the neoconservative Project for the New American Century (PNAC).[94] An essay in the same volume by Robert Cooper, a former Blair foreign policy adviser, serving Foreign Office diplomat, and adviser to Javier Solana, the EU's high representative for foreign and security policy, argued that the world was divided into three kinds of state: postmodern, modern, and premodern. In Cooper's view, the EU and United States are, more or less, in the postmodern camp and are obliged, for their own security, to cooperate in dealing with Al Qaeda and other terror bases in premodern states.[95] In so doing, they need to use any means necessary, including "force, pre-emptive attack, [and] deception," a series of strategies associated with Anglo-American aggression in Iraq in 2003.

Among its past fellows, the GMF's Transatlantic Fellows Program cites a roster of prominent figures from academic, political, and business life, including G. John Ikenberry (Princeton), Christopher Makins (Atlantic Council), Lee Feinstein (CFR), Ellen Bork (PNAC), Barry Posen (MIT), Cindy Williams (MIT), and John Harris (*Washington Post*).[96]

GMF is actively doing, in its own way, what some Americans claim that the U.S. government is not—a long tradition in American philanthropy. The context of the GMF's programs may be set by its president's writings. In an important article in *The National Interest*, President Craig Kennedy advanced the argument for more effective attempts by the U.S. administration to combat anti-Americanism and better promote the country's image.[97] Also in 2003, Kennedy was one of twenty-nine prominent Americans—including Lynne Cheney, William J. Bennett, James Q. Wilson, and Walter Russell Mead[98]—who contributed to a right-wing volume, *Terrorists, Despots, and Democracy: What Our Children Need to Know*. Its central argument was that the terrorist attacks of September 11, 2001, were sourced in the hatred of American values and freedoms and had *no relation whatever* to American foreign policy. Any arguments to the contrary, the volume stridently argued, were misguided and unpatriotic.[99]

In his article in *The National Interest*, Kennedy argued that anti-Americanism was being inadequately tackled by the American administration; indeed, the United States has a "public diplomacy crisis" of rising anti-Americanism in Europe, as erstwhile allies turn against the United States "in droves." The United States needed a "serious campaign to open European minds to our positions," drawing on how historically the *CIA and Ford Foundation* battled anti-Americanism during the Cold War. In particular,

Kennedy focused on the anticommunist Congress for Cultural Freedom (CCF), which has been unfairly portrayed as a "CIA front."[100] Its principal achievement, despite its failure completely to stem the tide of European anti-Americanism, was to "nurture a nucleus of thinkers and activists who were open to American ideas and willing to engage in serious discourse on the major issues of the day."[101]

In the wake of 9/11 and the Iraq War, it is vital, according to Kennedy, to recognize the correctness of Robert Kagan's views vis-à-vis American military strength and European weakness.[102] While there are differences of opinion and worldview, there are also important areas of cooperation and convergence—especially on terrorism and globalization—upon which the United States should try to make "more palatable" U.S.-European differential capabilities, "by building a base of support for active engagement with America." Kennedy advised the Bush administration to take four steps: first, public diplomacy to mobilize public opinion; second, more overseas travel to Europe by administration officials to *debate* policies and issues; third, more financial resources for public diplomacy information officers; and finally, to ensure that the kind of public diplomacy engaged in be active, explanatory, and combative and not merely an exercise to "re-brand American foreign policy, re-brand diplomacy," as Colin Powell's efforts had tried in vain to do.[103]

Recommending a strategy that resembles and complements the programs of the GMF, Kennedy urged the administration to "support those European political leaders and intellectuals who are willing to take the increasingly unpopular stand of backing America." We need to ensure both that the "good news" gets out about American policy and also "to knock down slander of the United States in a comprehensive and timely fashion." As an example of such "slander," Kennedy points to "unfounded" allegations of torture and mistreatment of prisoners at Guantanamo Bay: in fact, they were only "shackled and blindfolded [as] reasonable precautions . . . while the detainees were being transported."[104] The administration's diplomatic machinery alone, however, is too slow, inflexible, and unskilled to meet current needs.

These sorts of challenges require serious intellectual combatants. This means a critical mass of writers, thinkers and diplomats who can engage editorial boards, join the television talkshow circuits, participate in internet chatrooms, operate websites—not to mention debate Europe's scholars, business leaders and university students alike. Above all, it means developing a broader, non-partisan network of like-minded individuals on both sides of the Atlantic who are dedicated to the cause of keeping the idea of the West and its ever expanding community of liberal democracies alive.[105]

PRINCETON PROJECT ON NATIONAL SECURITY (PPNS)

Hoping to emulate the impact of George Kennan's "containment" concept, the Princeton scholars G. John Ikenberry and Anne-Marie Slaughter received Ford and Carnegie funding for their attempt comprehensively to resurrect American power in the wake of the Bush administration's war on Iraq. Its political significance lies in the fact that the project was close to Democratic opponents of the Bush administration, including Vice President Joseph Biden. Indeed, several former Princeton Project participants and leaders were appointed in 2009 to the Obama administration, including Anne-Marie Slaughter, who heads up the State Department's policy planning staff; James Steinberg, Kurt Campbell, and Philip Gordon in the State Department; and Michael McFaul at the National Security Council.[106] Robert Cooper, the British diplomat, was also a PPNS participant.

PPNS, funded to the tune of $240,000 by the Ford Foundation, in addition to funds provided by the Carnegie Endowment for International Peace and GMF, developed the basis of an "alternative" national security strategy to that of President George W. Bush, as proclaimed in the latter's 2002 national security strategy. Although not a blueprint for specific policies, the PPNS's *Final Report* claims to supply the underlying principles to guide future American administrations' national security strategies. Given its scholarly credentials and the policy-related experience of its participating individuals and organizations, the report has been of some significance in its contribution to the development of post-Bush bipartisan national security thinking.

PPNS is an example of scholarship in the service of the state (broadly conceived). Its scholarly claims of social-scientific rigor and thorough analyses of history[107] were compromised by the requirement to produce a document that hoped to guide "hard-headed" policy influentials. Its critical attitude to the Bush administration underlined its own *relative* "centrism," in contrast to the former's excesses and extremism. Its more or less completely uncritical overt and covert belief in the United States as the "good," peace-loving, freedom-promoting, "well-intentioned" but "misunderstood" or "envied" nation underlines the PPNS's nationalistic-patriotic intellectual underpinnings. Its underlying liberalism was highlighted by the uncritical claim that "American values" were/are universally applicable and therefore ought to be spread worldwide. The underlying narrative of America as "victim" of foreign military and terrorist aggressions—from Pearl Harbor in 1941 to 9/11—as the source of America's desire to be the world's leader, reflects the self-image of the most unreflective U.S. foreign policy makers. The report's characterization of all violent opposition, particularly in the Islamic world, to U.S. foreign policy as "a global insurgency with a criminal core" is further evidence of the same, as is its sidelining of scholarly research that yields evidence of the rationality rather than religiosity of such opposition.[108]

PPNS was a group of organic intellectuals intimately connected with an American hegemonic project to reshape the post-9/11 world. This project works by embedding American values, practices, and interests into existing and new international and regional organizations, expanding concepts of U.S. security to foreign ports and territories, penetrating other societies that constitute possible future threats, increasing American military spending in the context of building new international alliances, and institutionalizing the rules of preventive war. In short, the Princeton Project urges America to take the lead in creating a liberal global order protected by a "concert of democracies" operating outside the UN system but (apparently) upholding the latter's values.

The *Final Report* bears all the hallmarks of a product of the liberal-internationalist community, reading as a reasonable, apparently nonideological analysis and set of proposals. Its constituent working groups took over two years to come to their conclusions. The document is reasonable enough to critique the idea that there is one *single* threat to the United States around which to construct a unified framework for national security. The "war on terror" cannot supply the rationale to counter global climate change, natural disasters, and pandemics, for example. Multiple threats require multiple strategies and tactics. The report concedes that other states and peoples might see things differently than the United States and that other states ought to be consulted before American-led action. It argues against reflexive unilateralism and promotes the development of internationally agreed-upon rules for preventive wars. It argues for a two-state solution to the Israel-Palestine question, for talks with Syria and Iran, and for the integration of China into the American-led global order. It argues for the greater effectiveness of U.S. power by *combining* soft power with its hard power. It is argued here, however, that the above merely made the PPNS's proposals more worrying, as they were more likely to gain broader political acceptance: their very "reasonableness" being more superficially palatable than the Bush administration's mixture of evangelism and ideology—especially given the pervasive sense of crisis in the U.S. war on Iraq.

According to the PPNS's own rationale, "we"—the United States or the world, it is not entirely clear—exist at "a moment of critical global transitions." The project's aim was to "strengthen and update the intellectual underpinnings of U.S. national security strategy."[109] According to Anne-Marie Slaughter,[110] the Princeton Project was based on the work of "leading U.S. academics and policy makers and informed by consultation with top thinkers around the globe" and formally launched in May 2004. In attendance, among other notables, was the former national security adviser and secretary of state Henry Kissinger.

Ambitious in vision, the project's organizers tried to replicate the achievements of Princeton's George F. Kennan, the scholar who headed the State Department's Policy Planning Staff and the renowned architect of the anticommunist "containment" doctrine. The PPNS was a self-conscious attempt "to write a collective 'X article,'" to replicate Kennan's (then anonymous) 1947 *Foreign Affairs* article, which publicly launched the doctrine of containment. Of course, the world is more complex than it was in 1947, and Kennan's intellectual power was practically unmatchable. Hence, the project became a collective endeavor that ultimately involved around four hundred scholars, policy makers, former officials, businessmen, and other influentials. Nevertheless, the aim of the report was nothing less than to "set forth agreed premises or foundational principles to guide the development of specific national security strategies *by successive administrations in coming decades.*"[111]

From May 2004, the project convened and published seven working groups' findings on a range of national security challenges. The seven groups were grand strategy, state security and transnational threats, economics and national security, reconstruction and development, anti-Americanism, relative threat assessment, and foreign policy infrastructure and global institutions. Seventeen working papers were commissioned "on critical security topics." A series of nine conferences followed in the United States and abroad—including at the Council on Foreign Relations, Oxford, the Brookings Institution, the universities of Texas and Tokyo, and the Truman

National Security Project—to solicit input on numerous working papers and on the draft strategy. The project culminated in the production and dissemination of a ninety-page *Final Report* on national security, *Forging a World of Liberty Under Law*. Acknowledging that there were numerous other ongoing efforts to develop grand strategy for the United States, the project aimed comprehensively to link all efforts together and "to build on overlapping areas of consensus in charting America's future course."[112] PPNS, therefore, saw itself as strategic in elite consensus building, hoping thereby to exercise wider influence.

The PPNS claimed to be above party politics, as it was headed by George Shultz, a former secretary of state in the Reagan administration and close confidant of Condoleezza Rice, another former secretary of state, and Tony Lake, a former national security adviser to the Clinton administration. Its nonpolitical character is further suggested by its funding by David Rubinstein (a leading financier with the Carlyle Group), the Ford Foundation, the German Marshall Fund for the United States, and the Carnegie Endowment for International Peace. It was launched at an event on Capitol Hill sponsored by the New America Foundation, presided over by the Republican realist Senator Charles (Chuck) Hagel and the Democratic internationalist Senator Joe Biden.

A detailed analysis of the links of the sixteen leaders of the PPNS—i.e., the executive director, the two co-chairs, and the thirteen members of the steering committee—shows their close links with the Ivy League universities, Council on Foreign Relations, and the foreign policy agencies of the American state (mainly pre–Bush II era).[113] This evidence, while not unexpected, is important, because it boosts the Gramscian argument that PPNS represents a group of organic intellectuals who tend to see the problems of state and society from the perspectives of the dominant elites and institutions that sustain them. The above institutions are, as Robert Brym argues, vital agencies of socialization that nurture intellectuals, develop their modes of thought and, importantly, provide the bases of their successful integration into elite institutions. Intellectuals not so institutionally integrated, it is argued, are much more likely to exhibit radical and critical thought and action.[114] Although casting themselves as "outsiders"—people whose voices are unheard in the White House—the evidence suggests that the PPNS's leaders were completely immersed in policy organizations that reside very close to the centers of American elite power. As is argued below, PPNS cannot sustain a claim to be a genuine alternative—a counterhegemonic force—as its orientations and outlook were so close to those of private elite and statist forces and even shared the underlying view of the Bush administration that American values are universal and should be exported to the rest of the world.

Some 398 individuals are listed in the PPNS's final report as having participated in the project since May 2004. Alongside each name appears an affiliation—usually one but sometimes two—that represents that person's qualification for participation. Before setting out the main results of that analysis, it is worth listing a few notable participants: Henry Kissinger (President Nixon's national security adviser and secretary of state), Zbigniew Brzezinski (President Carter's national security adviser), Stephen Krasner (then head of the State Department's policy planning staff), Richard Haass (former head of the policy planning staff in the State Department in the Bush administration and currently president of the CFR), and Fareed Zakaria (the editor of *Newsweek International*). Prominent scholars include John Mearsheimer (Chicago), John Lewis Gaddis (Yale), Graham T. Allison (Harvard), Walter Dean Burnham (Texas), and Stephen Walt (Harvard). William Kristol (editor of the *Weekly Standard*), Charles Krauthammer (*Washington Post*), Robert Kagan (Carnegie Endowment for International Peace), and Barry Rubin (Interdisciplinary Centre, Israel, and *Middle East Review of International Affairs*) represented their respective neoconservative viewpoints in the project's various consultations and conferences. Contributors from the "left" of the academic-political spectrum included Bruce Cumings (Chicago), Emily Rosenberg (Macalaster), Tony Judt (NYU), and Ian Roxborough (SUNY).

The project's 398 participants operated, in effect, partly to reinforce the essential liberal-internationalist character of its leadership group and to open some space for critiques from out-and-out (conservative) realists such as Stephen Walt and John Mearsheimer and neo-conservative "Wilsonian realists" such as Kristol, Krauthammer, and Kagan. PPNS was an Establishment project to "replace" the Bush agenda with something more palatable to leadership groups within both main parties. Its overall conservatism underlines the words of the leading neoconservative, William Kristol: the impact of the neoconservatives has been such that there is no going back to isolationism, no way to drift away from democracy promotion or Iraq.[115] That is, even if the PPNS is evidence of a galvanization of centrist forces in the American foreign policy establishment, the right has shifted the center itself further rightward, one of the effects of the conservative ascendancy starting in the Reagan era. Indeed, it appears from the PPNS's report that their principal claim is that they can do a lot better than Bush and the neoconservatives in securing America, fighting criminal terrorism, promoting democracy, and so on, despite retaining the underlying values and assumptions of the Bush administration.

ANALYSIS OF FORGING A WORLD OF LIBERTY UNDER LAW: U.S. NATIONAL SECURITY IN THE TWENTY-FIRST CENTURY

Securing the homeland against hostile attacks or fatal epidemics, building a healthy global economy, and constructing "*a benign international environment*" grounded in security cooperation and the spread of liberal democracy should constitute Washington's basic objectives, according to the PPNS's *Final Report*. It was published in July 2006, in the very middle of Bush's second term (2004–2008), when criticism of the U.S. war on Iraq was commonplace across the political spectrum. Disenchantment with the Bush strategy was reflected in the emphatic victory for the Democrats during the midterm elections of November 2006—in which they gained control of both the Senate and the House of Representatives—which many predicted signaled the death of the Bush Doctrine of unilateralism, preemption, preventive war, and militarism.

The following sections consider the report's uses of history, its attachment to democratic peace theory, its attitude to the United Nations, and the role of global networks in American power.

The report's view of "history" is instructive: Pearl Harbor taught Americans interdependence and that unchecked foreign aggressors would eventually threaten the United States: "Rather than recoiling in isolation from great power politics, we decided . . . to play an active and leading role in the world" (PPNS, 16). That is, an innocent America was rudely awakened by an unprovoked military attack on its territory by a power to which it had done nothing, a version of U.S.-Japanese relations that may be comforting though not entirely accurate.[116]

The postwar "transformation of the Soviet Union from ally to adversary" and the threat of economic depression further strengthened American resolve behind "global involvement" (PPNS, 16). The uncritical assertion of the "Soviet threat" as a key cause of America's very neutral-sounding "global involvement" is also worrying, given the weight of historical scholarship on the question.[117] According to the report, it was NSC-68 that brought together all the strands of an enduring national security strategy and stressed the necessity of building a "healthy international community," as the United States "needed then, as we need now, a 'world environment within which the American system can survive and flourish'" (PPNS, 16). That the drive to develop and sell to the American public the aggressive message of NSC-68 was led by the militaristic Committee on the Present Danger receives no acknowledgement in the *Final Report*.[118]

Combined with such realizations and a response in terms of containment, the Truman administration inaugurated an era of international institution building to generate a "benign" international environment (PPNS, 15). The IMF, World Bank, United Nations, and NATO, as well as the Marshall Plan, which catalyzed European recovery and integration, helped to create and maintain a state of affairs that "served the interests of many other countries, making it easier to pursue our interests as well." In those days, the "United States led but listened, gained by giving, and emerged stronger because its global role was accepted as legitimate" (PPNS, 16, 22).

This is a version of history presented as uncontested, suggesting that American power is benign, largely reactive and defensive, and relatively enlightened rather than narrowly construed and self-serving. Taking from the past what is best for adaptation to the present appears to animate the *Final Report*. The Truman era is a "golden era" of relative prosperity, security, and order, which we need, in today's conditions, to reinvent, as "the world seems a more menacing place than ever" (PPNS, 11): "it means safeguarding our alliances and promoting security cooperation *among liberal democracies*, ensuring the safety of Americans abroad as well as at home, avoiding the emergence of hostile great powers *or balancing coalitions* against the United States, and *encouraging liberal democracy and responsible government worldwide*" (PPNS, 16; emphasis added).

The Princeton Project was persuaded of the efficacy of democratic peace theory: democracies do not fight each other, and thus the best hope for the world is democratization (PPNS, 25). Therefore, build alliances of liberal democracies, prevent other great powers or coalitions from threatening the United States, and promote democracy. Critiques of this view are left unaddressed.[119]

This sounds similar to the "neoconservative" orientations of the Bush administration and, of course, to thinking within the *Truman* administration.[120] This is understandable, according to Stephen Walt, as liberal internationalists and neoconservatives share a belief in the essential goodness of American power and the necessity of its use for global improvement.[121] That is why many liberal internationalists—some of them involved in the Princeton Project—supported the Iraq war.[122] Both groups also want only America and its allies to own and control weapons of mass destruction.[123] They differ, however, on the role of international institutions, with neocons skeptical, given liberals' stubborn desire for observing international law and, thereby, hindering the realization of American interests. It is clear, though, that the Princeton Project recognizes the limitations of the United Nations, for example, and calls, first, for "radical surgery"—abolition of the Security Council veto—to permit military interventions in sovereign states and, second, for a new organization of liberal democracies that would, in the failure of the United Nations to act, militarily enforce the United Nation's "values."[124]

The overlaps between the Princeton Project's Final Report and Bush's 2002 national security strategy (and the core beliefs of Bush's neocon allies) are many and interesting. Where that national security strategy and the neocons argued for spreading democracy, the Princeton Project argues for spreading "Liberty under Law."[125] Where the national security strategy wanted "a balance of power that favors human freedom," PPNS promotes "maintaining a balance of power in favor of liberal democracies." Both agree that defending and promoting freedom/liberal democracy requires "continued high level of U.S. defense spending" (PPNS, 30). Bush's national security strategy emphasized preventive war, which PPNS endorses against "extreme states" after approval from the United Nations or "some broadly representative multilateral body."[126]

To the PPNS, the UN system is broken and needs reform. Barring reform, the United States should build a new "Concert of Democracies" to enforce international law and deter and intervene against aggressors, brutal states, terrorist havens, and so on. The concert of democracies would be an American-centered alliance that would feature military burden sharing. In practice, the concert of democracies is likely to be an alliance of the United States, United Kingdom, Australia, Canada, New Zealand, and, possibly, India. It is similar to an alliance centered on the English-speaking countries—an Anglosphere[127]—the evolution of a hangover from late nineteenth-century and early twentieth-century Anglo-Saxonism.[128] This reappeared as Federal Unionism in the late 1930s and early 1940s, specifically between the United States and Britain but including its white dominions and Scandinavia.[129] Its racism was underlined by the machinations among its sponsors to gerrymander power away from populous India in a future federal assembly—including techniques borrowed from the U.S. deep South used to disenfranchise African Americans. The proposed concert of democracies may well represent an updated version of this tradition. That is, it appears to be part of an imperial project.

Empire has become in many neocons' and others' eyes perfectly acceptable today. An empire of liberty is not really an empire at all. An empire that promotes and extends democracy is the very antithesis of the old colonial system. And democracies do not fight wars against other democracies. These ideas are endorsed by the PPNS's *Final Report*. There is an expansive sense of "America" in the *Final Report* when it argues that "U.S. borders [should] be defined for some purposes as extending to the port of shipment rather than the port of entry. . . . [American officials should also] . . . strengthen the quality and capacity of a foreign government to control its territory and enforce its laws," a necessary corollary to "defining our borders beyond those established by land and sea" (PPNS, 57). "The Princeton Project seeks to help America to grasp this opportunity to lay the foundations for advancing America's interests on every front, rather than just vanquishing one enemy [global terrorism] . . . *a long-term strategy should strive to shape the world as we want it to be*" (PPNS, 58; emphasis added).

One of the means by which American interests are to be realized is through the power of *global networks* "of national, regional, and local government officials and nongovernmental representatives to create numerous channels for [democratic] nations and others to work on common problems and to communicate and inculcate the values and practices that safeguard liberty under law" (PPNS, 7). The aim is to create intersections between "international institutions and domestic governments . . . institutions providing incentives and pressure to help conquer dysfunctional levels of corruption and bolster the rule of law" (PPNS, 23).

Despite denials, therefore, of an imperial project, the levels of global leadership, global military engagement, degree of penetration of overseas nations—through border, port, and other security cooperation and supervision—interventions through public diplomacy and education—and political warfare—for nipping threats abroad in the bud all suggest that the PPNS effectively endorses an imperial approach to safeguarding American security. Kennan would, surely, have approved.[130]

The *Final Report* of the Princeton Project received wide attention: it was launched on Capitol Hill by Republican Senator Charles Hagel and then-Senator (and now) Vice President Joseph Biden and presented at conferences across the United States normally co-sponsored by the Council on Foreign Relations and at private meetings between Ikenberry, Slaughter, and Senate staffers. Congressmen were lobbied to organize Princeton Project events in their home districts, visits were made to the United Nations to discuss the report, and events were held in China and Europe.[131]

PPNS offered an "alternative" within a new consensus on U.S. engagement with the world and its remaking post-1989 and post-9/11; this is a reordering of the world more specifically under a U.S.-led global system and requires the redefinition of roles of global institutions, alliances, and so on. This process, triggered after 1989 and ongoing since the 1990s and especially after 9/11 includes developments under Bush as well as Tony Blair's thinking on "international community": i.e., it stands rhetorically as "alternative" to Bush in theory but in practice able to go along; it is liberal imperial at its core.[132]

The PPNS report's recommendations were and are an integral part of the liberal-imperial project, not its rejection. It had to be this way, given the objectives of the project, its leadership, and participants as well as the scholar-activists' desire to be taken seriously by policy makers; all of this affected the project's design, leadership, membership, funding, and networks. It was oriented to the U.S. state and therefore had to enter its intellectual frameworks and underpinnings if it was to sound "realistic" as an "alternative" to the state or an opposition party in waiting.[133] President Obama's national security strategy (May 2010) bears more than a passing resemblance to the Princeton Project's *Final Report*.[134]

Surveilling Islamism

Understanding Islamic societies, movements, and ideas today are significant foundation concerns, especially after the decline of area studies in the wake of the end of the Cold War.[135] This section examines some evidence of this recent development in foundations' efforts simultaneously to support the war on Islamic terror and smooth the paths to complete globalization.

"There is rarely a direct link between terrorism and poverty and exclusion. But it is evident that terrorists draw much of their support and justification from those who are, or *perceive themselves* as, unjustly impoverished." So wrote the president of the Rockefeller Foundation in 2002.[136] In addition to those programs, RF also launched a number of area studies–type initiatives to illuminate the nature of modern Islam as a precursor, or in addition, to further interventions in the war on terror and anti-Americanism.

In May 2004, RF allocated $700,000 to a series of conferences on "Muslim Worlds and Global Futures," the title suggesting an interest in examining the Muslim "mind" and its effects on the globalization process.[137] Further initiatives funded by RF on aspects of the "Islamic question" include a series of meetings, new studies, and research fellowship programs. RF also awarded $50,000 to the American Sufi Muslim Association toward the cost of the "Cordoba Dialogues, an interfaith effort to heal the relationship between Islam and America."[138] The Asian Resource Foundation in Thailand was granted $252,000 for its research fellowships program for "young Muslim scholars in the region," entitled *Islam in Transition in Southeast Asia: A View from Within*.[139] Other initiatives explored how Middle Eastern Islam looks from African and Asian perspectives or the nature of "Radical Islamic Organizations in Central Asia," or they are pointedly combative—the Sisters in Islam group, Malaysia, was funded for its meeting in 2003, "Muslim Women Challenge Fundamentalism: Building Bridges Between Southeast Asia and West Asia [i.e., the Middle East]."[140]

Inherent in these initiatives is the idea that the *principal* cause of terrorism and anti-Americanism is *insufficient knowledge and understanding* between communities or a failure to communicate. The initiatives suggest that the foundations, echoing the Bush (and Obama) administrations, believe that the problem lies in people's hearts and minds rather than in any desire to retain national cultures or autonomy from American domination. As Conway told delegates to the International Symposium of the World Conference on Religion and Peace, we must act now to "bridge the potential fissures that terrorism can create. Civilized societies should not fall victim to a manipulation of human understanding." Here, terrorism itself is given an *independent* causal role in spreading misunderstanding between peoples, rather than being seen in any way as *symptomatic* of significant globalization processes.[141]

The Carnegie Corporation has focused on the "problem" of Islam and globalization for some time, even prior to 9/11. For example, in June 2000, CC awarded $237,000 to the University of California–Santa Cruz for "research on Globalization and Islam."[142] This grant should be seen in the context of CC's funding of other studies of the effects of globalization on national self-determination and "ethnopolitics": to UCLA ($312,000 in early 2001), Yale ($445,000 in early 2001), UC–San Diego ($260,000 in 2002), and the University of Pennsylvania ($248,000 in 2000).[143] In effect, this helps strengthen an existing network of American Islamicists, a contemporary version of Cold War students of communism.

Post-9/11, however, a more sharply defined investment strategy has been forged at Carnegie. Its International Peace and Security Program is more pointedly aimed at "global engagement," as "the United States and other states face new global threats and opportunities." In particular, CC focuses on the problems posed by "states at risk for instability" that may be attacked by new "nation-building" measures, a policy now espoused, according to CC, by the Bush administration in Iraq and Afghanistan. According to Carnegie, there are, "on the horizon," "other candidates for external intervention by both the United States and other members of the international community," presenting CC with an opportunity to support efforts at "generating policy-relevant scholarship on the challenges posed by states at risk; and promoting new multilateral approaches to confronting these challenges."[144]

CC funded a plethora of scholars and institutes to study Islamic ideas, political Islam, and terrorism. For example, the University of Maryland was awarded $25,000 to finance a workshop on "non-state actors, terrorism and the proliferation of the weapons of mass destruction"; Robert A. Pape was granted $100,000 to research "The Strategic Logic of Suicide Terrorism"; and the National Academy of Sciences given $220,000 to study "U.S.-Russian challenges in countering urban terrorism."[145] Domestically, there is a growing interest in Arab and Muslim communities in America: in 2003, CC granted Louise Cainkar $100,000 for "A Sociological Study of the Islamicization of Chicago's Arab Community: Implications for Democratic Integration."[146]

Additionally, like Ford, CC also considers the principal cause of anti-Americanism to be in misunderstanding and backs several initiatives to extend understanding. For example, in March 2002, Boston University was awarded $100,000 for its radio stations to develop "programming on Islam and foreign policy," and in 2003, the American University in Beirut received $94,900 "toward a program to promote understanding between the United States and the Islamic world." Likewise, the Brookings Institution received $11,000 in 2004 toward "creating new dialogues between the US and the Muslim world."[147] The ultimate aim of these efforts is indicated in the title of a grant ($100,000) for the scholar Carrie Rosefsky Wickham, in 2003, to research "The Path to Moderation: Lessons from the Evolution of Islamism in the Middle East."[148]

Between 2007 and 2009, Carnegie granted $9.6 million to a range of universities and think tanks as part of its "Islamic Initiative." To build up cadres of Middle East experts engaged with public discourse and policy makers, in 2009 CC gave George Washington University's Institute of Middle East Studies $475,000. The SSRC was granted $3 million in 2009 to "mobilize academic expertise on Muslim regions and communities, with a special set of grants for policy-relevant work on Iran, Pakistan and Afghanistan." The Aspen Institute's program for U.S. congressional representatives to learn of the "contemporary dynamics in Muslim states and networks" received support from CC to the tune of $720,000 in 2008. Squarely located in the heart of the war on terror was the $500,000 CC grant to the Chicago Project on Suicide Terrorism, to "evaluate causes and countermeasures to terrorism, including the fastest growing form of terrorism (suicide attacks), as well as the dynamics of radicalization and strategies such as the 'decapitation' of terrorist groups." The Chicago grant was conditional upon outreach work with "government, academic, media and public forums." Finally, Harvard was awarded $200,000 by Carnegie to develop an online database on "contemporary Islam's emerging schools and identities," including debates on themes ranging from "personal conduct to rights and law, secularism, and the role of women . . . to reflect the most accurate picture of contemporary Islam."[149]

Conclusion

The Big 3 foundations constitute powerful forces for supporting American power. They promote capitalist globalization (or "smart globalization,"[150] as the Rockefeller Foundation now terms it), encourage amelioration strategies to assist (some of) those unable to compete in the global marketplace, and sponsor elite-led organizations that claim to give a voice to those unheard in the halls of power. Or, rather, they sustain forums through which globalization might be "reformed" or humanized. The programs are significant because they assume that there is no alternative to globalization, even though it generates, by its "normal" functioning, huge social and economic inequalities within and between nations and has led to impoverishment on a massive scale.

Interpreted as promoting *market* democracies, democratic peace theory, as the post–Cold War concept of U.S. power, scientifically legitimized America's continued global preponderance. Indeed, DPT—the successor to the doctrine of containment—offered American elites the opportunity to "shape the political character of the entire world for generations to come," according to Larry Diamond. In words that sound prescient a decade after 9/11, Diamond effectively expressed the political functionality of DPT for extending American power. Even more significantly, Tony Lake institutionalized DPT in Clinton's democratic enlargement and engagement programs. In emasculated form, DPT served as the legitimating rhetoric for the U.S. invasion and occupation of Iraq.

The major foundations were critical to the networks that relaunched DPT and articulated it with the Clinton administrations. Their publications in respected policy-oriented journals further refined the thesis and added to its scientific legitimacy. By the mid-1990s, DPT had attained political commonsense status among policy makers. Despite complaints by proponents of the democratic peace that their theory had been hijacked by the Bush administration, it is likely to remain a key element in the U.S. foreign policy arsenal. This was signaled in the very depths of the crises engulfing the Bush administration, in 2006, with the publication of the *bipartisan* report endorsing DPT, by the Princeton Project on National Security. It is now, arguably, central to the Obama "doctrine."

In the post–Cold War and post-9/11 world of American power, the Big 3 continue to play significant roles in maintaining and developing the concepts and infrastructure of foreign policy knowledge networks that are central to the exercise of America's global role. They are at the heart of dense networks of think tanks, research institutes, universities, and media organizations and close to the leaders of both main political parties and to relevant state agencies. They are to knowledge networks what central banks are to the financial system: absolutely critical in maintaining flows of *particular* people and *particular* ideas. As "soft" and "smart" power[151] become ever more relevant to the exercise of American power, nonstate actors such as the Big 3 are likely to become even more significant to maintaining and extending America's global reach.

9 | CONCLUSION

This study has tracked the major American foundations from the early part of the last century to the first decade of this one. During that time, the United States has grown from a society that was, on the whole, inward looking and parochial, relatively content within its own borders—or rather, content with expanding its frontiers to their continental limits—to one that considers the management of the very global order itself as not just a national interest but its God-given duty. The United States has transformed from a global minnow to the world's lone superpower. Many factors have contributed to this transformation—economic, political, and military—but one that is generally neglected is the role of philanthropic foundations.

Rockefeller, Carnegie, and Ford in various ways marginalized "isolationism" as a major force in U.S. politics, were central to building the knowledge base of the U.S. state and key elements of society about the rest of the world, built or reformed aspects of the U.S. state's foreign affairs capacities during World War II, harnessed their power to the American state during the Cold War, and helped to develop the key political and security concepts that guided American power through the period since the collapse of the Soviet bloc. In the post-9/11 period, the major foundations continue to develop and innovate, forming the model for newer philanthropies as well as collaborating with them. This book has documented in some detail the vast array of foundation funding programs that acted upon the capacities of the American state as well as those of academia and elite publics to better comprehend the world that U.S. elites now view in proprietary terms.

The central argument, over and above restating the importance of elite dominance of U.S. foreign affairs, is that the foundations' manifest purpose—to address fundamental problems like poverty and development through better knowledge of their causes—played second fiddle when compared to their (officially secondary) purpose of creating national and global networks of intellectuals committed to a Progressive-era state-building project for globalist ends. American foundations and the networks they nurtured and constructed carried out statelike functions for a global order consciously built by the corporate leaders who created and led the Big 3 foundations.

Running through all of the foundation programs reviewed here, the idea of the "network" is a constant. The knowledge network is the foundations' principal instrument and achievement. It is virtually an end in itself, a technology of power that acts as a "force multiplier." Indeed, Ford's Peter Cleaves and Jeffrey Puryear noted the point in those very words in regard to programs in Chile (chapter 7). Networks achieve much when they are well funded and attractive to the brightest and best. They bring together scholars and practitioners in productive union. They bestow prestige on insiders and draw the boundaries of what constitutes valuable knowledge. They act as gatekeepers of ideas and approaches, certifying some and delegitimizing others. They determine what is current orthodoxy. In so doing, they end up being rather "conservative" even in their methods of innovating, preserving certain powerful continuities and interests while making changes that may not radically alter patterns of power and influence within academia, politics, or the state. *In effect, networks are the tangible evidence of how elite hegemony actually "works," how "power works" in ostensibly (and, to an extent, actually) "open" democratic societies.*

Networks thereby generate outcomes that are not publicly stated. That is, the promotion of elite hegemony within the United States is nowhere stated in foundation publications or Web sites. Yet, the results of liberal internationalist foundation-funded networks are clear: the effective hegemony of a globalist worldview across elite and attentive opinion in the United States within the leadership of the main political parties and the upper echelons of the state.[1]

The influence of networks was felt during the Cold War, as shown in chapters 4–7 in reviewing the activities of the Kissinger and Salzburg seminars for European elites and the building of networked academic associations in Asian, African, and Latin American studies, sometimes with devastating consequences. The examples of Nigeria, Indonesia, and Chile are especially significant in this regard. In Nigeria, Ford-funded economic planning ultimately produced little economic "development" but exacerbated ethnic political tensions that contributed to the civil war in the mid-1960s. In Indonesia, economists supported by Ford funds contributed to undermining the "anti-American" Sukarno regime and, indirectly at least, to the bloody massacres that occurred in the wake of Suharto's military takeover in 1965–1966. Indonesian economists—the so-called Beautiful Berkeley Boys—went on to frame broadly neoliberal economic policies that transformed the country. In Chile, the Chicago Boys ended up plotting with the military ahead of Pinochet's coup of 1973 and presiding over the conversion of Chile into a laboratory for neoliberal experimentation. Indeed, in each case, the foundations' experts tended to see the societies in which they worked as real-world laboratories for their technocratic schemes for modernization, normally without any knowledge of the societies and peoples themselves. In fact, in the case of the Michigan/MIT economist Wolfgang Stolper, a lack of knowledge was worn as a badge of objectivity, if not pride. There is in each case a distinct colonial mentality in the dealings of American (and other) experts with "their" Third World counterparts.

Such colonial mentalities are unsurprising. They have their counterpart in U.S. elites' attitudes to the general run of *American* citizens. Elitism is a core attitude among those who created the foundations and their trustees and is evident in the subtext of the everyday work of their officers. Of course, by the 1970s, foundations were discussing "empowering" the masses and building partnerships with "local" people. And today, "giving a voice" to those left behind by globalization is a core concern. Nevertheless, the determination of who constitutes "the masses," "local people," or unheard voices seems in the end, as with the World Social Forum, to remain within the power of foundations and other rich funders themselves, and they tend to select people who work for "respected" organizations normally led by elites who think and speak in a cosmopolitan and technocratic language comprehensible to program officers.

Foundation elites tend, as a default position, toward other elites. Consider the Ford Foundation's programs in the wake of large-scale protest by African American Africanists in the late 1960s (chapter 6). Ford's programs, according to its own reports, ended up empowering *some* African Americans, but almost exclusively those drawn from programs at elite, mainly white universities, further deepening and widening the gap between those universities and historically black colleges. Even further, Ford's programs tended to remain oriented to white students—in terms of the relative scale of funding. Even among black students, the program ended up creating a black fellowship network, a smaller version of the extant white network.

Unerringly, what is continuous and longest lasting in terms of foundation programs' influence is the *network*: its careful construction and nurturing, maturing, and development is given the most painstaking attention. Ultimately, the network is the end, not just a means to an end. Its production, maintenance, and "normal" operations and activities constitute power technology. It is within networks that concepts are either initially developed or co-opted and elaborated, refined and packaged, and made ready for use by practitioners. This was most clearly shown in chapter 8, in discussing the knowledge politics of democratic peace theory, a theory that had been around for some time but that only broke through into mainstream academia and politics on the basis of a combination of powerful foundation networks as well as catalytic events—the end of the Cold War and the devastating terrorist attacks on New York and Washington, D.C., on September 11, 2001. And *it is such catalytic events, combined with the networked production and refinement of ideas for use that produces powerful policy shifts and the repositioning of the American state to its domestic society and to the world.* This was also clearly the case in regard to Japanese aggression at Pearl Harbor in December 1941: dense liberal internationalist networks composed of foundations, think tanks, and other organizations nurtured over a period of two decades or more had produced the concepts, attitudes, theories, and policy-oriented and "public" language that predominated after Pearl Harbor. But catalytic events alone do not guarantee any particular outcome. *The role of powerful networks is to interpret the world after the event and to sell their version of cause and consequence to American publics, to draw the lessons for future policy, and to advance concrete plans for implementation.*

The network concept encompasses, combines, and synthesizes "public" and "private" domains, "society" and "state." The network is an alloy—neither entirely private nor public but a complex mixture, a hybrid form that may be peculiar to societies featuring a "weak" state. This book has shown how closely connected and interpenetrated were foundations and the American state. Indeed, foundation and other "private" elites of the Progressive era worked outside electoral politics and Congress, or rather around them, and worked directly with the federal executive. Because they viewed the state as embodying the very spirit of responsible citizenship, of civic patriotism, they wanted to modernize it, strengthen it, to make it

more effective in governing an increasingly complex America and order-
ing a "dangerous" world. The philanthropic foundations considered in this
book were fully representative of such attitudes and tendencies, part of a
Gramscian "state-spirited" and networked Establishment of power that accommodated several interconnected and like-minded components, not to
mention a "revolving door" among them (chapter 2). They also recognized
a division of labor among them, with each "assigned" a specific role in the
processes of building American hegemony.

The idea that the foundations are "independent" of the state must be revised. The evidence presented here strongly suggests this. However, something must be recognized: the "independence" fiction has some "reality" in
the life of the foundations. They choose to do what they do; they could do
otherwise. In their day-to-day lives, foundation trustees and officials do not
receive state directives, nor do they issue their own to anyone else. What
they have, and what binds them so closely to the state, however, is more
powerful and significant than any official directives: they have an organic
unity with the state and the rest of the Establishment, born of a shared
worldview underpinning the conviction that the United States is a society
with superior ideas, culture, and economic system, one that is destined and
duty bound to lead the world.

The foundation-state relationship, therefore, is not a conspiracy—it may
be quite secretive and operate "behind the scenes," but it is not a criminal
enterprise. It is, however, strongly undemocratic, because it privileges the
"right" people, usually those with the "right" social backgrounds and/or attitudes. This clearly jars in an open society like the United States, where
rank and background are supposed to constitute no barrier to representation. It also violates the norm of accountability, since foundation elites do
not operate through elections or elected representatives.

In promoting themselves as independent, foundations also proclaim
their aloofness from the worlds of business and the marketplace. Yet their
trustees have overwhelmingly been recruited from the ranks of the corporate community—Wall Street is and has been very well represented at Ford,
Rockefeller, and Carnegie. Unsurprising though that is, it undermines the
self-image of foundations as being above business concerns. They could
never really be beyond business: they are headed by businessmen, they were
formed by industrialists, and they invest in and receive income from the
engines of capitalist globalization. Yet, the fiction has some "reality." The
income foundations receive may be "invested" in schemes with little or no

chance of success. Foundations, as nonprofit organizations, can take risks that businesses in competitive markets may be unable, or less able, to take. But this may suggest, as some have, that foundations are a little like venture capitalists.

This raises a related question. Are not the three foundations chosen for this study quite different and competitive among themselves, which increases the pressure on them to take fewer risks and "achieve" more—produce better results—than their "fellow" philanthropies? There is certainly plenty in the record above to indicate that this is not a new issue. There is a degree of "philanthropy envy"; doing good for mankind is serious business, honoring most those seen to be leading the way with innovative and successful programs. But the focus of this book has been broad—trying to paint a "big picture" while presenting detailed cases to illustrate salient features of American philanthropy over a century or so. That is not to suggest that the foundations are identical, however, but merely to point out that the blurring of distinguishing lines is a by-product of the approach taken here, suiting the purposes of *this* book—to examine the overall picture of the Big 3 foundations' activities and effects over a long timeframe.

Nevertheless, there is an implicit claim that more binds the Big 3 than divides them. Captivated by liberal internationalism, their ties were amplified by *defining their opponents* as backward looking, narrow minded, or parochial—anyone on either the left or right opposing American interventionism and empire building. This includes Robert Lynd in 1940, who warned of the dangers of corporate-led war mobilization for civil liberties; the marginalization of the historian-activist Charles Beard once he criticized increasing U.S. belligerence in the late 1930s; African American supporters of African independence in the 1950s; and the Marxist left in Chile in the 1970s. C. Wright Mills's proposed study, *The Cultural Apparatus*, was rejected for funding by Ford, as they feared it would be "another *Power Elite*," a radical critique of the American power structure and its global consequences.[2] Such cases should be seen as casting light on the very large and sustained funding of think tanks and university programs that broadly advanced the liberal internationalist cause, as detailed in this book.

Another issue that arises concerns the character of the foundations' influence on research and researchers. It is sometimes argued that the approach taken here suggests that foundations "dupe" or "suborn" researchers or otherwise interfere with research results. There is no evidence that the Ford, Carnegie, and Rockefeller foundations have ever engaged in such activities. *No claim to that end is made in this study.* Indeed, this study has throughout endorsed the approach taken by Harold Laski when he noted that foundations do not control research: "It is merely the fact that a fund is within reach which permeates everything and alters everything." Furthermore, Laski argues, "the foundations do not control, simply because, in the direct and simple sense of the word, there is no need for them to do so. They have only to indicate the immediate direction of their minds for the whole university world to discover that it always meant to gravitate swiftly to that angle of the intellectual compass."[3] The point is that foundations operate structurally, technocratically, and from the top down, rarely, if ever, micromanaging research or researchers.

The top-down technocratic character of American philanthropy has hardly been dented, in practice, by the greater reliance on the rhetoric of empowerment. Consider two recent examples that illustrate the point and suggest that even newer philanthropies are continuing to advance along the same lines. First, consider the Rockefeller Foundation's focus on "*smart globalization,*"[4] suggesting that RF was previously somewhat less smart, hence its failure to achieve key development goals. What is "smart globalization"? It is recognizing that globalization is a revolutionary process engineering radical change. This does not sound especially insightful. Smart globalization accepts that there are upsides and downsides, winners and losers, and tries to maximize benefits and minimize costs. How would the foundations apply this insight of smart globalization to their funding practices? The answer to this is clearly the key. According to one document, the practical implications of smart globalization are "a closer interaction of foresight and development experts and practitioners . . . [so they] work more closely together to coherently address the multitude, interlocking global challenges of the 21st century." Stronger, better-networked experts and practitioners would "harness the creative forces of globalization to ensure that the tools and technologies [of progress] are accessible to more people, more fully, in more places." According to the same document, a smart-globalization "mindset has influenced and directed the ongoing work of the Rockefeller Foundation."[5]

This leads to a consideration of the second instance of top-down technocratic values at the heart of American philanthropy. The Gates Foundation (GF)—the world's largest foundation, even before Warren Buffet's donations, the interest on which will add $1.5 billion annually to the foundation's spending power—leads the way. Yet, despite its valuable programs of immunization and vaccination and the rhetoric of partnership and empowerment, the overall mindset remains elitist, top down, and expert led. As *Time* magazine noted in 2006, the Gateses are "shrewd about doing good . . . rewiring politics and re-engineering justice . . . making mercy smarter and hope strategic." In the same issue, *Time* noted that the Gateses are "*intellectually captivated* by the scientific challenge of *treating the diseases* of the poor" and hope to invest "resources and rigor into the fight just when scientists are inventing new tools. . . . They [Bill and Melinda] run the foundation like a business. . . . And both use the language of business to describe the human experience."[6] Roy Steiner, the deputy director of GF's agricultural development department, emphasizes that "we believe in the power of technology."[7] *To one armed with "science" and technology, the world resembles a laboratory and its people experimental subjects, and every problem requires ambitious high-tech solutions.*

Additionally, the recent "discovery" that Africa was left out of the 1960s "Green revolution" led to a joint venture between the Gates and Rockefeller foundations that incorporates profit-making investors such as Monsanto. Starting in 2006, they hope to replicate the "success" story in contemporary Africa.[8] In their program—Alliance for a Green Revolution in Africa (AGRA)—supported by President Barack Obama,[9] there is little or no recognition of some of the key failures of the Green revolution in India, including the exacerbation of rural poverty and inequality, higher levels of landlessness, and, therefore, greater migrations to already overpopulated cities.[10] Like the previous Green revolution, AGRA offers high-tech solutions that are likely to exacerbate the very problems they claim to be solving.[11]

What have been the effects thus far of the Alliance for a Green Revolution in Africa? It is still early days for AGRA, but an internal Gates Foundation memo noted that, despite the rhetorical focus on "smallholders," the strategy will "require some degree of land mobility and a lower percentage of total employment involved in direct agricultural production"—that is, land-ownership concentration and an exodus to the cities, where opportunities are few.[12] The promotion of subsidized fertilizers is also likely to aggravate future food production. It is also clear that ending African hunger may not be at the top of the list of the Gates Foundation's priorities. As a report by the Chicago Council on Global Affairs, funded by GF, noted, the United States must "reassert its leadership" in "spreading new technologies" to increase trade and, ultimately, "strengthen American institutions."[13]

The obvious question is: why are the Gates and Rockefeller foundations repeating the mistakes of the past? Don't they realize what happened before? The short answer is that they are fully aware of the consequences and failures of past policies and believe that they have learned lessons. But their commitment to high-tech expert-led solutions, free-market and "comparative-advantage" economics, and to American/Western power and global leadership soars way above the oft-expressed and lofty interest in feeding the hungry and poor of this world.[14] The foundations have a demonstrable "imperial or hegemonic planning mentality that excludes the necessary role of local knowledge" or people, as James Scott argues with reference to modern states.[15]

And herein lies the problem of American philanthropy, limiting the possibility of radical reform. The elitist, scientistic, technocratic, and market-oriented mindset that dominates America is virtually hard wired into the dominant structures of society, economy, and polity. American business culture gave life to scientific, industrialized foundations, leaving an indelible imprint on their instincts, approaches, and practices. Philanthropy—or philanthrocapitalism—today reflects its context while simultaneously and continuously constructing and reconstructing it in an age of rampant neoliberalism, the iron grip of which shows no signs of relaxing. *The mental images with which major foundations operate make the world only partially legible but almost wholly open to manipulation and reconstruction.*[16]

The Big 3 operate today in a more crowded field. The Gates Foundation dwarfs them. There are numerous conservative foundations—Coors, Scaife, Bradley—that fund right-wing think tanks, media, and lobbying organizations. Yet the Big 3 remain highly significant. They are active, well organized, dynamic, and experienced. Between them, they have a three-hundred-year-strong record of domestic reform and global institution building. Their example is emulated by newer philanthropies, multiplying the Big 3's influence.

To be sure, there is the possibility that American foundations will respond with "new" ideas about global hegemony, given the rise of new powers, actors, and peoples across the world. They are likely to promote empowerment, institutional reform, and political accommodation of rising powers like China and India but unlikely to champion a radical restructuring of the global order. They could look backward to alternative models of U.S. philanthropy—such as the radical American Fund for Public Service—that were innovative experiments in empowering those struggling to promote working-class welfare, immigrants' rights, and civil liberties for those fighting for radical social and economic reform. But this is also highly un-likely in the era of neoliberal philanthrocapitalism. The foundations remain primordially attached to the American state, a broadly neoliberal order with a safety net, and a global rules-based system as the basis of continued American global hegemony.

NOTES

1. The Significance of Foundations in U.S. Foreign Policy

1. *Time* (December 26, 2005/January 2, 2006). The Gateses were named two of *Time* magazine's three "Persons of the Year"; the other was Bono of the rock group U2.

2. Although there are many other significant American foundations, the Big 3 were simply the most globally engaged and, therefore, the most worthy of more or less exclusive attention, although chapter 8 also considers an aspect of the role of the German Marshall Fund.

3. Jacqueline Khor (associate director, Rockefeller Foundation), "Innovations in Philanthropy: The RF's Perspective," Knowledge@SMU, http://www.knowledge .smu.edu.sg/index.cfm.

4. Simon Bromley, *American Power and the Prospects for International Order* (Cambridge: Polity Press, 2008).

5. Edward H. Berman, *The Influence of the Carnegie, Ford, and Rockefeller Foundations on U.S. Foreign Policy* (Albany, N.Y.: SUNY Press, 1983).

6. Historians have also neglected the study of elites in America's evolution; see Steve Fraser and Gary Gerstle, eds., *Ruling America* (Cambridge, Mass.: Harvard University Press, 2005), 2.

7. Donald Fisher, "The Role of Philanthropic Foundations in the Reproduction and Production of Hegemony: Rockefeller Foundations and the Social Sciences," *Sociology* 17, no. 2 (1983): 206–233; Martin Bulmer, "Philanthropic Foundations and the Development of the Social Sciences in the Early Twentieth Century: A Reply to Donald Fisher," *Sociology* 18 (1984): 572–579.

8. Robert O. Keohane and Joseph S. Nye Jr., eds., *Transnational Relations and World Politics* (Cambridge, Mass.: Harvard University Press, 1973); Samuel P.

Huntington, "Transnational Organizations in World Politics," *World Politics* 25, no. 3 (1973).

9. Huntington, "Transnational Organizations," 344. Even Philip G. Cerny's more critical account of the roles of states and private actors in globalization processes is based on Lindblom's neopluralist perspective (Cerny, "Multinodal Politics," *Review of International Studies* 35 [2009]: 421–449).

10. Kenneth Prewitt, "The Importance of Foundations in an Open Society," in *The Future of Foundations in an Open Society*, ed. Bertelsmann Foundation (Guetersloh: Bertelsmann Foundation, 1999), 17–29.

11. Ibid., 9.

12. Helmut Anheier and Diana Leat, *From Charity to Creativity: Philanthropic Foundations in the Twenty-First Century* (Stroud, U.K.: Comedia, 2002); cited in H. Anheier and S. Daly, "Philanthropic Foundations: A New Global Force?" in *Global Civil Society 2004–05*, ed. Helmut Anheier, Marlies Glasius, and Mary Kaldor (London: Sage, 2005), 159.

13. Anheier and Daly, "Philanthropic Foundations," 160, 174.

14. Robert W. Cox, "Civil Society at the Turn of the Millennium," *Review of International Studies* 25 (1999): 10.

15. Khor, "Innovations in Philanthropy."

16. Peter Haas, "Epistemic Communities and International Policy Coordination," *International Organization* 46, no. 1 (Winter 1992): 3.

17. Inderjeet Parmar, "Catalysing Events, Think Tanks, and American Foreign Policy Shifts: A Comparative Analysis of the Impacts of Pearl Harbor and 11 September 2001," *Government and Opposition* 40, no. 1 (Winter 2005): 1–26.

18. Eldon J. Eisenach, *The Lost Promise of Progressivism* (Lawrence: University Press of Kansas, 1994).

19. Though it acknowledges their importance, foundations are not a central focus of Akira Iriye, *Global Community: The Role of International Organizations in the Making of the Contemporary World* (Berkeley: University of California Press, 2002). The vital roles played by private actors in global civil society building is part of a whole complex of roles involving states and intergovernmental organizations that is transforming world politics; see Cerny, "Multinodal Politics."

20. Ronald Radosh, *Prophets on the Right* (New York: Simon and Schuster, 1975); Manfred Jonas, *Isolationism in America, 1935–1941* (Ithaca, N.Y.: Cornell University Press, 1966); Selig Adler, *The Isolationist Impulse* (New York: Collier, 1961).

21. Nils Gilman, *Mandarins of the Future: Modernization Theory in Cold War America* (Baltimore, Md.: The Johns Hopkins University Press, 2003); George Rosen,

Western Economists and Eastern Societies (Baltimore, Md.: The Johns Hopkins University Press, 1985).

22. Manuel Castells, *The Informational City* (Oxford: Blackwell, 1994), 169–170.

23. D. Swartz, *Culture and Power: The Sociology of Pierre Bourdieu* (Chicago: University of Chicago Press, 1997), 101.

24. Barry Karl and Stanley N. Katz, "Foundations and Ruling Class Elites," *Daedalus* 116, no. 1 (1987): 1–40; Barry Karl, "Philanthropy and the Maintenance of Democratic Elites," *Minerva* 35 (1997): 207–220.

25. Swartz, *Culture and Power*, 225.

26. Robert J. Brym, *Intellectuals and Politics* (London: George Allen and Unwin, 1980); M. Reza Nakhaie and Robert J. Brym, "The Political Attitudes of Canadian Professors," *Canadian Journal of Sociology* 24, no. 3 (1999): 329–353.

27. Brym, *Intellectuals and Politics*, 19.

28. Q. Hoare and G. Nowell-Smith, eds., *Selections from the Prison Notebooks of Antonio Gramsci* (London: Lawrence and Wishart, 1971).

29. Robert F. Arnove, ed., *Philanthropy and Cultural Imperialism: The Foundations at Home and Abroad* (Boston: G. K. Hall, 1980).

30. Harold Laski makes this point well ("Foundations, Universities, and Research," in *The Dangers of Obedience and Other Essays* [New York: Harper and Brothers, 1930], 171).

31. Berman, *The Influence of the Carnegie, Ford, and Rockefeller Foundations*, 84.

32. Leslie Sklair, *Sociology of the Global System* (New York: Harvester Wheatsheaf, 1991).

33. Landrum R. Bolling, *Private Foreign Aid: U.S. Philanthropy for Relief and Development* (Boulder, Colo.: Westview Press, 1982), 1.

34. Ibid., 61–62.

35. Sutton, cited in ibid., 71.

36. Ibid., 68–69.

37. Robert F. Arnove, "The Ford Foundation and 'Competence Building' Overseas: Assumptions, Approaches, and Outcomes," *Studies in Comparative International Development* 12 (September 1977): 105–106.

38. Ibid., 113.

39. Kenneth W. Thompson et al., "Higher Education and National Development: One Model for Technical Assistance," in *Education and Development Reconsidered: The Bellagio Conference Papers, Ford Foundation, Rockefeller Foundation*, ed. F. Champion Ward (New York: Praeger, 1974), 203. Emphasis added.

40. Michael P. Todaro, "Education for National Development: The University," in

Education and Development Reconsidered: The Bellagio Conference Papers, Ford Foundation, Rockefeller Foundation, ed. F. Champion Ward (New York: Praeger, 1974), 204.

41. Kenneth W. Thompson and B. R. Fogel, *Higher Education and Social Change* (London: Praeger, 1976), 3.

42. Ibid., 51–52; italics added.

43. Ibid., 209–216.

44. Ibid., 13.

45. Robert F. Arnove, "Foundations and the Transfer of Knowledge," in *Philanthropy and Cultural Imperialism: The Foundations at Home and Abroad*, ed. Robert F. Arnove (Boston: G. K. Hall, 1980), 315.

46. Ibid., 320–322.

47. Helen Laville and Hugh Wilford, eds., *The U.S. Government, Citizen Groups, and the Cold War: The State-Private Network* (London: Routledge, 2006).

48. Patrick Dunleavy and Brendan O'Leary, *Theories of the State* (Basingstoke: Macmillan, 1987); Peter B. Evans, Theda Skocpol, et al., eds., *Bringing the State Back In* (Cambridge: Cambridge University Press, 1985); Ralph Miliband, *The State in Capitalist Society* (London: Quartet Books, 1973); for a direct test of all three theories, see Inderjeet Parmar, *Think Tanks and Power in Foreign Policy* (Basingstoke: Palgrave, 2004).

49. Michael Mann, *States, War, and Capitalism* (Oxford: Blackwell, 1988).

50. This should not be taken to mean that there are no such zero-sum relationships between state and society; it is argued that such relationships are not necessarily the more decisive ones in understanding "how power works" in U.S. democracy.

51. Godfrey Hodgson, "The Establishment," *Foreign Policy* (1972–1973): 4–5.

52. Ibid., 5.

53. Michael J. Hogan, "Corporatism: A Positive Appraisal," *Diplomatic History* 10, no. 4 (October 1986): 363–372; Ellis W. Hawley, "The Discovery and Study of a 'Corporate Liberalism,'" *Business History Review* 12, no. 3 (1978): 309–320.

54. Michael Wala, *The Council on Foreign Relations and American Foreign Policy During the Early Cold War* (Oxford: Berghahn, 1994).

55. Thomas Ferguson, "From Normalcy to New Deal: Industrial Structure, Party Competition, and American Public Policy in the Great Depression," *International Organization* 38, no. 1 (Winter 1984): 46.

56. Arthur S. Link and R. L. McCormick, *Progressivism* (Arlington Heights, Ill.: Harlan Davidson, 1983); William E. Leuchtenberg, "Progressivism and Imperialism," *Mississippi Valley Historical Review* 39 (1952–53): 483–504.

57. Eisenach, *The Lost Promise of Progressivism.*

58. Diane Stone, *Capturing the Political Imagination* (London: Frank Cass, 1996), 86.

59. William Drake and Kalypso Nicolaidis, "Ideas, Interests, and Institutionaliza-tion: 'Trade in Services' and the Uruguay Round," cited in ibid., 97.

60. Joseph A. Schumpeter, *Capitalism, Socialism, and Democracy* (London: Unwin, 1987), 262. Schumpeter argues that "the typical citizen drops down to a lower level of mental performance as soon as he enters the political field. He argues and analyzes in a way which he would readily recognize as infantile within the sphere of his real interests. He becomes a primitive again."

61. Benjamin Ginsberg, *The Captive Public: How Mass Opinion Promotes State Power* (New York: Basic Books, 1986).

62. Chadwick Alger, "The External Bureaucracy in United States Foreign Affairs," *Administrative Science Quarterly* 7, no. 1 (1962): 50–78.

63. Karl Marx, cited by Ralph Miliband, *The State in Capitalist Society* (London: Quartet Books, 1984), 162–163. Marx further noted that "the class which is the ruling material force of society, is at the same time its ruling intellectual force."

64. Inderjeet Parmar, "Engineering Consent: The Carnegie Endowment for International Peace and the Mobilisation of American Public Opinion, 1939–1945," *Review of International Studies* 26, no. 1 (2000). The consent of the governed is "organized. . . . The State does have and request consent, but it also 'educates' this consent, by means of the political and syndical associations; these, however," Gramsci concludes, "are private organisms, left to . . . private initiative"; cited in Parmar, *Think Tanks and Power in Foreign Policy: A Comparative Study of the Role and Influence of the Council on Foreign Relations and the Royal Institute of International Affairs, 1939–1945* (London: Palgrave, 2004), 18.

65. Hoare and Nowell-Smith, *Selections from the Prison Notebooks*, 146–147. The eighteenth-century conservative political theorist Edmund Burke noted that a key part of the state's stability was derived from a partnership "not only between those who are living, but between those who are living, those who are dead, and those who are to be born"; see his *Reflections on the Revolution in France* (1790; London: Penguin, 1986), 194–195.

66. Hoare and Nowell-Smith, *Selections from the Prison Notebooks*, 16.

67. M. A. C. Colwell, "The Foundation Connection," in *Philanthropy and Cultural Imperialism: The Foundations at Home and Abroad*, ed. Robert F. Arnove (Boston: G. K. Hall, 1980); Anheier and Daly, "Philanthropic Foundations," 171; Peter D. Bell, "The Ford Foundation as a Transnational Actor," in *Transnational Relations and World Politics*, ed. R. O. Keohane and J. S. Nye (Cambridge, Mass.: Harvard University Press, 1972), 121, 125.

68. Karl and Katz, "Foundations and Ruling Class Elites," 19–20.

69. Ibid.

70. Ibid.; W. Weaver, ed., *U.S. Philanthropic Foundations* (New York: Harper and Row, 1967); J. Bresnan, *Managing Indonesia* (New York: Columbia University Press, 1993), 78–83, 282; J. Bresnan, *At Home Abroad: A Memoir of the Ford Foundation in Indonesia, 1953–1973* (Jakarta: Equinox, 2006).

71. Anheier and Daly, "Philanthropic Foundations"; M. Edwards, *Civil Society* (Cambridge: Polity, 2009).

72. Inderjeet Parmar, "Anti-Americanism and the Major Foundations," in *The Rise of Anti-Americanism*, ed. B. O'Connor and M. Griffiths (London: Routledge, 2006), 169–194.

2. AMERICAN FOUNDATION LEADERS

1. Joan Roelofs, *Foundations and Public Policy* (Albany, N.Y.: SUNY Press, 2003).

2. Jules Abels, *The Rockefeller Billions* (New York: Macmillan, 1965), 361.

3. Joseph A. Schumpeter, *Capitalism, Socialism and Democracy* (London: Unwin, 1987), 262; Jose Ortega y Gasset, *The Revolt of the Masses* (1930; London: Unwin, 1961).

4. Robert D. Dean, *Imperial Brotherhood: Gender and the Making of Cold War Foreign Policy* (Amherst: University of Massachusetts Press, 2001).

5. B. Ginsberg, *The Captive Public* (New York: Basic Books, 1986).

6. Joseph F. Wall, *Andrew Carnegie* (New York: Oxford University Press, 1970), 641.

7. Emily Rosenberg, *Spreading the American Dream* (New York: Hill and Wang, 1982).

8. Richard Hofstadter, *The American Political Tradition* (London: Cape, 1967).

9. Joseph Nye, *Soft Power* (New York: Public Affairs, 2004).

10. Robert Divine, *Second Chance* (New York: Athenaeum, 1967).

11. In this, as in the case of civil rights in the 1960s, the foundations did not cover themselves in glory; see Richard Magat, *The Ford Foundation at Work* (London: Plenum Press, 1979).

12. Douglas Brinkley, "Dean Acheson and the 'Special Relationship': The West Point Speech of December 1962," *Historical Journal* 33 (1990): 599–608.

13. Paul Kennedy, *The Rise and Fall of the Great Powers* (London: Fontana Press, 1989), 313.

14. H. G. Aubrey, *The Dollar in World Affairs* (New York: Harper and Row, 1964), 13.

15. R. Hofstadter, "The Psychic Crisis of the 1890s," in R. Hofstadter, *The Paranoid Style in American Politics and Other Essays* (New York: Alfred A. Knopf, 1952).

16. Kennedy, *Rise and Fall of the Great Powers*, 317–318.

17. Roosevelt to the U.S. Congress, cited by Thomas G. Paterson, et al, *American Foreign Relations: A History Since 1895* (Lexington, Mass.: D.C. Heath and Company, 1995), 44. Interestingly, Roosevelt toured several Caribbean countries circa 1906 and inaugurated antimalaria and other public health schemes and built ports; this was later followed by Rockefeller philanthropy as new and based on human welfare. TR did the same for strategic and economic reasons and to protect American soldiers. This highlights a recurrent theme: how American philanthropy followed the state.

18. This is not too far from a Durkheimian analysis of the traumas resulting from the shifts from mechanical to organic solidarity in modern industrial societies, which is normally accompanied by intensified class and other conflict; see Emile Durkheim, *The Division of Labour in Society* (New York: Free Press, 1969).

19. Hofstadter, "The Psychic Crisis of the 1890s," cited by Thomas G. Paterson, *Major Problems in American Foreign Policy*, vol. 1: *To 1914*, 3rd ed. (Lexington, Mass.: D. C. Heath and Company, 1989), 393.

20. Ibid.

21. Indeed, this is a feature also of the so-called new philanthropy of Bill Gates and George Soros. The very drivers of capitalist globalization also claim to advance the best "cure."

22. Wall, *Andrew Carnegie*, 583.

23. Ibid., 717.

24. Matthew Josephson, *The Robber Barons* (London: Eyre and Spottiswoode, 1962), 361.

25. Wall, *Andrew Carnegie*, 541.

26. Ibid., 547.

27. Ceane O'Hanlon-Lincoln, *County Chronicles* (Mechling Bookbindery, 2004), 2:79.

28. Abels, *The Rockefeller Billions*, 156.

29. Ron Chernow, *Titan* (New York: Vintage, 1999), 575.

30. Ibid., 585, emphasis added. See also, Kirk Hallahan, "Ivy Lee and the Rockefellers' Response to the 1913–1914 Colorado Coal Strike," *Journal of Public Relations Research* 14, no. 4 (2002): 265–315.

31. Barbara Howe, "The Emergence of Scientific Philanthropy, 1900–1920," in Robert F. Arnove, ed., *Philanthropy and Cultural Imperialism* (Boston: G. K. Hall, 1980), 25–54.

32. Sheila Slaughter and Edward T. Silva, "Looking Backwards: How Foundations Formulated Ideology in the Progressive Period," in Robert F. Arnove, ed., *Philanthropy and Cultural Imperialism* (Boston: G. K. Hall, 1980), 71.

33. Ibid., 73.

34. Howe, "The Emergence of Scientific Philanthropy, 1900–1920," 26.

35. Preface, *Index to Reports of Officers*, Vol. 1, *1921–1951* (New York: Carnegie Corporation, 1953).

36. Carnegie Corporation *Annual Report* (1945), 17–18.

37. Carnegie Corporation *Annual Report* (1952), 19–20.

38. Root cited in Parmar, "Engineering Consent: The Carnegie Endowment for International Peace and the Mobilization of American Public Opinion, 1939–1945," *Review of International Studies* (2000): 26, 35.

39. Howe, "The Emergence of Scientific Philanthropy, 1900–1920," 25–54.

40. Parmar, "American Foundations and the Development of International Knowledge Networks," *Global Networks* 2, no. 1 (2002): 13–30.

41. Peter Collier and David Horowitz, *The Rockefellers* (New York: Holt, Rinehart and Winston, 1976), 8.

42. Allan Nevins, *Study in Power: John D. Rockefeller, Industrialist and Philanthropist* (New York and London: Charles Scribner's Sons, 1953), 1:2.

43. Collier and Horowitz, *The Rockefellers*, 13.

44. Nevins, *Study in Power*, 2:426.

45. Ibid.

46. Collier and Horowitz, *The Rockefellers*, 35. Emphasis added.

47. Ibid., 40, 56–57.

48. Ibid., 40–41.

49. Chief Justice White of the U.S. Supreme Court opined that Rockefeller's "very genius for commercial development and organization . . . necessarily involved the intent to drive others from the field and to exclude them from their right to trade, and thus accomplish the mastery which was the end in view." http://nationalhumanitiescenter.org/pds/gildedpower/text2/standardoil.pdf.

50. Abels, *The Rockefeller Billions*, 360.

51. Collier and Horowitz, *The Rockefellers*, 88.

52. Hallahan, "Ivy Lee and the Rockefellers' Response to the 1913–1914 Colorado Coal Strike," 280.

53. Chernow, *Titan*, 624.

54. Collier and Horowitz, *The Rockefellers*, 82.

55. Abels, *The Rockefeller Billions*, 306.

56. Collier and Horowitz, *The Rockefellers*, 143.

57. Ibid., 635.

58. Ibid., 152.

59. Ibid., 152.

60. Ibid., 158.

61. Wall, *Andrew Carnegie*.

62. Ibid., 789.

63. Ibid., 792.

64. Reynold M. Wik, *Henry Ford and Grassroots America* (Ann Arbor: University of Michigan Press, 1972); Anne Jardim, *The First Henry Ford* (Cambridge: MIT Press, 1970).

65. Jardim, *The First Henry Ford*, 153–154.

66. Henry Ford, *My Life and Work* (London: Heinemann, 1923), 206–207. "Let every American become steeled against coddling. . . . It is a drug. Stand up and stand out; let weaklings take charity," Ford argued (221).

67. Ibid., 210.

68. Cited in Clarence Hooker, "Ford's Sociology Department and the Americanizing Campaign and the Manufacture of Popular Culture Among Assembly Line Workers c. 1910–1917," *Journal of American and Comparative Cultures* 20, no. 1 (Spring 1997): 49.

69. Ford's Americanization programs were taken up and implemented across Detroit; Hooker, "Ford's Sociology Department," 49.

70. Martin Walker, *Makers of the American Century* (London: Vintage, 2001), 55.

71. The biographical data in this section are drawn from the excellent dissertation by Alexander Nunn, *The Rockefeller Foundation: Philanthropy and Effect* (unpublished B. SocSci Politics dissertation, University of Manchester, 1998; in author's possession). The relevant data are cited with Alex Nunn's kind permission.

72. Several trustees did not specify the precise number of club memberships in their *Who's Who* entries, merely noting several and ending with "and many more."

73. I. Parmar, *Think Tanks and Power in Foreign Policy* (Basingstoke: Palgrave, 2004); Mark L. Chadwin, *The Hawks of World War II* (Chapel Hill: University of North Carolina Press, 1968).

74. Larry L. Fabian, *Andrew Carnegie's Peace Endowment* (Washington, D.C.: CEIP, 1985).

75. Alger Hiss, *Oral History Memoir*, 50; Carnegie Corporation Project, Oral History Research Office, Columbia University.

76. Lawrence Shoup and William Minter, *Imperial Brain Trust* (New York: Monthly Review Press, 1977).

77. Divine, *Second Chance*.

78. Cleveland Amory, *The Proper Bostonians* (New York: E. P. Dutton and Co., 1947).

79. Waldemar A. Nielsen, *The Big Foundations* (New York: Columbia University Press, 1972), ix. Nielsen also noted that the Big 3 were a "a microcosm of . . . the Establishment, the power elite, or the American ruling class"; 316.

80. Ben Whitaker, *The Philanthropoids: Foundations and Society* (New York: William Morrow, 1974), 90.

81. Cited in Edward H. Berman, *The Influence of the Carnegie, Ford, and Rockefeller Foundations on U.S. Foreign Policy* (Albany, N.Y.: SUNY Press, 1983), 36.

82. Shoup and Minter, *Imperial Brain Trust*, 59.

83. McCloy was declared "the Chairman of the Establishment" by John Kenneth Galbraith, and rightly so: see Kai Bird, *The Chairman: John J. McCloy and the Making of the American Establishment* (New York: Simon and Schuster).

84. For a more thorough discussion of this concept, see Helen Laville and Hugh Wilford, eds., *The U.S. Government, Citizen Groups, and the Cold War: The State-Private Network* (London: Routledge, 2006).

85. Thomas R. Dye, "Oligarchical Tendencies in National Policy-Making: The Role of Policy-Planning Organizations," *Journal of Politics* 40, no. 2 (May 1978): 309–331.

86. David Rockefeller, *Memoirs* (New York: Random House, 2002), 419.

87. Abels, *The Rockefeller Billions*, 177.

88. Wall, *Andrew Carnegie*, 365.

89. Ibid., 392.

90. W. H. Greenleaf, *The British Political Tradition* (London: Methuen, 1983), 239.

91. Harold Laski, "Foundations, Universities, and Research," in H. Laski, *The Dangers of Obedience and Other Essays* (London: Harper and Brothers, 1930), 150–177. Laski laments the rise of positivism in the study of society and politics as well as the foundation-sponsored "study group" method that mimicked the methods of the natural sciences.

92. William G. McLoughlin, *Revivals, Awakenings, and Reform* (Chicago: University of Chicago Press, 1978), 169–170.

93. M. Richter, "T. H. Green and His Audience," *Review of Politics* 18, no. 4 (1956): 444–572; M. Richter, *The Politics of Conscience* (London: Weidenfeld and Richardson, 1964).

94. McLoughlin, *Revivals, Awakenings, and Reform*, 152.

95. Ibid., 153.

96. Rockefeller, *Memoirs*, 21; Frederick T. Gates, *Chapters in My Life* (New York: Free Press, 1977), 161.

97. Rockefeller, *Memoirs*, 11.

98. Gates, *Chapters in My Life*, 161–162.

99. Ibid., 163.

100. David Nasaw, *Andrew Carnegie* (New York: Penguin, 2006), 715–716.

101. Laski, "Foundations, Universities, and Research," 163.

102. Ibid., 174.

103. Chernow, *Titan*, 483.

104. Ibid., 485.

105. Ibid., 486.

106. Louis R. Harlan, *Separate and Unequal* (New York: Athenaeum, 1968), 80.

107. Quotation of William H. Baldwin Jr., president of the GEB; cited by James D. Anderson, "Philanthropic Control Over Private Black Higher Education," in Robert F. Arnove, ed., *Philanthropy and Cultural Imperialism* (Boston: G. K. Hall, 1980), 155.

108. Ibid., 151.

109. W. E. B. Du Bois, *Autobiography of W. E. B. Du Bois* (New York: International Publishers, 1968), 230.

110. John H. Stanfield, *Philanthropy and Jim Crow in American Social Science* (Westport, Conn.: Greenwood Press, 1985), 142.

111. Anderson, "Philanthropic Control Over Private Black Higher Education," 156.

112. Stuart Anderson, *Race and Rapprochement: Anglo-Saxonism and Anglo-American Relations, 1895–1904* (London: Associated University Presses, 1981), 18, 23.

113. Wall, *Andrew Carnegie*, 695.

114. Sondra Herman, *Eleven Against War: Studies in American Internationalist Thought, 1898–1921* (Stanford, Calif.: Hoover Institution Press, 1969).

3. Laying the Foundations of Globalism, 1930–1945

1. The epigraph to this chapter is from an internal memo by Joseph Willits, director of the division of social sciences, Rockefeller Foundation (January 6, 1942); box 270, folders 3219/3221.

2. Simon Bromley picks up the story in 1945, whereas this study shows that such views were held by influential Americans much earlier in the twentieth century; Bromley, *American Power and the Prospects for International Order* (Cambridge: Polity Press, 2008).

3. Nicholas Murray Butler, *Across the Busy Years*, vol. 1 (New York: Charles Scribners' Sons, 1939). In several respects, Barrow's analysis of the institutionalization of the corporate ideal in the American university system and the strategic role of Carnegie and Rockefeller philanthropy very nicely dovetails with the present work; see Clyde W. Barrow, *Universities and the Capitalist State* (Madison: University of Wisconsin Press, 1990).

4. Robert F. Arnove, ed., *Philanthropy and Cultural Imperialism* (Boston: G. K. Hall, 1980); Ellen Condliffe Lagemann, *The Politics of Knowledge* (Middletown, Conn.: Wesleyan University Press, 1989).

5. William Leuchtenberg, "Progressivism and Imperialism," *Mississippi Valley Historical Review* 39 (1953): 483–504.

6. Ronald Radosh, *Prophets on the Right* (New York: Simon and Schuster, 1975); liberal internationalists effectively discredited opponents of U.S. interventionism as "outside the [new] consensus, or the mainstream . . . as subversive of the existing order" (14).

7. E. S. Rosenberg, *Spreading the American Dream* (New York: Hill and Wang, 1982).

8. N. M. Butler, *Across the Busy Years*, vol. 2 (New York: Charles Scribners' Sons, 1940).

9. David C. Engerman, "New Society, New Scholarship: Soviet Studies Programmes in Interwar America," *Minerva* 37 (1999): 25–43.

10. William C. Olson and A. J. R. Groom, *International Relations Then and Now* (London: Routledge, 1991), 75–76.

11. Rockefeller Foundation Archives (hereafter RFA), Tarrytown, NY, RG1.1 series 200 200S Yale University–International Relations, box 416, folder 4941; funding notes, 17 May 1935 and 16 May 1941.

12. See *Yale Institute Annual Report* (1942), in RFA, RG1.1 Series 200 200S Yale University–International Relations, Box 417, Folder 4957.

13. RFA; see inter-office memo by J. H. Willits, 29.2.40; letter, Frederick S. Dunn (Director of YIIS) to Willits, 2.6.41; letter, Dunn to Willits, 11.8.44; and YIIS annual report, 1938–39, 3; all in boxes 416 and 417, folders 4944, 4947, 4955. See also William T. R. Fox, *The American Study of International Relations* (Columbia: University of South Carolina Press, 1966) for the policy-oriented character of YIIS, of which Fox was a member.

14. Olson and Groom, *International Relations Then and Now*, 99.

15. RFA, box 416, folder 4944, Memorandum, "Yale University—Research in International Relations," 6 March 1940.

16. Figures compiled from annual reports and other internal RF sources.

17. RFA, box 416, folder 4944, Memo, 29 February 1940. According to Fox, Dunn's motive, to advance practical knowledge to enhance U.S. national security, was what ensured foundation support. The RF's director of the Division of Social Sciences, Joseph H. Willits, wrote that Spykman's ideas showed wisdom, maturity, "hard-headedness, realism and scholarly standards"; cited in Olson and Groom, *International Relations Then and Now*, 50–51.

18. YIIS *Annual Report* (1942), 3–4.

19. Ibid., 1–4 (italics added).

20. RFA, memorandum, "A Security Policy for Postwar America," 8 March 1945, in box 417, folder 4948.

21. See review, "The Gyroscope of Pan-Americanism," November 1943, in box 416, folder 4946. Written by the historian Samuel Flagg Bemis, it was entitled *The Latin American Policy of the United States* and was published in 1943. Bemis claimed that U.S. policy toward Latin America was a benevolent, "protective imperialism." It was, he continued, "an imperialism against imperialism."

22. This was a veiled reference to the confidential work of the Council on Foreign Relations for the State Department. See RFA, box 417, folder 4947; see Dunn's covering letter to Willits, 23 December 1943.

23. Ibid.

24. RFA, see *Annual Report* (1941–1942), 18–19, 25.

25. RFA, see YIIS *Annual Report* (1945–1946).

26. RFA, *Annual Report* (1943), 14–15.

27. Louis Morton, "National Security and Area Studies," *Journal of Higher Education*, 34, no. 2 (1963): 142–147.

28. See David Reynolds, *Britannia Overruled* (London: Longman, 1991), 173; also Olson and Groom, *International Relations Then and Now*, 100.

29. John A. Thompson, "Another Look at the Downfall of 'Fortress America,' " *Journal of American Studies*, 26, no. 3 (1992): 401.

30. See Paulo Ramos, *The Role of the YIIS in the Construction of the United States National Security Ideology, 1935–1951* (unpublished Ph.D. dissertation, University of Manchester, 2003), 267.

31. RFA, box 416, folder 4945; Lambert Davis (Harcourt, Brace) to George W. Gray (RF). (So influential that it was also produced in Braille).

32. Ibid.

33. Olson and Groom, *International Relations Then and Now*, 99.

34. Ramos, *The Role of the YIIS*, 240.

35. Spykman, cited in ibid., 242.

36. Ibid., 243.

37. Ibid., appendix C, 372.

38. Ibid., 243.

39. RFA, box 417, folder 4948; "Radio Program Notice," 6 April 1945.

40. Olson and Groom, *International Relations Then and Now*, 106–111.

41. Olson and Groom claim that the publication of this journal was "one of the most significant events in the history of the field [of international relations]." Ibid., 118.

42. Earle was an academic at Columbia and at the Institute for Advanced Study at Princeton. During World War II, he served in the Office of Strategic Services, among other agencies. In 1951, he served as political consultant to Dwight Eisenhower. He died in 1954.

43. "Notes on the American Committee for International Studies," April 5, 1941, 1; in Carnegie Corporation (hereafter CC) Papers, box 18. The ACIS functioned from 1936 to 1941 and consisted of four institutional members—CFR, FPA, IPR, and the U.S. National Committee on International Intellectual Cooperation—and of nine academics appointed by the Social Science Research Council. Later, the ACIS was designated by the SSRC as its Committee on International Relations.

44. Edward Mead Earle, "National Security and Foreign Policy," *Yale Review* 29 (March 1940); Edward Mead Earle, "The Threat to American Security," *Yale Review* 30 (March 1941).

45. Earle, "The Threat to American Security."

46. Alfred Vagts, "War and the Colleges," *American Military Institute*, document no. 4 (1940); Vagts, "Ivory Towers Into Watch Towers," *The Virginia Quarterly* 17, no. 2 (Spring 1941).

47. "Notes on the American Committee for International Studies," 5 April 1941, 1–2; CC Grant Files, box 18.

48. Edward Mead Earle, "The Future of American Foreign Policy," *New Republic* (November 8, 1939); Edward Mead Earle, "American Military Policy and National Security," *Political Science Quarterly* 53 (March 1938); Edward Mead Earle, "Political and Military Strategy of the United States," *Proceedings of the Academy of Political Science* (1940).

49. Record of Interview (by telephone), Frederick P. Keppel (president, CC) and Earle, 20 December 1937, in CC Grant Files, Institute for Advanced Study. "Study of the Military and Foreign Policies of the US through 1943"; letter, Earle to Keppel, 29 November 1938; all in box 178.

50. Letter, Earle to Keppel, 29 November 1938, 3. In all, up to 1942 only Earle's work received over $56,000 from the CC. See the minutes of its Executive Committee for November 7, 1940; March 5, 1941; and October 3, 1941 for details. Peffer is way off the mark when he suggests that Earle received only $35,000.

51. Letter, Page to Charles Dollard, 23 October 1941, CC Grant Files, box 178. Page was a public relations pioneer at AT&T in the 1930s and 1940s. His father was Walter Hines Page, a one-time U.S. ambassador to Britain.

52. See Earle's report, "Memorandum Regarding Problems of Morale, Recreation, and Health in Connection with American Naval and Air Bases in the Caribbean Area," May 1941; CC Grant Files, box 135.

53. Record of Interviews, Keppel and Earle, 17 October 1941; and Dollard and Earle, 17 December 1941; CC Grant Files, box 135.

54. Letter, Frank Aydelotte (IAS) to Robert M. Lester (secretary, CC), 16 December 1940; CC Grant Files, box 178.

55. Letter, Frank Aydelotte to Walter A. Jessup (president, CC), 26 January 1942. The syllabus, entitled "War and National Policy: A Syllabus," was published by Farrar and Rinehart; CC Grant Files, box 178.

56. "Report on Grant," by Frank Aydelotte to Robert M. Lester, 8 August 1942; CC Grant Files, box 178.

57. Ibid.

58. William T. R. Fox, "Interwar International Relations Research: The American Experience," *World Politics* 2 (October 1949): 78; Olson and Groom, *International Relations Then and Now*, 99; Ken Booth and Eric Herring, *Keyguide to Information Sources in Strategic Studies* (London: Mansell, 1994), 16.

59. Letter, Earle to Sir Charles Oman (All Souls' College, Oxford), 4 January 1944; Earle Papers, box 36, at Seeley G. Mudd Manuscript Library, Princeton University.

60. The third edition of *Sea Power* was published in 1968 and the fifth edition of *Layman's Guide* in 1965. See Earle's report on the seminar 1942–1943 in CC Grant Files, box 178; Brodie's entry in *Who Was Who*, vol. 7.

61. N. Peffer, "Memorandum on Carnegie Grants in the Field of International Relations," 17 April 1942, 3–4, in CC Grant Files, box 187.

62. William T. R. Fox, *The American Study of International Relations* (Columbia: University of South Carolina Press, 1966), 27.

63. Inderjeet Parmar, *Think Tanks and Power in Foreign Policy* (Basingstoke: Palgrave, 2004); Lawrence Shoup and William Minter, *Imperial Brain Trust* (New York: Monthly Review Press, 1977); Max Holland, "Citizen McCloy," *Wilson Quarterly* 15, no. 3 (1991): 22–42.

64. CC, New York, Grant Files, box 187: International Relations; Rare Book and Manuscript Collection, Butler Library, Columbia University; N. Peffer, "Memorandum on Carnegie Grants in the Field of International Relations" (April 17, 1942). The journal, *Foreign Affairs*, had 15,000 subscribers by 1939.

65. Shoup and Minter, *Imperial Brain Trust*; Parmar, *Think Tanks and Power in Foreign Policy*; R. D. Schulzinger, *The Wise Men of Foreign Affairs* (New York: Columbia University Press, 1984), 61.

66. RFA, RG1 Projects series 100 International; box 97, folder 100S, CFR 1936–37; WH Mallory (CFR) to EE Day (RF), 11 January 1936. By 1945, there were several groups approaching the completion of their deliberations, including the Group on Legal Problems of Reconstruction and the Cartel Group. Other groups

included U.S.-Soviet Relations, The Export of Technology, and Compulsory Military Training. See RG1 100 International, box 97 folder 100S, CFR 1945, Application for funds, W. H. Mallory (CFR) to J. H. Willits (RF), 15 January 1945.

67. The group included the economists Alvin Hansen and Jacob Viner, the historians W. L. Langer and James Shotwell, and the lawyers and businessmen John Foster Dulles and Norman Davis.

68. Shoup and Minter, *Imperial Brain Trust*, 120–122.

69. W. G. Bundy, *The Council on Foreign Relations and Foreign Affairs* (New York: CFR, 1994), 22.

70. Shoup and Minter, *Imperial Brain Trust*; G. William Domhoff, *The Power Elite and the State* (New York: Aldine de Gruyter, 1990); Inderjeet Parmar, "The Issue of State Power: A Case Study of the Council on Foreign Relations," *Journal of American Studies* 29, no. 1 (1995): 73–95. The Moscow Agreement of October 1943 was the first meeting of the three big powers—the United States, Russia, and Britain—during World War II. It set up the European Advisory Commission that worked out the basic principles for the treatment of Germany: the destruction of German military power and of the Nazi party, the punishment of war criminals, the zones of control, and the arrangements for reparations payments.

71. RFA, RG1 Project 100 International; box 99, folder 897; letter, Bowman to Willits, 23 November 1943. The CFR memoranda had dealt with reparations (which the State Department had nothing on at all), forms of postwar aid to Russia, and on confederation in Russia.

72. Kirk was a member of the Yale Institute of International Studies, a War-Peace Studies Project research secretary, and an independent consultant to the State Department. RFA, memorandum of conversation, Kirk and Willits, 22 November 1943, in same file as Bowman's letter, 23 November 1943.

73. RFA, Interview, Pasvolsky and Willits; 3 December 1943, in same file as Bowman's letter, 23 November 1943.

74. Shoup and Minter, *Imperial Brain Trust*; RFA, letter, Edward Stettinius (undersecretary of state) to J. H. Willits (RF), 24 November 1943, in same file as Bowman's letter.

75. RFA, Fosdick to Mallory, 8 October 1946, as for Bowman, but folder 898.

76. Bundy, *The Council on Foreign Relations and Foreign Affairs*, 22.

77. RFA, Tracy B. Kittredge to Joseph H. Willitts, 12 November 1940. RFA, RG1 Project series 100 International, box 99, folder 100S, CFR–War Problems, 1939–1940, letter, Tracy B. Kittredge to Joseph H. Willitts, 12 November 1940.

78. RFA *Annual Report* (1940), 61. Rockefeller also funded Harold Lasswell's research on content analysis at the Library of Congress, Douglas Waples's press

studies at Chicago, and Paul Lazarfeld's radio research at Columbia, among other mass communications projects; see Christopher Simpson, *Science of Coercion* (Oxford: Oxford University Press, 1994), 22.

79. RFA, RG1.1 series 200 200R Princeton University–Public Opinion, box 270, folder 3216; Memorandum, 5 December 1939.

80. RFA, box 270, folder 3216; funding note, 12 July 1940.

81. RFA, box 270, folder 3216; "A Proposed Study of the Effect of the War on Public Opinion in the United States," attached to a letter from Cantril to John Marshall (Rockefeller Foundation), 13 November 1939.

82. RFA, box 270, folder 3218, "Application for Renewal of Public Opinion Study," attached to a letter to John Marshall. RFA, box 270, folder 3216; letter, Cantril to Marshall, 28 November 1939.

83. RFA, box 270, folder 3218; letter, Cantril to Marshall, 9 September 1940.

84. RFA, box 271, folder 3228, "Comparison of Opinions of Those Who Do and Do Not Listen to the President's Radio Talks: Confidential Report," by Hadley Cantril, 17 September 1941.

85. RFA, box 271, folder 3228, "The People Who Would Join a 'Keep-Out-of-War' Party: Confidential Report," by Hadley Cantril, 21 November 1941.

86. RFA, RG1.1 series 200S subseries 200; RF report on Cantril's work, "The Changing Attitude Toward War," 16, January 1941.

87. RFA, box 271, folder 3229, "Confidential Report to Rockefeller Foundation on Work of the Office of Public Opinion Research of Princeton University from 1940 Through 1943," 14 December 1943, by Hadley Cantril.

88. RFA, box 270, folder 3220, Interview, Cantril, Gallup, and Marshall, 28 May 1941.

89. RFA, box 270, folder 3221, letter, Cantril to Marshall, 30 April 1942.

90. RFA, box 270, folder 3224, Interview, Cantril and Marshall, 29 January 1943.

91. RFA, box 270, folder 3225, letter, Cantril to Marshall, 4 October 1943.

92. RFA, box 270, folder 3225, Interview, Cantril and Marshall 16 December 1943. See, for example, Franklin D Roosevelt Presidential Library (New York), PPF 8229–Hadley Cantril; letter from FDR to Cantril, 12 November 1942. For Cantril's political loyalty to FDR, see letter by David K. Niles to Grace Tully, 11 November 1942, in the same file.

93. RFA, box 270, folders 3219, 3221; letter, Marshall to Cantril, 21 March 1941; and Internal Memo by J. Willits, 6 January 1942.

94. RFA, box 270, folder 3218; letter, Evarts Scudder of CDAAA to Marshall, 27 November 1940, thanking him for the report. Cantril also supplied reports to several other special-interest groups, such as the National Association of Manufacturers, trades unions, and farm organizations. See RFA, box 270, folder 3224,

Memorandum, "Proposed Work of Office . . . " 10 February 1943. The CDAAA was, itself, an ad hoc group of CFR members led by William Allen White (editor of the *Kansas Emporia Gazette*) at the suggestion of FDR; see Michael Wala, *The Council on Foreign Relations and American Foreign Policy in the Early Cold War* (Providence: Berghahn Books, 1994).

95. Simpson, *Science of Coercion*, 23.

96. Mark L. Chadwin, *The Hawks of World War II* (Chapel Hill: University of North Carolina Press, 1968).

97. Inderjeet Parmar, "'Another important group that needs more cultivation . . . ': The CFR and the Mobilisation of Black Americans for Interventionism, 1939–1941," *Ethnic and Racial Studies* 27, no. 5 (2004): 710–731.

98. A. S. Layton, *International Politics and Civil Rights Policies in the United States, 1941–1960* (Cambridge: Cambridge University Press, 2000), 39.

99. H. Agar, *A Time for Greatness* (New York: Little, Brown, 1942), 42.

100. Sulzberger was the publisher of the *New York Times* and a Rockefeller Foundation trustee and executive committee member. Markel later became a public-opinion expert, publishing a book on the subject, *Public Opinion and Foreign Policy* (New York: Harper, 1949).

101. See Walter Lippmann, *Public Opinion* (New York: Macmillan, 1941); and Edward Bernays, "The Engineering of Consent," *Annals of the American Academy of Political and Social Science* 250 (March 1947).

102. Peffer, "Memorandum on Carnegie Grants in the Field of International Relations," 12.

103. "Memorandum for Counsel: Foreign Policy Association," June 27, 1952; in CC Grant Files, box 147, 2.

104. Peffer, "Memorandum on Carnegie Grants in the Field of International Relations," 12. By 1945, membership had increased to almost 28,000; see "Report on Work of the Foreign Policy Association," July 1944–1945, CC Grant Files, box 147.

105. "Memorandum for Counsel: Foreign Policy Association," 3.

106. Peffer, "Memorandum on Carnegie Grants in the Field of International Relations," 12. The resulting "Foreign Policy Reports" were sent by the CFR to its regional committees. The FPA's "Report on Japan as an Economic Power" was used by the State Department in its courses for foreign-service officers specializing on the Far East; see letter, Carnegie Corporation to McCoy, 18 January 1943, CC Grant Files, box 147.

107. Letter, CC to McCoy, 18 January 1943, CC Grant Files, box 147.

108. Peffer, "Memorandum on Carnegie Grants in the Field of International Relations," 14. The International Ladies Garments Workers' Union also distributed

one hundred copies of each Headline book to its educational committee; see FPA Report to the CC, October 1, 1940–April 30, 1941, 2.

109. "FPA Education Program" report, 21 May 1943, box 147.

110. Ibid.

111. FPA Report, October 1, 1940–April 30, 1941, 2.

112. See reports of FPA work for 1940–1941; 1941–1942 in CC files.

113. See FPA report to CC, September 1, 1943–July 1, 1944, 4.

114. "Memorandum on the Work of the Foreign Policy Association," attached to 1941–1942 FPA report to CC, 3–4.

115. FPA report on work, September 1, 1941–July 1, 1942; and "memorandum on the Work of the Foreign Policy Association," attached to that report.

116. "Memorandum for Counsel," 12–13.

117. Ibid., 11.

118. "Memorandum on the Work of the Foreign Policy Association," 1, for a favorable opinion from Undersecretary of State Summer Welles; and letter, quoting former Secretary of State Edward Stettinius Jr., 28 October 1946, from the FPA to the CC, box 147.

119. Lawrence T. Woods, *Asia-Pacific Diplomacy: Nongovernmental Organizations and International Relations* (Vancouver, B.C.: UBC Press, 1993), 7.

120. John N. Thomas, *The Institute of Pacific Relations, Asian Scholars, and American Politics* (Seattle: University of Washington Press, 1974), 4.

121. Woods, *Asia-Pacific Diplomacy*, 8.

122. Thomas, *The Institute of Pacific Relations, Asian Scholars, and American Politics*, 4.

123. Thomas, *The Institute of Pacific Relations, Asian Scholars, and American Politics*, 30, 5; see also Woods, *Asia-Pacific Diplomacy*, 33, 35.

124. Owen Lattimore, *China Memoirs. Chiang Kai-shek and the War Against Japan* (Tokyo: University of Tokyo Press, 1990), 35.

125. Lattimore was appointed wartime political adviser to Chiang Kai-shek by President Roosevelt and also joined the Office of War Information as head of its Asia-Pacific bureau. It was not "a bad thing," Lattimore wrote, "to have a person who knew China well to be engaged in propaganda work for the Pacific areas directed against the Japanese." *China Memoirs*, 167–168. The AIPR also received grants from the Rockefeller Foundation.

126. Edward H. Berman, *The Ideology of Philanthropy: The Influence of the Carnegie, Rockefeller, and Ford Foundations on American Foreign Policy* (Albany, N.Y.: SUNY Press, 1983), 46.

127. The AIPR even opened a Washington, D.C., office upon the outbreak of World War II, forging stronger government links "to facilitate cooperation in the war

effort." See Thomas, *The Institute of Pacific Relations, Asian Scholars, and American Politics*, 34. According to Woods, *Asia-Pacific Diplomacy*, 35, the AIPR was "a very useful sounding board" for governmental officials' ideas.

128. Figures calculated from CC *Annual Reports* for the entire period.

129. Compiled from Rockefeller Foundation annual reports.

130. W. Harold Dalgliesh, *Community Education in Foreign Affairs: A Report on Nineteen American Cities* (New York: CFR, 1946), 4. The AIPR also ran a study group in Cleveland, Ohio, and a small program in Detroit.

131. Ibid., 16.

132. Ibid.

133. Peffer, "Memorandum on Carnegie Grants in the Field of International Relations," 16. The AIPR was an institutional member of the ACIS whose work at the Institute of Advanced Study at Princeton led to the North Atlantic Relations conferences, in an attempt to create an Atlantic version of the IPR. See also Paul F. Hooper, "The Institute of Pacific Relations and the Origins of Asian and Pacific Studies," *Pacific Affairs* 61 (Spring 1988): 98–121.

134. See FPA reports in CC Grant Files, for 1940–1941, 1942–1942, and 1943–1944.

135. CEIP, *Division of Intercourse and Education Annual Reports*, 1937 and 1939.

136. CEIP *Annual Reports*, 1943, 1944, 1945.

137. Peffer, "Memorandum on Carnegie Grants in the Field of International Relations," 16.

138. Produced jointly with the FPA, 1941–1942.

139. Peffer, "Memorandum on Carnegie Grants in the Field of International Relations," 17.

140. Record of interview, Dollard to Wm. W. Lockwood and W. L. Holland, 6 March 1942; CC Grant Files, box 182 (AIPR).

141. Letter, Henry James to W. A. Jessup (both CC), 7 April 1942; and letter, Lockwood to Robert M. Lester (CC), 21 January 1943; CC Grant Files, box 182.

142. See CC annual reports. Peffer again understates the funding levels severely, with his figure of $309,000 (up to 1942).

143. Office of the President, Record of Interview, September 3, 1937; letter, Page to Keppel, October 15, 1937; box 126, Carnegie Corporation Grant Files: Council on Foreign Relations: Committees on Foreign Relations 1937–1940. The CC initiative was officially known as the "Cooperative Adult Education Scheme," although, in its annual reports, the CC referred to the plan as a "demonstration program in Adult Education." Up to 1942 alone, the CC donated $100,000 to this program; by 1945, a further $70,000 had been granted.

144. Memorandum by Walter H. Mallory, executive director of the CFR: "Project for Popular Education in International Affairs Proposed by the Carnegie Corporation," November 1, 1937, 2.

145. Memorandum by Phillips Bradley (associate professor of political science, Amherst College) to F. W. Keppel, 21 September 1937, 8.

146. *The Council on Foreign Relations: A Record of Twenty-Five Years, 1921–1946* (New York: CFR, 1947), 48. The original seven Committees were in Cleveland, Denver, Des Moines, Detroit, Houston, Louisville, and Portland (Oregon).

147. Percy Bidwell (director of studies), "A Seven-Year Survey of An Educational Project in International Relations, 1938–1945," CFR, in CC Grant Files, box 127.

148. Percy Bidwell's introduction to W. Harold Dagliesh, *Community Education in Foreign Affairs* (New York: CFR, 1946), iii–viii.

149. Bidwell, "A Seven-Year Survey," 3; "Report to the Carnegie Corporation on the Work of the Foreign Relations Committees of the CFR During the 1942–43 Season," box 127.

150. Percy Bidwell, "Report on the Work of the Foreign Relations Committees, Season 1941–42," box 127.

151. Bidwell, "A Seven-Year Survey," 5.

152. CFR *Annual Report, Report of the Executive Director* (1944–1945), 14.

153. Bidwell, "A Seven-Year Survey," 6–7.

154. Quotation is from "Memorandum for Counsel of Carnegie Corporation," 1–15, June 30, 1952. CC Grant Files, 1946–55; Dulles, letter to Miller, n.d. CC Grant Files, box 127; Bidwell, 1941–42, 8; Herbert Heaton, *A Scholar in Action: Edwin F. Gay* (New York: Greenwood Press, 1968), 237–241.

155. Letter, Wilson to Assistant Secretary of State Breckinridge Long, July 13, 1940; memorandum by Charles W. Yost, division of special research, to Leo Pasvolsky, 14 April 1942, 1.

156. Miller, *Man from the Valley* (Chapel Hill: University of North Carolina Press, 1971), 87.

157. "Notes on the American Committee for International Studies," 5 April 1941, 2; in CC Grant Files, box 18.

158. Proposal received and filed in CC Papers, September 3, 1940, box 18.

159. Report on Lynd Proposal (Summary), 22 October 1940, in CC Papers, box 18. Among the five who rejected the proposal were Charles E. Merriam and Quincy Wright, both of the University of Chicago, and Henry M. Wriston, the president of Brown University and a Carnegie trustee.

160. Report by Savage, 13 November 1940, CC Papers, box 18.

161. Lewis A. Coser, *Men of Ideas* (New York: The Free Press, 1965), 339.

162. E. C. Luck, *Mixed Messages* (Washington, D.C.: Brookings Institution Press, 1999), especially chapter 2, the title of which is "A Special Nation, Peerless and Indispensable."

163. I. Parmar, "Resurgent Academic Interest in the Council on Foreign Relations," *Politics* 21 (2001): 31–39; Butler, *Across the Busy Years*, vol. 2. Butler held the view that the United States was "the keeper of the conscience of democracy"; cited by Luck, *Mixed Messages*, 21.

164. National Security Council-68, "United States Objectives and Programs for National Security," the April 1950 seminal Cold War blueprint, the main author of which was Paul Nitze.

165. Nicholas J. Spykman, *America's Strategy in World Politics: The United States and the Balance of Power* (New York: Harcourt Brace, 1942).

166. J. Ruggie, "Third Try at World Order?" *Political Science Quarterly* 109, no. 4 (1994): 553–571.

167. C. N. Murphy, *International Organization and Industrial Change* (Cambridge: Polity Press, 1994); R.W. Cox, "Labor and Hegemony," *International Organization* 31, no. 3 (1977): 385–424.

168. J. T. Shotwell, "The ILO as an Alternative to Violent Revolution," *Annals of the American Academy of Political and Social Science* 166 (March 1933): 18.

169. D. Fisher, "Rockefeller Philanthropy and the British Empire," *History of Education* 7 (1978): 129–143.

170. Akira Iriye, *Global Community: The Role of International Organizations in the Making of the Contemporary World* (Berkeley: University of California Press, 2002).

171. G. J. Ikenberry, *Liberal Order and Imperial Ambition* (Cambridge: Polity Press, 2006), 53.

172. Ibid., 56, 57.

173. Akira Iriye, *Global Community: The Role of International Organizations in the Making of the Contemporary World* (Berkeley: University of California Press, 2002), 28.

174. A. Bosco and C. Navari, eds., *Chatham House and British Foreign Policy* (London: Lothian Foundation Press, 1994).

175. Andrew Williams concludes that the CFR, Chatham House, and Carnegie philanthropy "were part . . . of a transatlantic opinion-forming community." "Before the Special Relationship: The CFR, The Carnegie Foundation, and the Rumour of an Anglo-American War," *Journal of Transatlantic Studies* 1, no. 2 (2003): 233–251.

176. Parmar, *Think Tanks and Power in Foreign Policy*; Shoup and Minter, *Imperial Brain Trust*.

177. Bowman, cited in Parmar, *Think Tanks and Power in Foreign Policy*, 123.

178. Carnegie Endowment for International Peace, *Institutes of International Affairs* (New York: CEIP, 1953).

179. Parmar, *Think Tanks and Power in Foreign Policy*. See also K. Rietzler, "Philanthropy, Peace Research, and Revisionist Politics: Rockefeller and Carnegie Support for the Study of International Relations in Weimar Germany," *GHI Bulletin Supplement* 5 (2008): 61–79. Rockefeller enthusiasm for GAP waned when the latter felt that research at GAP had "taken the form of unsystematic, individual research by members of staff, according to their several interests and inclinations" (73).

180. P. C. Dobell and R. Willmott, "John Holmes," *International Journal* 33, no. 1 (1977–1978), 109–110.

181. T. Carothers, "A League of Their Own," *Foreign Policy* (July–August 2008); see also G. John Ikenberry and Anne-Marie Slaughter, *Forging a World of Liberty Under Law* (Princeton, N.J.: The Woodrow Wilson School of Public and International Affairs, Princeton University, 2006).

182. J. Lloyd, "The Anglosphere Project," *New Statesman* (March 13, 2000). Interestingly, this concept is supported by the historian Robert Conquest, the former critic of U.S. power Christopher Hitchens, and the former British prime minister Gordon Brown. The continuities between Anglosphere and Anglo-Saxonism are clear. The revival of such ideas is captured by Andrew Roberts, *A History of the English-Speaking Peoples Since 1900* (London: Phoenix, 2007).

183. M. W. Doyle, "Liberalism and World Politics," *American Political Science Review* 80 (1986): 1151–1169. The Princeton Project on National Security, headed by Ikenberry and Slaughter, is a champion of democratic peace theory (see chapter 8). Both Ikenberry and Doyle also acknowledge that Federal Union was an early expression of the underlying assumptions of democratic peace theory.

184. Minutes, "World Order Preparatory Group," first meeting, 17 July 1939; Lionel Curtis Papers, box 110–111; Bodleian Library, Oxford.

185. Letter, Streit to Curtis, 13 May 1939; Curtis Papers, Correspondence, box 16; letter, Curtis to Captain Nugent Head, 6 December 1945, Curtis Papers, Correspondence, box 34.

186. Parmar, *Think Tanks and Power in Foreign Policy*.

187. Ibid.

188. In particular, James T. Shotwell, the Columbia University historian and CEIP leader, was active in the formation of the ILO in 1919 and in the US labor

movement; Inderjeet Parmar, "Engineering Consent: The Carnegie Endowment for International Peace and the Mobilisation of American Public Opinion, 1939–1945," *Review of International Studies* 26, no. 1 (2000): 43.

189. K. Rietzler, "Unbroken Bridges: Why the Rockefeller Foundation and the Carnegie Endowment Supported the International Studies Conference in the 1930s," paper presented at the Transatlantic Studies Association conference (July 2008), 5. The American foundations were represented on the ISC's executive committee and successfully changed the ISC into a version of the Institute of Pacific Relations, orienting its national councils to policy-related questions.

190. G. Murray, "Intellectual Co-operation," *Annals of the American Academy of Political and Social Sciences* 235 (September 1944): 7. According to Murray, Carnegie and Rockefeller funding came second only to that of the French government.

191. See, for example, E. Richard Brown, *Rockefeller Medicine Men* (Berkeley: University of California Press, 1979).

192. E. J. Murphy, *Creative Philanthropy* (New York: Teachers' College Press, 1976).

4. PROMOTING AMERICANISM, COMBATING ANTI-AMERICANISM, AND DEVELOPING A COLD WAR AMERICAN STUDIES NETWORK

1. The Welch quotation in the epigraph is cited by Richard Barnett, *Roots of War* (Baltimore, Md.: Penguin, 1973), 19. The Kennan quotation in the epigraph is cited by S. Lucas, "Introduction: Negotiating Freedom," in Helen Laville and Hugh Wilford, eds., *The U.S. Government, Citizen Groups, and the Cold War: The State-Private Network* (London: Frank Cass, 2005), 9.

2. Paul Kennedy, *Rise and Fall of the Great Powers* (London: Fontana Press, 1989), 461.

3. To Ford Foundation trustees, a "healthy international environment" would only be produced if the "underdeveloped nations succeed in meeting the challenge before them" of defeating communist-inspired "revolutionary ferment"; Volker R. Berghahn, *America and the Intellectual Cold Wars in Europe: Shepard Stone Between Philanthropy, Academy, and Diplomacy* (Princeton, N.J.: Princeton University Press, 2001), 159.

4. T. McDowell, *American Studies* (Minneapolis: Minnesota University Press, 1948), 26.

5. David Campbell, *Writing Security* (Manchester: Manchester University Press, 1992); Alan Wolfe, *The Rise and Fall of the Soviet Threat* (Boston: South End Press, 1984).

6. Rockefeller, Carnegie, and Ford philanthropies were, of course, also subject to the charge of "un-Americanism" by various McCarthyite congressional committees

during the 1950s. The Ford Foundation is generally understood to have been engaged in combating anti-Americanism and communism during the cold war; Oliver Schmidt, "Small Atlantic World: U.S. Philanthropy and the Expanding International Exchange of Scholars After 1945," in J. C. E. Geinow-Hecht and F. Schumacher, eds., *Culture and International History* (Oxford: Berghahn Books, 2003), 121.

7. Foundations' annual reports.

8. Ben Whitaker, *The Foundations: An Anatomy of Philanthropy and Society* (London: Eyre Methuen, 1974); Giles Scott-Smith, *The Politics of Apolitical Culture: The Congress for Cultural Freedom, the CIA, and Postwar American Hegemony* (London: Routledge, 2002); Frances Stonor Saunders, *Who Paid the Piper? The CIA and the Cultural Cold War* (London: Granta, 1999).

9. Robert E. Spiller, "The Fulbright Program in American Studies Abroad: Retrospect and Prospect," in Robert H. Walker, ed., *American Studies Abroad* (Westport, Conn.: Greenwood Press, 1975), 8.

10. Ibid., 5.

11. Berghahn, *America and the Intellectual Cold Wars in Europe*, 170.

12. Melvin P. Leffler, *A Preponderance of Power* (Stanford, Calif.: Stanford University Press, 1992); Kathleen D. McCarthy, "From Cold War to Cultural Development: The International Cultural Activities of the Ford Foundation, 1950–1980," *Daedalus* (Winter 1987): 93–117.

13. Victoria de Grazia, *Irresistible Empire: America's Advance Through Twentieth-Century Europe* (London: The Belknap Press of Harvard University Press, 2005).

14. Marcus Cunliffe, "The Anatomy of Anti-Americanism," in R. Kroes and M. Van Rossem, eds., *Anti-Americanism in Europe* (Amsterdam: Free University Press, 1986); B. Appleyard, "Why Do They Hate America?" *Sunday Times* (September 23, 2001); R. Weikunat, "The Philosophical Origins of European Anti-Americanism," *Contemporary Review* (July 2002).

15. *Humanities Discussion Papers*; Trustee Subcommittee on Humanities and the Arts; Reports 016196, 5 March 1970; FFA.

16. Although American Studies programs had existed in the United States since the 1920s, they only became fully established—complete with a professional association, annual conferences, and a learned journal, for example—during the Cold War; Spiller, "The Fulbright Program in American Studies Abroad," 5.

17. Tremaine McDowell argues that American Studies would unify Americans through greater self-knowledge, undermine isolationist sentiment, and promote internationalism; McDowell, *American Studies* (Minneapolis: University of Minnesota Press, 1948), 31.

18. John W. Gardner, "Education in Values for Americans," part 1, in Carnegie Corporation (CC) Grant Files, "American Values 1948–50", April 24, 1950, in box 40, folder 14, 1.

19. Ibid., part 2, 1.

20. Ibid., part 2, 3–4.

21. Ibid., part 2, 9. Emphasis added.

22. Letter, Gordon W. Allport to John Gardner, September 28, 1948; box 40, folder 14.

23. Letter, Gardner to Allport, October 19, 1948; box 40, folder 14.

24. Gardner, "Education in Values for Americans," part 2, 14.

25. CC memorandum, "Grants for American Studies," September 1958; box 411, folder 11.

26. CC, "A Program of Research Grants for Historical Studies in the Field of American Civilization," January 5, 1949.

27. John W. Gardner, "Preliminary Notes for a Survey of Programs in American Studies," ca. 1948; CC Grant Files, box 40, folder 8; emphasis added.

28. CC memorandum, "Grants for American Studies," September 1958; box 411, folder 11.

29. Athan G. Theoharis, *Seeds of Repression* (Chicago: Quadrangle Books, 1971).

30. *Statement by Dean Rusk on Behalf of the Rockefeller Foundation and the General Education Board to the Special Committee on Foundations*, 39; Rusk Collection, box 4, folder 53; Rockefeller Archive Center, Tarrytown, New York.

31. Ibid., 43–44.

32. Scott Lucas, "A Document from the Harvard International Summer School," in J. C. E. Gienow-Hecht and F. Schumacher, eds., *Culture and International History* (New York: Berghahn Books, 2003), 258.

33. Inderjeet Parmar, "Conceptualising the State-Private Network in American Foreign Policy," in Helen Laville and Hugh Wilford, eds., *The U.S. Government, Citizen Groups, and the Cold War: The State-Private Network* (London: Frank Cass, 2005); see also Liam Kennedy and Scott Lucas, "Enduring Freedom: Public Diplomacy and U.S. Foreign Policy," *American Quarterly* 57, no. 2 (2005): 309–333.

34. George Kennan endorsed the seminar plan as having "a worthy, dignified and useful purpose" when he forwarded it to the Ford Foundation for support; Memorandum, John B. Howard to Joseph M. McDaniel Jr., "Harvard Summer School Foreign Students Project," May 24, 1951; PA55–9, reel 0942; Ford Foundation Archives (FFA), New York.

35. Lucas, "A Document from the Harvard International Summer School," 259. Kissinger was director of the seminar from 1951 to 1971.

36. Kissinger was involved in recent similar activities in behalf of the German Marshall Fund's transatlantic understanding programs; *Annual Report* (2003), 1–6.

37. Henry Kissinger, "Report of the Sub-committee on Academic Programs" (undated, October/November, 1950), in Lucas, "A Document from the Harvard International Summer School," 261–262. Emphasis added.

38. Lucas, "A Document from the Harvard International Summer School," 263. Emphasis added.

39. In one letter concerning grant applications to Ford, Kissinger offered to provide supporting references from Allen W. Dulles (CIA director) and C. D. Jackson, head of the Congress for Cultural Freedom initiative; Kissinger to Don K. Price (FF associate director), December 10, 1953; PA53–159, reel 1118 (FFA); see also Berghahn, *America and the Intellectual Cold Wars in Europe*.

40. Ford Foundation annual reports; see also, Ford Foundation, *American Studies Abroad*; report 004642, April 1969. In total, FF granted Kissinger over $390,000; FFA.

41. "Docket Excerpt. Executive Committee meeting September 27, 1956: International Programs: International Affairs: Harvard University International Seminar"; PA55–9; reel 0492 (FFA).

42. Ibid.

43. Ibid.

44. "Excerpt from Docket: International Affairs: Harvard International Seminar," October 29–30 1954; Grant file PA55–9; reel 0492; Ford Foundation Archives (FFA).

45. "Docket excerpt, Executive Committee Mtg. September 27, 1956: International Programs: International Affairs. Harvard University International Seminar"; Grant file PA55–9; reel 0492; FFA.

46. Ibid.

47. Inter-Office Memorandum, Bernard L. Gladieux to Joseph M. McDaniel, "Harvard International Seminar (-A351 Revised)," August 13, 1952; PA55–9, reel 0492 (FFA).

48. "Docket Excerpt . . . September 27, 1956"; Grant File PA55–9; reel 0492 (FFA).

49. "Docket excerpt, Executive Committee Mtg.," September 27, 1956 (FFA). Emphasis added.

50. It is an interesting use of language to refer to European dissent as "disturbance," suggesting, perhaps, that opposition to America rests largely on psychological and emotional factors internal to the individual.

51. Henry Kissinger, report on 1955 program; PA55–9; reel 0492 (FFA).

52. "Extracts of Letters from Past Participants," attached to a letter, Kissinger to Harold Swearer (FF), 4 November 1968; PA69–134, reel 2248 (FFA).

53. Letter, Kissinger to Harold Swearer (FF), 4 November 1968; PA69–134, reel 2248 (FFA).

54. Walter Isaacson, *Kissinger* (London: Simon and Schuster, 1992), 71.

55. J. Gedmin and C. Kennedy, "Selling America, Short," *National Interest* (Winter 2003).

56. Inter-Office Memorandum, "Harvard International Seminar", Bernard L. Gladieux to Joseph McDaniel, August 13 1952; PA55–9, reel 0942 (FFA).

57. The phrase "the faint odor of cultural imperialism" is from an interoffice memorandum, Richard C. Sheldon to W. McNeill Lowry, "American Studies," March 5, 1968, 2; PA69–134, reel 2248 (FFA).

58. Indeed, this was precisely how Kissinger and Elliott contextualized their own efforts; letter, Elliott to Don K. Price (Ford Foundation), 13 February 1954; PA55–9, reel 0942 (FFA).

59. "Clemens Heller: Founder of the 'Marshall Plan of the Mind,'" http://www .salzburgglobal.org/2009/history.cfm?goto=heller.

60. David E. Bell and McNeill Lowry, *Grant Allocation to Salzburg Seminar in American Studies, Inc.*, January 20, 1970; 3; PA55–216; reel 2081 (FFA).

61. Dexter Perkins, "A Proposal to Strengthen the Salzburg Seminar in American Studies," March 1960; PA55–216, reel 2081 (FFA). The fellows were selected by "responsible" men in Europe and officers of the U.S. Information Service; many alumni subsequently went on to take up Commonwealth Fund study scholarships in the United States, becoming networked in a tightly organized set of U.S. East Coast establishment organizations.

62. Letter, Grayson Kirk to Dexter Perkins (President, Salzburg Seminar), March 8, 1960; PA55–216, reel 2081 (FFA).

63. All quotes are from Paul M. Herzog (president, Salzburg Seminar), "Application to the Ford Foundation for a Grant for the Period 1970–1975," October 1969; PA55–216, reel 2081 (FFA).

64. Perkins, "A Proposal to Strengthen the Salzburg Seminar in American Studies," March 1960; PA55–216, reel 2081 (FFA).

65. Cited by Herzog, "Application to the Ford Foundation . . . "; PA55–216, reel 2081 (FFA).

66. Bell and Lowry, *Grant Allocation to Salzburg Seminar*, January 20 1970; PA55–216, reel 2081 (FFA).

67. Perkins, "A Proposal to Strengthen the Salzburg Seminar in American Studies."

68. Ibid., exhibit IV.

69. Ibid.

70. Bell and Lowry, *Grant Allocation to Salzburg Seminar*, January 20 1970; PA55–216, reel 2081 (FFA).

71. Perkins, "A Proposal to Strengthen the Salzburg Seminar in American Studies," exhibit XIV.

72. Ibid.

73. Letter, Daniel Bell to Dexter Perkins, March 1 1960; PA55–216, reel 2081 (FFA).

74. Perkins, "A Proposal to Strengthen the Salzburg Seminar in American Studies."

75. Espinosa's quotation in the epigraph to this section is cited in Giles Scott-Smith, Ali Fisher, and Inderjeet Parmar, "American Foundations, Public Diplomacy, and the Cold War: The Case of American Studies in the U.S., Britain, and the Netherlands," unpublished paper (2005), 1.

76. For details see D. Reynolds, "Whitehall, Washington, and the Promotion of American Studies in Britain During World War Two," *Journal of American Studies* 16, no. 2: 165–188.

77. R. Pells, *Not Like Us* (New York: Basic Books, 1997).

78. Letter, Richard P. Jackson to E. F. D'Arms (associate director, division of humanities, Rockefeller Foundation), July 13 1955; Rockefeller Foundation Archives, RG 1.2 series 401R, box 52, folder 454; Tarrytown, New York. Jackson was reporting to the foundation on a recent meeting to draw up a BAAS constitution, at University College, Oxford (July 12, 1955).

79. Letter, Frank Thistlethwaite to E. F. D'Arms (RF), 10 August 1955; RFA, RG 1.2 series 401 R, box 52, folder 454. No suggestion is made as to the motives of scholars in accepting or soliciting foundation grants. No charge is leveled that scholars produced research results foundations wanted nor that they robotically produced predetermined pro-American conclusions. It is argued that there was on the whole a coincidence of wants on the part of scholars and foundations, as Michael Heale argues. However, the foundations did narrow the space for other work, ideas, and scholars and thereby mobilize bias; Heale, "American History in Britain," paper presented at BAAS conference, Cambridge, April 2005. This is, indeed, confirmation of Laski's point, once again.

80. The conferences were held at Oxford and Cambridge to lend academic prestige: 1952, St. John's College, Cambridge; 1953, University and Magdalen Colleges, Oxford; 1954, Peterhouse, Cambridge; and 1955, University College, Cambridge; *Final Report: The American Studies Conferences in the United Kingdom 1952–1955*; RFA, RG 1.2 series 401R, box 76, folder 646.

81. Mark L. Chadwin, *The Hawks of World War II* (Chapel Hill: University of North Carolina Press, 1968). In 1957, Herbert Agar, another war hawk and leader of the Fight for Freedom, joined BAAS's Advisory Council; BAAS, Bulletin No. 4, April 1957; RFA, RG 1.2 series 401R, box 74, folder 644.

82. Fulbright Commission, *Final Report: The American Studies Conferences in the United Kingdom 1952–1955*, 7; RFA, RG 1.2 series 401R, box 74, folder 646.

83. In the extreme case of Germany after 1945, American Studies was promoted by the cultural officers of the U.S. Military Government and High Commission. Professor John A. Hawgood reports that much of the German interest in America in the "difficult years 1945–48 tended to follow the dollar. . . . All sorts of people in Germany discovered a hitherto unsuspected interest in the history and culture of the United States."; BAAS Bulletin No. 6, February 1958, 14; RFA, RG 1.2 series 401R, box 74, folder 645. Precisely Laski's point.

84. Fulbright Commission, *Final Report: The American Studies Conferences in the UK 1952–1955*, 10; RFA, RG 1.2 series 401R, box 74, folder 646.

85. Ibid.

86. Pells argues that such individuals were attracted to American Studies and an identification with an egalitarian vision of America on the basis of their non-establishment social origins—they were Welsh or Scottish, working or lower middle class, or Jewish; *Not Like Us*, 117.

87. Letter, Thistlethwaite to D'Arms, 10 August 1955.

88. Memorandum to the ad hoc committee on American Studies, Richard P. Taylor, Executive Secretary, "Proposed Formation of a Council or Association of American Studies," April 18, 1955; RFA, RG 1.2 series 401R, box 52, folder 454.

89. Taylor was replaced as executive secretary in 1956 by Dr. W. L. Gaines, who had previously worked in the intelligence section of the U.S. embassy in London; Excerpt, E. F. D'Arms's "Diary of Trip to Europe," May 7, 1956; RFA, RG 1.2 series 401R, box 52, folder 454. Gaines felt that BAAS was "on a sound basis and should prove a valuable means of promoting American Studies."

90. Fulbright Commission, *Final Report*, 14.

91. Letter, D'Arms (RF) to Frank Thistlethwaite, August 23 1955; RFA, RG 1.2 series 401R, box 52, folder 454.

92. Letter, Taylor to D'Arms, October 31 1955, RFA, RG 1.2 series 401R, box 52, folder 454. Taylor was executive secretary of the U.S. Educational Commission (Fulbright Commission), United Kingdom, and treasurer of the RF's grant-in-aid to University College, Oxford.

93. Letter, Thistlethwaite to D'Arms, 9 August 1956; RFA, RG 1.2 series 401R, box 52, folder 454.

94. Letter, Thistlethwaite to D'Arms, 9 August 1956; RFA, RG 1.2 series 401R, box 52, folder 454. By this time, BAAS was effectively administered from the Department of American Studies at the University of Manchester.

95. Interview, E. F. D'Arms and Thistlethwaite, October 2, 1956; RFA, RG 1.2 series 401R, box 52, folder 454.

96. BAAS memorandum (by Thistlethwaite), "Memorandum for the Rockefeller Foundation on the Needs of the British Association for American Studies," n.d. but circa 1956; RFA, RG 1.2 series 401R, box 52, folder 454.

97. E. F. D'Arms diary note, February 27, 1957; RFA, RG 1.2 series 4021R, box 52, folder 454.

98. Letter, Marcus Cunliffe to John H. Greenfield, Asst. Comptroller, Rockefeller Foundation, February 1, 1965; RFA, RG 1.2 series 401R, box 52, folder 457.

99. For the negotiated character of the founding of BAAS, see Ali Fisher and Scott Lucas, "Master and Servant? The U.S. Government and the Founding of the BAAS," *European Journal of American Culture* 21, no. 1 (2002): 16–25. Fisher argues elsewhere that, despite the protracted negotiations between British Americanists, the State Department, and the Rockefeller Foundation, their respective aims were "congruous to those of the [American] State"; Ali Fisher, "Sought by the U.S. Government, Facilitated by Philanthropy," paper presented at BAAS conference, Cambridge, April 2005, 3.

100. *American Studies Abroad, with Particular Reference to the ACLS Program*; Report 004642, FFA; 6.

101. Ibid., 57.

102. *Humanities Discussion Papers*, Trustee sub-committee on Humanities and the Arts, 5 March 1970; Report 016196; FFA.

103. *American Studies Abroad*, 56–58.

104. Ibid., 22–23.

105. Memo, Richard C. Sheldon to W. McNeill Lowry, 5 March 1968, reel 2248, PA69–134, FFA.

106. "American Studies," Howard R. Swearer to Messrs. Bell, Sutton, Kohl and Gordon, 19 February 1968, reel 2248, PA69–134, FFA.

107. "Grant-in-Aid to the EAAS Towards Its General Support and Conferences"; RFA, RG 1.2 series 700, box 17, folder 148. $6,000 was awarded in August 1956.

108. Paper attached to "Grant-in-Aid to the EAAS . . . "; RFA, RG 1.2 series 700, box 17, folder 148.

109. Letter, Robert Spiller to John Marshall (RF), 6 February 1959; RFA, RG 1.2 series 700, box 17, folder 148.

110. *American Studies Abroad*, 161. Giles Scott-Smith notes, however, that two Dutch

professors funded by a combination of Ford and U.S. state grants were "forced to leave their positions because of left-wing radicalism"; Scott-Smith, "The Ties That Bind: Dutch-American Relations, U.S. Public Diplomacy, and the Promotion of American Studies Since the Second World War," *Hague Journal of Diplomacy* 2 (2007): 299.

111. Cited by Marcus Cunliffe, "American Studies in Europe," in Robert H. Walker, ed., *American Studies Abroad* (Westport, Conn.: Greenwood Press, 1975), 50–51. Cunliffe was citing a (justly critical, in his view) review of one of his own books.

112. Giles Scott-Smith, "The Congress for Cultural Freedom in Retrospect," *Storiografia* 6 (2002); Saunders, *Who Paid the Piper?* Although Scott-Smith argues that the foundations were "bit players" in CCF in terms of funding, the aim above is to show that Ford did provide some funding and, even more, that Ford, CCF, and the CIA shared similar outlooks—and personnel—in regard to fighting America's enemies in the Cold War.

113. Scott-Smith, "The Congress for Cultural Freedom in Retrospect," 183. CCF was formed in Berlin in 1950; key founders included Michael Josselson, James Burnham, Sidney Hook, Arthur Koestler, and Melvin Lasky.

114. Saunders, *Who Paid the Piper?* 142.

115. Berghahn, *America and the Intellectual Cold Wars in Europe*, 220–221.

116. Giles Scott-Smith, "The Congress for Cultural Freedom, the End of Ideology, and the 1955 Milan Conference: 'Defining the Parameters of Discourse,'" *Journal of Contemporary History* 37, no. 3 (2002): 437–455.

117. Ibid., 442.

118. For the definitive study of this subject, Hugh Wilford, *The CIA, the British Left, and the Cold War* (London: Frank Cass, 2003).

119. Scott-Smith, "The Congress for Cultural Freedom," 449. Schmidt argues that the Bilderberg conferences were "largely sponsored by the Carnegie Endowment"; Schmidt, "Small Atlantic World," 122.

120. Berghahn, *America and the Intellectual Cold Wars in Europe*.

121. Militant Tendency, *CIA Infiltration of the Labour Movement* (London: Militant Tendency, 1982), 30.

122. Francis X. Sutton, Inter-Office Memorandum to Messrs. McGeorge Bundy and David Bell, "Congress for Cultural Freedom," September 21, 1967; Report 002784 (FFA).

123. Sutton, "Confidential: Information Paper, Congress for Cultural Freedom," September 1967; Report 002784 (FFA).

124. Berghahn, *America and the Intellectual Cold Wars in Europe*, 241.

125. William Appleman Williams, *Some Presidents, from Wilson to Nixon* (New York: New York Review, 1972), 22.

126. Ford Foundation, *American Studies Abroad*, April 1969; Report 004642; FFA.

127. Letter, Elliott to Price, 13 February 1954; PA55–9, reel 0942 (FFA).

128. Inderjeet Parmar, "Institutes of International Affairs: Their Roles in Foreign Policy-Making, Opinion Mobilization, and Unofficial Diplomacy," in Diane Stone and Andrew Denham, eds., *Think Tank Traditions* (Manchester: Manchester University Press, 2004), 19–34; Parmar, "American Foundations and the Development of International Knowledge Networks," *Global Networks* 2, no. 1 (2002): 13–30. See also Lewis Coser, *Men of Ideas* (New York: The Free Press, 1965).

5. THE FORD FOUNDATION IN INDONESIA AND THE ASIAN
   STUDIES NETWORK

1. J. K. King, *Southeast Asia in Perspective* (New York: Macmillan, 1956); W. Henderson, ed., *Southeast Asia: Problems of United States Policy* (Cambridge, Mass.: MIT Press, 1963).

2. Secretary of State Cordell Hull noted that "the successful defense of the United States, in a military sense, is dependent upon supplies of vital materials which we import in large quantities from this region of the world"; cited in Lawrence Shoup and William Minter, *Imperial Brain Trust* (New York: Monthly Review Press, 1977), 147.

3. Memorandum E-B34, 7 March 1941, CFR, *War-Peace Studies*.

4. King, *Southeast Asia in Perspective*, 7. King, and the CFR study group that contributed to his book, funded by Carnegie, noted that Southeast Asia was "an interconnected strategic unit" whose "loss" would divide the air and sea routes from the Pacific to the Indian oceans.

5. President Sukarno was a founder member of the Non-Aligned Movement and hosted the Bandung conference of 1955.

6. Memorandum by Dyke Brown to Rowan Gaither, "Asian Studies Proposal of Stanford University," 3 April 1951; reel 0402, grant 05100035; FFA.

7. *Survey of Asian Studies*, prepared by the Ford Foundation, 1951; reel 0402, grant 05100035; FFA.

8. The Korean War, which broke out in June 1950, was the trigger for the release by President Truman of NSC-68, written by Paul Nitze, among others, a few months earlier. NSC-68 called for a massive program of American rearmament and hailed the adoption of militarized containment and "rollback" of the Soviet Union. Secretary of State Dean Acheson noted that NSC-68 aimed to "bludgeon

the mass mind of 'top government' " to support rearmament and intervention; cited by Noam Chomsky, *Deterring Democracy* (New York: Hill and Wang, 1992), 90. See also Jerry W. Sanders, *Peddlers of Crisis* (Boston: South End Press, 1983).

9. Between them, Malaya and Indonesia supplied 90 percent of the world's rubber and 55 percent of its tin, resources which were militarily valuable way beyond their value in dollars; King, *Southeast Asia in Perspective*, 9.

10. The Communist Party Indonesia (PKI) had around three million members and another twelve million supporters through a range of youth, student, labor, and peasants' organizations.

11. David Ransom, "Ford Country: Building an Elite for Indonesia," In S. Weissman, ed., *The Trojan Horse* (San Francisco: Ramparts Press, 1974), 93–116.

12. Ian Chalmers and V. R. Hadiz, eds., *The Politics of Economic Development in Indonesia* (London: Routledge, 1997), 18–19.

13. J. Bresnan, *Managing Indonesia* (New York: Columbia University Press, 1993), ix, 301. Bresnan was Ford's assistant representative in Indonesia (1961–1965), representative (1969–1973), and head of Ford's Asia and Pacific office (1973–1981). As a result, he became very familiar with the economists who transformed Indonesia (and their Ford connections). Finally, the Rockefeller Brothers Fund and the Henry Luce Foundation financed Bresnan's research.

14. *Memorandum* by John Bresnan (FF), "The Ford Foundation and Education in Indonesia," (for internal circulation), August 6, 1970; 005509. More recently, Bresnan has justified Ford's roles in Indonesia; Bresnan, *At Home Abroad: A Memoir of the Ford Foundation in Indonesia, 1953–1973* (Jakarta: Equinox, 2006).

15. George McTurnan Kahin, *Southeast Asia: A Testament* (London: RoutledgeCurzon, 2003), 1. Neither Kahin nor Bresnan ought to be seen as cynical self-servers or reactionaries but as authentic *liberals* operating in a particular structural context created, in part, by the Ford Foundation's own "politicized" programs.

16. Edward H. Berman, *The Influence of the Carnegie, Ford, and Rockefeller Foundations on U.S. Foreign Policy* (Albany, N.Y.: SUNY Press, 1983); Robert F. Arnove, ed., *Philanthropy and Cultural Imperialism: The Foundations at Home and Abroad* (Boston: G. K. Hall, 1980); Inderjeet Parmar, "Engineering Consent: The Carnegie Endowment for International Peace and the Mobilisation of American Public Opinion, 1939–1945," *Review of International Studies* 26, no. 1 (2000).

17. Martin Bulmer, "Philanthropic Foundations and the Development of the Social Sciences in the Early Twentieth Century: A Reply to Donald Fisher," *Sociology* 18 (1984): 572–579; Barry Karl and Stanley N. Katz, "Foundations and Ruling Class Elites," *Daedalus* 116, no. 1 (1987): 1–40; Barry Karl, "Philanthropy and the

Maintenance of Democratic Elites," *Minerva* 35 (1997): 207–220; and H. Anheier and S. Daly, "Philanthropic Foundations: A New Global Force?" in *Global Civil Society 2004–05*, ed. Helmut Anheier, Marlies Glasius, and Mary Kaldor (London: Sage, 2005).

18. Peter D. Bell, "The Ford Foundation as a Transnational Actor," *International Organization* 25, no. 3 (1971): 117. Such analyses implicitly accept the "modernization" thesis, with or without reservations that do not fundamentally challenge that paradigm's assumption that the way to build a modern economy and eradicate poverty and "underdevelopment" in the Third World is to transfer Western capital, as well as modes of thought, organization, and technologies that, in the hands of "modernizing elites" would transform societies; Richard Magat, *The Ford Foundation at Work* (New York: Plenum Press, 1979); Nils Gilman, *Mandarins of the Future* (Baltimore, Md.: Johns Hopkins Press, 2003); Bresnan, in a memoir, notes he was "intellectually committed to social modernization by way of economic development" when he arrived at the Ford Foundation's filed office in Jakarta in 1961; Bresnan, *At Home Abroad*, 2007.

19. As Truman's assistant secretary for Far Eastern affairs, and just prior to taking up the presidency of the Rockefeller Foundation in 1952, Rusk encouraged American institutions to "open . . . [their] training facilities for increasing numbers of our friends from across the Pacific"; cited in Parmar, "American foundations and the development of international knowledge networks," *Global Networks* 2, no. 1 (January 2002): 18.

20. William Greenleaf, *The Ford Foundation: The Formative Years* (unpublished internal report, 1958), chapter 2, 43; report 013606; FF archives.

21. Point Four was a U.S. foreign aid project aimed at providing technological skills, knowledge, and equipment to poor nations throughout the world. The program also encouraged the flow of private investment capital to these nations. The project received its name from the fourth point of a program set forth in President Truman's 1949 inaugural address. From 1950 until 1953, Point Four aid was administered by the Technical Cooperation Administration, a separate unit within the Dept. of State. During the administration of President Eisenhower, it was integrated into the overall foreign aid program.

22. It is clear from the records that Ford wanted it to appear that the need for a survey had arisen spontaneously from Stanford's own scholars rather than from Ford itself; see Memorandum, Dyke Brown (FF) to Rowan Gaither (FF), "Conference with Carl Spaeth" (Stanford), 21 February 1951; reel No. 0402, grant 05100035, Leland Stanford Junior University, "Survey of Asian Studies"; FF archives.

23. Letter, H. Rowan Gaither Jr., Associate Director (Ford Foundation), to J. E. Sterling (President, Stanford University), 27 April 1951; reel 0402, grant 05100035, Leland Stanford Junior University, "Survey of Asian Studies"; FF archives.

24. Ford argued that "if the personnel bottleneck in the United States is to be smashed, incentives must be provided to attract the most promising scholars into the field," a perfect illustration of Laski's structural explanation of foundations' influence; *A Survey of Asian Studies*, 16. The Asian Studies networks envisaged would be composed of "centers in selected underdeveloped countries with corresponding 'cousin' establishments in the United States"; *A Survey of Asian Studies*, 25.

25. Memorandum, Dyke Brown to Rowan Gaither, "Asian Studies Proposal of Stanford University", 3 April 1951; reel 0402, grant 05100035.

26. Letter, Spaeth to Gaither, 30 March 1951; reel 0402, grant 05100035; FF archives.

27. Memorandum, Dyke Brown to Rowan Gaither, "Asian Studies Proposal of Stanford University," 3 April 1951.

28. *Ford Foundation Directives for the 1960s. Supporting Materials Volumes I and II. Program Evaluations, 1951–1961*; December 1961; report 011193; FF archives.

29. Ford Foundation, "ITR Program Grants. Summary Sheet, Calendar Years 1951 Through 1966," in Section 3, ITR Finding Aid/Notebook; FF archives.

30. William Greenleaf, *The Ford Foundation*, chapter 6, 28–29.

31. Appendix, "South and Southeast Asia," to *Report of the Trustees Ad Hoc Committee on the Overseas Development Program*, March 28/29 1963; ITR box 035769; FF archives.

32. Minutes, Trustee and Executive Committee meetings, December 12–13–14, 1957; ITR box 035805; FF archives.

33. International Training and Research, *Reports 1956*; ITR box 035805; FF archives.

34. International Training and Research, Foreign Area Studies, Docket Excerpt, March 14–15, 1966; PA61–47, reel 1887.

35. *A Survey of Asian Studies*, 26–29.

36. The "Techniques of Soviet Indoctrination and Control" project encompassed a broad, global Cold War strategy, including countries such as Japan, Italy, Iran, and India.

37. Kahin the was author of a well-received study, *Nationalism and Revolution in Indonesia* (Ithaca, N.Y.: Cornell University Press, 1952), and a New Deal liberal. To Ford, their plans would be more successful if they used people experts like Kahin to win Indonesians' "confidence" and generate the basis of *Indonesian* applications for Ford grants; Meeting Notes by Dyke Brown (FF) for John Howard (FF), June 4, 1952; FF International Training and Research, box 036139:

Indonesia—General Correspondence, 1952. The U.S. ambassador in Jakarta, Cochran, suspected that Kahin was (too) close to the (pro-Western and generally anti-Sukarno) Socialist Party of Indonesia; letter, Samuel P. Hayes Jr., Head of ECA Mission, Jakarta, to Carl Spaeth (FF), May 21, 1952; ITR box 036139: Indonesia—General Correspondence, 1952. Cochran, Kahin thought, had been the main reason that the State Department temporarily withheld his passport; letter, PF Langer to Cleon Swayzee, April 15, 1953; reel 0408; PA54–6. In the same letter, Langer confirmed that Kahin, although politically "left of center . . . is certainly neither Communist nor pro-Communist."

38. "Copy and Excerpt: Journal of Cleon O. Swayzee: Response to Howard's cable of March 9 195- [final digit missing from copy, but most likely 1952]; reel 0408; PA54–6.

39. Kermit Roosevelt, a senior officer in the CIA's Middle Eastern division, had "expressed strong approval" of the Indonesian project. This was May 1953. By the summer of 1953, Roosevelt was directing the CIA's successful coup that ousted the democratically elected Dr. Mohammed Mossadegh. In his own account of the matter, Roosevelt claimed that the coup was to prevent a communist takeover; Kermit Roosevelt, *Countercoup* (New York: McGraw-Hill, 1979); Excerpt from Memorandum dated 26 May 1953 from Cleon Swayzee to Carl B. Spaeth, "Conversation with Mr. Kermit Roosevelt on the Langer Proposals"; reel 0408; grant PA54–6.

40. FF Inter-Office Memorandum, Clarence E. Thurber to Central Files, "Telephone Conversation with George Kahin, Concerning Country Study on Indonesia," August 31, 1954; reel 0408; PA54–6. Emphasis added.

41. Memorandum by Kahin to C. O. Swayzee, BOTR, Ford Foundation: "Contemporary Indonesia Project: A Study of Indonesian Government and Politics," attached to a letter, Kahin to Swayzee, June 6, 1953; reel 0408; PA54–6.

42. Kahin, *Southeast Asia*, 141. This suggests that Kahin's original objection was tactical and not principled; indeed, he suggested a study that would subject Indonesia to far wider and deeper American surveillance than had originally been proposed.

43. Board on Training and Research Docket, "Co-ordinated Country Studies on Soviet Techniques of Indoctrination and Control," 5 May 1953; reel 0404, grant 54–6.

44. Kahin Memorandum, 1–2.

45. Ibid., 2.

46. Ibid., 5.

47. Ibid., 6.

48. George McT. Kahin, "Cornell Modern Indonesia Project: Report for the Period July 1, 1954—September 30, 1955," 4; submitted October 30, 1955; reel 0408; PA54–6 [hereafter MIP Report].

49. Ibid., 6–7.

50. At the national level, CMIP had obtained the support of President Sukarno and leading government ministers; ibid., 2.

51. Ibid., 13.

52. Ibid., 16.

53. Ibid., 17.

54. Internal Ford Memorandum by A. Doak Barnett to Thurber, Howard, and Everton, "Barnett-Everton Trip to Cornell, March 8–9," March 10, 1960; reel 0408; PA54–6.

55. Letter, Kahin to Clarence Thurber (Ford Foundation), December 31, 1957; reel 0408; PA54–6.

56. Letter, Kahin to Clancy Thurber, February 9, 1962; reel 0408; PA54–6.

57. Letter, Kahin to John Everton, March 14, 1961; reel 0408; PA54–6.

58. Letter, Elmer Starch (FF) to Kahin, 10 September 1954; reel 0408; PA54–6.

59. Letter, Paul F. Langer to Cleon O. Swayzee, July 13, 1953.

60. Memorandum, "Excerpt from Draft Minutes of Meeting of May 5, 1953," in which the "sensitivity" and "danger" of studying communism in Indonesia was noted several times, as was the necessity of never publicly using the actual title of the project, "Soviet Techniques of Indoctrination and Control"; reel 0408; PA54–6. For CIA and State Department consultations and the quotation on U.S. vital interests, see Memorandum by Paul F. Langer to Philip E. Mosley, Carl Spaeth, and Cleon O. Swayzee, "Implementation of the Proposed Coordinated Country Studies"; reel 0408; PA54–6.

61. Letter, Langer to Swayzee, 13 July 1953; in reel 0408; PA54–6.

62. Ibid.

63. Frank L. Kidner, executive officer of the project "A Proposal to the Ford Foundation for a Grant-in-Aid Covering Teaching and Research in Economics and Related Fields in Social Sciences Between the University of California and the University of Indonesia," March 25, 1958; reel 0679; PA58–309.

64. Docket Excerpt, Board of Trustees Meeting, "University of California, Development of Training and Research in Indonesia," March 21–22 1958; reel 0679; PA58–309.

65. Docket Excerpt, Board of Trustees Meeting, March 21–22, 1958.

66. David Ransom, "The Berkeley Mafia and the Indonesia Massacre," *Ramparts* (October 1970): 37–42.

67. Press Release, University of California, Office of Public Information, July 10, 1956.

68. "Application to the Ford Foundation for a grant for financing research and training services and assistance by the University of California to the University of Indonesia in economics and related fields," 30 April 1956; reel 0695; PA56–190.

69. Program Letter no. 3; Country: Indonesia; by John Howard, 22 December 1954; Report 006574.

70. "Application to the Ford Foundation . . . ," 2–3; reel 0695; PA56–190.

71. Letter, Clark Kerr (Berkeley Chancellor) to John Howard (FF), May 18, 1956; reel 0695; PA56–190.

72. *Annual Report*, 1959–1960, University of California—University of Indonesia Economics Project, 4–5; reel 0679; PA58–309.

73. Ralph Anspach, "Monetary Aspects of Indonesia's Economic Reorganization in 1959," *Ekonomi Dan Keuangan Indonesia* (February 1960); Bruce Glassburner, "Problems of Economic Policy in Indonesia, 1950–57", available in multilith; *Annual Report*, 1959–1960; reel 0679; PA58–309.

74. Ford Foundation, *Annual Report*, 1959–1960 (New York: Ford Foundation), 5–6.

75. Ford Foundation, "Indonesia: Program Report," 1958; 7; 003236.

76. Ford Foundation, *Annual Report*, 1959–1960, 6–7.

77. Sumitro Djojohadikusumo, "Recollections of My Career," *Bulletin of Indonesian Economic Studies* 22, no. 3 (December 1986): 29.

78. Richard W. Dye (Ford Foundation), *The Jakarta Faculty of Economics*, January 1965, 5; 000374.

79. "Ford Foundation Supported Activities in Indonesia: Status Report," December 1961, part 1; i–ii; 011174.

80. "Ford Foundation Supported Activities . . . ," December 1961, part 1; ii, 2; 011174.

81. Ibid., December 1961, part 1; ii, 5; part 2, p.3.

82. Bresnan, *At Home Abroad*, 107.

83. "Ford Foundation Supported Activities . . . ," December 1961, part 2; 2.

84. Thee Kian Wie, "In Memoriam: Professor Sumitro Djojohadikusumo, 1917–2001," *Bulletin of Indonesian Economic Studies* 37, no. 2 (2001): 176. There was a "flying lecturers" program that reached universities throughout Indonesia.

85. "Ford Foundation Supported Activities . . . ," December 1961, part 2; 1–2.

86. Ibid., 3.

87. *The Ford Foundation in Indonesia: Ford Foundation Staff Comments on Ramparts Article*, October 1970; 2; 012243.

88. *Excerpts from Ramparts/Comments on Ramparts Excerpts* (By F. Miller); attached to 012243.

89. *Attachment 1, Excerpts from Ramparts* . . . ,4; 012243.

90. R. Robison, *Indonesia* (Sydney: Allen and Unwin, 1986), 110–111; emphasis added.

91. *Excerpts from Ramparts* . . . ; 012243.

92. C. B. Mahon, "Comments on Indonesia," 1952, 8; 006326.

93. Edwin G. Arnold and Dyke Brown, "Burma and Indonesia," September 21, 1952, p. 1, 43; 003367.

94. Robison, *Indonesia*, 110.

95. Ransom, "The Berkeley Mafia," 42.

96. The article was published in *California Management Review* 1 (Fall 1958): 20–29; it tried to "make a reasonable case for the western system as opposed to the Russian and Chinese systems" (21).

97. G. McT. Kahin and Audrey Kahin, *Subversion as Foreign Policy* (Seattle: University of Washington Press, 1995).

98. Ransom, "The Berkeley Mafia," 41.

99. Richard W. Dye, *The Jakarta Faculty of Economics*, January 1965; 4; 000374.

100. Ford did, however, contact several other scholars and Ford officials; *The Ford Foundation in Indonesia: Ford Foundation Staff Comments on Ramparts Article*, October 1970; 012243.

101. Letter, Michael Harris (Ford rep. in Jakarta) to F. F. Hill (FF, New York), 23 January 1958; reel 0679; PA58–309. As Ford's John Howard noted in 1957, "The Department of State has encouraged us and organizations like your own to proceed with our activities in cooperation with the Indonesian institutions concerned"; letter to Paul S. Taylor (chairman, Institute of International Studies, UC-Berkeley), December 18, 1957; reel 0697; PA58–309.

102. *The Ford Foundation in Indonesia: Ford Foundation Staff Comments on Ramparts Article, October 1970*; 012243.

103. John Bresnan (*Managing Indonesia*, 281) himself argues that without the Western-oriented Ford-funded economists, Indonesia would probably have become much more aligned with "Marxism-Leninist" regimes.

104. Bresnan, *At Home Abroad*, 121.

105. F. Miller (FF representative, Jakarta), "The Ford Foundation and Indonesia: 1953–1969. Retrospect and Prospect", 4; 6; 11; 006567. Emphasis added.

106. Bresnan, *Managing Indonesia*, 83. Emphasis added.

107. Memorandum by John Bresnan (FF), "The Ford Foundation and Education in Indonesia," (for internal circulation), August 6, 1970; 005509.

108. Peter Dale Scott, "The United States and the Overthrow of Sukarno, 1965–1967," *Pacific Affairs* 58, no. 2 (Summer 1985): 239–264.

109. Ibid., 246.

110. Ibid., 247.

111. Pauker's "personal ties with Indonesia's economic elite—the so-called 'Berkeley mafia'" were confirmed at his funeral in September 2002; Michael D. Rich, "Guy Pauker: A Eulogy," September 21, 2002. http://www.rand.org/pubs/papers/2006 /P8073.pdf.

112. Guy J. Pauker, "Toward a New Order in Indonesia," *Foreign Affairs* (April 1967): 503, 505. In a previous article, Pauker had sounded the alarm over the imminent Soviet takeover of Indonesia; Pauker, "The Soviet Challenge in Indonesia," *Foreign Affairs* (July 1962): 612–626.

113. Ransom, "Ford Country," 101–102.

114. Scott, "The United States and the Overthrow of Sukarno, 1965–1967," 249. PSI and Masjumi student groups had been involved, in collaboration with the Army, in anti-Chinese riots in 1963, "in the very shadow of SESKOAD" (249).

115. Memorandum by John Bresnan (FF), "The Ford Foundation and Education in Indonesia," (for internal circulation), August 6, 1970; 005509. For challenges to the notion of a communist coup, see George McT. Kahin and Audrey Kahin, *Subversion as Foreign Policy* (1995); R. Cribb and C. Brown, *Modern Indonesia: A History Since 1945* (New York: Longman, 1995).

116. F. Miller (FF representative, Jakarta), "The Ford Foundation and Indonesia: 1953–1969. Retrospect and Prospect", 5, 15, 16, 17, 20, 22; 006567.

117. Ibid., 7; 006567.

118. F. Miller, "Development Experience During Periods of Social and Political Change: Indonesia," March 1970, 1; 006568.

119. Letter, Miller to George Gant, April 10, 1966; in 01224.

120. In an article in 1990, the journalist Kathy Kadane demonstrated that CIA and State Department officials in Indonesia had supplied the Indonesian army with lists of names of up to five thousand communist leaders, "from top echelons down to village cadres," to ensure the annihilation of the PKI; Kathy Kadane, "Ex-Agents Say CIA Compiled Death Lists for Indonesians," *Washington Post* (May 21, 1990). The CIA director in the Far East, William Colby, suggested that the program was the Indonesian equivalent of the Phoenix Program he pioneered in Vietnam to try to destroy communist organization there.

121. Letter, Miller to Gant, April 10, 1966; 01224.

122. Kahin, *Subversion as Foreign Policy*, 230. Kahin shows that the United States supplied weapons "to arm Moslem and nationalist youth in Central Java for use against the PKI," as part of the Indonesian army's policy "to eliminate the PKI" (230).

123. Bresnan, *At Home Abroad*, 116.

124. F. Miller to Eugene Black, "April Visit to Indonesia," May 19, 1966; copied to Mc-George Bundy and F. Champion Ward; 012244.

125. Cribb and Brown, *Modern Indonesia*, 115n1.

126. Bruce R. Glassburner, ed. *The Economy of Indonesia*. (Ithaca, N.Y.: Cornell University Press, 1971).

127. "Background and Justification," Ford Foundation, Request number ID-1284; PA68–737; reel 4996.

128. Memorandum, David E. Bell (FF International Division) to McGeorge Bundy, June 18, 1968; 3; PA68–737; reel 4996.

129. Walter P. Falcon, "Conversation with Professor Widjojo, Saturday, December 1, 1973 (Gillis and Falcon)," December 5, 1973; PA68; reel 4996.

130. Memorandum, Theodore M. Smith, "Economics: Discussions with Adriennus Mooy," September 6, 1978; PA68–737; reel 4996.

131. Gustav F. Papanek (Harvard Development Advisory Service), "Indonesia," October 22, 1968; PA 68–737; reel 4996. Papanek noted that economic failures had resulted in "increasing criticism of the government and particularly of the economists who had dominated its policies" (1).

132. Chalmers and Hadiz, *The Politics of Economic Development in Indonesia*, 18.

133. Bell, "The Ford Foundation as a Transnational Actor," 116. As Bell argues, the Ford Foundation often operates as "an opening wedge for the United States Agency of International Development."

6. FORD, ROCKEFELLER, AND CARNEGIE IN NIGERIA AND THE AFRICAN STUDIES NETWORK

1. The source of the first epigraph to this chapter is from Arnold Rivkin, "Nigeria's National Development Plan," *Current History* 43 (December 1962), 323–324. Rivkin was the epitome of the state-private network in action, moving easily from the International Cooperation Administration (administering Marshall aid in Europe), to MIT's Ford and Carnegie-funded Center for International Studies (CENIS, as founding head of its African Economic and Political Development Project), to adviser and negotiator on Nigerian aid and development in the Kennedy administration, to the World Bank's main Africa expert; see L. Grubbs, "Bringing 'The Gospel of Modernization' to Nigeria: American Nation Builders and Development Planning in the 1960s," *Peace and Change* 31, no. 3 (July 2006): 279–308. Rivkin had also served on the Africa Area Group of President Eisenhower's Committee to Study the Military Assistance Program, better known as the Draper Committee. The second epigraph to this chapter is from L. Gray Cowan, "A Summary History of the African Studies Association

1957–1969," in PA61–47; reel 1887; Ford Foundation archives. Cowan was a Columbia University Africanist, founder, fellow, and executive secretary and president of the ASA.

2. Memoranda by USAID officials to State Department and President Kennedy, in 1961, cited by Grubbs, "Bringing 'The Gospel of Modernization' to Nigeria," 306n24.

3. W. W. Rostow's *The Stages of Economic Growth: A Non-Communist Manifesto* (Cambridge: Cambridge University Press, 1960) was written during a year at the University of Cambridge and funded by a grant by the Carnegie Corporation. Rostow's book became the bible of American development and modernization thinking; see David Milne, *America's Rasputin* (New York: Hill and Wang, 2008), for details.

4. Grubbs, "Bringing 'The Gospel of Modernization' to Nigeria," 297.

5. Rupert Emerson, "The Character of American Interests in Africa," in Walter Goldschmidt, ed., *The United States and Africa* (1958; New York: Praeger, 1963), 5.

6. Ibid., 29.

7. Ibid., 12–13; Bowles cited in ibid., 13.

8. Ibid., 6, 13.

9. Ibid., 19. James Coleman notes the British missionaries' complete monopolization of Nigerian education, the content of which effectively alienated Nigerians from their own history, languages, and cultural practices; James Coleman, *Nigeria: Background to Nationalism* (Los Angeles: University of California Press, 1958), 114–115.

10. Emerson, "The Character of American Interests in Africa," 31.

11. Ali A. Mazrui, "The African University as a Multinational Corporation: Problems of Penetration and Dependency," *Harvard Educational Review* 45, no. 2 (May 1975): 191–210.

12. Cited in Emerson, "The Character of American Interests in Africa," 32.

13. Mary L. Dudziak, *Cold War Civil Rights* (Princeton, N.J.: Princeton University Press, 2000).

14. In 1963, one hundred years after emancipation, the United States was still two years away from congressional legislation outlawing practices such as literacy tests, poll tax requirements, and grandfather clauses that denied Southern blacks the franchise.

15. Donald Fisher, "Rockefeller Philanthropy and the British Empire," *History of Education* 7 (1978): 129–143; E. Richard Brown, "Public Health in Imperialism: Early Rockefeller Programs at Home and Abroad," *American Journal of Public Health* 66, no. 9 (September 1976): 897–903.

16. *A Survey of Sources at the Rockefeller Archive Center for the Study of Twentieth-Century Africa* (Sleepy Hollow, N.Y.: RAC, 2003), 1–10.

17. Such networks also created communities of Western-oriented consumers, strengthening those networks; Mazrui, "The African University as a Multinational Corporation," 199.

18. Alan Pifer, Speech to Trustees, "The African Setting," 19 March 1959, 2; CCNY Policy and Program—Commonwealth Program (Africa) 1956–1975, folder 2; CC Archives, Columbia University, New York.

19. Arnold Rivkin, *The African Presence in World Affairs* (New York: Free Press, 1963), x.

20. Ibid., ix.

21. Ibid., ix–x.

22. Memorandum, Pifer to Gardner, "Possible African Program," 14 June 1957; attached to CCNY Policy and Program—Commonwealth Program (Africa) 1956–1975, folder 2.

23. Memorandum to CC by Alan Pifer, "State Department Conference on Africa South of the Sahara, At Washington, DC—Attended by AP," 28 October 1955; CC Grant Files Series 1, U.S. Department of State, 1939–1955.

24. Pifer, "Some Notes on Carnegie Grants in Africa," 5.

25. E. J. Murphy, *Creative Philanthropy: The Carnegie Corporation and Africa, 1953–1973* (New York: Teachers' College Press, 1976), 34.

26. Ibid.

27. Ibid.

28. Jane I. Guyer, *African Studies in the United States: A Perspective* (Atlanta, Ga.: African Studies Association Press, 1996), 63.

29. Edward H. Berman, "The Foundations' Role in American Foreign Policy: The Case of Africa, Post-1945," in Robert F. Arnove, ed., *Philanthropy and Cultural Imperialism* (Boston: G. K. Hall, 1980), 213; D. Court, "The Idea of Social Science in East Africa," *Minerva* 17 (1979): 250.

30. Wilbert J. LeMelle (Ford Foundation deputy representative in Eastern and Southern Africa), "The Development of African Studies: A Survey Report," 13; 10 September 1970; report number 003622.

31. Carol A. Dressel, "The Development of African Studies in the United States," *African Studies Bulletin* 9, no. 3 (December 1966): 69–70.

32. Guyer, *African Studies in the United States*, 52. Boston, Columbia, Indiana, Michigan State, Stanford, UCLA, Pennsylvania, Wisconsin, and Yale were also listed as resource centers.

33. L. Gray Cowan, Carl Rosberg, Lloyd Fallers, and Cornelis W. de Kiewiet, "Confidential Supplement to Report on the State of African Studies," prepared for the

Ford Foundation, 8 August 1958, acc. 000625; FF archives. For example, a grant of $50,000 for five years to Howard was justified thus: "It is in a particularly good position to provide a broad objective view of African problems to American Negro and native African students who sometimes approach the field with a strong emotional or political bias"; Executive Committee Meeting Excerpt, "Howard University Program in African Studies," ITR, 21 March 1957, PA54–49, reel 0420; FF archives.

34. LeMelle, "The Development of African Studies," 14.

35. Ibid., 2, 7, 9, 10.

36. Ibid., 3, 7.

37. Ibid., 15.

38. Ibid., 13.

39. Gwendolen M. Carter, "The Founding of the African Studies Association," *African Studies Review* 26, nos. 3/4 (September–December 1983): 5.

40. Record of interview between JP and Dean Rusk (RF), Kenneth Thompson (RF), Don Price (Ford), and Howard Johnson, 22 October 1953; CC Grant Files series 1, U.S. Department of State, 1939–1955.

41. R. A. Hill, *The FBI's RACON: Racial Conditions in America During World War II* (Boston: Northeastern University Press, 1995).

42. Carter, "The Founding of the African Studies Association," 6.

43. Jerry Gershenhorn, "'Not an Academic Affair': African American Scholars and the Development of African Studies Programs in the United States, 1942–1960," *Journal of African American History* 94, no. 1 (Winter 2009): 44–68.

44. Ibid., 51–52.

45. Memorandum by Pearl T. Robinson to David R. Smock, "Evaluation of General Support Grant to the African Studies Association," 18 September 1974, p. 1; PA61–47, reel 1887, Ford Foundation Archives. Ford later invested further amounts in excess of $350,000 for oral data archives, development of research materials, and the work of the Research Liaison Committee (1).

46. *Summary Report of the Conference on the Position of Problems of the American Scholar in Africa*, 18–19 November 1966; CC file, African Studies Association, 1957–1976.

47. Pearl T. Robinson memorandum, 2–3; PA61–47, reel 1887.

48. Memorandum by Lynn E. Baker, U.S. Army Chief Psychologist, Human Factors and Operations Research Division, to Colonel William G. Sullivan, "22 December 1964 Meeting with Members of the NAS Advisory Committee on Africa," 23 December 1964; CC, African Studies Association file, 1957–1976. Advisory Committee members present were C. W. de Kiewiet (chair, and former president of Cornell University) and Wilton Dillon (National Research Council's

international division). In addition, the Rockefeller Foundation was represented by John McKelvey and Columbia University by Gray Cowan.

49. Memorandum, distributed by Charles R. Nixon to all UCLA Faculty African-ists, Discussion of Proposal for an Army-Sponsored University Consortium for African Studies, n.d: "General Statement of the Problems to Be Dealt with and the Recommended Action to be Taken for the Further Development of Support for Research on Africa," 4–5 February 1965; CC, African Studies Association file, 1957–1976.

50. Letter, James Coleman to Lynn E. Baker, 25 January 1965; CC, African Studies Association file, 1957–1976.

51. George E. Lowe, "The Camelot Affair," *Bulletin of the Atomic Scientists* (May 1966), http://books.google.com/books?id=UggAAAAAMBAJ&pg=PA44&vq =Lowe&dq=Soviet+intelligence+sponsored+social+movements+Vietnam&lr =&as_brr=3&hl=pl&source=gbs_search_s&cad=0#v=onepage&q=Lowe&f =false.

52. Memorandum, Wilton S. Dillon to Charles Wagley (Institute of Latin American Studies), Melvin J. Fox (Ford Foundation), John J. McKelvey (Rockefeller Foundation), and L. Gray Cowan (Columbia University), 16 December 1964; memorandum, Lynn E. Baker, attached to Dillon's, of which there were just three pages in Ford archives—quotes taken from section entitled "Social Psychology, Sociology, and Ethnological and Humanistic Science: Special Program Plan B", 32–34; both attached to Inter-Office Memorandum, Melvin Fox to John B. Howard and Cleon O. Swayzee, 2 March 1965; in PA61–47, reel 1887.

53. *Summary Report of the Conference on the Position and Problems of the American Scholar in Africa*, 18–19 November 1966; 16–17; CC, African Studies Association file, 1957–1976.

54. Ibid., 19.

55. Letter, Frederic Mosher (of CC) on behalf of Alan Pifer, to Gwendolen Carter, 11 August 1965; letter, Carter to Pifer, 25 June 1965; in CC Grant Files series 2, African Studies Association—Conference on African Nationalist Movements, 1964–1966. Mosher adjudged that Carter's letter had been written before the fall of Project Camelot and replied, "I think the idea of channeling possible Army funds to projects through the Corporation is a genuinely bad one" and feared for the future conduct of oral history projects in Africa.

56. Letter, Pierre L. van den Berghe (University of Washington, Seattle) to Cowan, 30 September 1966; PA61–47, reel 1887; FF archives.

57. Inter-Office Memorandum by Pearl T. Robinson to David R. Smock (Ford Foundation), "Evaluation of General Support Grant to the African Studies Association," 18 September 1974; PA61–47, reel 1887.

58. Ibid., 2.

59. Ibid., 3

60. Ibid.

61. Ibid., 4.

62. Rupert Emerson, Joseph Nye, Robert Rotberg, and Martin Kilson of the Harvard Department of Government signed a letter protesting the behavior of Black Caucus members and denying any racism at anytime of the ASA's leaders; letter, Emerson et al. to Cowan, 20 October 1969; CC, African Studies Association, box 386, folder 1.

63. Cowan, "A Summary History of the African Studies Association 1957–1969," PA61–47, reel 1887, 23.

64. Ibid., 20; see also Melvin Fox, "Evaluation of Grants to African Studies Association Research Liaison Committee 1966–1975," December 1979; PA61–47, reel 1887.

65. Inter-Office Memorandum, Robinson, 8. Although Ford did change its own approach at least temporarily, there were some who preferred to place the blame entirely on the shoulders of the ASA. Robert Edwards, for example, suggested that the problem was both societal—"an accumulation of past oversights and injustices in the society at large"—and specific—"short-sightedness and insensitivity on the part of the A.S.A.'s leadership," implying a bystander role for Ford; Robert Edwards to David R. Smock, "Re-Evaluation of Grants to the African Studies Association," 24 September 1974; PA61–47, reel 1887. Edwards had previously served in the State Department's Office of UN Political Affairs.

66. Memorandum, Stackpole to Pifer, 21 October 1969; CC, African Studies Association, box 386, folder 1.

67. Bundy cited in a report, n.d. but ca. 1969, on Ford grants to Yale and Howard to establish Afro-American studies programs; PA69–518, reel 2004, 20; FF archives.

68. Letter, Norman W. MacLeod (assistant to Ford's treasurer) to Franklin H. Williams, 29 April 1970; in PA70–001, reel 4020.

69. Inter-Office Memorandum, Craig Howard to William D. Carmichael, "Middle East and Africa Fellowship Program for Black Americans," 7 September 1979, 2; PA669–0617, Reports, reel 3735.

70. Minutes of the African Heritage Association Executive Committee, n.d. but 1970; and AHSA—Report of the Program Committee, May 1970; both in PA70–001, reel 4020; FF archives.

71. Report on Ford grants to Yale and Howard to establish Afro-American studies programs; PA69–518, reel 2004.

72. Inter-Office Memorandum, Craig Howard to William D. Carmichael, "Middle East and Africa Fellowship Program for Black Americans," 7 September 1979; PA669–0617, Reports, reel 3735. The program disbursed $987,648 over ten years.

73. Attachment to Request No. ID-1242, n.d. but ca. 1975; in PA69–617, reel 3735; FF archives.

74. Inter-Office Memorandum, Craig Howard, 4.

75. Ibid., 4.

76. Ibid., 7–8.

77. Ibid., 12.

78. Ibid., 10.

79. Immanuel Wallerstein, "The Evolving Role of the Africa Scholar in African Studies," *African Studies Review* 26, no. 3/4 (September–December 1983): 157. For an excellent analysis of CIA programs in Africa (particularly chapter 9), see Hugh Wilford, *The Mighty Wurlitzer: How the CIA Played America* (Cambridge, Mass.: Harvard University Press, 2008).

80. A. Olukoshi, "African Scholars and African Studies," *Development in Practice* 16, no. 6 (November 2006): 534–535.

81. Ibid., 541.

82. Wallerstein, "The Evolving Role of the Africa Scholar in African Studies," 159.

83. Murphy, *Creative Philanthropy*, 68.

84. Until 1962, Ibadan was a satellite college of London University and subject to its control in terms of curriculum development, admissions and assessment standards; Mazrui, "The African University as a Multinational Corporation," 195.

85. Eric Ashby, quoted in Murphy, *Creative Philanthropy*, 78.

86. Murphy, *Creative Philanthropy*, 80–81. Carnegie also funded the formation of the Nigerian Committee of Vice-Chancellors with an award of $102,000 (80).

87. Coleman confirms the conservative nationalism of Oxbridge-educated Nigerians; *Nigeria: Background to Nationalism*, 247.

88. Aboyade, *Development Burden and Benefits*, 302.

89. Ibid., 305.

90. R. A. Adeleye, "The Independent University, 1962–68," in J. F. Ade Ajayi and Tekena N. Tamuno, eds., *The University of Ibadan, 1948–73* (Ibadan: Ibadan University Press, 1973), 73.

91. Ibid., 77.

92. J. F. Ade Ajayi, "Postgraduate Studies and Staff Development," in J. F. Ade Ajayi and Tekena N. Tamuno, eds., *The University of Ibadan, 1948–73* (Ibadan: Ibadan University Press, 1973), 161.

93. Olatunji Oloruntimehin, "The University in the Era of the Civil War and Reconstruction," in J. F. Ade Ajayi and Tekena N. Tamuno, eds., *The University of Ibadan, 1948–73* (Ibadan: Ibadan University Press, 1973), 100.

94. Cranford Pratt, John E. Swanson, and Rose E. Bigelow, *An Evaluation of the General Development Grant and the Staff Development Grants of the Ford*

Foundation to the University of Ibadan, 1958–1972; September 1973; 2; Reports, 002325; FFA.

95. Ibid., 14, 30.

96. Request for Grant Action (OD-1985), "Development of a Program in Behavioural Sciences"; 13 July 1967; reel 1391, PA67–481; FFA.

97. C. G. M. Bakare, Behavioural Sciences Research Programme, University of Ibadan: Ford Foundation Grant (670–0481), Terminal Report, May 1972; 9; reel 1391, PA67–481; FFA; $221,000 was granted to the unit.

98. Letter, Alexander Leighton (Harvard) to Mr. Heaps (Ford), 16 January 1966; reel 1391, PA67–481; FFA.

99. T. Adeyo Lambo, "Proposal Presented to the Ford Foundation for a Behavioural Science Research Programme Within the Department of Psychiatry, University of Ibadan," August 1966; reel 1391, PA67–481. Emphasis in the original.

100. Arnold Rivkin, "Nigeria: A Unique Nation," *Current History* 45, no. 268 (December 1963): 329–334. The African center at MIT that Rivkin headed, funded by Carnegie, was clearly wedded to developing a market economy and the elimination of subsistence and exchange economies, which were seen as a "drag on the rate of economic growth." See "Proposal for a Project on Economic Development and Political Change in Africa South of the Sahara," 6, CENIS at MIT, July 1958; in box 672, folder 6, MIT Sub-Sahara Africa, Research on Center for International Studies (1958–1967); CC archives.

101. Rivkin, "Nigeria: A Unique Nation," 329.

102. Arnold Rivkin, "Nigeria's National Development Plan," *Current History* 43, no. 256 (December 1962): 321.

103. Hakeem I. Tijani, *Britain, Leftist Nationalists, and the Transfer of Power in Nigeria, 1945–1965* (New York: Routledge, 2006), 7, esp. 51–66. See also, O. Awolowo, "Nigerian Nations and Federal Union," in R. Emerson and M. Kilson, eds., *The Political Awakening of Africa* (Englewood Cliffs, N.J.: Prentice-Hall, 1965), 61–65. Awolowo argues that Nigeria must be a federation given its fundamental ethnic and regional divisions, some of which, especially in the Northern Region, had been fostered by deliberate British policies (64). In the same volume, consider the pro-British attitudes of Chief S. L. Akintola and Tafawa Balewa, the latter becoming prime minister of independent Nigeria in 1960. Akintola thanked Britain's "benevolent imperialism" for creating Nigeria and for her parliamentary democracy, liberal education, and law and order; Akintola and Balewa, "Nigeria Debates Self-Government," in R. Emerson and M. Kilson, eds., *The Political Awakening of Africa* (Englewood Cliffs, N.J.: Prentice-Hall, 1965), 67. As a result, Akintola argued that Nigeria would never sever ties with Britain but cooperate on the basis of "mutual trust, reciprocal goodwill, and mutual understanding"

(68). The more radical W. E. B. Du Bois noted that such Nigerians had been, "through bribery and deception . . . so manipulated by the British Empire as to regard the British mainly as benefactors"; W. E. B. Du Bois, *The World and Africa* (New York: International Publishers, 1969), 327.

104. H. H. Smythe and M. M. Smythe, *The New Nigerian Elite* (Stanford, Calif.: Stanford University Press, 1960).

105. Tijani, *Britain, Leftist Nationalists, and the Transfer of Power in Nigeria.*

106. Rivkin, "Nigeria's National Development Plan," 326.

107. Wolfgang F. Stolper, *Planning Without Facts: Lessons in Resource Allocation from Nigeria's Development* (Cambridge, Mass.: Harvard University Press, 1966), xx.

108. Ibid., 3.

109. To Stolper, Nigeria is "primitive" (ibid., 18), unsophisticated (6), and lacking in "aesthetic or artistic values" (108).

110. Ojetunji Aboyade, *Development Burdens and Benefits: Reflections on the Development Process in Nigeria* (Ibadan: Development Policy Centre, 2003), 15.

111. Ojetunji Aboyade, *Foundations of an African Economy* (New York: Praeger, 1966), 154. Aboyade was a member of the economics department of the University of Ibadan and succeeded Stolper as head of the Federal Economic Planning Unit, 1962–1963. In 1963–1964, he was a research fellow at the University of Michigan's Center on Economic Development, of which Stolper was director, funded by a Rockefeller Foundation travel grant. Aboyade was a sympathetic critic.

112. Ibid., 155–156, 154.

113. Stolper, *Planning Without Facts*, 5.

114. Clive S. Gray, ed., *Inside Independent Nigeria: Diaries of Wolfgang Stolper, 1960–1962* (Aldershot: Ashgate, 2003), 19, 70.

115. Ibid., 72.

116. Coleman, *Nigeria: Background to Nationalism.*

117. Aboyade, *Foundations of an African Economy*, 75.

118. Ibid., 157.

119. Ibid., 160. For a radical critique, see Chinweizu, *The West and the Rest of Us* (Lagos: Pero Press, 1987), esp. 136–144.

120. Du Bois, *The World and Africa*, 331.

121. Gray, *Inside Independent Nigeria*, 225.

122. E. Wayne Nafziger, "The Political Economy of Disintegration in Nigeria," *Journal of Modern African Studies* 11, no. 4 (1973): 505–536.

123. Tijani, *Britain, Leftist Nationalists, and the Transfer of Power in Nigeria*, 75, citing a U.S. report entitled "The Political, Economic and Social Survey of Nigeria" (1951). Under Point 4 programs, Nigerian Foreign Service Officers were trained

in "diplomacy, ethics, and the essence of western values" at the Department of State and the British embassy in Washington, D.C.; they also received lectures on "Issues in International Relations," at the Johns Hopkins School of Advanced International Studies (77, 90).

124. "Testimony of Arnold Rivkin Before the Committee on Foreign Affairs House of Representatives Eighty-Seventh Congress Firs Session on H.R. 7372 The International Development and Security Act, June 26 1961"; box 672, folder 5, MIT Sub-Sahara, Research on (CENIS 1958–1967); CC archives.

125. Stolper, *Planning Without Facts*, 269.

126. Nafziger, "The Political Economy of Disintegration in Nigeria," 516–518.

127. Richard Sklar, "Contradictions in the Nigerian Political System," *Journal of Modern African Studies* 3, no.2 (August 1965): 204.

128. Reginald H. Green, "Four African Development Plans: Ghana, Kenya, Nigeria, and Tanzania," *Journal of Modern African Studies* 3, no. 2 (August 1965): 260.

129. Ibid., 259. Emphasis in the original.

130. Ibid., 275–276.

131. Without formally evaluating the impact of Stolper's plan, Ford funded from 1968 the training of Nigerian economic planners to draft the Second Development Plan. They failed to discuss procedures for recruiting Nigerian civil servants to economics fellowship positions in the United States—mainly Harvard and Williams College—and received criticism from the authorities; Curt C. F. Wolters, Project Specialist in Social Sciences, "Evaluation: Fellowship Program to Train Nigerian Economic Planners," 9; 4 April 1973; reel 1398; PA68–0799. $120,000 was granted to the program that trained twelve economists.

132. Coleman cites a British colonial education policy document which stated in 1925 that the role of education in Nigeria was to "strengthen the feeling of responsibility to the tribal community"; Coleman, *Nigeria: Background to Nationalism*, 117.

7. THE MAJOR FOUNDATIONS, LATIN AMERICAN STUDIES, AND CHILE IN THE COLD WAR

1. The source for the chapter's first epigraph is Naomi Klein, *The Shock Doctrine* (London: Penguin Books, 2008), 70. The CIA dubbed Pinochet's coup "Operation Jakarta"; see Greg Grandin, "Plumping for Pinochet," *The Nation* (January 21, 2002), http://www.thenation.com/doc/2002012/grandin/print. The source for the chapter's second epigraph is OLAC [Office of Latin American and the Caribbean] Social Science Conference, "The Interplay Between the Foundation and the Grantee," December 7, 1973, 6; Report 010152; FF archives.

2.   OECD, "Chile Should Create More and Better Jobs to Cut Poverty and Inequality," June 2009, http://www.oecd.org/document/49/0,3343,en_33873108_39418658 _42514801_1_1_1_1,00.html. Chile is one of the most unequal societies in Latin America: between 1980 and 1989, the share of wealth owned by the wealthiest 10 percent of the population increased its share from 36.5 percent to 46.8 percent.

3.   Patricio Silva, "Technocrats and Politics in Chile: From the Chicago Boys to the CIEPLAN Monks," *Journal of Latin American Studies* 23, no. 2 (May 1991): 385.

4.   Ibid.

5.   William J. Barber, "Chile con Chicago: A Review Essay," *Journal of Economic Literature* 33, no. 4 (December 1995): 1942.

6.   As J. Ramos argues, "We no longer talk about whether a centrally-planned or market economy is better, but rather what the best combination of the two in a mixed economy would be." Cited in Veronica Montecinos, "Economic Policy Elites and Democratization," *Studies in Comparative International Development* 28, no. 1 (Spring 1993): 46n86.

7.   Eduardo Silva, "The Political Economy of Chile's Regime Transition: From Radical to 'Pragmatic' Neo-Liberal Policies," in Paul W. Drake and Ivan Jaksic, eds., *The Struggle for Democracy in Chile*, 2nd ed. (Lincoln: University of Nebraska Press, 1995), 98–127.

8.   Fred Rosen, ed., *Empire and Dissent: The United States and Latin America* (London: Duke University Press, 2008), 38.

9.   Fredrick B. Pike, *Chile and the United States, 1880–1962* (Notre Dame, Ind.: University of Notre Dame Press, 1963).

10. According to one source, U.S. military forces have intervened in the region on at least ninety occasions since America's declaration of independence; NACLA, *Subliminal Warfare: The Role of Latin American Studies* (New York: NACLA, 1970), 1.

11. Earl T. Glauert and Lester D. Langley, eds., *The United States and Latin America* (London: Addison-Wesley Publishing Company, 1971).

12. Ball, in ibid., 153.

13. Pike, *Chile and the United States, 1880–1962*, 303.

14. Ibid., 296.

15. Marvin O. Bernstein, *Foreign Investment in Latin America* (New York: Alfred A. Knopf, 1966), 7.

16. "U.S. Private Investment in Latin America 1880–1961," in *Yanqui Dollar: The Contribution of U.S. Private Investment to Underdevelopment in Latin America* (New York: NACLA [North American Congress on Latin America], 1971), 8.

17. Ibid., 12.

18. U.S. Department of the Interior (Bureau of Mines), *Minerals Yearbook 1969* (Washington, D.C., 1971).

19. U.S. Department of Commerce, *Survey of Current Business, October 1970* (Washington, D.C.).

20. J. Petras and M. Morley, *The United States and Chile* (London: Monthly Review Press, 1975), 8–10.

21. Peter Kornbluh, *Chile and the United States: Declassified Documents Relating to the Military Coup, September 11, 1973,* http://www.gwu.edu/~nsarchiv/NSAEBB /NSAEBB8/nsaebb8i.htm. The quote is taken from handwritten notes from a meeting between CIA Director Richard Helms and President Richard Nixon.

22. Petras and Morley, *The United States and Chile,* 11.

23. Helen Delpar, *Looking South: The Evolution of Latin Americanist Scholarship in the United States, 1850–1975* (Tuscaloosa: University of Alabama Press, 2008), 26.

24. Mark T. Berger, *Under Northern Eyes: Latin American Studies and U.S. Hegemony in the Americas, 1898–1990* (Bloomington: Indiana University Press, 1995), 2.

25. Delpar, *Looking South,* ix.

26. Berger, *Under Northern Eyes,* 173.

27. Delpar, *Looking South,* ix.

28. Ibid., xi. Between 1945 and 1959, there was a definite lull in federal and foundation interest in Latin America; the Cuban revolution revived that interest.

29. Ibid., 156.

30. Ibid., 160–161.

31. Ibid., 162.

32. Reynold E. Carlson, "The Development of the Social Sciences in Latin America," The Ford Foundation, New York, November 1965; Report 000100; FF archives.

33. Ibid., 3–4.

34. Ibid., 12.

35. Carlson, 13.

36. Ibid., 19.

37. Delpar, *Looking South,* 166–168; C. Wright Mills, *Listen, Yankee* (Tuscaloosa: University of Alabama Press, 1960); W. A. Williams, *The United States, Cuba, and Castro* (New York: Monthly Review Press, 1962).

38. According to Ford's annual reports, neither NACLA nor the URLA received any funding between 1966 and 1976. Conversely, LASA received $392,000 during that period.

39. Juan Gabriel Valdes, *Pinochet's Economists: The Chicago School in Chile* (Cambridge: Cambridge University Press, 1995). Valdes acknowledges the generosity of Rockefeller's hospitality at their villa at Bellagio, Italy, when writing up his book. Jeffrey Puryear also notes that the Institute of Latin American Transnational Studies, where Valdes worked while in exile during the Pinochet years, was partly funded by the Ford Foundation; Jeffrey Puryear, *Thinking Politics: Intellectuals and Democracy in Chile, 1973–1988* (Baltimore, Md.: Johns Hopkins University Press, 1994), 45n25.

40. Clearly, dependency theory is broad and encompasses Marxist and non-Marxist variants. In this chapter, the version of dependency theory referred to is the original ECLA version outlined in the text above; for a very good review, see Heraldo Munoz, ed., *From Dependency to Development* (Boulder, Colo.: Westview Press, 1981).

41. John Strasma, "A Note on Chilean Economics in 1960," in PA61–372A, reel 3126; FFA.

42. Peter D. Bell, Inter-Office Memorandum, "Santiago Office Report on Fiscal Year 1970," to Harry E. Wilhelm, 4 November 1970; 5; Report 012288; FF archives.

43. Ibid., 4–5.

44. "Chile 1964: CIA Covert Support in Frei Election Detailed; Operational and Policy Records Released for First Time," National Security Archive news release, September 27, 2004, http://www.gwu/~nsarchiv/news/20040925/index.htm. It is noted that the national security adviser at the time, McGeorge Bundy, was aware and supportive of CIA financial backing, to the tune of $2.6 million, of the Frei presidential campaign and of an additional $3 million for negative campaigns against Salvador Allende. Bundy commended the CIA on its work during the Frei campaign.

45. Bell, Inter-Office Memorandum, 20.

46. Ibid., 6.

47. *University of Chile–University of California Cooperative Program Comprehensive Report 1965–1978*, July 1979; PA76–115, reel 3086; FFA.

48. Bell, Inter-Office Memorandum, 6.

49. Carl B. Spaeth and John Howard, *Spaeth/Howard Report on Latin American Studies*, June 1964; report 001556; 7; FFA.

50. Bell, Inter-Office Memorandum, 4.

51. Rorden Wilkinson, *The WTO* (London: Routledge, 2006); Douglas A. Irwin, "GATT Turns 60," April 9, 2007, http://www.freetrade.org/node/608.

52. Bell, Inter-Office Memorandum, 7.

53. OLAC [Office of Latin American and the Caribbean] Social Science Conference, "The Utilization of Social Science," 6 December 1973, 23; Report 010152; FF archives.

54. Milton Friedman, *Capitalism and Freedom* (Chicago: Chicago University Press, 1982), vi.

55. Economists at the University of Chile were not interested in an exclusive arrangement with just one U.S. university, especially one associated so strongly with a free-market tradition; Valdes, *Pinochet's Economists*, esp. chap. 4.

56. Catholic University faculty also opposed the plan because Chicago economics was seen as ignoring social justice seen by many as central to the mission of a Christian university; ibid., 125.

57. Ibid., 138.

58. Ibid., 165.

59. Ibid., 144n48.

60. Ibid., chap. 1.

61. Ibid., 161.

62. Ibid., 186.

63. Murray Yudelman (RF), Diary Excerpt of meeting with Albion W. Patterson, 2 October 1956; RFA 1.2; 309S, box 32, folder 268; Catholic University Economic Research Center.

64. Interview, NSB (RF) with Theodore W. Schultz—Chairman, Department of Economics, University of Chicago, 27 July 1956; RFA 1.2; 309S, box 32, folder 1.

65. Diary Note, by Montague Yudelman, of a meeting with Professor T. W. Schultz, 29 November 1956; RFA 1.2; 309, box 34, folder 283.

66. *The Chile Project: First Report to the Catholic University of Chile and the International Cooperation Administration*; 20 July 1956; by the Department of Economics, University of Chicago; RFA 1.2, 309S, box 32, folder 268.

67. Ibid., 11–12.

68. Sergio Molina, for example, was finance minister from 1964 to 1968.

69. For full details, see Valdes, *Pinochet's Economists*, chap. 10.

70. Interview, CMH (RF) with Grunwald, 8–10–12–15 May 1961; RFA 1.2, 309S, box 35, folder 291.

71. Ibid.

72. Veronica Montecinos, *Economists, Politics, and the State: Chile 1958–1994* (Amsterdam: CEDLA, 1998), 137–138.

73. Grant Allocation, RF to University of Chile—Institute of Economic Research, 3 April 1957; RFA 1.2, series 309, box 34, folder 283.

74. Grant Allocation, RF to University of Chile—Graduate School of Economics, 22 October 1959; RFA 1.2, series 309, box 43, folder 283.

75. Letter, Grunwald to Yudelman, 22 February 1957; RFA 1.2, series 309S, box 34, folder 283.

76. Interview, CMH (RF) with Grunwald, 8–11–12–15 May 1961; RFA 1.2, 309S, box 35.

77. Interview, Montague Yudelman and Grunwald, 11 January 1957; RFA 1.2, series 309S, box 35, folder 291.

78. William D. Carmichael, "Education in the Field of Economic Development and Administration in Argentina and Chile," November 1965; Report 000117; 79; FFA.

79. John Strasma, "A Note on Chilean Economics in 1960," in PA61–372A, reel 3126; FFA.

80. Ibid.

81. John Strasma, "Background," memo on economics at the University of Chile, November 1965; PA61–372, reel 3126.

82. Ibid., 4–6.

83. Ibid., 14–17.

84. Request for Grant Action, Graduate Program in Economics, University of Chile; 2; PA61–372, reel 3126; FFA.

85. Carlos Massad, Research Program 1964–1965, ESCOLATINA, University of Chile, 7; 19; 24; PA61–372, reel 3126; FFA.

86. Ibid., 19–27.

87. "A Report to the Ford Foundation," by Roberto Maldonado, director of the Institute of Economic Research and Planning, and Edgardo Boeninger, dean of the Faculty of Economics; PA61–372, reel 3126; see appendices; FFA.

88. Ibid.

89. John Strasma, "Survey of Student Leader Opinion of the School of Economics of the University of Chile, 1967," in PA61–372A, reel 3126; FFA.

90. John Strasma, Inter-Office Memorandum, "A footnote on ESCOLATINA," to Peter D. Bell, 11 January, 1971; PA61–372A, reel 3126; FFA.

91. John Strasma, Inter-Office Memorandum, "ESCOLATINA Situation and Outlook for 1972," to Peter D. Bell, 17 December 1971; PA61–372A, reel 3126; FFA.

92. John Strasma, "Some Program Notes Towards a History of the Graduate Program (ESCOLATINA), 1957–1972," written 24 January 1972; PA61–372A, reel 3126; FFA.

93. Inter-Office Memorandum, William D. Carmichael to John S. Nagel and Donald Finberg, "University of Chile, Faculty of Economics (Institute of Economics and INSORA), 24 August 1965, 1–2; 7; PA61–372A, reel 3126.

94. John Strasma, Inter-Office Memorandum, "Comments on Interim Narrative Report by the Institute of Economics and Planning, University of Chile (PA 61–372A)," to Peter D. Bell, 25 January 1972; 1; PA61–372A, reel 3126; FFA.

95. John Strasma, Inter-Office Memorandum, "Comments on Interim Narrative Report by the Institute of Economics and Planning, University of Chile (PA 61–372A)," to Peter D. Bell, 25 January 1972; 14; PA61–372A, reel 3126; FFA.

96. Peter D. Bell, Inter-Office Memorandum, "Recommendation for Grant Modification, University of Chile, Graduate Program of Latin American Economic Studies (ESCOLATINA (PA61–372A)," to William D. Carmichael, 3 February 1972; PA61–372A, reel 3126; FFA. Kalman Silvert also questioned any continued support for ESCOLATINA, given changed political conditions; see Silvert, Inter-Office Memorandum, "Modification ESCOLATINA (PA 61–372-A)," to William D. Carmichael, 13 March 1972; PA61–372A, reel 3126; FFA.

97. Memo, Peter S. Cleaves, "ESCOLATINA," to Peter T. Knight, 29 March 1973; PA-372A, reel 3126; FFA.

98. Inter-Office Memorandum, Lovell S. Jarvis, "Final Reporting and Evaluation, University of Chile, Graduate Program in Economics (ESCOLATINA), (PA61–372A)," to Peter D. Bell, 2 January 1974; 3; FFA.

99. Memo, Peter Hakim, "Recommendation for Closing of Grant, University of Chile, Graduate Program in Economics (ESCOLATINA)," to William D. Carmichael, 2 January 1974; PA61–372A, reel 3126; FFA.

100. Montecinos, *Economists, Politics, and the State*, 32–33.

101. Lovell S. Jarvis, Inter-Office Memorandum, "First Annual Report of Institute of Economics, Catholic University," to Peter Hakim, 19 June 1973; PA72–107, reel 3954; FFA.

102. Jeffrey Puryear, Inter-Office Memorandum, "Second Annual Reporting, Catholic University, Institute of Economics (PA72–107)," to Peter Hakim, 21 June 1974; PA72–107, reel 2857; FFA.

103. Letter, Willard J. Hertz (Ford, acting secretary), to Vice Admiral Jorge Swett Madge (Rector), Pontifical Catholic University of Chile, 29 August 1975; PA72–107, reel 3888; FFA.

104. Jeffrey Puryear, Inter-Office Memorandum, "Recommendation for Closing—Institute of Economics—Catholic University of Chile (PA72–107 and A)," 10 May 1978; PA72–107, reel 2857; FFA. Puryear notes that Ford was "guilty of naivete" in this memorandum, though it remains a source of some mystery.

105. Norman R. Collins, Inter-Office Memorandum, "Pontifical Catholic University of Chile, Postgraduate Program in Agricultural Economics (70–629)," to Peter D. Bell, 2 November 1973; PA70–0629, reel 4276; FFA. The roles of the Chicago

boys in the Pinochet regime are explored in detail in Carlos Huneeus, "Technocrats and Politicians in an Authoritarian Regime: The 'ODEPLAN Boys' and the 'Gremialists' in Pinochet's Chile," *Journal of Latin American Studies* 32 (2000): 461–501.

106. Alain de Janvry, Inter-Office Memorandum, "Programo Postgrado de Economia Agraria, Catholic University of Chile," 21 September 1973, to Peter Bell; PA70–0629, reel 4276.

107. Norman R. Collins, Inter-Office Memorandum, "Pontifical Catholic University of Chile, Postgraduate Program in Agricultural Economics (70–629)," to Peter D. Bell, 2 November 1973; PA70–0629, reel 4276; FFA.

108. Alain de Janvry, Inter-Office Memorandum, "Graduate Program in Agricultural Economics (PPEA) at the Catholic University," to Peter D. Bell, 19 November 1973; PA70–0629, reel 4276; FFA. According to Huneeus, ODEPLAN, dominated by the Chicago boys, signed fourteen institutional agreements with Catholic University from 1973 to 1989, transferring US$12.6 million to the university (465).

109. Letter, Peter D. Bell to Fernando Martinez, 3 January 1974; PA70–0629, reel 4276; FFA.

110. Alain de Janvry, Inter-Office Memorandum, "Graduate Program in Agricultural Economics at the Catholic University of Chile," to Peter D. Bell, 18 March 1974; PA70–0629, reel 4276; Peter Hakim, Inter-Office Memorandum, "Annual Reporting, Catholic University of Chile, Agricultural Economics (PA70–629A)," to William D. Carmichael, 23 April 1974; PA70–0629, reel 4276; Reed Hartford, Inter-Office Memorandum, "Final Evaluation, Pontifical Catholic University of Chile, Agricultural Economics," to Norman R. Collins, Peter Hakim, and Lowell S. Hardin, 15 June 1977; PA70–0629, reel 3865; FFA; and, finally, James Trowbridge, Inter-Office Memorandum, "Final Evaluation: Pontifical Catholic University of Chile, Development of a Graduate Teaching and Research Program in Agricultural Economics—(PA700–0629A)," to William D. Carmichael, 8 April 1985; PA70–0629, reel 4932; FFA.

111. Jeffrey M. Puryear, Inter-Office Memorandum, "Recommendation for Closing—Institute of Economics—Catholic University of Chile," to Richard W. Dye, 10 May 1978; PA72–107, reel 2857; FFA.

112. Lovell Jarvis, Inter-Office Memorandum, "CEPLAN Seminar on Income Distribution and Economic Growth," to Peter D. Bell, 10 April 1973; 6; PA71–0369, reel 3905; FFA.

113. Ibid.

114. Peter D. Bell, Memorandum, "Pontifical Catholic University of Chile, Center for National Planning Studies," to Carlson, Dye, Funari, Himes, and Nicholson, 29 September 1972; PA71–0369, reel 3905; FFA.

115. John Strasma, Inter-Office Memorandum, "CEPLAN," to Peter D. Bell, 13 April 1971; PA71–0369, reel 3905; FFA.

116. Ford's Richard Dye suggested that the CEPLAN group were "outstanding young economists" that Ford had funded from their very beginnings in 1968; letter, Dye to Frank Bonilla, 2 June 1972; PA71–0369, reel 3905; FFA.

117. Lovell S. Jarvis, Inter-Office Memorandum, "Authorization of Quarterly Payment to the Center for National Planning Studies (CEPLAN), Pontifical Catholic University," to Peter D. Bell, 27 December 1973; 2; PA71–0369, reel 2677; FFA.

118. Ibid.

119. Jeffrey M. Puryear, Inter-Office Memorandum, "Final Evaluation of CEPLAN (PA71–369)," to Peter D. Bell, 17 May 1974; PA71–369, reel 2677; FFA.

120. Jeffrey M. Puryear, Inter-Office Memorandum, "Recommendation for Closing (CEPLAN) (PA71–389A)," to Richard W. Dye, 31 January 1977; PA71–0369, reel 2677; FFA.

121. Peter D. Bell, Inter-Office Memorandum, "The Aftermath of the Military Coup in Chile," to William D. Carmichael, 22 November 1973; 6; Report 010668; FFA. In a report of April 1974, Bell estimated that up to half of all Marxist professors had been dismissed from the universities; Bell, Inter-Office Memorandum to William Carmichael, "Review of the Foundation's Program in Chile and Staff Deployment for the Southern Cone," 1 April 1974; 2; Report 008957; FFA.

122. "OLAC and the Social Sciences," December 5 1973; no report number; FFA.

123. Peter D. Bell, Inter-Office Memorandum, "The Aftermath of the Military Coup in Chile," to William D. Carmichael, 22 November 1973; 4; Report 010668; FFA.

124. Jeffrey M. Puryear, "Higher Education, Development Assistance, and Repressive Regimes," *Ford Foundation Reprint* (New York: Ford Foundation, 1983), 2.

125. Susan Cantor, Inter-Office Memorandum, "The Ford Foundation's Experience in Assisting Refugees," to Bruce Bushey, 27 February 1979; 1; Report 004654; FFA.

126. U.S. Department of State Fact Sheet, November 15 1973, by Jack J. Kubisch, http://www.gwu.edu/~nsarchiv/NSAEBB/NSAEBB8/ch10-05.htm.

127. Susan Cantor, Inter-Office Memorandum, "The Ford Foundation's Experience in Assisting Refugees," to Bruce Bushey, 27 February 1979; 1; Report 004654; FFA.

128. Puryear, "Higher Education, Development Assistance, and Repressive Regimes," 16.

129. Ibid., 7.

130. The three organizations so funded were the Latin American Studies Association, the Latin American Social Science Research Council (CLACSO), and the World University Service; Cantor, Inter-Office Memorandum, "The Ford Foundation's Experience in Assisting Refugees," 2.

131. Ibid., 7.

132. Richard W. Dye, Inter-Office Memorandum, "Report on My Visit to Chile—March 20–23," to William D. Carmichael, 26 March 1974; Report 008958; FFA.

133. Ibid.

134. Kalman Silvert, Inter-Office Memorandum, "Chile," to William D. Carmichael, 26 March 1974; 2–5; report 008959; FFA (emphasis added).

135. Dye, Inter-Office Memorandum, "Report on My Visit to Chile."

136. Puryear, "Higher Education, Development Assistance, and Repressive Regimes," 12. Emphasis added.

137. Decades later, William Carmichael noted that Ford's senior leadership was, by the 1970s, of the view that "we ought to be concerned about the nature of the governments in countries in which we were heavily engaged," explaining further why Ford stayed in Chile; "Interview with Bill Carmichael," *Alliance* 14, no. 2 (June 2009): 30.

138. Nita Manitzas, "The Ford Foundation's Social Science Program in Latin America," December 1973; no report number cited; FFA.

139. Kalman Silvert, "Looking Backward to Santa Maria," 3 June 1974; no report number cited; FFA.

140. "OLAC Social Science Conference: The Social Sciences in Latin America," 5 December 1973; 3–5; no report number cited; FFA.

141. "OLAC Social Science Conference: The Social Sciences in Latin America," 5 December 1973; Sunkel quote, 9; Bell quote, 15; no report number cited; FFA.

142. "OLAC Social Science Conference: The Interplay Between the Foundation and the Grantee," 7 December 1973; no report number cited; Carmichael, 16; FFA.

143. "OLAC Social Science Conference: Concluding Discussion," 7 December 1973; no report number cited; Lagos, 8; FFA.

144. "OLAC Social Science Conference: Concluding Discussion," 7 December 1973; no report number cited; Peter Cleaves, 9; FFA. Emphasis added.

145. Nita Rous Manitzas, "Evaluation of the Southern Cone DAP," February 1980; Report 011879; FFA. DAP is an abbreviation of "delegated-authority project."

146. Ibid., 6.

147. Ibid., 10.

148. Ibid., 12.

149. Elizabeth Fox (with the "cooperation of Nita Manitzas"), *Support for Social Sciences Research in the Southern Cone* [no publication information provided], 13; http://idl-bnc.idrc.ca/dspace/bitstream/123456789/36041/1/75106_v1.pdf.

150. P. Cerny, "Embedding Neoliberalism," *Journal of International Trade and Development* 2, no. 1 (2008): 1–46.

151. Fox, *Support for Social Sciences Research in the Southern Cone*, 10.

152. Silva, "Technocrats and Politics in Chile," 386.

153. Fox, *Support for Social Sciences Research in the Southern Cone*, 47.

154. Ibid., 48. Ford funded CIEPLAN to the tune of $125,000 per annum between 1978 and 1980, while the UNDP awarded it approximately $85,000 per annum.

155. Patricio Meller and Ignacio Walker, "CIEPLAN: Thirty Years in Pursuit of Democracy and Development in Latin America," paper for "Ownership in Practice" workshop, OECD Development Forum, Paris, September 27–29, 2007, http://www.oecd.org/dataoecd/3/59/39370440.pdf. In actual fact, growth with equity was hardly a new formulation for Christian Democrats—it was the approach favored by Foxley back in the 1970s; see Lovell Jarvis, Inter-Office Memorandum, "CEPLAN Seminar on Income Distribution and Economic Growth," to Peter D. Bell, 10 April 1973; PA71–0369, reel 3905. In the memo, Jarvis summarizes a paper written by Foxley and Munoz in which the authors largely ruled out income redistribution in conditions of low productivity and economic growth (6).

156. Meller and Walker, "CIEPLAN: Thirty Years in Pursuit of Democracy and Development in Latin America," 4.

157. Ibid., 10.

158. Interview with PBS Commanding Heights program, at http://www.pbs.org/wgbh/commandingheights/shared/pdf/int_ricardolagos.pdf. Lagos argued that distributive questions had to follow economic growth, not precede it. He also noted that this had nothing to do with being left or right wing: "It's simply sound economic policies now." Lagos fits the template of technocrat described by Miguel Centeno and Patricio Silva: "fluency in international discourses and an implicit (and often explicit) discomfort with nationalist language . . . emphasis on economic growth and the implied inevitability of following the dictates of the international market . . . rejection of conflict as unproductive . . . dismissing the inherent antagonism between classes or groups." Miguel Centeno and Patricio Silva, eds., *The Politics of Expertise in Latin America* (Basingstoke: Macmillan Press, 1998), 3–4.

159. Fox, *Support for Social Sciences Research in the Southern Cone*, 52.

160. Ibid., 71.

161. Jeffrey M. Puryear, *Thinking Politics: Intellectuals and Politics in Chile, 1973–1988* (Baltimore, Md.: Johns Hopkins University Press, 1994), 50, quoting Jose Joaquin Brunner, a Chilean social scientist.

162. Ibid., 51. Puryear argues that had it not been for foreign funding, "the [research] centers might not have existed at all"; 51.

163. Ibid., 52.

164. Ibid., 37.

165. Osvaldo Sunkel, "Consolidation of Chile's Democracy and Development," *Discussion Paper* 317 (Institute of Development Studies, 1993), 2.

166. Christian Democrats such as Foxley, Patricio Aylwyn, Robert Zahler, among others, established the Chilean Institute of Humanistic Studies as a means of keeping alive their political activity; Puryear, *Thinking Politics*, 40.

167. Indeed, the negotiated settlement that led to civilian rule also institutionalized the power of the military as well as its guaranteed bloc of representatives in the Senate. In practice, along with the guaranteed position of the business community in a market democracy, this meant that the settlement created a centrist polity commanding the confidence of international investors but with relatively minor social protection for the poor; the project-planning mentality of neoliberalism had become a permanent fixture in Chile. Emanuel de Kadt, "Poverty-Focused Policies: The Experience of Chile," *Discussion Paper* 319 (Institute of Development Studies, 1993), 19.

168. It is also important to bear in mind that the experience of exile also played a role in redefining political strategies in Chile; see Alan Angell and Susan Carstairs, "The Exile Question in Chilean Politics," *Third World Quarterly* 9, no. 1 (January 1987): 148–167.

169. Puryear, *Thinking Politics*, 57.

170. Ibid., 58.

171. Ibid., 60.

172. Patricio Silva, "Technocrats and Politics in Chile," 399, argues that leftists accept relegating the role of the state in economic policy and courting foreign investment. Osvaldo Sunkel also came to accept the inevitability and irreversibility of globalization; the most anyone could do, he argued, was to minimize the disadvantages and maximize the advantages through economic and social progress; Sunkel, "Consolidation of Chile's Democracy and Development," 5. Sunkel told PBS: "I think we have also come to accept the workings of the market as a fact of life. . . . We have to be competitive in world markets"; Sunkel, PBS interview, http://www.pbs.org/wgbh/commandingheights/shared/pdf/int_osvaldosunkel .pdf. For a radically different take on this matter, see James Petras, "The Metamorphosis of Latin America's Intellectuals," *Latin American Perspectives* 17, no. 2 (Spring 1990): 102–112.

173. Huneeus, "Technocrats and Politicians in an Authoritarian Regime," 472.

174. Ibid., 469. See also, Paul W. Drake, "International Factors in Democratization," Estudio/Working Paper 1994/November 1994, presented at the Center for

Advanced Study in the Social Sciences, Juan March Institute, Madrid, November 4, 1993.

175. Puryear, *Thinking Politics*, 170–171. Emphasis added.

8. AMERICAN POWER AND THE MAJOR FOUNDATIONS IN THE POST–COLD WAR ERA

1. Carl Boggs, *Imperial Delusions: American Militarism and Endless War* (Lanham, Md.: Rowman and Littlefield, 2005), 32, 86.

2. P. G. Cerny, "Embedding Neoliberalism," *Journal of International Trade and Development* 2, no. 1 (2008): 1–46.

3. Christopher Hitchens, "Defending Islamofascism," *Slate* (October 22, 2007), http://www.slate.com/id/2176389. Hitchens equates Islamic fundamentalism with the fascist regimes of Italy and Germany in the 1930s and 1940s.

4. Thomas Friedman, *Longitudes and Attitudes* (London: Penguin, 2003), 5.

5. With Warren Buffet's donations to the Gates Foundation, the latter annually grants around $3 billion; Maureen Baehr, "New Philanthropy Has Arrived—So What?" in S. U. Raymond and M. B. Martin, eds., *Mapping the New World of American Philanthropy* (Hoboken, N.J.: John Wiley and Sons, 2007), 82.

6. "It is evident that terrorists draw much of their support and justification from those who are, or *perceive themselves* as, unjustly impoverished." So wrote the president of the Rockefeller Foundation in 2002. The current global financial crisis has also depleted foundations' income.

7. James M. Scott and Kelly J. Walters, "Supporting the Wave: Western Political Foundations and the Promotion of a Global Democratic Society," *Global Society* 14, no. 2 (2000): 256.

8. R. F. Arnove and N. Pinede, "Revisiting the 'Big Three' Foundations" (unpublished paper in possession of author).

9. H. K. Anheier and S. Daly, "Philanthropic Foundations: A New Global Force?" in *Global Civil Society 2004/5* (London: Sage, 2005), 169, argue that foundations hold "substantial investments in the global capital market [which is] considered responsible for many of the social and economic imbalances that global civil society seeks to address."

10. "Break-out Session Globalization, INSP Plenary Meeting," March 22, 2002.

11. James D. Wolfensohn, *Development and Poverty Reduction* (Washington, D.C.: International Bank for Reconstruction and Development/World Bank, 2004).

12. Joseph Stiglitz, *Globalization and Its Discontents* (London: Penguin, 2002).

13. Ibid.; Stephen Gill, *Power and Resistance in the New World Order* (Basingstoke: Palgrave, 2003).

14. David Hamburg, CC president (1983–1997), cited by Arnove and Pinede, "Revisiting the 'Big Three' Foundations," 10; emphasis added.

15. Arnove and Pinede, "Revisiting the 'Big Three' Foundations, "13.

16. Richard Peet, *Unholy Trinity: The IMF, World Bank, and WTO* (London: Zed, 2003), 14.

17. Arnove and Pinede, "Revisiting the 'Big Three' Foundations," 19. That there are alternatives—based on fair trade, as opposed to free trade, etc.—see Peet, *Unholy Trinity*.

18. Arnove and Pinede, "Revisiting the 'Big Three' Foundations," 29.

19. Rockefeller Global Inclusion Program, October 2003; www.Rockfound.org.

20. Ford Foundation Web site, www.Fordfound.org; grant awarded in 2003.

21. S. Sharma, "Microcredit: Globalisation Unlimited," *Hindu Business Line*, March 5, 2002, http://www.thehindubusinessline.com/2002/01/05/stories/2002010500111200.htm. Grameen Bank interest rates were also far higher than commercial rates, at around 20 percent, another point of criticism.

22. Arnove and Pinede, "Revisiting the 'Big Three' Foundations," 22.

23. The Prince of Wales International Business Leaders Forum received $100,000 to "build, study and promote mutually advantageous business links between large corporations and small or microenterprises worldwide"; http://www.Fordfound.org.

24. D. Rockefeller, "Why We Need the IMF," *Wall Street Journal*, May 1, 1998.

25. http://www.Fordfound.org; granted in 2003 to the Third World Network, Berhad, Malaysia.

26. See, for example, the report of the Foundations of Globalisation International Conference, University of Manchester, November 2003, http://www.les.man.ac.uk/government/events/foundations_finalreport.pdf.

27. Ford granted $350,000 to Yale University in 2003 to fund "the research practice and outreach activities of the Center for Cities and Globalization and to strengthen an interdisciplinary network on globalization."

28. The Philanthropic Initiative, Inc., *Global Social Investing* (Boston: TPI, Inc., 2001), 4–5, 37–42.

29. All three grants in 2003; Ford Web site; TPI, *Global Social Investing*, 20.

30. Ford gave $153,000 to Internews Interactive, Inc., as part of its "Bridge Initiative on Globalization," to assist the WSF to communicate with the World Economic Forum.

31. Suzanne Charle, "Another Way: Leaders of a Global Civil Society Chart an Alternative to Globalization," *Ford Foundation Report*, Spring 2003.

32. Ibid. Michael Edwards, *Civil Society* (Cambridge: Polity Press, 2004), 14, argues "humanizing capitalism" is the WSF's principal role.

33. Jose Gabriel Lopez, "Green Globalization," *Ford Foundation Report*, Summer 2003.

34. *CC Grants for Globalization Initiatives*; CC Web site.

35. Grant to the LSE Foundation, 2003; Ford Web site.

36. http://www.ilps-news.com/central-info-bureau/events/mumbai-resistance-2004 /why-mumbai-resistance-2004/.

37. MumbaiResistance Against Imperialist Globalization and War; http://www .mumbairesistance.org.

38. *The Guardian*, January 17, 2004; L. Jordan, "The Ford Foundation and the WSF," January 15, 2004, at http://www.opendemocracy.net. The WSF did accept Ford-funded delegates. WSF is also run by a co-opted, rather than elected, organizing committee; see M. Morgan, "Overcoming the Imperial Subject: The WSF and Counter Hegemonic Strategies for a Post-Political Age," paper presented at IR conference at METU, Ankara, June 18–20, 2008.

39. Firoze Manji, "World Social Forum: Just Another NGO Fair?" *Pambuzka News* 288 (January 26, 2007), http://www.pambazuka.org/en/category/features/39464.

40. Owen Worth and Karen Buckley, "The World Social Forum: Postmodern Prince or Court Jester?" *Third World Quarterly* 30, no. 4 (2009): 649–661. Worth and Buckley show that high proportions of WSF participants and leaders have post-graduate qualifications and daily Internet access, in contrast to the masses of the poor and excluded they claim to be representing (654).

41. R. Cox, "Civil Society at the Turn of the Millennium," *Review of International Studies* 25 (1999): 11–12.

42. M. Buckley and Robert Singh, eds., *The Bush Doctrine and the War on Terrorism* (London: Routledge, 2006); Center for Strategic and International Studies, *Democracy in U.S. Security Strategy* (Washington, D.C.: CSIS, 2009), v.

43. A. L. George and A. Bennett, *Case Studies and Theory Development in the Social Sciences* (Cambridge, Mass.: The MIT Press, 2005), 37–38.

44. J. Lepgold and Miroslav Nincic, *Beyond the Ivory Tower* (New York: Columbia University Press, 2001), 113. They take the quotation from Jack S. Levy, "Domestic Politics and War," *Journal of Interdisciplinary History* 18 (1988): 653–673. Levy's study was partly financed by the Carnegie Corporation.

45. This is acknowledged by Doyle in part 2 of his article, "Kant, Liberal Legacies, and Foreign Affairs," *Philosophy and Public Affairs* 12, no. 4 (1983); in Ford Foundation records, see letter, Doyle to Laurice H. Sarraf (grants administrator,

International Affairs Programs, Ford Foundation), 20 July 1983; in PA795–677, reel 3751.

46. Grant number 07990618; reels 3038; 5376–78; Ford Foundation archives, New York.

47. Michael Doyle and Miles Kahler, "North and South in the International Economy: A Re-Examination," in PA795–677; reel 3751.

48. In his *Ways of War and Peace*, Doyle (1997) acknowledges the support of several organizations, including a Social Science Research Council/MacArthur Foundation Fellowship in International Peace and Security, and of the Belfer Center on Science and International Affairs at Harvard (on which more below). Doyle also noted that the MacArthur Foundation consciously set out to develop ideas that challenged Cold War realist thinking; Michael Doyle, private communication with the author; undated but ca. May 2009.

49. M. W. Doyle, "Liberalism and the Transition to a Post-Cold War System," in A. Clesse, R. Cooper, and Y. Sakamoto, eds., *The International System After the Collapse of the East-West Order* (Dordrecht: Martinus Nijhoff, 1994), 98–101.

50. Michael W. Doyle, "Liberalism and World Politics," *American Political Science Review* 80 (1986): 1151–1169.

51. Larry Diamond, *An American Foreign Policy for Democracy* Progressive Policy Institute Policy Report (1991), http://www.ppionline.org/ppi_ci.cfm?knlgAreaID=450004&subsecID=900020&contentID=2044. Emphasis added.

52. Ibid.

53. In one part of the speech, Clinton's words were lifted directly from Diamond's report: "Democracies don't go to war with each other. . . . Democracies don't sponsor terrorist acts against each other. They are more likely to be reliable trading partners, protect the global environment, and abide by international law"; speech, "A New Covenant for American Security," Georgetown University, December 12, 1991; http://www.ndol.org.

54. Securitization is used here as defined by the Copenhagen School: "Once 'securitized,' an issue will evoke images of threat, enemies, and defense and allocate the state an important role in addressing it—thus the politics surrounding the issue will be transformed"; Deborah Avant, "NGOs, Corporations and Security Transformation in Africa," *International Relations* 21, no. 2 (2007), 144.

55. C. Buger and T. Villumsen, "Beyond the Gap: Relevance, Fields of Practice, and the Securitizing Consequences of (Democratic Peace) Theory," *Journal of International Relations and Development* 10 (2007): 433.

56. Lake, quoted in ibid., 435; emphasis added.

57. W. G. Hyland, *Clinton's World* (Westport, Conn.: Praeger, 1999), 23.

58. Anthony Lake, "Remarks of Anthony Lake," September 21, 1993, http://www
    .mtholyoke.edu/acad/intrel/lakedoc.html.

59. Strobe Talbott, "The New Geopolitics," U.S. Department of State Dispatch, No-
    vember 14, 1994.

60. J. Kruzel, "More a Chasm Than a Gap," *Mershon International Studies Review* 38
    (1994): 180.

61. T. Smith, *A Pact with the Devil* (New York: Routledge, 2007).

62. Larry Diamond, *Promoting Democracy in the 1990s: Actors and Instruments, Is-
    sues and Imperatives*, December 1995, http://wwics.si.edu/subsites/ccpdc/pubs
    /di/di.htm. Emphasis added.

63. E. D. Mansfield and J. Snyder, "Democratization and the Danger of War," *Inter-
    national Security* 20 (1995): 5–38.

64. Council for the Community of Democracies, *CCD: The First Five Years 2001–
    2005*, http://www.ccd21.org.

65. T. Carothers, "A League of Their Own," *Foreign Policy* (July–August 2008).

66. See http://belfercenter.ksg.harvard.edu/project/58/quarterly_journal.html?page
    _id=146&parent_id=46.

67. S. E. Miller, "*International Security* at Twenty-five," *International Security* 26
    (2001): 5–39, n16.

68. See the "Acknowledgments" to M. E. Brown, S. M. Lynn-Jones, and S. E. Miller,
    eds., *Debating the Democratic Peace* (Cambridge, Mass.: The MIT Press, 1996).

69. The original idea came from McGeorge Bundy, the Ford Foundation president
    and former national security adviser to presidents Kennedy and Johnson, who
    wanted to establish a number of university-based international security centers
    across America. Ford's endowment to Harvard's Center grew to $6 million in
    1979; it was originally granted in 1974. See http://belfercenter.ksg.harvard.edu.

70. Bruce Kuklick, *Blind Oracles: Intellectuals and War from Kennan to Kissinger*
    (Princeton, NJ: Princeton University Press, 2006).

71. Carnegie Corporation (2007) *Annual Report*. Emphasis added.

72. Graham Allison, "Message from the Director," http://belfer.ksg.harvard.edu
    /about/welcome.html.

73. Miller, "*International Security* at Twenty-five," 5, 12, 13, 34; William Jefferson
    Clinton, "State of the Union Address, 1994," http://www.let.rug.nl/usa/P/bc42
    /speeches/sud94wjc.htm.

74. Brown, Lynn-Jones, and Miller, *Debating the Democratic Peace*, xiv.

75. E. O. Goldman and L. Berman, "Engaging the World," in *The Clinton Legacy*, ed.
    C. Campbell and B. A. Rockman (New York: Chatham House, 2000), 236, ar-
    gue that Clinton dropped "democratic enlargement" and retained "engagement"

because of "a set of academic arguments that democratization was often a con-flict-prone process."

76. Strobe Talbott, "Democracy and the National Interest," *Foreign Affairs* 75 (1996): 47–64. In note 2, Talbott cites academics on democratic peace, including John Ikenberry, David Lake, and Christopher Layne.

77. Mansfield and Snyder, "Democratization and the Danger of War," 34.

78. E. D. Mansfield and J. Snyder, *From Voting to Violence* (New York: W. W. Norton, 2000), 41.

79. John M. Owen IV, "Iraq and the Democratic Peace," *Foreign Affairs* 84 (2005): 122–127.

80. Barack Obama, *Pan American Day and Pan American Week* Press Release, April 14, 2009; R. McMahon, "The Brave New World of Democracy Promotion," *Foreign Service Journal* (January 2009): 31–39.

81. Owen, "Iraq and the Democratic Peace." Other journals were also important in the development and discussion of democratic peace theory. *World Politics* published articles by Randall Schweller (1992), C. R. and M. Ember and Bruce Russett (1992), and John Oneal (1999). The *Journal of Democracy* defended and promoted the implementation of DPT. For example, Morton Halperin (director, PPS, at State, 1998–2001, and senior director for democracy at the NSC,1994–1996) co-wrote articles on how the major powers increasingly were "guarantee-ing democracy" where it was actively undermined, while the political scien-tist James Lee Ray provided a robust theoretical and methodological defense of DPT. M. H. Halperin and Kristen Lomasney, "Toward a Global 'Guarantee Clause,'" *Journal of Democracy* 4 (1993): 60–64; M. H. Halperin and Kristen Lomasney, "Guaranteeing Democracy," *Journal of Democracy* 9 (1998): 134–147; J. L. Ray, "The Democratic Path to Peace," *Journal of Democracy* 8 (1997): 49–64.

82. Francis Fukuyama, *The End of History and the Last Man* (London: Hamish Ham-ilton, 1992). References to the democratic peace and Michael Doyle appear in the book (for example, 262–263) but not in the original article in *The National Interest* (1989), from which the book took its inspiration.

83. B. W. Jentleson, "In Pursuit of Praxis," in *Being Useful*, ed. M. Nincic and J. Lep-gold (Ann Arbor: University of Michigan Press, 2000), 129–149.

84. Condoleezza Rice, "The Promise of Democratic Peace," December 11, 2005, http://www.washingtonpost.com/wp-dyn/content/article/2005/12/09/AR2005120901711.html.

85. For a comprehensive analysis of anti-Americanism, see Brendon O'Connor, ed., *Anti-Americanism*, 4 vols. (Westport, Conn.: Greenwood, 2007).

86. GMF was originally founded by a West German government grant in 1972 in appreciation of U.S. Marshall Plan assistance; headquartered in Washington, D.C., it also maintains five offices in Europe—Belgrade, Berlin, Bratislava, Brussels, and Paris; GMF *Annual Report, 2003*; http://www.gmfus.org.

87. "Partnerships," GMF Web site, at http://www.gmfus.org.

88. Ibid.

89. GMF *Annual Report, 2003*, 1–6.

90. Rubin held that post in President Clinton's second administration (1995–1999); he was a partner at Goldman Sachs from the early 1970s and is a former trustee of the Carnegie Corporation.

91. GMF *Annual Report, 2003*, 7–10.

92. Ibid., 11.

93. Mark Leonard, ed., *Re-Ordering the World* (London: The Foreign Policy Centre, 2002).

94. Inderjeet Parmar, "Catalysing Events, Think Tanks, and American Foreign Policy Shifts: A Comparative Analysis of the Impacts of Pearl Harbor 1941 and 11 September 2001," *Government and Opposition* (Winter 2005): 1–25.

95. Robert Cooper, "The Post-Modern State," in Mark Leonard, ed., *Re-Ordering the World* (London: The Foreign Policy Centre, 2002), 11–20. Since then, Cooper has published *The Breaking of Nations* (New York: Atlantic Monthly Press, 2003). For a critical analysis, see Inderjeet Parmar, " 'I'm Proud of the British Empire': Why Tony Blair Backs George W. Bush," *Political Quarterly* 76, no. 2 (2005): 218–231.

96. "Transatlantic Fellows Program: Past Fellows"; GMF Web site. Other past fellows have included the former president of Bulgaria, Peter Stoyanov; Todd Stern, a former Clinton White House Staff member; and numerous French, German, Italian, and other public figures.

97. Jeffrey Gedmin and Craig Kennedy, "Selling America, Short," *National Interest* (Winter 2003).

98. Cheney is the wife of George W. Bush's vice president, Richard Cheney; Bennett was President Ronald Reagan's "drug tsar" and current head of Americans for Victory Over Terrorism (AVOT); Wilson is a conservative former Harvard academic; Mead is a senior fellow at the CFR.

99. Thomas B. Fordham Foundation, ed., *Terrorists, Despots, and Democracy* (Washington, D.C.: Thomas B. Fordham Foundation, August 2003).

100. Giles Scott-Smith, *The Politics of Apolitical Culture: The Congress for Cultural Freedom, the CIA, and Postwar American Hegemony* (London: Routledge, 2002).

101. Gedmin and Kennedy, "Selling America, Short."

102. Robert Kagan, "Power and Weakness," *Policy Review* (June 2002). In GMF's *Annual Report, 2003*, Kennedy notes the importance of greater recognition of the need for European military development, within NATO, and America's increasing appreciation of "soft power," such as foreign aid and better knowledge of "skills . . . to operate effectively in the Islamic world."

103. Gedmin and Kennedy, "Selling America, Short." Colin Powell was secretary of state in the first George W. Bush administration (2001–2004). Immediately following 9/11, Powell commissioned the Madison Avenue advertiser Charlotte Beers to rebrand US foreign policy; she resigned in 2002.

104. Kennedy omits mention of the failure of the U.S. administration to grant the protections of the U.S. constitution to detainees and violations of the Geneva Convention.

105. Gedmin and Kennedy, "Selling America, Short."

106. President Obama's national security strategy, published in May 2010, bears a close resemblance to the PPNS *Final Report*.

107. The PPNS's *Final Report, Forging a World of Liberty Under Law* (2006), claims that its conclusions are drawn from the findings of "both reason and social science" (58). http://www.princeton.edu/~ppns/report.html.

108. PPNS, *Final Report*, 9; R. Pape, "The Strategic Logic of Suicide Terrorism," *American Political Science Review* 97, no. 3 (2003): 343–361.

109. http://www.wws.princeton.edu/ppns/mission.html.

110. Anne-Marie Slaughter, currently director of the State Department's policy planning staff, was dean of the Woodrow Wilson School of Public and International Affairs and professor of international politics at Princeton University. Prior to this, she was a professor of politics at Harvard. She is a board member of the CFR. She recently wrote *A New World Order* (Princeton, N.J.: Princeton University Press, 2004). G. John Ikenberry is a professor of politics at Princeton.

111. http://www.wws.princeton.edu/ppns/mission.html. Emphasis added.

112. Lake and Shultz, "Foreword" to the PPNS *Final Report*, 2.

113. For full details, see Inderjeet Parmar, "Foreign Policy Fusion," *International Politics* 46, no. 2/3 (March 2009): 177–209.

114. R. Brym, *Intellectuals and Politics* (London: Allen and Unwin, 1980).

115. W. Kristol, "Postscript—June 2004: Neoconservatism Remains the Bedrock of U.S. Foreign Policy," in Irwin Stelzer, ed., *Neoconservatism* (London: Atlantic Books, 2004), 75–76. Yet Kristol's assessment may be overblown: neocons' rhetoric became broadly acceptable only after 9/11, when it offered conservative Americans and liberal interventionists a ready-made language with which to wield influence.

116. J. A. Thompson, "Another Look at the Downfall of 'Fortress America,'" *Journal of American Studies* (December 26, 1992).

117. M. P. Leffler, *A Preponderance of Power: National Security, the Truman Administration, and the Cold War* (Stanford, Calif.: Stanford University Press, 1992); G. A. Kolko, *The Politics of War: Allied Diplomacy and the World Crisis of 1943–1945* (London: Weidenfeld and Nicolson, 1969); D. Campbell, *Writing Security* (Manchester: Manchester University Press, 1992).

118. J. W. Sanders, *Peddlers of Crisis: The Committee on the Present Danger and the Politics of Containment* (Boston: South End Press, 1983).

119. S. Rosato, "The Flawed Logic of the Democratic Peace Theory," *American Political Science Review* 97, no. 4 (2003): 585–602.

120. Andrew O'Neil, "American Grand Strategy: The Quest for Permanent Primacy," in B. O'Connor and M. Griffiths, eds., *The Rise of Anti-Americanism* (London: Routledge, 2006).

121. Stephen Walt, "Woodrow Wilson Rides Again," http://bookclub.tpmcafe.com /blog/bookclub/2006/oct/10.

122. J. Der Derian, "Decoding the National Security Strategy of the United States," *Boundary* 30, no. 3 (2003): 19–27.

123. Walt, "Woodrow Wilson Rides Again."

124. Ibid., 7.

125. Ibid., 2, 4.

126. Ibid., 4.

127. John Lloyd, "The Anglosphere Project," *New Statesman* (March 13, 2000). Interestingly, Christopher Hitchens, writing about Robert Conquest, a champion of the Anglosphere, now considers the idea positively: see the *Wall Street Journal*, February 3, 2007.

128. S. Anderson, *Race and Rapprochement* (London: Associated Universities Presses, 1981).

129. I. Parmar, *Think Tanks and Power in Foreign Policy* (Basingstoke: Palgrave, 2004), 71–72, 195–196.

130. *Policy Planning Staff Memorandum*, Washington, May 4, 1948, National Archives and Records Administration, RG 273, Records of the National Security Council, NSC 10/2. Top Secret; RG 59, Records of the Department of State, Policy Planning Staff Files 1944–47: lot 64 D 563, box 11.

131. E. Quinones, "Project Aims to 'Kindle Debate' on U.S. National Security," *Princeton Weekly Bulletin* (October 16, 2006).

132. Yet deeper still, it is clear that postwar modernization theory itself—as championed by Walt Rostow, for example—was based on an explicit belief in the

inevitable relative decline of American power over time. This emphasized the need on America's part to ensure the globalization of American values and institutions within a benign international environment enabling the United States to flourish; see Simon Bromley, *American Power and the Prospects for International Order* (Cambridge: Polity Press, 2008).

133. Indeed, the American social sciences were "born in the service of the modern state, and they evolved in a way that left them quite closely, if often invisibly, tied to the purposes and institutions of states." Lisa Anderson, *Pursuing Truth, Exercising Power: Social Sciences and Public Policy in the Twenty-first Century* (New York: Columbia University Press, 2003), 5.

134. http://www.whitehouse.gov/sites/default/files/rss_viewer/national_security_strategy.pdf.

135. David Szanton, ed., *The Politics of Knowledge: Area Studies and the Disciplines* (Berkeley: University of California Press, 2004).

136. RF *Annual Report* (2002); emphasis added.

137. http://www.rockfound.org; *Global Inclusion Program*, 2004. The goal of the Global Inclusion Program is "to help broaden the benefits and reduce the negative impacts of globalization on vulnerable communities, families and individuals around the world."

138. RF Web site; *Assets and Capacities Program*, 2003.

139. RF Web site; *Southeast Asia Regional Program*, 2004.

140. RF Web site; Bellagio Program, 2003. No details of level of financing are available.

141. "Statement by Gordon Conway, President, The Rockefeller Foundation," October 25, 2001; RF Web site.

142. CC *Grants for Globalization Initiatives*; International Peace and Security Program; CC Web site.

143. Ibid.

144. CC *International Peace and Security Program: Global Engagement*; CC Web site.

145. CC Grants, *International Peace and Security Program*, 2004; CC Web site.

146. CC Grants, *Carnegie Scholars Program*, 2003; CC Web site.

147. CC Grants, *Special Opportunities Fund*; CC Web site.

148. CC Grants, *Carnegie Scholars Program*, 2003; CC Web site.

149. All grant information is for the CC grants database at http://carnegie.org/grants/grants-database.

150. David Jhirad, Claudia Juech, and Evan S. Michelson, "Foresight for Smart Globalization," *Foresight* 11, no. 4 (2009): 1013; http://www.altfutures.com/pro_poor_foresight/Foresight_For_Smart_Globalization.pdf.

151. For the definitive works on soft power, see Joseph Nye, *Soft Power* (New York: Public Affairs, 2004); and I. Parmar and M. Cox, eds., *Soft Power and U.S. Foreign Policy* (London: Routledge, 2010).

9. CONCLUSION

1. Ronald Radosh, *Prophets on the Right* (New York: Simon and Schuster, 1975), argues that American expansionism was opposed on both the left and right wings of U.S. politics.

2. Edward H. Berman, *The Influence of the Carnegie, Ford, and Rockefeller Foundations on American Foreign Policy* (Albany: State University of New York Press, 1983), 31.

3. Harold Laski, "Foundations, Universities, and Research," in Harold Laski, ed., *The Dangers of Obedience* (New York: Harper, 1930), 171, 174.

4. RF *Annual Report* (2008); http://www.rockefellerfoundation.org/uploads/files /901c639d-bf3f-43d2-9975-5d98d02d0be8-rfar_2008.pdf.

5. David Jhirad, Claudia Juech, and Evan S. Michelson, "Foresight for Smart Globalization," *Foresight* (2009): 1.

6. "Persons of the Year," *Time* (December 26, 2006). Emphasis added.

7. Raj Patel, Eric Holt-Gimenez, and Annie Shattuck, "Ending Africa's Hunger," *The Nation* 21 (September 2009). According to the *Seattle Times* (October 17, 2006), "at the core [of the Gates Foundation] is faith in the power of science and technology to improve lives," http://seattletimes.nwsource.com/html/business technology/2003308397_gateshires17.html.

8. Maureen Baehr, "New Philanthropy Has Arrived—Now What?" in Susan Raymond and Mary Beth Martin, eds., *Mapping the New World of World of American Philanthropy: The Causes and Consequences of the Transfer of Wealth* (Hoboken, N.J.: Wiley and Sons, 2007), 82.

9. Obama's appointee to the Food and Drug Administration, Michael Taylor, was vice president for public policy at Monsanto from 1998 to 2001 and champion of biotechnology policies in the Clinton administration; Isabella Kenfield, "Monsanto's Man in the Obama Administration, with an Eye on Africa," http://www .foodfirst.org/en/node/2515.

10. Patel, Holt-Gimenez, and Shattuck, "Ending Africa's Hunger."

11. Eric Holt-Gimenez, "Out of AGRA: The Green Revolution Returns to Africa," *Development* 51, no. 4 (2008): 464–471. Holt-Gimenez shows how AGRA focuses on market-led, genetically engineered crop strategies.

12. Patel, Holt-Gimenez, and Shattuck, "Ending Africa's Hunger."

13. *Renewing American Leadership in the Fight Against Global Poverty and Hunger* (Chicago: Chicago Council on Global Affairs, 2009). AGRA is now allied to the Millennium Challenge Corporation set up by President George W. Bush.

14. Tanya Kersson, "Gates Agriculture Speech Highlights Sustainability but Falls Short," October 26, 2009, http://www.foodfirst.org/en/node/2608. There are also strong concerns about the technocratic character of the Gates Foundation's global health programs, the annual expenditures of which actually exceed the budget of the World Health Organization; D. McCoy, G. Kembhavi, J. Patel, and A. Luintel, "The Bill and Melinda Gates Foundation's Grant-Making Programme for Global Health," *Lancet* 373 (May 9, 2009).

15 James C. Scott, *Seeing Like a State* (New Haven, Conn.: Yale University Press, 1998), 6.

16. Ibid., 7.

INDEX